FLYING BETWEEN HEAVEN AND HELL

WEATHERING STORMS

ROGER BLAIR JOHNSON

Address all inquiries to:
REBOH@cox.net
Road Scholar Publishing Group LLC

ISBN: 978-0-9671100-3-5

Editor: Road Scholar Publishing Group LLC
Cover Design and Interior Layout: Fusion Creative Works

PREFACE

Without question my second year of high school was one of the worst, yet one of the best, most enlightening, years of my life. Revealing the reason for that dichotomy is what motivated me to write this memoir.

It was in my sophomore year of high school when my father began his very physically and emotionally abusive attacks on me (prior to that year my mother was the only one who was the target of his alcohol fueled rage). That was also the year when my father began to teach me to fly.

It's hard to understand what my sisters, mother, and I endured month-in and month-out, as my father would attack his wife, with his kids as witnesses. We saw the absolute hatred in his eyes, actions, and words as he fought and fought with our mother, one time almost to the death. Though my sisters never experienced my father's backhand upon their face, my mother and I did, many times, as well as having to brace our mind, heart, and soul to endure his horribly malevolent and cussword laced verbal attacks. Unless you've been a recipient or witness to this kind of domestic hell, it's hard to understand the affect that this abuse and fighting can have upon a person. To this day the effects of those dark days upon my psyche still linger; I never hated a human more than I hated my father during his drunken rages.

Conversely, it's hard to understand the elation I felt when I began to learn to fly, with my father as my instructor. My spirits soared to astronomical heights with each takeoff as my father began to teach me his craft in that year of both heaven and hell. Becoming an aviator, like my father, was a wonderful escape from the depths of personal and family hell and took me to a world where distant horizons, always changing, could be visited; my father was so magical, so angelic, and wonderful as both an aviator and instructor that I have never loved anyone more than he in the world of aviation.

This memoir is more than just a tattling of my father's and mine dysfunctional relationship through life and it's certainly not meant to be a "Mommie Dearest" diatribe. It's more a fusion of the many elements: emotional; environmental; social; mechanical of two lives who have flown hundreds of thousands of miles and tens of thousands of hours in a multitude of aircraft, both very small and very big, very fast and very slow, over a period of 70 years.

This book not only reveals a dark and dramatic secret of my father's, as confessed on his deathbed, it also illuminates the covert world of the aviator, possibly on a level never before brought to light. It takes you behind the closed cockpit door and into the professional and personal lives of aviators as they battle the storms conceived of both mother and human nature as they circumvent the globe and experience the best and worst that the world has to offer. This memoir is an adventure, a journey through peoples' lives which are filled with joy and laughter, sadness and pain, terror, splendor, good, evil, and finally, most importantly, redemption on the grandest of transcendental understanding.

Lastly, but certainly not least, this book is meant to offer hope to anyone, young or old, who may be in the throes of a depression so deep and dark that you think you will never escape. Before I learned to fly, I too was there, on a level to which I contemplated suicide, almost daily. Though it was my learning to fly that raised me out of the detritus of one of the most horrible periods of time in my life, it was what my mother taught me at the age of seven that truly saved and shaped my life as an aviator, a person, and as my father's son.

PROLOGUE

WEATHERING STORMS

Right after we took off, I relinquished the flight controls to Austin and let him fly. He is as natural a pilot as was his late grandfather, and he immediately began banking to and fro above the well-watered forests near the airfield from which we just departed. Millions upon millions of dark-green, chlorophyll-intoxicated leaves emerged from the branches of a slightly less number of trees; there was no question that spring was in full bloom.

As I let my youngest son explore the boundaries of his nascent aviator's skills over the seemingly impenetrable carpet of green below, I gazed upon the distant horizon. The day's dry air offered unlimited in-flight visibility, and as my eyes looked far ahead, my heart contradicted their gaze as it searched far in my past, reminding me of the significance of this flight.

I had begun to experience déjà vu from the moment I woke up that morning and prepared to leave for the airport with my very enthusiastic son. Once airborne and as my heart retraced my life's steps in getting to this euphoric moment, I suddenly realized that it had been thirty-four years since I first took flying lessons from my father. Now, here I was with my wonderful child, sharing an experience that I felt so privileged to have made into a career.

I don't know how old I was when the tradition of my father giving me an airplane ride on or near my birthday began, but somewhere in my distant youth, that tradition ignited. As the days to those wonderful, annual moments of flight approached, I was tortured by time. I swear the tick of the clock drastically slowed as the days remaining waned toward the flight. But when the aircraft's engine started, a quantum reversal in the space-time continuum always seemed to occur, as it felt to me that no sooner had the wheels left the ground on takeoff than we were touching down before I could fully grasp the surreal experience of the actual ascent. Those youthful flights were usually an hour in length, and though my dad never failed to take me, there was one caveat to the whole experience . . . I had to ask him to take me flying as he never, *ever*, extended the offer.

My dad was big on the desire theme of life: "Desire and attitude. Buck, desire, and attitude—that will take you far." He used to say that unrelenting desire is what made a successful career.

So, in the month of May, as my fiftieth birthday rapidly approached, my eleven-year-old son asked me if I would take him for a ride in a friend's Super Cub. Although Austin had previously been on many flights, and in a multitude of different aircraft, that was the first time he had ever asked me for an airplane ride. There was no delay in my saying yes, as that was about as good as it could get for me with regard to receiving a birthday gift—sharing the magic of flight with my own child. Could this be the beginning of me passing the torch to my son?

The morning of the flight with Austin dawned clear and chilly as a moisture-laden weather system had moved through the area the previous day, taking very grayish, heavy, and low-lying clouds with it. The passing cold front left the Earth unclothed, causing the trees to shiver with each gently blowing breeze.

My son's excitement was contagious and had fully infected me by the time we started up and taxied. As we made our way to the grass strip's only runway, I told Austin, via the intercom, when I flew as a teenager many times I pretended to be a fighter pilot preparing to go into battle while taxing my mount for takeoff.

The previous night's deposit of dew upon the grass runway's blades gave obvious hint to the left-right deviations of our takeoff roll as the history of our passing was temporarily impressed upon the turf. Though not extreme, the miscues of my feet upon the rudder pedals alluded to my lack of currency in this type of aircraft. It had been thirty years since I last flew a Super Cub with any regularity before recently being reunited with that same make and model aircraft owned by a friend and colleague, who so graciously allowed me to borrow it for this flight.

The low angle of the sun above the horizon, the sound of the engine, and the chill of the air rushing in and around the open cockpit reminded me of the many morning takeoffs that I'd performed while towing banners during the summers of my college years. Possibly because my eleven-year-old son was sitting right behind me, his youth energizing the both of us, or maybe just because this takeoff reminded me of one particular day, many years ago, when a fellow banner tow pilot and I departed in our banner-towing Cubs with aerial battle a certainty . . .

KITE WARS

Flashback to late May, 1977. I was only nineteen years old and beginning my first season of aerial advertising (banner towing) with Paramount Air Service, located at Cape May County Airport, in Rio Grande, New Jersey.

It was a typically busy midmorning at the airport as I gassed up my clipped-wing cub, nicknamed the *Silver Slipper*, in preparation for the day's towing. My buddy, Jeff, also being assigned a clipped-wing cub for the day's flying, pulled up next to me on the flight line and waited to do the same with his aircraft. As the new guys that summer, we were the last to be able to get our aircraft fuel so that we could snatch banners from the grass and earn some beach, bar, and babe money.

I finished feeding my beast and was attaching three grappling hooks while Jeff took his turn fueling his ride when the owner of the business, Mr. Andre Tomalino, drove up, rather rapidly, and waddled over to Jeff and me. He had a pensive look on his face, as he usually did when something was pissing him off. He shepherded Jeff and I together, and in a very bold and outspoken manner told us that we, "the company," had lost a banner over Diamond Beach (it's a beach on Wildwood Crest, in Southern Wildwood) due to a kite (kite string will cut through a banner's tow rope like a hot knife through butter). Mr. Tomalino told us that the banner pilot who reported the loss said there were a lot of kites near/over Diamond Beach. He then told us, since we hadn't yet started towing, to go scout out the situation and, if we had to, "take them out."

I asked Mr. Tomalino, "When you say 'take them out,' what exactly do you mean . . .?"

At that seemingly stupid question – at least I gauged it was stupid due to the immediately quizzical look and then subsequent frown upon Andre's face – he said, "I don't care if you have to shoot them down, I don't want any more of my banners being lost due to those kids and their kites."

Well, you don't have to tell two nineteen-year-old college kids full of piss, vinegar, and hormones, twice that they have creative license in taking down those "sons of bitches communist kids' kites."

In no time, Jeff and I neared Diamond Beach, the southernmost beach on Wildwood Island, from where most of the day's banners start their northbound run headed up said island or beyond, depending upon how far north the advertiser wants his particular banner towed. Since the airspace above Diamond Beach was so pivotal to Paramount's towing operation, it had to be held at all costs, and nothing less than unconditional surrender by the enemy would suffice!

And because Jeff was older than me by a year, and was the finest natural pilot I have ever known (other than my father), I deferred the lead to him and flew about fifty yards off, and slightly behind, his left wing.

I have to admit a certain adrenaline rush as we alighted from the runway bound for certain battle. As I usually did when flying my banner aircraft, I imagined that I was flying some sort of World War I or II fighter aircraft, and today, Jeff and I were flying Sopwith Camels and heading toward Richthofen's Flying Circus . . . I make no excuses for my vivid daydreaming, it made life that much more colorful.

As we approached the beach from the northwest at 500 feet above the ground, I was amazed at the enemy's numbers. In my rather imaginative mind back then (and no, I didn't do drugs), I envisioned that the kites were barrage balloons and needed to be taken out; but with so many, it was intuitively obvious that we had our work cut out for us.

At this point, I must say that I never gave thought to any possible ramifications for this up-and-coming duel—not in regard to the FAA and its regulations, any local laws/regulations forbidding kite killing, or to the possibility of injury to those flying the kites, neither the tethered ones nor those powered by their Lycoming engines. (The term *kite* is often given to the type of aircraft that Jeff and I were flying because they are built with a light metal frame and covered in fabric.) Though I can't fully speak for Jeff, as we never really talked about our personal feelings after this event, I think I can safely say that we just never gave it a second thought. Our boss had told us to go take out the kites, and that's what we were going to do. Andre's immediate wrath was far more real than the FAA's, and I go back again to the aforementioned, "We were nineteen-year-old college kids" phrase. In addition, I think I might have rationalized that I was under the "corporate veil" or some idealistic college bullshit such as that and could not be legally prosecuted for my actions.

To digress a bit, the reason the kites were a factor that day, versus most other days, was due to the rather strong wind from the northwest. A cold front had come through, and with it, the winds shifted from an onshore sea breeze to an offshore blow. In the limited time I had been towing, I was told that this would happen periodically, the kites being "blown" out to sea, and to avoid the kite string that tethered these seemingly innocuous vehicles of flight. I don't really understand the aerodynamics of it, but the string from a kite stays relatively low over the ground, and then as it nears the spot over where the kite is flying, it rises dramatically upward; it's not linear at all. As you tow a banner down the beach and are crabbed into the wind, your banner is driven out to sea; and invariably, if you are not careful, the kite string comes between the banner and the aircraft and, as the twine runs its course across the tow rope, slices it, and the banner drops to the sea. When the kites are few and sporadic,

avoiding them is usually not a big deal and easily done. But that day
. . . whoa . . . it was like revenge of "The Kite Kids from Hell.' There
was no way to really avoid them without flying too far offshore
or avoiding the beach altogether, leaving the advertisers feeling as
though they weren't getting their money's worth.

So, there we were, Jeff and I, and I had no idea how to "down a
kite." I threw out my grappling hook with the intention of snagging
one, and then I watched, mesmerized, as Jeff just literally smashed
into one with his propeller. Hmmmm, I never thought of being
that straightforward, but I have to say that made short work of the
kite. Now mind you, all the kites back then were the standard box
kite, the plastic bat-wing style, or the traditional triangular-paper-
and-wood one that defines our thoughts of what a kite looks like.
After Jeff's initial smashing success, I tried to drag one from the sky
and failed miserably. Meanwhile, Jeff had quickly spun around and
taken out another. In no time, he was going to be an ace.

Ya know, his aggressiveness was actually surprising to me, as on
the ground I swear this guy was one of the most laid-back and non-
threatening individuals I've ever known. But Lord, put him in an
aircraft and, jeez, he turned into a killing machine!

As I watched "Baron von Richthofen" go for his third kill, I was
startled when I accidentally slammed into a kite myself. I hadn't
seen it because this one was flying much higher than the others, and
I had been "hawking the fight" while Jeff waded right in amongst
the pesky critters.

As the Baron took out his third kite, I decided to fly over
the beach to see what kind of miscreants had decided to invade
Diamond Beach and challenge Andre's air supremacy. I was amazed
as I zoomed over the beach to see all the kids below—well, those

actually flying kites—desperately reeling in their weapons! One kid had a trailer that he towed on his bike, and on it was a drum/spool type thing that appeared to hold all his kite string, which he could wind in with bicycle pedals, literally a winch type of setup. I looked to see where his twine headed so I could locate his kite, and quite literally you could see it—the kite—descend as it was being pedaled in. With such a setup, I knew this kid was a true professional, and I had to tip my hat to him! And though I knew he would be back one day to do certain harm to our banners, I just couldn't take out his kite. I had looked into the enemy's eyes, albeit from a few hundred feet up, and decided to be chivalrous and grant him a reprieve.

After what I was assumed was Jeff's fifth kill, the skies were quickly clearing of the vermin and Jeff and I headed back to the airport, feeling totally victorious—with Jeff unofficially crowned as ace of the base. We taxied up to our operations area on the ramp without any fanfare and with no sign of our Italian leader. Thusly we began, again, our day of gassing up and rearming for banner towing.

The rest of the day was pretty routine and though there were a few kites flying off some of the other beaches, it was light resistance at best and not very well organized. We had broken the back of the enemy and once again Paramount Air Service had air superiority over the South Jersey beaches; life was good.

Until the day I towed my last banner and left for the USAF, four years or so later, I never again saw that many kites in one place. Their first attempt, the Communist Kite Kids of Wildwood, was their last . . . their limited numbers disappeared into the many numbers of law-abiding beachgoers and "Shoo Bees" of the shore.

The story doesn't end there though since there was a revenge of sorts by the kite kids. One day, as I was heading to Ocean City with a banner in tow, and while still over the back bays off Sea Isle, Jeff came zooming by me and did a barrel roll, pulling nothing but a tow rope. It seems he had lost his vigilance while towing a banner off Sea Isle, and a kite got it. Chalk one up for the kids. I'd lay money down that it was that bugger with the little trailer and big spool of twine. Ultimately, in my four years of flying for Paramount, I never lost a banner to a kite . . . mercy has its rewards.

CHAPTER 1

While most kids languish in their early years trying to decide what to do for a living, that was not the case for me. I knew at a relatively young age that I wanted to be a pilot, I just never thought I could fly, though I hoped and prayed as such. Maybe because I saw the escape that flying afforded my father from his miserable existence while at home did I yearn to do the same—fly to escape. My biggest problem (as I saw myself becoming a social misfit as I matured, thanks to growing up in the psychological hell fostered by my parents) was I had no self-confidence or belief in myself that I could ever rise to the position of being an airline captain like my father. Nor, even if I felt so inclined to be an airline pilot, did I have a clue as to how I should shape my life so as to achieve that lofty goal.

However, in hindsight, I can see clearly that providence continually bathed me as I grew with the sovereignty of God directing my every footstep toward my childhood dreams. It truly is amazing the amount of times my father tried to divert me into this career or that one, only for his motives to be thwarted while many other unplanned and career-enhancing events occurred outside of his manipulation. Providence, God, has taken me beyond my dreams and aspirations and has allowed me to become a B-777 captain for one of the greatest airlines in history. I do not hold any human accountable for where my career has marched—no, I give God the glory for my good fortune. Very rarely did I ever think of what my future steps should be to get me to where I am now because my forethoughts for most of my life usually extended only to today and very rarely beyond tomorrow. However, like most people, I did have some pretty grandiose dreams, which I shared with God on the many evenings I sat on a South Jersey beach gazing at the sand, sky and sea. Never, *ever*, did I expect to actually get to visit the exotic places that existed over the eastern horizon as I watched tiny flashing lights far up in the sky fly into a rising sun.

The seed of my faith, which I feel has shepherded and protected me all my life, was planted well before I ever took my first airline flight. My introduction to a God greater than the demigod of whom my father believed he was occurred very early in my adolescence when my seemingly non-Christian mother taught me to recite the Lord's Prayer at the age of seven:

Our Father in heaven, hallowed be Your name. Your kingdom come. Your will be done, on earth as *it is* in heaven. Give us this day our daily bread and forgive us our debts, as we forgive our debtors. And do not lead us into temptation, but deliver us from the evil one. For Yours is the kingdom and the power and the glory forever. Amen. (Matthew 6:8–13, NKJV)

What prompted her to do this, I have no idea, as she never manifested any semblance of the Christian faith herself; but whatever her reasons, she felt compelled to get me to commit to memorizing the Lord's Prayer and praying it every night before I went to bed. As of this writing, except for a few occasions, I have never broken from that covenant with her.

I don't know if she taught my sisters to pray the same, and oddly, I never actually heard her say it after she taught it to me, so maybe to her it was always said in the privacy of her own personally tortured soul.

As for my father, for most of his life he was a practicing pagan, many times telling me as he drowned himself in his beloved beer that it was "nectar from the gods." There is no doubt he worshipped his godly beer almost more than flying and certainly more than his wife and kids.

I firmly believe it was my faith in the Father of the Lord's Prayer that protected me from the hell that infused my home when my daily drunken father would morph into one of his "moods" and railed against his wife or me. And it was that prayer that was the catalyst that has taken me on a long, slow dance with God and the Christian faith. The meaning, intent, and promise of God's words in the Lord's Prayer, and my belief in them and Him, have caused me to persevere through many trials, tribulations, and periods of intense emotional grief as the years have quite literally flown by.

As odd as it may sound, given what I revealed thus far, there was a genuine blessing and silver lining in being my father's son. The silver lining of which I speak is the amazingly incredible aviation adventures that have intertwined, woven, and coalesced my father's and my lives together in spite of our often personal repugnance of each other.

Many, many, times while growing up, my father said to me, "In life, every knock is a boost," to which my mother would add, "Every dark cloud has a silver lining."

If I've heard those phrases once, I've heard them a thousand times. Usually, they were stated at the worst possible time for me to hear them if only because they'd be sternly quoted, in tandem if both parents were near. That was my parents' way of cheering me up.

But to be honest, as the years went by and as I would discover, they were true words of wisdom.

Though my parents were terrible at parenting, being raised in our household was not all bad. For one, I was born into a wonderfully aviation-graced womb, in which I was continually nourished while still in the embryonic stage of my own aviator development. In addition, because of having to live with such horribly and fundamentally flawed parents, my faith became a beacon of hope that I might not have seen had I enjoyed a saner upbringing. Finally, learning how to live with both parents' extreme moods helped me to work well with certain types of "greatest generation" grumpy and crusty captains when I eventually became employed in the airlines.

CHAPTER 2

My aviation career – and please excuse me as I am not trying to sound boastful or prideful – but my career itself, at least when I compare it to most pilots with whom I've spoken over the years, has been a kind of Camelot affair. I started flying at fifteen, towed aerial advertising banners above the South Jersey beaches in Super Cubs during the summer months of my college years, went on from there to fly F-4s and F-16s in the USAF/ANG, and then as a natural progression from the military, I went into the airlines and have been a captain on both the MD-11 and the B-777. As I write this, I am still with the airline for whom I was hired in early 1988, and I can say without hesitation that so far it's been a wonderfully fantastic and blessed ride, particularly considering that many times when I was in my teens, I very seriously contemplated suicide.

Cradling, caring, and feeding me aviation lore while I was still developing a sense of airmanship and in the aeronautical womb were my father and a few of his colleagues and friends. Occasionally, a "whiskey front" (an impromptu alcohol-fueled party) would blow through the immediate neighborhood and cause these denizens of the sky to land and take refuge on our patio or in some local American-style pub. Like a fly on the wall, I would listen to these sky gods talk about their craft, as they eagerly drank their high-octane fuel of choice. The more fuel they drank, the more their physical actions became animated, as their hands and arms sprang to life, mimicking the flight paths of the suddenly reincarnated mounts in which they flew during the heyday of their glory years: biplanes, T-6s, P-51s, F-86s, F-100s, F-105s, DC-3s, DC-4s, and 6s and finally, three- and four-engine jets were reconstituted in situ. Esoteric air battles of World War II and the Cold War were re-enacted as were airline flights of desperation, daring or passion, all in vivid, colorful detail . . . including sound effects. So many aerial fights and flights of fancy, no doubt embellished, were recalled on those severe weather "daze" with much jet fuel consumed in their telling and all for me to see and hear; my respect for these knights of the air was immense as they were truly wonderful men and pilots and the crème de la crème of Brokaw's greatest generation.

Being unabashedly biased, the best of the lot was my father. However, before I discuss the complexities of what made him so incredibly amazing as an aviator, I must tell you of another amazing pilot who was both a colleague and friend of my dad's and a man whom God used to help shape my own career.

Robert Grace lived behind my house in Linwood, New Jersey. He was so laid-back and modest, yet my father said Bob was one of the best stick-and-rudder pilots with whom he ever flew; coming from my father, that was a great, and very rare, compliment. I can honestly say I believe that my dad was jealous of Bob because he flew fighter aircraft for most of his adult life and may have been more of a naturally gifted pilot than the old man himself. All I know is that anytime my father spoke of Mr. Grace, it was with a reverence that he never bestowed upon any other aviator.

Mr. Grace started his career flying P-51s in World War II and then, after the war, came back to New Jersey and flew a variety of fighter aircraft in the Garden State's Air National Guard: F-84 (both models – Thunderstreak and Thunderjet); F-100 (again both models); and then the ultimate testosterone producer in men, Republic F-105 Thunderchief.

When Bob was hired as a flight ops test pilot with the FAA, the same position as my father, I don't know, but it was sometime in the mid 1960s.

While flying full-time with the FAA, Bob also continued to fly part-time in the locally based Air National Guard unit where he flew whatever fighter jet they operated at the time (every few years or so, they would reassign the unit based at Atlantic City Airport a different type of fighter).

One day one of those aforementioned whiskey fronts happened to blow into my backyard, and I couldn't have been happier as that day was truly a silver lining in contrast to ever-thickening dark clouds that began to tighten their grip on my house and the souls within it during this period of time. My father and a few of his colleagues voluntarily grounded themselves for a Friday afternoon and evening to "refuel." As the sun faded, emotional spirits soared as the liquid spirits were consumed in vast quantities. Being in my early teens, I felt gifted by God as these amazing aviators told their stories, as I had so many wonderful storytellers around me, allowing me to be privy to a world that only they, the angels, and God could know.

I remember this one particular occasion because Mr. Grace was party to an interesting tale that I will never forget. Bernie Hughes, the originator of the story, was also a flight ops test pilot who had flown P-47s in the war, and who, like Bob, flew all the same fighters in the same Air National Guard units. Mr. Hughes recanted the story, no doubt to quell my incessant badgering of the pilots as they were mingling about for flying stories of daring, adventure, and fancy.

After Mr. Hughes took a nip of his Scotch, he began to tell of the day that Bob Grace almost had to bail out of an F-84 whose engine had flamed out as they were returning from a mission flown off the New Jersey coast. Continuing his narrative and his nipping, Bernie said that as they neared Atlantic City and while still above 10,000 feet, Mr. Grace's engine quit for no apparent reason. Bob immediately set up a glide, headed toward the Atlantic City Airport, which is actually ten miles northwest of the city, and, as he rather quickly lost altitude (F-84s do not glide well), had diverted most of his attention to trying to start the F-84's only engine. Down Bob descended, and, as Bernie told the story, he flew alongside Bob, trying to keep him abreast of their position, and more importantly of their altitude since Bob was so intent on getting the jet's engine running. Bernie was afraid Bob would lose track of his height above the ground and might possibly get too low to bail out should the engine not start at a reasonable-enough altitude.

Bernie said to Bob, as they went through 3000 feet, "Ya know, Bob, you may have to jump out of that thing."

Bob did not respond.

From three to two to finally a thousand feet, Bernie was calling out altitudes and telling Bob to get out of the jet; silence was Bob's answer.

Finally passing one thousand feet, Bob said he got the engine running and was waiting for it to spool up to speed so he could develop usable thrust and climb. At 500 feet, Bob's descent stopped, and he climbed to 1,500 feet and landed straight in on runway 31, now only a few miles straight ahead.

Concluding the story, Bernie said to Bob, "Ya know, Bob, I've never told you this before, but you are my hero for going so low to save that jet. I would've punched out much sooner!"

For Bernie to say that Bob was his hero was a big deal for Bernie, because quite simply, Bernie had a really big ego, and my father always thought Bernie's biggest hero was Bernie himself.

As my father and I listened to the end of Bernie's short story, Bob chimed in, "Bernie, to this day, I have never told anyone this, other than God Himself, but do you know why I never ejected that day?"

Bernie, in a look of surprise as he added more jet fuel to his gas tank said, "I assumed you wanted to save the jet."

"No, that's not why. To be honest, I didn't care about the jet at that point. No, the real reason I stayed so long in the cockpit was because I had never armed the ejection seat prior to getting in the jet, so I couldn't have ejected if I wanted to . . . so let me tell you, I had a lot of personal motivation to get that engine started."

And with that, Bob took a sip of his scotch and gave a quick wink to me while my dad and Bernie belly-laughed, and I vowed to myself that if I ever flew fighters, I would always arm my ejection seat prior to getting into the cockpit.

While that heretofore untold story is cute, it is just a lead-up to one of the coolest thing's I've ever heard a pilot do—maybe not the smartest, but what Bob did in the early 1980s in a Convair 880 rivals the gutsiest move ever made by an aviator, other than what Maverick did in the movie Top Gun (you'll have to watch the movie to get that).

The magnum opus of Bob's flying career, and an event any pilot would relish to claim as an accomplished feat (but without the scrutiny of the FAA), came in the summer of 1980. In my heart, it remains the gutsiest move of any pilot I have ever known in my life, even to include Maverick's infamous spilt S.

On a sultry August day, Nan 42, an FAA-owned CV-880, was being flown by Captain Bob Grace, Captain Jess Terry, and Flight Engineer Louie DeStefano to Oklahoma City, Oklahoma; the aircraft had been purchased by the Navy and was being delivered.

As my father drove with Bob to work that day, my dad said, "You don't have a hair on your ass if you don't do something special as you depart."

Bob, like an eternal young boy in spirit, assured my father that he had "something special" in mind.

Taking off on runway 13 and trailing the signature black smoke emanating from its four CJ805 General Electric jet engines, Bob flew the aircraft out past Atlantic City, about ten miles to the southeast, and then turned around to come inbound on runway 31, heading in the opposite direction from which he departed. He was flying at 1,500 feet and 250 knots.

My father, and all the flight test boys, loved the CV-880. It was an old jet by then, but it was like the fighter jet of four-engine jets, so said my father. It was fast, at least for a four-engine transport jet, and had an aura and mystique that few big jets of that day carried despite test pilot guys having practically flown the aircraft around the world testing this or that thing. In fact, my father flew Nan 42 to Alaska, landing at various airports up there that weren't used to seeing four-engine jets; in that trip, the old man and his crew participated in the rescue of a family that made an emergency landing in a Piper Comanche, on a sand bar, near Bethel (Alaska).

So, as Nan 42 powered to the northwest in a stately fashion, all the flight test pilots that weren't flying that day, and various other FAA employees, were either on the ramp or on the roof of the massive flight ops hangar, watching the flyby and paying silent tribute.

Then as the sleek four-engine jet approached midfield its nose rose, first through ten, then twenty degrees of pitch and as the aircraft climbed more black smoked squirted out the back as power increased to support the rather rapid climb. And then the aircraft began a right roll and climbed some more, and rolled even more, until it was soon upside down. And then as the nose fell slightly, the black smoke lessened, and the aircraft continued to roll; and the nose fell some more, and she rolled some more. Soon, Nan 42 was at level flight at 1,500 feet and near 250 knots after having done a barrel roll.

Louie DeStefano told me later that it was about as perfect a barrel roll as could have been flown. He said he was looking at his flight engineer's instrument panel, which faces away from the front of the aircraft and as he did so, he'd noticed a slight increase in "seat-of-the-pants pressure," G force, but, what really caught his attention was the change in the light pattern on his panel. When he looked forward, he about threw up because they were completely upside down and, upon seeing that they were inverted, he got instant vertigo. As he looked away, his first reaction was to grab his coffee and pencils, which were sitting on his flight engineers panel. He was, in his words, "amazed that the pencils never moved and my coffee remained level in its cup, never spilling."

After that grand event, to the shock and awe of the observers below, Nan 42 continued on to Oklahoma City. Jess Terry, the other captain, not being privy to Bob's mischievous intentions, was not happy that they just rolled an FAA-owned CV-880 above an FAA-owned airport and test center; repercussions were sure to follow. (They did—it took Bob two years to get his flying privileges back.)

Tex Johnston, a test pilot for Boeing in the 1950s, achieved great fame by rolling "Dash 80" (the prototype for the four-engine B-707) over Lake Washington, near Seattle, in August of 1955. Actually, two rolls were done, and Tex has received much acclaim for that event over the years.

With a much smaller crowd of spectators observing Bob, but with no less the same swashbuckling swagger, he did something that I've not heard done since Tex Johnston's infamous maneuver. He may have had to do the tap dance of his life in front of his boss and the higher-ups to get his flying privileges reinstated, but in my humble opinion, it was worth it.

CHAPTER 3

"Your father is a man of mystery," my mother once said. She said this because she knew very little of his adolescent life, previous marriage, or of the three children from that first marriage. In fact, when my dad divorced his first wife, in the early 1950s, he never his ex-wife nor the children from that marriage again. Also, just as heat is the energy source that drives a hurricane, most of the maelstroms of torment in my father's sandblasted soul were almost continuously fed by an emotional fermentation process caused by a closely held secret that brought wave upon wave of fervent distress into his psyche. What my father told me on the day he passed away, regarding a tryst between him and his mother and the topic of that meeting, permanently put to rest the nagging question in my heart as to what caused most of his repressed anger; I am the only person to whom he ever confided this secret. Finally, swirling along with the aforementioned innuendo of sin by his mother, and the grief it generated in his heart, were his deep-seated feelings of insecurity due to his own father's parental indifference and alcoholism, and a Napoleon complex due to his diminutive physical dimensions.

This trilateral assemblage of dysfunction created a bipolar, but amazingly well-functioning, aviator who was very effective at compartmentalizing the various extremes of his past and present while he flew. Once safely on the ground, however, and off duty, my father would begin to imbibe, daily, on tremendous quantities of alcohol, and then he could either be an attentive and charming father and husband or morph into a banshee or ghoul and reign extreme upon his castle and its inhabitants. His moods when not at work were as unpredictable as the movement of hurricanes, but in the aviation arena, he was steadfast with an easygoing and very laid-back temperament.

Without question, and even as broken as he was when not flying, my father was and is the greatest aviation hero of my life. Though his misdeeds on the ground as both a father and husband could be considered, at best, dysfunctional, his skill in the aviation realm was beyond all reproach. When strapped into an aircraft, I swear angels possessed his spirit, and he flew and spoke as if God Himself took delight in manipulating His creation. I have never known a human who could articulate their craft as well as he whilst instructing, or equally manipulate the controls of his flying machine with such forethought, skill, cunning, and grace. He was my mentor, as I grew wings of my own, and let there be no doubt, though my father officially began to teach me his trade when I was fifteen, the actual indoctrination and edification began many, many years earlier. There were times as an adolescent when I got to fly with him while he was working, and I listened as he and his buddies talked shop, or more personal still, when I was freshman in high school and we began the tradition of our backyard patio talks with him telling me personally of his stories of aviation romance and adventure while he slowly drank himself to sleep.

It was at Christmas in my first year of high school when my father bought me a book called Fate Is the Hunter. I was an avid reader back then since books were a cerebrally exciting form of escape from my home life and an absolute enjoyment since the earliest days of my youth. The impact of that book cannot be understated; it was truly a silver lining during a dark Christmas season that showed no joy, only derision and a deepening sarcasm and bitterness (as if it could get any worse) between my mother and father. In a very slow, subtle, and persistent way the contents of it began to change and shape my life. It took me from being in my dreadful and oftentimes emotionally oppressive and spirit-killing house to flying around in an opportunity and action-filled world with a heavy dose of adventure and drama and topped off with awe. What that magnificent man (Ernest Gann, the author of the book) and his flying machines did, and where he went, captivated me more than any other career in the world. But what struck me like a lightning bolt, in one of those "Aha!" moments, after reading the book, was the fact that I had my own Ernest Gann, albeit a sometimes very drunk and potentially nasty one, living under my roof.

Since Fate Is the Hunter caused an epiphany, I began to take time in the early evenings, before I went out with friends, or after returning home later in the evening, to ask my father to tell me stories of his flying adventures. Generally, no matter what mood he may have been in at the time and no matter how drunk, the one thing that my father always loved to do was reminisce about his past. He could be in the foulest of moods, but if I began asking him about his flying life, it usually dulled the emotional cutting torch he might be wielding at the time.

Like the beer he drank, the stories would flow as long as I was willing to listen. Most of his stories were told to me outside our house, on the patio, late in the evening, and under the protective sword of Orion with the faint glow of its companion constellations softly illuminating his steely eyes. He was usually smoking a cigar and drinking a beer while the muffled notes from big band greats playing on the stereo indoors softly filled the spaces between audible pauses in his rambling musings. Hearing him talk of his worldwide escapades was truly the most marvelous gift an aviation-interested child could have since it was like having a never-ending Fate Is the Hunter book read to me, if not melodramatically acted out, over many, many nights as I haphazardly bounded along in my teenage years.

CHAPTER 4

In the spring of 1940, Kenneth Blair Johnson graduated from high school in Bedford, Massachusetts, and even though he had a scholarship offered to him from the Boston College of Fine Arts, he told his father he first wanted to have a go at flying. Harry was all for Ken taking flying lessons versus going to college, particularly since his son would have majored in the fine arts, which Harry thought was a weak man's vocation. His mother, Elsie, on the other hand, was caught betwixt her love for her son and his desires, and her fear of losing her only child in an aircraft accident. Being the matriarch, however, didn't blunt the coup d'état by the men who were successful in causing Elsie to hold in abeyance her maternal fears and allow Ken to have a chance to spread his wings.

After arguing for his son's desires, in July 1940 Harry plunked down $5000 on the counter of Wiggin's Airways, a flight school located at East Boston Airport (now called Logan). That money was more than just a down payment on flying lessons for an immature young man steeped in a devil-may-care attitude, it was the seed money for his growth, at least that was his father's hope. By taking to flight, Harry hoped the responsibility of being an aviator would cause his son to turn the corner from adolescence to manhood. The final product, though it would come after many years of cavorting amongst the wind-tossed clouds with both cherub and gremlin alike, was a sort of male Sybil: Ken demonstrated incredible angelic qualities when surrounded by the stratosphere, but this heavenly air went stale when alcohol-fueled insecurities tormented him while on the ground.

I have no doubt that had he chosen a career in the fine arts he would have been a constantly tortured soul, rapidly drinking himself to death, as his genius melted into insanity. And with that said, there is no doubt to me that hell is under our feet as my father was so badly tortured by persistent and furtive Hades-borne demons clinging to and influencing him when his feet were actually grounded to terra firma. I believe it was by providence that he chose a profession that allowed him at least some freedom from pain while he was airborne.

And airborne he was . . . a lot. When I began to fly at the age of fifteen, my father was fifty-two and had already been in the air for 24,000 hours (almost three years) of his life and showed no signs of letting up. By the time he whispered his last words to me on his deathbed, at the age of seventy-nine, he said he had accumulated approximately 35,000 flight hours; his flying career spanned fifty-seven years, from biplanes to four-engine jets, from NDBs and four-legged ranges to GPS navigation, and from Boston to circling the globe.

The first of the old man's extraordinarily large amount of flying time began after Wiggin's went to the bank with the five grand that Harold gave them for his son's flight training.

After earning his pilot's license, the old man kept going and earned his instructor rating and soon after began teaching students while employed by Wiggin's. Eventually he began to teach instrument flying too, and after America became officially involved in

World War II, Ken was transferred to Springfield, Missouri, where he taught basic flying training and aerobatics in a Waco UPF-7 biplane.

Fulfilling his contract with Wiggin's in early 1943, he then joined the Army Air Corps, got married to his first wife, and was promptly shipped out to Finschhafen, New Guinea, to captain C-47 cargo aircraft. In my father's own words, it was not glamorous duty, and he greatly envied the swashbuckling fighter pilots of the day.

When the war ended, my dad, Ken, came back to the States in November 1945, and like so many thousands of other jubilant servicemen, he was happy the conflict ended but anxious about the prospects of battling tens of thousands of other pilots against the backdrop of a dearth of domestic airline flying positions.

In 1946, Meteor Air Transport (MAT) emerged from a business model drawn on the back of a napkin by a dreamer, Bob Morrow, and into reality. The non-sked[1] started its operations at Teterboro Airport, then just a cinder strip, which was (and still is) located just north of Newark, New Jersey, and across the Hudson River from New York City. (In fact, Meteor's main hangar and attached offices are still there, though the airport itself is much bigger and now is a huge hub for corporate aircraft.) Ken was one of the first pilots Meteor brought onboard, being hired so quickly because of his young age, twenty-five, yet high amount of flying time as a captain—particularly in the C-47 (the C-47 was the military version of the Douglas DC-3).

Hired as a DC-3 captain in May, 1946, at the rate of seventy-five dollars per week, Kenny (that was his nickname) flew his first trip on the nineteenth of that month. It was unlike any trip he had

---

1. Non-sked—the Civil Aeronautics Board's efforts to limit competition on transcontinental routes were seriously challenged by scores of new airlines that emerged after World War II. These nonscheduled airlines, or "non-skeds," carried cargo and passengers on irregular or charter services.

ever flown up until that point and was one heck of an introduction to the world of flying in the non-skeds.

At 2 p.m. local time my father, with Mike Segan as his co-pilot and mechanic, flew from Teterboro, New Jersey, to Mobile, Alabama.

In Mobile, they loaded up on flowers and flew to Chicago's Midway Airport.

They flew VFR on top[2], my dad said, as it was easier than flying IFR. Approaching Chicago, they were asked to climb to a higher altitude due to IFR traffic, but my father refused because he said he saw the traffic, a TWA DC-3, and that there was not going to be a conflict (as a point of note, my father had at least 20/15 vision if not 20/10 for most of his younger (under sixty) life). The controller[3] and he got into a pissing contest because my dad refused to climb and the controller said he was going to alert the authorities about my father's intransigence. Being true to his word, the controller—that is, a CAA[4] representative—was there to "happily" greet my father upon their arrival at the Midway ramp.

As the cargo was unloaded from the aircraft, my dad and the CAA representative went for breakfast in the terminal cafe to discuss

2. VFR on Top is defined as air traffic control authorization for an aircraft operating under Instrument Flight Rules (IFR) to do so in visual meteorological conditions (VMC) at any appropriate visual flight rules (VFR) altitude. A pilot receiving this authorization must comply with the VFR visibility, distance from cloud criteria, and the minimum IFR altitudes.

3. Air Traffic Controllers are personnel responsible for the safe, orderly and expeditious flow of air traffic in the global air traffic control system. Usually stationed in air traffic control centers and control towers associated with certain airports, they monitor the position, speed, and altitude of aircraft in their assigned airspace visually, by radar, or by time separation over checkpoints and give directions to the pilots by radio.

4. In 1938, the Civil Aeronautics Act transferred federal responsibilities for non-military aviation from the Bureau of Air Commerce to a new, independent agency, the Civil Aeronautics Authority. The CAA, was responsible for air traffic control, safety programs, and airway development. The CAA eventually became what it is now known today – The FAA (Federal Aviation Administration.)

the matter at hand. In the end, the CAA gentleman said this was a nonevent and bid my father adieu; theirs was a friendship of mutual respect that would continue to grow throughout the ages as they each matured in their relative positions. Sadly, though, some of their meetings would take place after a couple of fatal Meteor aircraft accidents.

With the unloading of the DC-3 complete, and a quick "power nap" by the crew, the boys were off yet again, this time to Beaufort, South Carolina, to pick up another load of flowers.

Arriving at 6 p.m., the aircraft was refueled and once again loaded with the South's sweet fragrance and tangible beauty. Pressing on, in spite of the coming night, they launched into a lovely evening sky with a waning sun off their left wing and headed for Providence, Rhode Island.

As twilight became night, they could visibly see evidence of a squall line encroaching upon their route of flight as they began to fly over Southern New Jersey. Almost continual fat, straight-down (from cloud to ground) lightning bolts or thinner, cracked-glass types of arcs shredded the balmy spring night air, and the ADF[5] needles on their instrument panel swung wildly with each discharge. Staying in visual conditions, Kenny elected to land short of the tempests, picking Atlantic City Naval Air Station as his port in the storm.

While normally a fairly routine act for most pilots and flights, landing an aircraft on that night turned out to be one of the more difficult landings my father ever had to do, though he wouldn't know it until much more of his flying life was behind him.

Every time the tower assigned him a runway upon which to land, the wind shifted with such fierceness, ferocity, and quickness

---

5. An Automatic Direction Finder (ADF) is an aircraft radio-navigation instrument that automatically and continuously displays the relative bearing from the aircraft to a suitable radio station or transmitting beacon.

that tower told him to abort. He tried every runway available, some multiple times, and with each approach nature decided to change her mind with regard to which way she wanted the wind to blow. Exasperated, my father told the tower he'd pick the runway and be responsible for the result. Eventually, he landed on runway 31[6], but the ride wasn't over yet!

Sounding like bullets, the windblown rain began to pelt the aircraft's sides as they taxied to parking, reminding my dad of the many tropical rainstorms he'd flown through a year earlier while in the Army Air Corps. Upon entering the ramp, the tempest fully enveloped them, and they were under the belly of the beast. To keep the aircraft from being damaged by such continuously shifting, strong, and severely gusting winds, Ken had to "fly" the aircraft while on the ground. By constantly manipulating the flight controls, the engines, and brakes, he tried to keep it pointed as best as he could into the wind so it wouldn't take off prematurely or get blown over and/ or off the ramp. Up to this point in his young life, it was the flight of his career and as usual, with seemingly boundless energy, enthusiasm, and a zest that surely only the angels could have infused, my dad popped out of the aircraft after the storm and performed his patented Irish jig dance to celebrate.

Gassing up, Dad and Mike blasted off into clearing skies and a brightening horizon as they went on to finish leg four of their five-leg whirlwind tour of the eastern half of the United States.

---

6. Runway 31—runways are identified in cardinal numbers related to their compass magnetic orientation. Hence runway 31 equates to a magnetic heading of 310 degrees (sometimes the actual runway heading is not exact). If there are two runways on the same airport that are parallel the left runway is designated 31L and the right 31R. If three runways, the middle one is 31C.

Just past sunrise, the Providence, Rhode Island, ramp readily accepted the brightly colored and sweet-smelling flowers. However, the ramp crew gave the very overripe and earthy-smelling flyboys a wide berth whenever they came near as the pair prepared for their last leg.

With the fueling complete and the cargo unloaded, they took off and turned westerly into a maturing day and quickly made their way home. Sliding into bed slightly less than two days after he left, my father was thoroughly exhausted when he got home but, conversely, thoroughly excited about his career choice.

His next trip began on June 6, and its itinerary was thus: He left New York City's LaGuardia airport in a C-47 (Military version of the DC-3) with Mike and twenty-eight passengers, fourteen of whom were to deplane in Salt Lake City with the remaining fourteen continuing on to San Francisco; there was no plan as to what Mike and my Dad were going to do once they got to San Francisco. My father had never flown transcontinental before, let alone over the Rockies, but such was his confidence that he never gave pause to think he shouldn't be flying the trip, let alone with twenty-nine other people. He said in wartime, he'd done so many things where the "regulation books were thrown out the window" that this airline flying seemed tame in comparison.

The flights to Salt Lake City and then San Francisco proceeded as follows:

1. LaGuardia to Chicago Midway

Good weather en route and an uneventful flight, so said my dad.

2. Midway to Omaha, Nebraska

West of Des Moines, Iowa, they encountered a huge line of thunderstorms. This time, instead of landing, they flew right through them. My father said back then they didn't have airborne or ground-based weather radar to guide them safely around weather, so sometimes the only option was to try and punch through the storms. In preparation for such drama, he lowered the aircraft's landing gear, turned on the interior cockpit lights to full bright, lowered his seat, and went to METO[7] power on the engines.

3. Omaha to Cheyenne, Wyoming

Uneventful.

4. Cheyenne to Salt Lake City, Utah

West of Cheyenne is where the Rockies begin, and my father said he climbed to 12,000 feet to clear them. He said the C-47 actually performed better than the DC-3 when it came to altitude/load capability, and he was glad he was flying a C-47 on this trip. They navigated back then using ADFs and Adcock ranges (also known as "four-legged range[8]").

With good weather in Salt Lake, they dropped off half of their fares, refueled, and then flew non-stop to San Francisco to liberate the remaining folks.

Now mind you, this flight into Salt Lake City and then beyond was done without any sleep for the crew; every stop between Teterboro and San Francisco was done for fuel and/or dropping off passengers, not rest.

---

7. METO power is the maximum power an engine is designed to produce continuously. Takeoff power is normally limited to 5 minutes or less on a reciprocating engine. In jet engines METO power is called Max Continuous with generally the same limitations.

8. Four Legged Range or Adcock Range is the low-frequency radio range (LFR), also known as the four-course radio range, LF/MF four-course radio range, A-N radio range, Adcock radio range, or commonly "the range," was the main navigation system used by aircraft for instrument flying in the 1930s and 1940s, until the advent of the VHF omni-directional range (VOR), beginning in the late 1940s. It was used for en route navigation as well as instrument approaches and holds.

Arriving in San Francisco just as the sun was rising above the low-slung mountains east of the city, a cuddling blanket of low-lying fog greeted the boys as they too crested the same mountains as the sun; somewhere in front of them their destination was submerged under a thick, velvety in appearance, white blanket of cloud. The view before them was surreal. It appeared as if an unseen hand had delicately tacked a slightly undulating, puffy, white carpet from one side of the bay to the other. The ground close to sea level was obscured from view, but the shoulders and peaks of the higher hills and mountains in the immediate bay area were above the fog's tops and stood radiant in the morning sunshine, as did some of the loftier reaches of the cityscape sculpting the vast bay's perimeter.

San Francisco Airport had a four-legged range approach to runway 28, and it was for that approach they were cleared as they neared the field. Being dog-tired, yet faced with the necessity of having to fly a to minimums[9] approach would probably have been daunting to most pilots. But Ken used to teach instrument flying as a relative youngster at Wiggin's, so this instrument approach with a six-hundred-foot overcast ceiling was a nonevent.

With the unloading of the passengers complete, the intrepid aviators put their aircraft to bed and then headed downtown in search of a bed for themselves. They found a reasonably priced hotel near present-day Fisherman's Wharf and after a few beers at the Buena Vista Hotel settled in for a well-deserved night's sleep.

Feeling totally refreshed, Ken and Mike arrived at the aircraft the next morning to begin their long flight home. As providence would have it, a note on the door of the aircraft, left by the Golden

---

9. Fly to Minimums—every instrument approach has a minimum altitude to which the aircraft may descend until the runway is sighted and it is deemed safe to land.

Gate Travel Agency, said they (the travel agency) had twenty-eight Marines eager to go to Seattle and wanted to know if my father would take them there. Desperate to make some money for their pubescent airline, the boys readily accepted the fares, and the next day at 8 a.m. sharp, they departed for Seattle, with one stop planed in Medford, Oregon, for fuel.

Arriving at Boeing Field a little past midday, they liberated the Marines from the confines of the well-used C-47 and once again put the aircraft to bed for the night. With an adventurous heart, my father and his charge headed downtown to Seattle proper in search of a hotel and a local newspaper.

Working on a tip given to him by the travel agency when they were in San Francisco, Kenny looked in the shipping news section of the paper to see what ships would be coming into port in the next couple of days and from where the crews were based. He located a ship with a New York-based crew and called the receiving company to find out if any of the ship's crew would want to fly back to New York in his C-47.

My dad said right after the war airline seats were at a premium because so many people were flying here and there, readjusting to postwar demographics. It was extremely difficult to find an open airline seat, and my father, now armed with this information, intended to try and turn a profit by going right to the consumer with an offer of twenty-eight cramped and uncomfortable seats in which he would whisk them across the country.

The representative of the shipping company asked my father how much he wanted for the flight to LaGuardia. My dad said $150 per person, thinking that was about all the crew would be willing to pay; the ship's officer said that was a bargain because the airlines were asking $300 or more, and that's if you could even find a seat.

The next day, twenty-eight weary, rubbery-legged merchant mariners boarded the claustrophobic confines of the C-47 and headed east for the long flight home. It was an overcast and dreary day when they took off, but soon, the C-47 climbed above the muck and mire of the lower atmosphere and broke out on top into brilliant sunshine with Mt. Rainer standing sentinel just off their right side. My father said the passengers all cheered when they got "on top" and were greeted with the effervescence of the snowcapped peak sparkling in the morning's rays.

Flying through the day and into the night, they were all exuberant – the passengers because they were going home, and the pilots because they were doing what they loved.

They landed in LaGuardia after five legs of uneventful flying.

After deplaning their passengers, they flew the short hop across both the East and Hudson rivers to their home base in Teterboro, officially ending their adventure.

In just two trips with his company, newly minted, twenty-five-year-old airline Captain Kenneth Johnson had flown from the top to the bottom of his nation and landed at airports lapped by the respective oceans upon each of its flanks. In those transcontinental crossings, he had carried safely families, immigrants, refugees, soldiers and sailors, and citizens. They all represented and contributed to the literal and figurative DNA that made up what was – and is – the body of America. In addition, the cargo he carried on his first trip may have made its way into some of his passenger's hands as expressions of love as they were welcomed home from long and far-away journeys.

In the immediate post-World War II years, and since their incorporation, Meteor struggled to gain a secure beachhead in the American economy. Nonsked airlines were a dime a dozen back then due to the huge number of surplus cargo/passenger aircraft dumped on the market by the military. Many two-bit financed dreamers threw their hats into the ring, trying to get rich in the lightly regulated nonsked business.

If you ask me what were the two best traits of my father, I'd have to say they were his eternal optimism and his unbelievable strength to overcome adversity when things were at their worst. He seemingly thrived on hardship, and in fact, when there was nothing wrong in his life, that's when he was at his worst.

As Meteor struggled to gain a business brand name and a continuous, positive cash flow, my father, who was now the chief pilot, was determined to keep the pilots' morale up since paychecks were sometimes either very low or bounced. So, to meet the individual needs of his workforce, the old man asked everyone to pool their earnings; and then each pilot would announce his most pressing financial obligation, and then the dollar amount equal to that need was doled out. If you ever saw the movie It's a Wonderful Life when they were trying to keep the bank from going under, it was exactly the same at Meteor during that financially stressful time.

When my dad told me stories of those hard times, his eyes glowed, and he gently smiled. You could tell he relished the hardship and the struggle, and he said those hard times pulled the pilot group so much closer together, like a big family.

During those dark days, while the airline struggled, my father said he and the airline's founder, Bob Morrow, formed a very tight friendship that transcended the workplace. My dad spoke with reverence of Bob every time his name needed mention in one of my father's stories, and the two remained close friends for many, many years and until Bob's untimely passing.

One of the lowest points in Meteor's early years came when my dad spent twenty-four hours in a jail in Reno, Nevada, for not being able to pay a fuel bill for a C-46 he flew in on a charter. Mr. Morrow wired money from his own personal account to the gas company, Texaco, and with that, all charges were dropped and the crew departed.

Though it was the end of a war that caused the beginning of Meteor, it would be the beginning of another that saved it. When the Korean War broke out in 1950, the military needed troop and material transport yesterday, and Lord knows there was a plethora of nonskeds willing to offer their services. Meteor, with its massive twin-engine C-46s and reliable DC-3s was able to slip nicely into this gravy train of government-financed logistics.

As serendipitous as the Korean War was, another more smoldering and longer-lasting war of subterfuge, intimidation, and espionage began to worsen. This war, in which the world was its stage, and which would extend Meteor's addiction to the government's financial teat after the end of the Korean "conflict" was the Cold War. The construction of the DEW line and the requisite material needed to build the radars' and operators' quarters, and also the resupply of the sites once they were built and manned, in addition to the requirement for increased troops and material in Europe, was another way in which Meteor's aircraft were utilized. In fact, it was the need for troops and war-fighting material in Europe that caused Meteor Air Transport to buy DC-4s to garner a bid from the Military Air

Transport Command, which called for regular troop carriage and material resupply service to certain American bases in Europe.

As the decade of the 1950s ticked slightly past the middle, Meteor's staple, bread-and-butter flights were nightly trips on behalf of the Big Three automobile manufacturers and DC-4 flights on behalf of Uncle Sam. Monday through Friday nights C-46s and DC-3s beat a well-worn path to the industrial cities of the Midwest – Detroit, St Louis, Chicago, Toledo, et al. Once there, the aircraft picked up urgently needed auto parts and delivered them to dealers and automobile assembly plants in the New York area or between a few of the larger Midwestern cities previously mentioned. As a supplement to this regular income, Meteor's twin-engine aircraft continued to fly charter flights to the West Coast, much in the same fashion as the ones my father flew when he first got hired.

For their part, the DC-4s would alight from Teterboro and fly to one of a few East Coast military bases where they would load up with either troops or cargo. Once loaded, the aircraft and crew would then fly to Gander, Newfoundland, where more fuel and a navigator were taken on board before hopping over the North Atlantic and landing in Shannon, Ireland to drop off the naviga-tor. Once again gassing up and checking the European weather, to include their destination and an alternate, the DC-4 then flew on to its final destination, wherever in Europe that was. After arriving at their destination, the crew went to the hotel while the aircraft was unloaded of its cargo or passengers; the DC-4's return flight was manned by a crew that had arrived within the previous day or two.

Of all the flying he did while at Meteor, my father said he loved the European flights in the DC-4s the most. He told me many sto-ries of his European and other worldwide adventures, but I'm sorry to say that the finer details of most of them have been carried away by the gentle breezes that eavesdropped upon our conversations.

There is one story, though, that I shall never, ever forget. If anything, what my father had to do to get his aircraft and crew safely to the ground, while on the following story's flight, further defines his supreme aviator persona and gives much credibility to my earlier statement about how he was always at his best when things were at their worst.

This amazing adventure began when my father and his crew were flying into Châteauroux-Déols Air Base, France, on a late fall's evening in 1956.

When telling me about his escapades while flying in Europe, my father often mentioned a seemingly ubiquitous and perpetual fog as one of the main or supporting characters in his tales. However, when I began to fly to England, and other destinations in Europe myself, I can't say I ever saw anything close to those Jack-the-Ripper, menacingly thick, London-type fogs that infiltrated many of my father's experiences. With each trip over there being devoid of even a heavy mist, I began to wonder if the old man was radically embellishing his stories to make them more profound.

But serendipity came to the rescue of my dad's integrity while I was on a trip to Wales, UK, in June 1997 and visiting an old coal mine. An elderly tour guide said that back "in the old days," almost every home and factory in England, if not in all of Europe, used to burn coal for heat and/or production of goods. This dependence upon coal for home and industrial related heating started in earnest with the beginning of the Industrial Revolution in the mid- to late-1700s and continued until legislation in the mid-20th century mandated cleaner burning fuels.

Further explaining the link between coal and fog, the guide said that when the homes burned coal for heat, usually during the colder months, and if the air was moist (humid), all this particulate matter floating about in the atmosphere was ripe for being coalesced. During the day, while the sun was high and the temperatures fairly warm, the sky would appear very hazy; but at night, when it cooled, malicious fogs would come out of hiding and appear ominously across entire counties, if not even countries. To add even more mayhem to this brew, if a low-pressure system was bringing in the moist air, it often brought with it an inversion. This was particularly bad as the inversion caused the warm coal smoke to settle back on the neighborhoods from whence it came, thusly polluting the polluters with a double dose of their own poisonous exhaust. These inversion-enhanced fogs could be so thick there were times when you couldn't see across the street. The dangerous health effects from these acidic fogs are pretty obvious, and in 1956, Britain enacted its first Clean Air Act, but the actual cleaner air wouldn't come until well after my dad's regular trips over there ended.

So back we go to the fall of 1956 as we reimmerse ourselves in my father's story . . .

As the Meteor DC-4 neared Châteauroux Air Base, the whole of Europe was blanketed in low clouds and fog. Just getting into Shannon, so said my dad, was a dicey affair as they had gone down to minimums in mist and drizzle as they approached; after departing for Châteauroux, the weather finally did go below minimums.

As they continued to their destination and checked the weather, their alternate[10], London Heathrow, went below minimums as did

---

10. Generally, when an aircraft is on an IFR (Instrument Flight Rule), flight plan it is required to have a back-up, alternate, airport that it can go to if the destination airport goes below minimums or closes.

all the other alternate airports that they normally would have used while flying into Châteauroux – Prestwick, Brussels, Frankfurt, Paris, etc. Everywhere they checked, the weather was below minimums.

Amazingly enough, the weather at their destination continued to hover just above minimums, so they held out hope that they would be blessed with a relatively easy arrival.

Not.

As they were being vectored for a GCA, Ground Controlled Approach, the radar controller told them that the weather had just gone below minimums; in fact, he said it was WOXOF[11].

Their options were now very limited. As they held[12] over the field, they used their radio to talk to the meteorologists in the military base below them and checked the weather at various airports in Europe. As the weather reports from around Europe began rolling in from the Teletype, it was becoming intuitively obvious that they were screwed. Every airport within range of their now-somewhat-depleted fuel supply was reporting weather that was either at or below minimums, and those airports that were much farther away but with weather that was decent were forecasting rapidly deteriorating conditions.

In the final analysis of the weather aspects of this flight, the good news was that they had the fuel to go somewhere; but the bad news was they simply had nowhere to go that was better than where they were now when time was factored in, at least according to the forecasters.

---

11. Early aviation weather term meaning indefinite ceiling which means the clouds are at ground level and the visibility is almost zero due to fog.

12. Essentially the aircraft preforms a small racetrack pattern in the sky, holding over a radio beacon. ATC will direct aircraft to hold if too many aircraft are trying to get into an airport at the same time, usually because the weather is bad and traffic flow slows.

In his evaluation of a game plan for a successful conclusion to their flight, my father said he "knew" Châteauroux Air Base. He was the captain on the company's first flight to the base and continued to fly there month in and month out. He knew its runway, the controllers, and the lay of the land around the airport. He felt comfortable there. So, after evaluating all the weather information, the facilities of the other airports with similar weather, and looking at all the other options available to them (there really weren't any), my father said he was going to shoot a GCA approach to a blind landing.

Probably the biggest factor in causing my father's reticence to leave Châteauroux was the fact that he trusted their GCA controllers, and he said the GCA, in his opinion, was the greatest invention since paid toilets. But then my father had many, many moments of fleeting hyperbole where he said a lot of things were the greatest invention since paid toilets, so I am not actually sure where on the pecking order of superlatives the GCA actually stood. And to be honest, as I write this, I never quite understood what it was about paid toilets that made my father love them so, as I never got into an in-depth conversation with him on the subject. But I can tell you on this night, the GCA was right up there with beer, aircraft and paid toilets.

Briefing the crew on the approach, he said he would monitor what heading it was that kept them on course as they neared "minimums" and once the controller said they were at minimums (whereupon the controller would no longer give directions) he would hold that heading as best as he could until landing. Concurrent with managing the heading, he said they needed to hold whatever average rate of descent it was that kept them on glideslope and continue with that descent rate once the controller went silent. Continuing, he briefed the boys that they had a lot of fuel so if the first approach was not going well, they could go around for another try, and another, and another until they nailed the numbers as precisely as they could. He finally added that there was very little wind that would affect them on this approach, so at least they had that going for them; and looking on the bright side, he said, "Since it is dark, we have a good chance of seeing the runway lights before we land." There was not one dissenting voice among the crew for my father's game plan.

Sticking to the plan, they got vectored out of the holding pattern and onto GCA final. With their gear and flaps down and slowed to final approach speed, they established contact with the final GCA approach controller. This controller told the DC-4 crew that they were approaching the glideslope and to not acknowledge further radio calls. Upon seeing the bright greenish dot, which was the actual raw data radar, return of the Meteor DC-4 on his cathode ray tube (CRT) reach a downward descending, much lighter green line that represented the three-degree Glideslope of the GCA, the controller said, "Begin descent." With that call, the flight engineer pulled off a bit of power on the engines, and my father lowered the aircraft's nose so as to begin a 500 to 600 feet per minute rate of descent toward an intensely black abyss.

Thus began an approach whose success or failure would define my father for his lifetime.

As they flew down an invisible, radar-derived glideslope into a night so thick with fog that some trains would refuse to leave their stations, the only way the crew on the DC-4 knew they were actually airborne was due to the various readings on their flight instruments indicating such. Vestibular, inner-ear sensations belied their actual aircraft's flight path and movement, causing the pilots to think they were in either a left bank or a right bank, pointing steeply toward the ground, or climbing rapidly when in actuality, they were wings level and in a precisely controlled descent, albeit blindly, toward what they hoped would be a lovely reunion with a runway. To land on the runway would be magic, but secretly, my father said any landing close to the runway and its relatively flat environment and one that didn't spell catastrophe for the crew would have been acceptable in his eyes; hence the adage, "Any landing you walk away from is a good one!"

The GCA controller's radarscope is split into two distinct presentations. The top part of the display, the glideslope, is represented by a slightly descending whitish green line on one part of the controller's radarscope, the length of which is measured in miles and altitude (horizontal and vertical axes, respectively). Below the glideslope is an absolutely straight horizontal line that indicates the final approach course to the runway, again represented in miles from the runway. The GCA controller, by cross-referencing the bright-green dot on the CRT, uses his/her radio to give heading and descent information to the aircraft, such as, "Turn right to 271 degrees, on course, slightly high on glideslope," etc. With each radio call by the controller, the pilot of the aircraft would turn in the appropriate direction and maintain that GCA-directed heading as best he/she could. Were it just a heading that the pilot had to fly, the GCA would be a relatively easy approach to fly. But to get down below the clouds, you flew a glideslope too. So, adding another dimension, the vertical, puts a little more dynamic stress on the approach and both the pilots' and controllers' respective duties. However, unlike the azimuth, where a specific heading was given to fly in the vertical plane (no pun intended), the controller simply states where the green dot is in relation to the glide slope line on the CRT and trend information. So, a GCA controller's calls might go like this:

"MATS 4, no need to acknowledge further radio calls, check gear down, six miles from the runway, on course, approaching glide slope."

"Begin descent, come left to 270, going slightly right of course."

"On Glideslope, come left to 269, slightly right of course."

"Going slightly high on Glideslope, come right to 270, on course."

"Holding slightly high on Glideslope, on course."

"Four miles from touchdown, on course, on Glideslope, you are cleared to land."

"Come left to 269, going slightly right of course, going slightly below Glideslope."

"Come right to 270, on course, slightly below Glideslope, correcting."

"Three miles from touchdown, on course, on Glideslope."

And down you flew, increasing your descent rate, or slowing it to try to match the glideslope as best as you can, and making little "baby steps" with the flight controls to maintain the controller-directed headings and descent as best as you can.

When I began to fly these approaches myself in the USAF, I thought the attention to detail in flying would be too difficult for me to handle and that I would fail miserably. But after some practice, I felt comfortable enough to fly the approach down to minimums; but beyond that, I wanted to see the runway for landing. The thought of actually flying the GCA blind, to landing, caused me to shudder every time I flew a practice GCA (or the two "real" weather GCAs I flew in an F-4 while going into Navy bases).

I cannot imagine what it was like for my dad to fly at 120 knots in a lumbering DC-4 on that miserable night. The F-4, and then the F-16 that I flew in the USAF, flew at 165 to 145 knots, respectively, and they were nimble and responsive and had ejection seats. I knew if worst came to worst, I could punch out (eject) and get a nylon letdown. Not so for the old man and his crew. Their asses were tied to whatever fate their skills and the controller's were able to achieve. Those are the times when no amount of pay is enough and when you secretly, or openly, wished you had thought about your career choice with greater detail and forethought.

The pilots flying these approaches back then did not have the luxury of an autopilot to use for the actual approach, autopilots being used only for cruise phase of flight during this period of aviation development. Consequently, the approaches were manually flown, using the pilot's hands, legs, feet, eyes, ears, intuition, and brains to guide the aircraft to a safe landing. Flying this type of approach takes attention to detail to the extreme when it comes to manipulating the flight controls and interpreting the aircraft's flight instruments. The control yoke, which controls movement of the ailerons and elevator is constantly being manipulated by the pilot to meet the parameters required to stay on course and on glide slope. If the heading is one degree off the pilot will make a slight bank, to correct, and then bank back slightly to hold the bank angle and then add input to the ailerons in the opposite direction to roll back to level flight to hold the new heading once achieved. In tandem with aileron movement, the rudder pedals may or may not be pushed depending upon their need to maintain coordinated flight. The elevator, too, is adjusted if the aircraft is slightly high, or low, on the glide slope. In this case, the yoke is either pushed, or pulled, gently, in order to lower or raise the nose in order to increase or decrease the rate of descent, or ascent, in order to get back on glide slope. But, almost immediately after the yoke is pushed or pulled in order to get on the correct glide path, it is readjusted again, ever so slightly, so as to remain on the correct glide path. The throttles are constantly manipulated too, usually in concert with an increase or decrease in elevator input to maintain the correct airspeed for the approach. Every input of one flight control can slightly, or greatly, depending upon which flight control it is and to the extent it was moved, upset the aircraft's heading or rate of descent or airspeed and thusly require a corrective movement of the other flight control(s). For the approach to be successful, unyielding attention must be paid to the flight instruments and GCA directives and then the required flight control inputs made to cause the aircraft to conform to the proper flight path while maintaining the correct approach speed. There is a rhythm that develops between the hands and feet of the pilot, somewhat mimicking those of a conductor as he/she directs the orchestra to its crescendo. In a similar way, the pilot, the leader of his band of brothers (the other crew), directs his thundering aircraft to its climax, which occurs with a successful landing; to say the least it's mentally exhausting and requires a tremendous amount of cognitive and fine motor skill.

The GCA controller was the key to the success of the approach. He/she was part-human and part-machine since they had to know their own ground radar's idiosyncrasies, as well as those of the aircraft they were controlling. If that wasn't enough, they had to be able "read" the temperament of the sometimes emotionally fickle pilot(s) with whom they were talking. Some pilots were "mechanical" in their flying, and when the controller said turn to this heading or that one, they would "snap" to it and correct now. Other, more laid-back flyboys may be more lackadaisical about their corrections. In every case, the controller would have to adjust his/her instructions and anticipate appropriately for each different aircraft and/ or pilot flying so as to be able to safely guide their charges home. Finally, as they goaded the green dot across their scopes, they had to keep in mind that that little "blip" on their scope represented a real aircraft in which sat real people who could die in a firestorm of debris if they were accidentally flown into the ground.

So, as I said, not only did they have to be masters at mechanical ingenuity, these GCA controllers had to became instant Dr. Phils as they sensed the pilot's reactions to their instructions, gauging whether they were guiding a type A personality or a type B. My father said a good GCA controller was worth more than his weight in gold; after I began flying GCAs in the USAF, I couldn't have agreed with him more.

The approach itself on that black, mucky and moisture-laden night, according to my dad, was about as good as you could get when it came to being "On course, on Glideslope."

Once they reached minimums, the controller told them they were going below minimums and should be able to see the runway. They did not.

So, downward they flew into an opaque, completely black, and misty kind of fog hell. Though his duties officially ended at 200 feet above the runway, the GCA controller provided guidance to the limits of his radar and display screen. Amazingly, the DC-4 continued on course, but went slightly above glideslope as they neared the runway—but still, they pressed in for the landing.

When flying, there are times when fate can quickly descend upon you and be either like a soft and gentle paramour, wanting to free you from harm—or conversely like a truculent ex-spouse from hell, intent on your destruction. This night, in my father's case, fate was caressing him sweetly, as if he was in a dream in which a delicately framed and lightly perfumed French beauty wrapped herself around him, whispering barely audible romantic exhortations in his ears in between her gentle good-luck kisses.

My dad said this night was even darker than any he'd ever experienced, and his eyeballs hurt from looking desperately for any kind of light as they got close to the runway. It was all to no avail and the landing was totally blind and the touchdown, when it came, unexpected. They knew, via reference to the altimeter, they were getting close to the ground and then very shortly after the glance at the altimeter they glimpsed the diffused illumination of one runway light, which came into view on the left side cockpit window, and then they touched down.

The actual touching of the gear to the concrete was not harsh with the ground effect slowing their sink rate just a bit before the actual smack of the gear against the concrete. Temporarily shocked by the landing, they all sat there wondering if this was the actual touchdown or a prelude to greater mayhem. But when they saw the runway's lights, ever so faintly, out of each side of the cockpit, the pilots swung into instinctive action to slow their forward progress. They landed on the left side of the runway, close enough to cause my dad to urgently steer right as they slowed, but how far down the runway's length they couldn't tell. The brakes were applied in direct proportion to my father's ability to keep the wheels from skidding since he feared they might go off the runway's end.

Silence infiltrated the cockpit once they stopped as each man thanked whatever entity he thought was responsible for their safe arrival.

The ironic part of the whole approach is what happened after landing—when the copilot finally regained his composure enough to announce to tower that they had landed. The controller didn't believe him. He said you'd have to be crazy to land in such a fog. So, a surreal conversation ensued for a couple of minutes between the tower and the aircraft, where one did not believe the other had landed, even though the one claiming he had landed had actually landed and couldn't understand why the other didn't believe them. The stalemate was broken when the radar shack called the tower to verify that the DC-4 had actually landed and not crashed somewhere, as the aircraft was not showing up on their radar. Tower finally acknowledged to the radar shack that they were talking to an aircraft that claimed they had landed somewhere on the airport, but they weren't exactly sure where.

Because of their unease about their exact position and just plain inability to see the runway lights and markings well, my father told the tower that he would not taxi off the runway unless a "follow me truck" was sent to guide them. In anticipation of this request, the controller said they had already dispatched one and that he should be there shortly. As they waited for their shepherd, all the aircraft's engines were shut down. That they did this, shut down the engines, was fortuitous.

The arrival of the "seeing eye Jeep" was announced to the Meteor crew by a rather violent jolt to the aircraft; the airman had run into the right main wheels of the DC-4 while he was looking for it! It is a good thing that the engines had been shut down since the jeep driver would possibly be sporting a new haircut. My dad said they deplaned to find the source of the bump and discovered a rather perplexed and unhurt airman shaking his head, as he examined his Jeep. With the aircraft's tire taking the brunt of the impact, no harm was done to either vehicle and after coming to his senses the airman slowly guided the DC-4 to its overnight roost.

CHAPTER 5

In 1956, Meteor earned 3.2 million dollars in revenue, a sum that was more than twice what the airline made the year before. Costs were growing too, but the revenue outpaced them, and they operated in the black until the USAF Military Air Transport Command made it a stipulation, in their latest charter contracts in 1957, that all passenger-carrying aircraft had to be pressurized.

By 1957, most, if not all, of the major airlines were operating an all-pressurized fleet of DC-6s, Lockheed Constellations, or turbo-props and flying above most of the bad weather associated with the lower altitudes. Meteor's DC-4s were not pressurized, nor were their other two aircraft types (C-46 and DC-3). To compete with the other nonskeds and keep the lucrative military contracts, Meteor needed the newer pressurized aircraft.

Unfortunately, given their razor-thin profit margin and inability to get generous financing like the flag[13] airlines of that period, there was no way the company could afford to buy the aircraft they needed without some drastic cost-cutting and cash accumulation.

---

13. A flag carrier is an airline that, being locally registered in a given state, enjoys preferential rights or privileges accorded by the government for international operations. The term also refers to any carrier that is or was owned by a government, even long after their privatization when preferential rights or privileges continue.

So, management asked the employees to take a deferment in seniority, longevity and cost-of-living-based pay increases for one year. They wanted to use the money saved in this endeavor to increase their cash reserves to get the required financing for the purchase of the newer aircraft.

Relatively shortly after Meteor's genesis, my father had asked ALPA, the airline pilots union of the day, to come on the property and organize the Meteor pilots. He did this, he said, because it tended to give the appearance of a financially sound, responsible and mature company to the business world.

The company could not arbitrarily defer the pilot's pay, like it could the non-unionized employees, due to the contract in place between the two entities, so my father, since he was the head of flight ops and the chief pilot, was spearheading the union talks. My dad thought that since he was so well-liked by the pilots and since he had actually asked ALPA to organize Meteor's pilots in the first place that the union's acceptance of this one-year deferment would be easily obtained.

He figured wrong. The head of the local union, under the advice of ALPA National, rejected the deferment plan, and after more, rather tense negotiations, the pilots went on strike.

It would not be a long strike. In early 1958, six months after the beginning of their labor strife, Meteor Air Transport closed its hangar doors forever.

My father was never bitter about any of the pilots who went on strike, as he respected them all for their flying ability and dedication to their profession. However, until his dying day, he had nothing but guttural contempt for the union bosses. Whatever happened in the backroom, closed meetings between him and the union, I'll never know because we never talked about it, but his absolute hatred of union management was born in those last days at Meteor.

The handwriting for Meteor's impending doom was on the wall as soon as the pilots began walking the picket line, and my father did not let the grass grow under his feet. While he was tending to the operations of a dying airline by day, at night, he and my mom, his second wife, were busily typing out and mailing resumes to more than a hundred companies and airlines.

Ken's career was eclectic, to say the least, in part because at this juncture in his life, he did something few men would have done when approaching a midlife crisis. He, like my mother when she went west to Los Angeles after high school, took the road less traveled when selecting his next flying position. In retrospect, and according to him, my father never wavered in the belief that he chose the correct course of action after Meteor failed. In his eyes, that road played out handsomely as he aged.

While still in the employ of Meteor, he was offered flying positions at Pan American Airlines, Mohawk Airlines, and Collin's Radio. Many of his colleagues from Meteor went to other airlines, nonsked or flags; but for my father, the airlines had lost their luster. The thought of having to begin again and being "tail-end Charlie" on another airline's seniority list was either too much for him to handle at this point in his life, or his ego and pride got in the way, or it was all of the above combined that prompted him to go down the less traveled path (as compared to his colleagues). At any rate, my father chose Collin's Radio as his next employer, for no reason other than it was not an airline and he would be a captain in their relatively small flight department.

Collin's Radio was based in Cedar Rapids, Iowa. It was a kind of corporate flying position where he would fly a Beech 18 or Convair 240 and demonstrate the technologies of the day, as Collin's was steeped in the world of aircraft avionics development, engineering and sales.

My dad said the flying for Collin's was enlightening and fun, though it didn't pay very well. The company's aircraft were equipped with the cutting-edge avionics technology of the day, and he and Bill Stevens would fly around the country either together or separately, demonstrating the company's wares to airlines, aircraft manufacturers, and the military. Ken was so good at the art of BS, and so charming, that he was a natural in sales, though he didn't actually like having to try to sell the products. He always said their products were so good they sold themselves, he just enjoyed flying aircraft with nice equipment and carousing with Bill on layovers as they canvassed the country demonstrating their equipment.

However, as much as my father loved the trips and the flying with Collin's, he was gone, a lot; and this change in venue, in both employers and residence, destroyed the family dynamic and with it, the family itself.

CHAPTER 6

I am not sure what came first: (1) my father habitually and incessantly accusing my mother of having an affair, even though he had no proof and quite possibly because of his own insecurity, or (2) the fact that my mother, June, did begin an affair at some point after moving to Cedar Rapids because she hated Dad's drinking, his job, him, and also because she hated the idea of having kids and a family in the first place.

When my father hired June as a stewardess in 1952, she was living a carefree life in Los Angeles, and she thought the flight attendant position was going to be the avenue to a wonderful world of exciting travel and romance.

Her first year at Meteor Air Transport was somewhat what she wanted as she traveled to places she'd only read about. But after being hired, she came under constant pursuit by my father and his charm. She eventually succumbed to his romance and courtship, and they married in 1953, just as she became pregnant with Linda, the first of her three children.

My mother was twenty when she married, and my father was thirty-two; it was her first time around and his second. They had totally different ideas of how they wanted to live out their lives together, and I really wondered how much they talked about anything of importance before they tied the knot. My dad's idea entailed June being a stay-at-home mom and housewife, and my mother's was a life with no kids and traveling around the country, if not the world.

How ironic it was then that a little more than two years after leaving her hometown of Bloomfield, New Jersey, that June would end up back near it, living in a house in the suburbs, pregnant with her first child. Then to add more salt to the wound, after a couple of more years, she's pregnant with her second child. She hated it. For my mother, it was a kind of purgatory made barely palatable by my father's status as the head of flight ops and the prestige that brought him and consequently her. She didn't have to work, and she could parade around her hometown on the odd occasion, since it was a few miles south of where she lived, and celebrate her "success" with old friends who were still living at home and hoping to achieve the ever-elusive American dream . . . whatever that really is.

And then Meteor goes bust, and almost overnight, the fabric of what held her sanity intact, and her ability to cope with her husband and kids, vaporized.

Moving to Cedar Rapids was a wicked reality check for her. No matter where Ken lived he always used his flying as an escape from the "real" world of raising a family or dealing with his wife. My mother didn't have that luxury. Every morning when she woke up the view out the window was the same and there was no room service. In fact, she was the room service provider to children that were always demanding her attention and were an ever-present reminder that she was not succeeding in achieving her dreams.

Unlike my father, my mother was stuck in Podunk City and to add insult to injury, she had to get a job to help make ends meet financially. (Ken was still paying child support for the three kids of his first wife)

On an average Monday morning, my father would kiss his wife on the forehead then walk out the door and fly to Dallas, Los Angeles, Denver—wherever—showcasing, through the use of demonstration flights, Collin's Radio's technologically superior avionics. When the sun set, the salesmanship continued in lounges and restaurants, as my father and his sales crew further whetted the appetites of the potential customers.

On that same Monday morning, my mother would wake up, again, after having gotten up at 2 a.m., to feed a newborn (me), her third child who was born shortly after arriving in Iowa. Then while carrying her son around the house with her, she would make her husband coffee and some toast, kiss him goodbye, and tend to her oldest daughter, now six years old, helping her get ready for kindergarten, all the while attending to the middle child's early morning needs. And if that was not enough, she had to get herself ready for work, drop her two daughters off at school and the youngest at the babysitter's. In the afternoon, it was the reverse of the morning's routine. Even if you loved and embraced motherhood, that would be hard work on an average day. For my mother, whose dreams never included kids, it seemed like she had been condemned to hell. And every weekday was Groundhog Day, a repeat of the previous day, week in, week out, month in, and month out.

And of course, my father would come home from his trips exuberant, full of tales of adventure and of his life on the road. He'd excitedly tell of the glorious places he'd been, interesting people he'd met, and the excesses of the rich and famous, as he cavorted with them in his or their flying machines or dined in their mansions or on their yachts. How and why he never saw the glow of life in my mother's eyes dim as he told of his exciting life and she reflected on her daily routine, I'll never know. But with each week in Cedar Rapids, my mother slowly died.

Eventually, the differences in their lifestyles got the best of her, and a few months after I was born she had a nuclear kind of emotional meltdown and had to be committed.

We lived with our Aunt Aileen and Uncle Billy near Denver while my mother rehabilitated in Cedar Rapids and my father divided whatever time off he got from work between seeing his kids out west and a convalescing wife in Iowa. While we lived with my aunt and uncle, my mother tried to pawn us off to her sister. Aileen and Billy, though grateful to have the time with their nieces and nephew, were afraid that if they took custody of us, one day, June might want her children back and they'd have been devastated if they had to give us up; so, in pain, they declined my mother's "generous" offer.

A little after our year in Denver, my sisters and I boomeranged back to a now certifiably well mother in Iowa.

What goes on in the mind of a person who has been institutionalized for a year is beyond my comprehension. When you stand back and realistically evaluate how incongruent my mom's lifestyle, prebreakdown, was versus what her dreams were, it's no wonder she went over the edge, particularly when her spouse was bebopping in and out of the house, traveling and doing what she so much desired. What I do know, based upon her actions after being released, is that she planned on changing the status quo to better fit her desires.

CHAPTER 7

In life, timing can be everything. My dad getting hired by Meteor so soon after putting in his application, getting the chief pilot position, getting hired by Collin's just as he lost his position at Meteor—all his life, my father was blessed by impeccably good timing, particularly when it came to his career.

The same cannot be said for my mother. When she decided to bring her lover back to our house on Seely Avenue in Cedar Rapids while my father was on one of his many trips, she had no idea that a severe winter storm had truncated Ken's travels plans.

The comedian Henny Youngman once joked, "The cheating man asked the married woman, when her husband began to open the front door of her house, 'Quick, Quick, where's the backdoor?!'

"The woman said, 'There isn't one!'

"The now-very -scared man then exclaimed, 'Where do you want one!'"

Well, this was pretty much what my father experienced on that fateful night, for all of us, so long ago.

Quickly wrapping up that rather awkward meeting with my mother's paramour, my father left his house, forever, and endeavored to find another job far, far away.

The bad news didn't end with my mother's ill-timed indiscretion. Shortly after my father realized his marriage was dust, Harry (my dad's father) was diagnosed with terminal cancer and died within the year. It was a one-two punch that was only made bearable by his continued flying and drinking.

By good fortune, blind luck, or God's mercy upon my father's aching heart, in 1961 the FAA had just begun filling positions for flight test pilots at their relatively new NAFEC (National Aviation Facilities and Experimental Center) test center based at Atlantic City Airport in Pomona, New Jersey. Bill Stevens had gotten word that the FAA was looking for high-time, experienced captains, so both he and my dad flew out there and interviewed. Dutch Osterhout, an extraordinarily suave and debonair chief pilot who had the swagger and looks of an aging Errol Flynn, with the requisite beautiful young wife, hired them both on the spot.

NAFEC was a dream come true for the old man since it was like an aircraft smorgasbord. During my father's years there, the FAA operated a Gulfstream I, multiple DC-3s, a couple of DC-6s, multiple Convair 580s, a Convair 440 (and on odd occasion a 340), a Convair 880, a couple of B-727s, a Sikorsky S-76 helicopter, and finally, a diminutive Aero Commander 540. In addition, they leased various other smaller piston engine aircraft through the years and, at one point, borrowed an A-4 fighter from the Navy for wake turbulence testing. All the aforementioned aircraft were based either together or at one time on the flight test facilities ramp for use in research and development flying. And all the flight test pilots were qualified to fly all the aircraft, with the exception of the A-4. (Only one pilot had been checked out to fly it, a wonderful man named Keith Biehl.)

Like the aircraft, the pilots at NAFEC were a varied bunch. Initially, all of them were World War II/Korean War veterans who had flown many types of aircraft prior to their employment at NAFEC. As my father's tenure continued, the greatest generation gave way to the oldest of the baby boomers or the generation between the two. Many of Ken's colleagues had flown fighters or bombers during the wars, and some even continued to fly as traditional guardsmen in F-105s, F-100s, F-84s, F-8 Crusaders, or whatever fighter or heavy aircraft one of the Air National Guard or Navy Reserve units in the tristate area was operating. Further still, one pilot, Bernie Hughes (who I previously mentioned), did triple duty as a test pilot with Curtiss, a flight ops test pilot with the FAA, and finally flew F-105s in the local Air National Guard unit.

It was a potpourri of epic aviation proportions, this confluence of men and machine, or so my father felt. He loved the flight test position because, he said, it wasn't routine and with the passing of each new day, he was afforded a new adventure in the realm of aviation.

It would take a dedicated book to document all the adventures and tales in which my father was exposed in his thirty-five flying years as an FAA flight ops test pilot. But those adventures were simply a by-product of NAFEC's primary mission: to develop, test fly, and investigate, evaluate, or solve aviation-related issues.

Though he didn't know it at the time, NAFEC[14] was to be my father's last place of employment, and where he would spend the next thirty-seven years of his life.

---

14. NAFEC, National Aviation Facilities Experimental Center. This comprehensive facility tested and developed a multitude of aircraft/airport safety equipment and flight operating procedures. It was started by the FAA in the early 1960s and is still very much a cornerstone of aviation safety; it is now called the William J Hughes Technical Center and includes comprehensive development of ATC procedures/facilities.

CHAPTER 8

To this day, catching a whiff of the exhaust from a jet aircraft immediately reminds me of the night my father, sisters, and I waited at JFK airport in the winter of 1964 for my mother to arrive from Chicago. All of us were excited because after more than two years apart, we were going to be a family again, this time living in a small house in Absecon, New Jersey, near my father's place of employment. As kids, the only way my sisters and I could control our youthful energy while waiting was to alternate between running outside and then inside whatever terminal it was in which we waited. The smell of the effluent from the day's jets as they taxied to and from the runways permeated the chilly winter's air and my lungs, and the memory of the smell brings pleasant thoughts of that night. My father had gotten custody of us kids after he and my mom divorced, and we hadn't seen my mother since leaving Cedar Rapids. Like waiting for a pot to boil, it seemed to take forever for her flight to arrive, being delayed a few hours due to a winter storm in the Midwest.

If my mother and father thought their second time around, their second marriage to each other, was going to be better than their first, I suspect they were each grievously disappointed.

Initially, life was bliss after the emotional reunion at the airport, and my mother made huge strides in being an affectionate and happy wife and mother; but somewhere along the way to that happy Hollywood ending, their marriage turned out to be a train wreck of epic proportions, and even worse than their first attempt. The true tragedy was the collateral, emotional damage inflicted upon their children, since instead of divorcing again, they decided having regular scream fests was a better and healthier alternative.

In my adolescent years, and while we lived in Absecon, the police made regular visits to our house in order to mediate the toxic couple. In most cases, the domestic disputes were horrifically verbal, profanity laced, and loud; the experience of which no child should have had to endure once, let alone hundreds of times. There were many fights, however, when the war of words between the two combatants was just not powerful enough to support their side of their argument so they resorted to physical violence—my mother throwing objects and my dad his fists. Probably the most traumatic fight for me while I was still very young was when I stabbed my father in the back with a pair of scissors as he strangled my mother, her face turning a darker shade of blue while my father's hands gripped each side of her neck with vengeance. I was seven at the time, and the wound in my father's back, though not very deep, did draw blood and then, shortly thereafter, tears from my father's eyes as he dramatically apologized over and over to my gasping mother. We, my parents and I, all huddled on the living room floor crying; and through sobbing breaths, my parents promised they would stop the fighting—that promise being broken maybe a week later. It's no coincidence that that was around the same time when my mother taught me the Lord's Prayer, my first real silver lining in those dark shadows of hell.

Such frequent and extreme domestic disputes did not come without a cost to the unwilling and innocent spectators (children). It was during those times, the early years in Absecon, where my sisters and I learned to compartmentalize the heinous fights and put the horrific memories of them into secret boxes in our heads, choosing, fight after fight after fight, to forget the emotional pain. But, like a young person who has received multiple concussions during their youth, the repeated blows to the brain do eventually cause permanent damage (though it can't be seen with the eyes) that isn't manifested until later in life. Linda, Gail, and I were gutted psychologically, often and very deeply, by the amazing display of hatred demonstrated by our parents as they fought. Our friends and neighbors couldn't physically see the damage being inflicted upon our psyche with each altercation, but, it was there, in our hearts and heads, getting worse with each emotional blow. So, it only stood to reason that it was just a matter of time before each of us kids would begin to show society our brokenness, due to the cumulative effects of living in hell; the symptoms were different for each of us, but, let there be no doubt as Linda, Gail, and I entered our high school years we would each manifest the scars from our childhood.

I can't speak for my sisters, but as for me and for most of my life I've always woken up happy, no doubt because, as I mentioned earlier, my mother often said that every dark cloud had a silver lining. For me, mornings were the silver linings from the dark clouds of the fights from the previous evening. With the sunrise of each new day, the bright rays of light rushed into the house to illuminate the shadows, causing gloom to scurry away. Generally, every morning

of those days in Absecon, my parents were usually found convers-
ing over coffee, happily, and acting as if nothing had happened the
night before. It was so perplexing to see their uplifted spirits, but
because they actually seemed like they were getting along, it raised
my mood and allowed me to believe with each new morning, there
was a brighter future for our family.

Oddly, on the "mornings after the fights" my parents never, ever,
apologized for their amazing display of emotional horror of the evening before. My mother would never, ever try and comfort us kids
and in fact acted with total indifference towards her children as all
of our emotional nerves began to calm during "the morning after."
My father, for his part, might make a funny face or throw out a
funny quip or two as he read the morning paper, drank coffee and
light heartedly chatted with his wife. And, like his wife, he never
attempted to show any physical or emotional affection towards his
kids nor was he contrite, as he should have been, since he was always
the instigator of the fights.

Simply put, there was no love demonstrated with-in our house
either before, during, or after the fights or for that matter on any
given day, and never was, during all of mine and my sisters' lives
(while living at home). When my mother first arrived, after their
remarriage, there is no doubt she tried to be something she was
not…a loving human. But, as the days extended in Absecon and my
parents began to fight again, my mother morphed back into what
she always was: unfeeling, unaffectionate, and distant. She was per-
functory in her duties as a wife; cooking and cleaning were done as if
on autopilot and the only stimulus that seemed to arouse her moods
was her music, which was usually played in nauseating repetition;
it was usually the music associated with the most popular play on

Broadway at the time. If I came home with a bruise somewhere on my body, as I usually did since I was very active outside (as were most kids during that time in America), the look in my mother was one of disgust because it meant she had to extend herself to actually helping one of her kids. One day I came home with two seriously smashed fingers due to being hit with a baseball. I tried to tell her they were broken, if only because when they were hit, they both went 90 degrees sideways, to the left; I immediately bent them back towards a more normal look after seeing their unusual displacement from the other 3 fingers. When I got home, and told my mother I broke my fingers, she said I didn't, that they were just sprained. I tried to explain the situation, as my fingers swelled up to gross sizes, but the evidence and testimony I gave were unconvincing. It was only due to my father seeing the size of my hand when he came home from work, and his insistence to my mother that I needed to see a doctor, that she finally took me; both fingers were broken, one of them in two places and a cast was put on my right arm that extended up to my elbow.

Unlike my mother, my father could actually be more soft, but it was only on the rare occasion. Where my mother always seemed distant, my father actually existed quite frequently in the here and now and, unless he was drunk or in a mood, was actually approachable and could be kind. His problem was his alcoholism, the drinking which started as soon as he got home from work around 5, and by 7 pm he was on his way to becoming another person altogether; if only he could have stayed sober it would have made life at home much more tolerable and sane.

Finally, with regards to any possible loving bond between the siblings, at least while we all lived in my parent's house, the was none. Linda, Gail, and I all lived separately, there was no affection, no warmth, no true integration between the 3 of us. When my parents fought, we each retreated to our rooms, Gail and Linda together in the room they shared and me to my room, usually hiding in my closet with my fingers in my ears. My sisters never invited me to be with them, nor did I ever impose upon them with my presence as I was usually met with protests when I did try to enter the hallowed hall of main estrogen production in our house. It actually wasn't until we all left our parent's house well behind, as we aged, that we eventually became much more loving to each other as siblings, but that would take many years.

You can only have so many Groundhog Days, the fighting and dysfunction, before the reality begins to sink in that nothing is ever going to change. So, as I aged, I quite literally believed that the only future I had was in a prison cell or an early grave, in spite of my hopeful prayers to God. My dreams of a flying career I gave to God to contemplate upon since I never did actually articulate to anyone but Him what I wanted to be; the weariness of dealing with my neglectful parents left me believing that I just wasn't good enough to be successful in anything in life. God, however, planned otherwise.

I did acquire a very active interest in aviation as I matured and badgered my father much as my adolescent years passed, asking if I could go flying with him, my persistence was his fault since he always used to quip, "The squeaky wheel gets the oil." Probably the greatest thing I ever did in my preteen life, aviation-wise and with my dad, was when I got approval to fly with him and his colleagues in a DC-3 to an air show at McGuire AFB. We took off from Atlantic City for the twenty-minute flight to the AFB where we were dropped off. While there the group of us sat outside a Gulfstream I,

G-1, which was on static display, and answered questions for the air show attendees. It was very cool to be so young, ten years old, and hanging around my father and his colleagues. I really felt like one of the boys that day. This air show hosted the USAF Thunderbirds, which at the time were flying the "thunderingly" loud F-4 Phantom.

Whether by providence, luck, or influence, 13 years after this airshow I would find myself being trained in the F-4.

From that wonderful adventure, a few months later, my dad got approval for me to fly with him to Leesburg, Virginia, in a Piper Tri-Pacer. The FAA bought the small, single-engine Tri-Pacer with the sole intention of having my father crash it for a safety movie being made by the FAA. Cliff Robertson, a famous movie actor and avid pilot, was there as the movie's narrator and FAA spokesman.

Excitement built during the day as my father made repeated test approaches and landings as the cameramen positioned and then re-positioned their cameras to record every angle and bit of the antici-pated demolition of the aging Tri-Pacer. Unfortunately, my father's crash test dummy moment was not near as dramatic as I hoped, with him basically just destroying the aircraft's gear in a simulated "bad crosswind" controlled landing: the aircraft bounding off the runway and into a deep ditch. After waiting all day in the hot sun, and after countless dry runs, I was hoping for a balled-up and smok-ing airframe with my father emerging victoriously unscathed; I got one out of the two.

As my years progressed toward my teens, and even penetrating them, the biggest flying thrill I would consistently experience was my yearly birthday flights in one small type of aircraft or another. I so loved those father-son flights and my time with my dad when we flew. Part of the reason I enjoyed those flights was because I began to realize that my father, when immersed in the realm of aviation, was different, i.e., when he was flying or at work. He was always so calm, happy, and lovely in spirit, and never did he show anger or agitation.

When I was in eighth grade, my English teacher, Mrs. Galupo, asked our class to write a short story about something that was near and dear to our hearts. By serendipity, I had just flown with my father on my fourteenth birthday flight. I really enjoyed that flight, more so than most of the others because we did acrobatics in a Citabria. I wrote as best as I could, careful to be very descriptive about the experience of flight. I dug deep in my soul to articulate on paper the wonderful emotional effect that flying had on me and the joy it brought to my heart. About a week after turning in the papers, Mrs. Galupo said she loved my story so much she insisted that she read it out loud in class. I cringed as my words were vocalized and audibly dispersed to my classmates and expected ridicule from some of them when she finished. Instead a few kids in the class, even a couple of the tougher guys, came up to me and said they liked the story and thought it was cool that I got to go fly. I was blown away that my words could move someone to appreciate something that I really loved doing. There is no question that when Mrs. Galupo read that story aloud in class, it was the tie that bound my love of flying with an incessant desire to, one day, share that love through the written word.

Without question, the watershed moment with regard to my father and I, when I really began to see his true and wonderfully divine nature while immersed in the world of aviation, was in August of 1972.

Oddly, it started out with the potential downfall to many a man who has endeavored upon a noble career path but then falls prey to a fatal attraction. The woman in this case was my neighbor.

A family of four girls had recently moved into a newly built house right across the street from our newly built house. The one who was my age, Dana, was absolutely beautiful, with blonde hair, blue eyes, a svelte swimmer's body, and the kind of tan that comes from spending most of your summer days on the beach.

Though it took awhile, as the summer of 1972 drew to a close I finally got the courage to ask Dana for a date. I almost dropped dead when she said yes, whereupon I got that giddy exuberance that belongs almost exclusively to youth as I pondered the prospect of taking her to the boardwalk to practice my night moves.

In the late afternoon of the blessed day on which Dana and I were to go out, as I was heading downstairs, I saw my father coming out of his bedroom all dressed up for what I perceived was work. (He usually wore a tie when he was going to work, and just prior to walking out the door, he usually doused himself with enough Old Spice cologne to fumigate the place.)

"Hey, Dad, are you going flying?" I asked, kinda shocked as he rarely flew local flights on Friday evenings.

"Yeah, Buck." He called me Buck, short for Buck Rogers. "Al and I are going flying for a few hours this evening."

"Can I go?!" was my flippant, unrehearsed, and impulsive reply, temporarily forgetting that I had my first date with a vision of beauty scheduled for that evening. I also knew full well that the odds were ninety-nine million to one that the answer would be his patented.

"Son, I wish I could take you, but you know how it is, the government doesn't normally allow anyone to fly on their aircraft." If I heard it once, I heard it a thousand times, but, I never failed to ask and my father never seemed to get exasperated with my asking.

I continued heading downstairs to ready myself for this lucky girl when my dad said, "Well, let me call Al and see if he is okay with it, and if he is, then you can go."

I had a bowel movement. I can honestly say that, without hesitation, I immediately forgot about Dana and our date and focused all my temporal energy into an ESP-type of mental projection directed toward Al (Mr. Bazer) in the hopes it would make him agreeable and allow me to go flying with them. I continued downstairs and waited patiently on the couch while my dad called Al from his bedroom.

After a few anxious moments on my part and a brief chat on my father's, he hung up the phone, casually walked downstairs, and simply said, "Okay, you can go."

I will admit I did not call Dana and tell her I couldn't make the date, as we had to go and my father waited for no one when he walked out the front door—if you were not on his train when it left the station, you were left at the station . . . period.

I would like to say I felt bad about knowing I was going to stand her up, but to ease my conscious somewhat, I asked my mom to tell Dana, if she should call or come over, that I went flying with my father.

I admit I felt a certain kind of grown pride and coolness in saying that I was "going flying with my father," and I know I had a grin that beamed from ear to shining ear as I left the house and jumped into the car.

I was so excited, so happy, so giddy. Girls did not exist, nor did boats nor motorcycles. Nothing but aircraft occupied my mind as I proudly rode shotgun while my dad and I went to "work" together; seriously . . . it just didn't get any better than that!

At the airport, my father quickly ushered me out from the operations building and into the waiting CV-440 aircraft. It turns out the aircraft was not the FAA's, it was being leased, so technically, my father said, I was allowed to go flying on it. At that point, I couldn't have cared less who owned it and for what reason!

Once the aircraft's main door was closed and my dad and Al were seated, respectively, in the pilot's and copilot's seats, I was directed to sit on a hard, iron board type of fold-down "jumpseat" situated just behind the pilots' seats and in the narrow and short companionway, which connected the cockpit to the cabin. I was pretty short at fourteen, so I was not able to see directly over the nose and down as much as I would have liked, but no matter, I was part of the crew. There were some knobs and glowing dials related to some unknown type of instruments to my immediate left, so I was content to pretend that it was my job to monitor those instruments for the boys up front and let them know if anything went amiss . . . not that I had a clue what in the hell that stuff did and what would be the indication if they actually went "amiss."

In addition to having my own jumpseater's instrument panel, my dad let me wear a headset so I could hear all the ATC communications. That singular act of courtesy on my dad's part added even more of an air of camaraderie and personal involvement to this flight on my part as now I truly felt that headset made the three of us an intertwined team. Wow, this was sooo cool!

Cranking up the two big ol' radials on either side of us seemed a rather routine affair to the boys up front as the engines belched to life with an increasing succession of black puffs and deep-throated chugging, as each cylinder added to the smoke and sound emanating from the exhaust stack. While the engines were being started, I actually ran to the back and looked out the windows so I could get an up-close and personal view of a big radial coming to life. Very impressive!

The rumbling sound the engines made once started had a narcotic effect on my thoughts, as we taxied, causing me to think of Pan Am Clipper pilots of past as they taxied for a water takeoff in their Boeing Clipper ships. With all thirty-six cylinders of the two Pratt and Whitney R-2800s screaming in a baritone kind of way, we took off into a blazing, setting sun, the vibrations on the aircraft along with the engine noise being the pinch on my arm I needed to assure me that I was truly awake and that this was not a dream.

As we climbed away from the reality of our earthbound lives, I was mesmerized by the aura of the cockpit, and for the first time in my life, I was experiencing what it was like being immersed in the business end of an airliner type of aircraft and to experience what my father so enthusiastically made into a career choice. I had been in an aircraft many times before with him, but this time, it wasn't for an hour or so or in a small little aircraft. We—my dad, Al, and I—were actually on a project, doing something substantial for the FAA, and it felt cool to be a witness to my father's secret world.

It was on this flying adventure, with my father, where I truly noticed, without bias, that Ken was sincerely a different person when immersed with-in the world aviation. He was relaxed and playful, seemed to have no ego, and was so nice to everyone from the aircraft maintenance folks to the aeronautical and electrical engineers who worked on the projects, to the janitors who cleaned the facilities. He was on a first-name basis with almost everyone and always had a kind word to say or some funny quip. While deep insecurities haunted my father outside the gates of the airport, inside of them, I never saw the slightest hint of anger or any telltale trace of personality disorder. Additionally, he was very cool in demeanor, and it was evident by the way he flew his aircraft that he was extremely keen minded; you could tell that this was where he belonged. His movements were fluid, his speech purposeful, and his eyes' gaze deliberate and laser-like. Occasionally, he would look back at me and break into a huge grin or stick out his tongue or wink or stick his thumb on his nose and wiggle the other fingers. All those mannerisms were in his auto reflex repertoire, and he never added to or took away from them for as long as he was alive. God, I loved to be around my father when he was in "his" environment, and I was hugely proud of him too.

After flying around Washington DC for the better part of three hours, and doing multiple approaches and missed approaches into Washington National Airport (now Ronald Regan), and oddly enough holding in a holding pattern right over Dana's hometown at one point, we made our way back to Atlantic City and landed sometime after 10 p.m.

The proverbial after-flight cocktail (beer for my dad, Coke for me) took place at the Lew Mathis' Rugby Inn, in Northfield, New Jersey. It was the coolest American-style pub I'd ever been to back then, and the tradition of going to Rugby Inn for an après flight libation and flight debriefing or just for getting together and talking about aviation continued well into the 1990s.

Getting back to what started this thread, though Dana quickly forgave me for my date no-show, we were never to be an item. The upshot, however, was the wonderful bonding that my father and I experienced on that aforementioned flight. It truly was a watershed event with regards to his and my understanding each other.

In my father's eyes, my willingness to ditch a date with a hot girl to go flying showed him that I had a desire for something other than girls in my heart. And trust me, having a positive attitude and unrelenting desire were huge and mandatory attributes one needed to be successful in my father's eyes. So, even though I was not trying to bond with the old coot, he took this flight to heart as much as I did.

For me, I was quite a bit older and more situationally aware on this flight than on the previous ones, and more importantly, I saw my father flying as the captain. His demeanor really impressed me. I saw him in an environment where he was extremely nonchalant yet was fully in control and very professional. And though to the average person flying may seem rather complicated and dangerous, if anything, my father made operating an aircraft look easy, fun, and free-spirited.

Finally, and by far the brightest of silver linings up until this point in my life with regards to my personal relationship with my father, was this flight. During that time, God truly opened my eyes and allowed me to see my father as He, God, saw him and for why Ken was brought into existence—not to be a father or a husband, and really not even anyone's friend, but for the sole purpose of being an aviator.

As I said, Ken was extremely different when at work and inside an airport's confines than when not. Always, his colleagues would pour on the accolades about my dad when I was speaking one on one with them. They would constantly tell me of some wonderful flying feat they saw my father perform or some funny prank he would pull on one his colleagues. I think the most profound of the stories was the one Bill Purcell—an MIT grad, electrical engineer and FAA employee—told me one day.

In the late 1970s, my dad, Bill and others were taking off from Monrovia, in Liberia, and heading to Brazil in Nan 42, the aforementioned Convair 880 that Bob Grace rolled. They were doing worldwide testing of VLF/Omega signals and had been flying back and forth between South America and Africa, validating that the Omega/VLF signals could be used reliably over the mid/south Atlantic. My father was in the passenger cabin on this departure, taking a break from the flying on this leg, as the aircraft had two complete crews assigned to this rather-lengthy trip due to the crew's extended days on the road and the length of some of the duty days. Ken had flown the flight into Monrovia. As the aircraft climbed out, my dad pseudo-smoked an unlit cigar while sitting on a seat in the main cabin. Mr. Purcell said, after a few minutes of flying, my dad jumped out of his seat and flew into the cockpit to asked the pilots where they were going. Thus began a few minutes of head-shaking and double-checking, by all of the crew, as to the actual point to which they flying. It turned out the flying pilots had programmed the wrong latitude and longitude points into their INS for the first couple of fixes they should have been flying directly to. With potential tragedy, or at the very least embarrassment, by the FAA crew averted, my dad slid back into his passenger seat in the back to continue sucking on his cigar, the rest of the flight being uneventful.

As things settled in the cabin and the engineers began recording their data, Bill found time to ask my dad how he knew they were not going in the right direction since my dad was sitting in the back with the rest of the folks, and they didn't have a clue anything was amiss. My dad smiled impishly at Bill and, in a fatherly, old-sage type of voice, said, "After a few years in the air, you pretty much know where the sun should be in relation to your aircraft when flying to this or that destination. The sun wasn't in the right place, and I wanted to know why."

There was a prolonged drought of FAA-financed flying for me after that spectacular CV-440 flight, though I wouldn't actually think about it as I got to being busy as a high school kid. I did think flying was neat and had dreams of being an airline pilot, but I was too young to learn to fly then, and I became more interested in things I could do. But I can honestly say I never thought, after watching my dad perform his flying magic, that I was even close to being good enough to do what he did for a living.

CHAPTER 9

A couple of weeks before my sixteenth birthday, as my sophomore days in high school began to wane, my father asked me if I wanted to learn to fly. This came from out of the blue (no pun intended) since I had never once asked him if I could, though he did know I wanted a career as an airline pilot. In a New York second, I said yes, but I did ask "Why now?" since we'd never talked about it before. Evidently, he decided that I needed a change in lifestyle because he thought I was heading down a "bad road."

That bad road, according to my father, manifested itself in the form of me being very sullen, asocial, detached, and reclusive while at home, and evidently in school, too, as noticed by a teacher who sent a note to my parents stating such. If my parents were perfect, or at least more "normal," I could understand their concern, but what they didn't want to acknowledge was that the person I was becoming back then was a direct reflection upon their negligent parenting and dysfunctional personalities and marriage. I had no desire to live in such a dark emotional world—no one does—but to cope with the bitterness of their war-of-the-roses marriage[15], as demonstrated

---

15. War of Roses marriage—relating to the dark, comedic movie starring Michael Douglas and Kathleen Turner and chronicles their battles as they go through a very bitter divorce.

by their still frequent and wickedly visceral fights, and compounded by my father's extremely random and mean-spirited attacks on me, I went "inside myself" to survive my home life.

Without question, my sophomore days in high school were the vilest, some of the darkest of all clouds, in all of my years while living at home, and with the exception of a couple of instances as an adult, the worst so far in my life. My mother had entered a severe depression as the summer of 1973 ended, just as my father decided that I was to be a new target, besides my mother, for his seemingly unprovoked verbal and sometimes physical assaults. My mother's rapid slide into an extremely dark mental state exacerbated an already depressing home life now that my father decided to emotionally and mentally shred me. School could have been a temporary refuge, but for some reason, some guy in a couple of my classes decided to dovetail onto my father's abuse and bully me, thusly leaving me with no way out of my personal hell. Fighting back against my father only enraged him even more, whereupon his attacks become even more violent. Standing up for myself against the bully was somewhat fruitless since I was relatively small as a young teenager, and the bully at school was training to be a boxer and about six inches taller than me. During the times when I attempted to stand my ground against him, I was left with a bloody mouth, nose, or severe loss of breath after a shot in the stomach. The teachers in the gym class, where he usually attacked me, never wanted to go beyond just breaking up the fight, refusing to send us to the principal where maybe the root cause could have been discovered and corrected. The sum total of all the crap that was going on during that period effectively demolished my self-esteem, so I accepted the beat-downs, on both fronts, with resignation and retreated inside of myself, trying to survive until better days.

Oddly, and in spite of my plight, and what saddened me the most during those days, was to watch the life and spirit in my mother drain as the essence of who she was slowly seep into the ether of another reality. While my mother would never have won an award for personal warmth or charm, she still was human and deserved a modicum of Christian love and respect. In those days, on most days, she was less than human, more like a zombie, who stared with blank eyes and an expressionless face and always spoke rhetorically on the rare occasion when she actually did speak to me. An answer on my part never elicited any sign of emotion or genuine, logical, verbal response. There is no doubt she did hear me when I responded, she just didn't really seem to care what I said. I so badly wanted to help her, but I was trying to cope myself, and there was nothing I could do. And even if I did take action, no doubt my father would have thwarted it. It was only when my father left on one of his many trips that year that my mother began to "wake up," and I could see a faint glimmer in her eye and some sign of genuine life. Unfortunately, upon my father's return she went back into an emotional abyss from which no one could reach her.

You didn't challenge my father while in his castle. If I had not seen how different he was when at work, how nice and charming and almost angelic he was while flying, I never would have believed a human could be so bipolar when drunk and/or in a mood. As a freshman in high school, one day, I was hitting golf balls in my immediate neighborhood. I was using a 9-iron to hit a ball down the street into an empty lot and then back again to the empty lot next to our house. One of my golf shots back toward my house was errant, and the ball smashed through the kitchen's glass door, completely shattering the entire glass pane, scattering shards on the floor, and causing my mother to scream in shock since she was making dinner at that time. Fearing a death sentence from my father's wrath, I was shocked that his response was laughter; he said I must have hit a great shot. Contrast that to a few months later when I used one of his plastic buckets—he had five of them—such as you might use when you wash a car. I had filled the bucket with water and went down the street to launch Bangsite rockets with a friend. When I got back from the junior NASA experience, my father was waiting in the garage. Though the bucket was not harmed in any way by the rocket launching, my father royally reamed me for unauthorized use of one of his precious buckets; to this day, I have no idea how he even knew I had spirited one away, unless he counted them upon his return home each evening; they were kept high upon a shelf and almost out of sight.

The previous examples, though minor in their actual impact upon my life, are but two of many, many dichotomous occasions when I was in high school or college, and beyond, when my father (and this occurred usually in the evening, and 97 percent of the time he was drunk) would, without provocation, rip me to pieces emotionally but then be incredibly contrite, nice and even complimentary to me the next day. In the evening, during his abhorrent attacks, if I challenged him, he could get physical, so I usually just stood by his side while he told me how worthless and good for nothing I was and that I would never amount to anything. He then might continue on saying that I would never be able to get a real girlfriend or, when I did get a girlfriend, the only reason she wanted to be with me was to be near him (no, I'm not making this up). Many, many times he said I'd never be good enough to be pilot or that when I did begin to fly, I wouldn't be able to make it into a career and that I should just join the Army. On and on he would "vent" cusswords being contorted in various, amazing combinations and used to buttress his attacks on every facet of my life. The abuse lasted until he was either too drunk to continue or he simply ran out of steam, or both.

Never, ever once did my mother come to my aid during those beat-downs or after, since she usually hid in her bedroom listening, over and over to Johnny Cash's songs, chain-smoking, drinking gallons of coffee, and no doubt taking her mind to another time and place. I am truly surprised she never tried to kill herself, given the fact that she'd been institutionalized in the past and because I can surely say that many, many times I wanted to slit my wrists or OD on something to end my miserable life. It was a horrible existence, that sophomore year, and though things got a bit better for me after I began to fly and then went to college, my father's random attacks would continue until I left for the USAF after graduating college.

I am absolutely and positively convinced that my faith in God, the Father of the Lord's Prayer, as taught to me by my mother many years prior, is what sustained me through all those years of hell. I have zero doubt that Jesus held me tight and comforted me as my parents verbally raked each other over the coals while I hid in my closet when still a child. And I have zero doubt that it was God who gave me strength to stand tall in my father's presence while he castigated me for no apparent reason through my high school and college years.

Most of us feel we are free to live our lives any way we choose. I too used believe we had total free will in our lives. As I've aged though, I am firmly convinced that providence has a sometimes soft, sometimes harsh, but always persistent influence in our lives to see that God's will be done. I don't think we immediately realize the manipulations of His hand on our behalf, but nonetheless His active, life-long presence in our lives is real. The less we fight His direction, and in fact embrace it, the more peacefull our walk and certainly the less mysterious. Why God chose to deliver me from my misery in those waning days of my sophomore year, I don't know, but He did; no doubt he was answering quiet prayers of desperation. The fact that my father asked me, and without us ever discussing it beforehand, if I wanted to fly was miraculous in and of itself, specifically in the timing. The positive emotional effect upon me when I began to fly cannot be measured, but what's even more miraculous were the other two life-changing and uncharacteristic parental decrees that my father made just as I began to fly—decrees that, in addition to my newfound wings, would profoundly move me in a more positive direction toward my goal of being a professional aviator.

CHAPTER 10

The first flight I ever took with the intention of becoming a pilot, my father being the instructor, took place on May 10, 1974, in N2011Z. The aircraft was a really beat-up 1964 Cessna 150 owned by a friend of my father's, Jack DiStefano. The aircraft was temporarily based at KACY, Atlantic City's main airport, the location of my father's place of employment in the town of Pomona, New Jersey.

I flew nine hours with him, between May 10th through 26th. We lost a week in between those dates due to wind and rain conditions that precluded a neophyte like me from operating, but we pretty much flew every chance we could after my dad got off work. We always practiced our takeoffs and landings at Woodbine Airport, a sleepy, old, ex-Navy World War II auxiliary field with three runways for me to choose from, about fifteen to twenty miles west, southwest of Atlantic City Airport.

Two amazing and wonderfully profound events occurred in those nine hours: (1) I was in even greater awe and had much more respect for my father as a pilot than at any point in my life; and (2) I was born again (though not in the manner in which the Bible belt folks think).

Unless you've ever received flying training, it's hard to explain the exact qualities that make a person a great instructor. Some are tangible—knowledge, personal flying ability, and communication skills being a few—but then there is a certain je ne sais quoi that takes one from simply being good to being exceptional.

My dad was exceptional, phenomenal, extraordinary, and prescient as a pilot and instructor . . . give me the superlatives of the superlatives and that was my father as an instructor. Yes, I may sound like the king of hyperbole, without the paid toilets, but there was not one time in those nine hours when I saw my father excited, worried, scared or anxious, but there were many times when I was. He spoke deliberately, calmly, encouragingly and generally softly, and I listened excitedly, partially or sometimes not at all. Many times he was there with a deft touch on the yoke, correcting one of my errors, or a nudge on the rudder pedals to keep us straight, or maybe just a softly directive voice, urging me to continue pulling into a departure stall when every living cell in my body screamed at me to lower the aircraft's nose. He was my very own guardian angel, naturally equipped with his own wings, which seemingly supported our aircraft when its own wing stopped levitating us. I do not attribute his laid-back nature to superior flying ability on my part but to his omniscience as an instructor. The fact that he was able to bolster my confidence from negative numbers to slightly above zero in those nine hours is a testament to his coaching ability and angelic aviation pedigree.

I never felt truer love for my father than I did during those first nine hours of flight. Yes, he could be an extreme asshole while drunk and in a "mood," but when daylight came and all the tormenting gremlins scurried back into their hiding places in his psyche, he put on tiny little white wings, hopped into an aircraft, and was truly, unquestionably angelic in nature. His bipolar existence never ceased to amaze me, but I thank God, above all, that my father was so exceptional at teaching a craft in which he himself was also exceptional in performing. I was in absolute awe of this man, and to this day, I have not loved or admired any person in the realm of aviation more than him.

As for being born again, there is no human way for me to convey how liberating and rejuvenating to my soul and spirit flying was. Quite simply, it saved me, and I cannot thank God enough for His grace in choosing to liberate me, if at least temporarily, from my earthly hell at that time through the use of 2011Z. Though flying offered only a short-term physical escape, the more I flew, the more lasting the positive emotional effects. The relief that flying offered me came at a time when I'd grown to loathe my life and humanity. I loved the view that the birds had, the feeling of superiority over the mere mortals below me, and best of all, flying made me feel like I was in control of my destiny and isolated from the issues that plagued me while I was on the ground.

In addition, I love the mechanical devices involved in aviation. From the earliest days of my youth, I have loved the switches and dials and knobs and instruments that abound in the cockpit of an aircraft. There were many times as a kid when, during bad weather, nature-incarcerated days at home, I would draw instruments and dials on the inside of big boxes and then sit with the box over my upper body pretending to be in an X-15 or space capsule on my way to the moon or Planet X.

Finally, and with a deeply personal glimpse of my psyche, I love the physical beauty of aircraft in the same way I love the physical lines of a beautiful and shapely woman. Each represents a beautiful work of art with their curvaceous lines, causing me to feel an endorphin rush with each extended glance.

On so many levels, flying was a connection to all of the disassociated parts of my heart, mind, and soul, binding them together, allowing me to have hope that a future beyond the torment of my home was possible.

And then the nonpareil moment of my lifetime came when, on May 26, my dad deplaned from 2011Z after we had done some warm-up touch and had gone at Woodbine, and said, "It's time for you to take her up by yourself son." In other words, to fly solo, alone.

Prior to my solo, I was just a piece of worthless crap and a loser to my dad, a dream-killer and drag to my mother, an ancillary friend to my friends, or, lastly, an irritant to the bully at school while invisible to most of my other schoolmates and teachers. But with that solo flight, my life changed forever. By God's grace, He did not answer the many prayers I prayed months earlier for death. Oh, He brought me closer to heaven all right and certainly gave me wings of my own, but only in the most unexpected and wonderful of ways in which God can so divinely do. That solo flight instantly elevated me above the detritus that had shaped my sophomore year and helped me to rise (both literally and figuratively) above it with very powerful and positive results to my persona.

Sixteen days before my solo flight on the 26th, I was flying blind emotionally, spiritually, and mentally. I was immersed in clouds of gloom and depression so oppressive I couldn't see a way out; I had lost hope. Then I began to take flying lessons, and the clouds began to brighten with each flight and though I was still lost I gained vision and hope with each flight until the day I soloed. On that day, when I soloed, I became an aviator, not on the same level as my father, but I had burst out of the dark clouds that had surrounded me for so long and flew into a wonderfully glowing silver lining that would, in a very powerful and positive way, change me for the rest of my life.

CHAPTER 11

With the initial phase of my flying training complete, my father's plan was now to allow me to fly as much as I wanted, by myself, using Jack's 150, the same aircraft in which my father had been teaching me. Then as I edged closer to the age of seventeen, the minimum age required to get a private pilot license, Jack DiStefano was to begin to instruct me in earnest, and with greater frequency, so that I could fulfill all of the mandatory FAA flying/training prerequisites required to take my private pilot's checkride.

So after that initial flurry of instruction and being soloed, I spent most of my flights that summer flying alone, enjoying the supremely wonderful and liberating feeling of flight and the breathtaking views the birds keep a secret from us mere mortals; well that's the truth of what I was doing.

The façade I showed the rest of the world and my father was that I was practicing for my private pilot's license with every flight of fancy that I took. I had a year to prepare for my checkride, so I had quite a bit of time to goof off before I came under the judgmental and discerning eye of both Jack and an FAA evaluator. (At that time, I did not know that my father was going to give me my private pilot checkride.)

In those early days of my avian gestation, I would ride my bike from my suburban-embedded home located next to the marshes and bays of South Jersey with a view of Atlantic City outside the kitchen window, to a cozy, forest-secreted grass strip. That's where Jack's aircraft were normally bedded down. Knocky's is what I always called the very well-hidden airport, in honor of the owner's name, but the official FAA designated name was Nordheim's Flying K.

The airport was surrounded on all sides by thick woods, but in the greater scheme of things, it was only about four miles south of the much larger and busier Atlantic City Airport where the FAA, New Jersey Air National Guard, and a few general aviation aircraft called home.

Knocky's, had two grass runways that crossed roughly midfield to each other, at about a thirty-five-degree angle and from the air they resembled a narrow X. Those runways, in contrast to Atlantic City's 10,000-foot main, and two mildly shorter subordinate concrete landing surfaces, were only 2,400 and 1,600 feet long, depending upon how you measured them and they were all grass; in fact, the whole airfield was nothing but grass with one very old, big, and wooden hangar located on its western side.

In all, maybe ten aircraft called Nordheim's Flying K their permanent home. All but one, 2011Z being the exception, were tail-draggers[16] and aged, and other than N28432, a beautiful 1940 Luscombe 8A, I never saw any of the other aircraft fly; in fact, I never saw an owner of any of them either. On the odd occasion after

---

16. Tail Dragger—most aircraft built and flown today are tricycle gear and sit relatively flat with a nose wheel in front of their main gear. A tail dragger does not have a nose wheel but instead sits slightly angled up, with its main wheels moved more forward than a tricycle gear aircraft, with the tail resting on a small tail wheel that supports the aft end of the aircraft.

coming back from flying 11Z, I used to walk around to each of the aircraft, which were all tied down in proximity to each other and near the only patch of trees on the field, and take a peek into their cockpits. I wished I could have owned any one of them, no matter what its mechanical health, as I would have poured my heart and soul into getting it fixed and cleaned up. But—sigh—my father said he never wanted to own an aircraft, and I certainly could not afford even the cheapest of the lot were it being offered for sale.

The owner of the airfield, Knocky, was a short, cantankerous and well-past-his-prime, white-haired man who, as he told me, bought the field years ago as a diversion after his retirement and to get away from his wife of a "thousand years." However, after getting to "know" the man, I believe his wife got the better end of the deal (with reference to his daily absences).

Knocky spent most of his days rebuilding (in vain it seems, since he never seemed to get it near completion) an old Stearman biplane, with which I was absolutely in love and secretly desired to own one day, or at the very least get to fly.

His entire hangar and all the artifacts in it reminded me of what his brain must have looked like—

nothing in the hangar was new, and everything that was in it was either scattered around or neatly placed and was an aviation relic of some type with a certain amount of sentimental, historical, practical or financial value attached to it; he didn't like to throw anything away, it seemed. There were many spare radial engines and propellers lying about or crated up, with other bits and pieces of air- craft, instruments, wheels, and other ancillary aircraft-related items occupying almost every nook and cranny of the building. I used to love just meandering through this archive of aviation "stuff." I used to pretend I was selecting parts to build my own flying machine and even though Knocky was a grumpy little troll, he never cared that I spent hours looking through his ancient collection of stuff, to include sitting in the Stearman and pretending to fly it.

Oddly, in spite of spending so much time near him, as I explored over and over every nook and cranny of his man cave, I can't say I ever had a meaningful conversation with him, no matter how hard I tried; so, in addition to his wife, I don't think he appreciated kids either.

CHAPTER 12

The second out-of-character, parental decree that occurred just as I began to fly was in my father's idea of choosing Jack DiStefano to be my primary flight instructor. (but only after my father had soloed me)

I can't remember the exact date when I first met Jack. I know that it was a Saturday, early summer in 1974, and I was sixteen years old. I had just come back from riding my dirt bike, and when I went to put it back in the garage, I found Jack and my father talking, each of them holding a can of beer. They were winding down, my dad said, from a fishing trip they had gone on early that morning in my dad's boat. Given that we had a refrigerator in the garage always full of brew, the fishing stories they told me that afternoon were quite impressive, if not woefully embellished.

Since my father very rarely socialized at home, I closely examined this stranger in my garage to see what special qualities he possessed that allowed him to stay in there and drink beers with Capt. Ahab; up until this point, I was about the only person who had ever drank with my old man in the garage. (Yeah, I was only sixteen, but my dad had a skewed sense of parenting; he always said the French kids drink wine...)

Fleshy is an often overused term in literary circles to visually describe a person, but in my travels, I have found very few people who actually fit that description. Jack, however, was the exception. He reminded me, somewhat, of a cartoon caricature. With his last name, DiStefano, hinting to his ancestral heritage (Italian) and food preference, you could tell he fulfilled his pasta cravings in grand style. However, the pasta tailings accumulated under his skin in an odd way. While his arms and legs seemed relatively normal in proportion to his rather smallish five-foot-seven-inch height, his stomach . . . whoa . . . it looked as if he had swallowed a keg of beer that had lodged in his gut. But given his ability to consume large quantities of the liquid, having a keg down there would probably have been answered prayer. But I digress . . . His mostly bald head seemed, like his gut, to have stored its fair share of unused calories, thusly making it very round and giving him two chins—one firm and the other, under the first, very pliable and prone to jiggle when he laughed, and also making it seem like his head was too big for his body (if that was possible given the aforementioned well-endowed belly). Finally, and by far his most positively striking feature, were his incredible blue eyes. Because he wore thick glasses, his eyes were magnified to the point that it reminded me of two planet Earths (due to the blue), as seen from space, closely chasing each other in orbit around a flesh-colored sun.

His wardrobe that day was pretty basic—a white T-shirt and jeans—and given the overhang of his belly above his pants, the tee shirt was not tucked in, which meant that it was more like a kilt draping the front half of his belly. He wore sneakers, and upon his head was a baseball cap. For as long as Jack was alive, the aforementioned ensemble was his standard dress when he was not at work.

The only thing that might change was the logo on his hat and/or T-shirt.

Audibly, he was as large as he was visually. He had a voice that announced his arrival long before his belly ever peeked around the corner. But his loudness was never due to arrogance or belligerence; it was just Jack being his jovial self. A belly laugh from him could shake the plaster from the walls, and it always made me smile when he started vibrating the area around him with his raucous chuckling.

While he may have been short on physical stature (we're talking height), Jack seemed larger than life because of his character. He was straightforward, honest and very in your face; there was nothing shy about him! Most people of an urbane, upper-crust personality might think of him as being obnoxious, or at the very least gauche. Because of his simple manner of dress and weight issue, they seemed to treat him like a second-class citizen, but he was not a mean or vindictive person, just naturally inquisitive, very intelligent, and full of fun. Finally, because he came armed with strong leadership qualities and a gregarious nature, I'm sure many people took him as being belligerent, given how blunt and loud he could be. However, when you really listened to and observed him, you would see that he was more like a big kid, full of enthusiasm and in love with the world, particularly aircraft.

Born to a blue-collar father in Cape May, New Jersey, in the early 1940s, he enlisted in the Navy at eighteen and became a crew chief on Sea Furies (Navy version of the USAF F-86). Though he was a quick study, his lack of social graces no doubt hindered his career advancement opportunities.

While he may have started out his formal career as a Navy mechanic, his true love was flying aircraft, not fixing them. So, while off duty and during his spare time, he began to fly light aircraft at a civilian airport near his Navy station in Rhode Island. His exuberance and love of flight did eventually carry over into his, however brief, Navy career, almost ending it with a court martial; while taxiing a Navy Sea Fury after performing some engine maintenance, he got the aircraft so fast on the taxiway he was able to lift the nose wheel off the ground, as if to takeoff. His superiors were not impressed. Talking himself out of harm's way, he managed to leave the Navy with an honorable discharge, A&P mechanic's license, and private pilot license. Then once on the civilian side of the fence, he used the GI Bill to get more flying time, ratings, and licenses (instrument and commercial) to include becoming a multiengine certified flight instructor.

When I met him, he was a mechanic for the FAA and where my father worked. He actually maintained the same aircraft that my father flew at that time. But, Jack really wanted to be a flight ops test pilot like my father, unfortunately his flying experience nowhere near met the minimum standards to be considered for such a position. Eventually, he left the mechanic group and went to work in Central Aircraft Dispatch (CAD), the official name of the area in which he worked; by the time I met him, he was in is his mid-thirties.

That night of our first meeting, I stayed silent as the two of them got drunker and drunker. As expected, the fishing trip stories they were telling took on preposterous lives of their own until they ran out of beer, and then reality hit and they parted company for the night.

I wasn't the most charming teenager when I was sixteen, and I definitely was not very extroverted. Jack's in-your-face, sunny personality and very funny wit was almost 180 degrees opposed to who

I was back then. He told stories with huge doses of drama and animation, and in spite of his uncouthness, I immediately liked him. He was so funny and laughed so naturally and so often that I felt like I was around a comedian. When he told a story, his passion, exaggeration, and wide-eyed, arm-swinging expressions caused me to feel as if I was immersed in it and not just listening. I felt like I was a young kid with a storybook coming alive before me when Jack went into one of his "war stories" about this or that flying adventure, and I was usually peeing my pants laughing by the end of them—and he had so many!

While my dad was an aviation God in my eyes, and his stories were awe-inspiring, he spoke from a podium and place that made him and his career seem untouchable. But Jack . . . he was tangible and real and down to earth.

At sixteen, in the grip of raging hormones and hugely insecure, Jack was aviation reality with humor and possibility. He brought flying, if not life itself, down to earth for me and made me begin to think that I was capable of being somebody. Simply put, Jack was human and kind and nice to me at a time when I distrusted people and myself; he was my personal door to the land of the living and a silver lining that showed itself whenever I was around him.

I didn't know it at the time, but my dad had an ulterior motive when he invited Jack to our house that day. What I thought was just the byproduct of a fishing trip, the garage meeting was actually part of the scheming that my father and Jack had done while on a DC-3 trip. The old man's purpose was to introduce me to Jack as a way of breaking the ice between two such disparate personalities because my father knew that one day, in the not-so-distant future, Jack and I were going to begin spending a lot of time together.

CHAPTER 13

I mentioned earlier that my father made three momentous, out-of-the-ordinary (for him) parental decisions that changed the course of my life. The first two I just elaborated upon—learning to fly and being introduced to Jack. The third and final life-changing decree handed down by the old man was his sending me to summer camp, a decision that came about because I was "arrested" by the police shortly after I began learning to fly.

The Reader's Digest version of the story is as follows:

One weekend, as summer approached, I was riding my dirt bike through a trail in the woods with my friend Randy riding as a passenger. Another friend was riding his motorcycle right behind us. I hit a bump while going pretty fast, and Randy flew off the back of my bike. Gordon, the other rider, went into a sideways skid to avoid hitting Randy, but it was all for naught as the left side of Gordon's swing arm, near the rear wheel axel, hit Randy smack-dab on his ass.

I can't say I laughed, but I still have the visual of that ass smack down in my synapses, and I thought Randy was going to be a bit sore but fine. Well, when Gordon and I tended to him, he kept moaning about his ass being broken. I can't say I was an expert on what constituted a broken ass at that time, and I had no desire to personally examine manually, or visually, the area in question, so while Gordon tried to comfort Randy, I ran to the nearest house and called for an ambulance.

To cut to the chase, Randy was taken away in an ambulance and me in a cop car, since the police said I was riding on city property, hence trespassing; Gordon, rightfully so, took off before the police got there.

While Randy's black-and-blue butt (I took his word for the actual color) healed, my mom maintained a lighter shade of red from stewing over the fact that she had to take me to juvenile court. The judge was actually a very cool guy, and though he tried to sound threatening, he openly laughed when I told him that although I had concern for Randy's ass, I was reluctant to examine it for broken bones. After being admonished, briefly, by the court of law, I was told to keep my nose clean for the next six months, and if I did, my record would be expunged.

I walked out of court happy with the experience, feeling like I was a more mature and seasoned teenager, while my mom wanted to throttle me because she was still embarrassed. She said I made her look like a bad mother because she had to answer to the judge as to why I was riding my motorcycle where I was when Randy got hurt. Well, I kinda thought like saying, "Ya know, if the shoe fits . . . " However, I decided to let that thought stay silent as my mouth had too much of a tendency to get me into trouble.

When my father got home from work that night, he informed me that I had to go to summer camp. Where I went was up to me, but the fact that I was going "somewhere" was written in stone.

I can say unequivocally that I didn't want to go and initially put up a fight. But that night, the old man, as usual, got drunk and sternly warned me that fighting him on this would be pointless and would draw severe consequences, so off to camp I was going.

What I wouldn't realize until much later in life was that forcing me to go to camp, when tied to my flying and friendship with Jack, would have positive implications on my life far beyond which my father or I could ever have realized at that time. Though I can't thank my father enough for his wisdom, I really praise God (again!) since I feel He is the one who used my father as a tool to achieve His will for me.

The bright side of this summer camp edict was I could go where I wanted in as far as the type of camp; it just had to be located out of the tristate (Delaware, Pennsylvania, New Jersey) area. So, the next day, I bought a Boy's Life magazine and searched the classifieds section for ideas as to what types of camps were available and their locations.

As a fan of scuba diving, in which I had gotten my certificate the previous year, I was leaning toward some sort of scuba/water themed camp. I had grown up watching both the TV series Sea Hunt and Flipper and loved the adventures in the episodes as well as that of the Jacques Cousteau/National Geographic specials that aired randomly on one of the three main broadcasting networks. Back then, I felt that scuba diving was almost as liberating as flying, and I really thought if flying didn't work out, that I might want to be a treasure diver one day, as far-fetched as that may seem.

After much classifieds ad scouring and vetting, I settled on Camp Hugo on Marathon Island in the Florida Keys. I looked on a map to see where Marathon was and determined that since it was located relatively near Key Largo, which was where Flipper was filmed, I would enjoy the same clear, turquoise-tinted water that looked so beautiful on our color TV in each Flipper episode.

The arrangements were made, money sent, and off I went, in silent screaming, protest on an Eastern Airlines B-727 to Miami at the end of the first week in July 1974 to a southern camp with a Jersey attitude.

While most of the details of my many adventures in my three weeks at Camp Hugo have sifted through my rather porous memory, the finer points need not be mentioned anyway, I must state, emphatically, that going to the camp changed me in the most wonderful of ways. Even though I may not have shown it externally, the initial experience of leaving and being so far away from my home was terrifying. While my parents were not going to win a presidential award for good parenting, they were all I had known up to that point and Lord there was no telling if they were going to be at the same address when I got back. I was scared to death. But as the days in Marathon ticked by and I observed all the other kids, from all parts of the country, and though we all spoke with such junior bravado and machismo, I realized that deep down we were all a bit timid and scared and nervous. And so, realizing that it was normal to feel how I did, I began to grow out of my rather small, insecure South Jersey shoes and had one life-changing epiphany after another. With each new scuba diving adventure, or fish caught on the reefs and then cooked on a beach over an open campfire, or the occasional late-night camp breakouts I organized so we could play pinball at the local Holiday Inn, I realized I didn't need my parents to survive. Being away from the tumultuousness of my father's alcoholism and dysfunction brought peace to my life, and once out of his influence and dark shadow, I began to realize that I had a developing skill set of my own that would offer me the chance to be a success at something in life. The crowning glory of those three weeks was my being selected as top camper, and eventually, after I got home, the camp owners asked me if I wanted to come back the next summer and become a counselor in training (my room and board being paid by the camp). The incredible self-confidence gained in just those three weeks cannot be underscored enough and was the third wonderful silver lining that bound, like a three-stranded cord, the previous two (silver linings) which occurred during the same period. Truly, God had heard my prayers of desperation during those sophomore days of hell and was very active at this point in my life, in changing me for the better.

The story that comes next does not necessarily add to the aviation theme of this book. I have added it because throughout my life, and like my father, I have a love for both the sea and the air above it. Both mediums over the years have offered me refuge, safety, awe, enjoyment, and above all splendor; and though I chose flying as a trade, I could easily and most willingly have slipped the noose of having a "normal" job and the social mediocrity that befalls most people after college or high school and migrated down to some obscure Caribbean island and made a life living on a sailboat, diving for treasure, and looking for my lost shaker of salt.

A TALE OF TWO DIVERS

"Ask the animals, and they will teach you, or the birds of the air, and they will tell you; or speak to the earth, and it will teach you, or let the fish of the sea inform you. Which of these does not know that the hand of Lord has done this?" (Job 12:7–11).

In the summer of 1974, four very excited sixteen-year-olds donned their scuba gear, jumped off the back of their dive boat, and entered the turquoise-colored ocean. They were anchored over a very small patch of coral called Coffin's Patch. Coffin's Patch was well inside the almost continuous stretch of coral that runs the length of the Florida Keys and was a great second dive site because it was in shallow water (which kept the chances of decompression sickness at bay), and since it was off the beaten path off the normal popular dive sites, usually, the only sea creatures swimming about were its own undersea residents.

The nascent aquanauts, all being prisoners of Camp Hugo, had been diving all day, and this was their last dive before heading to dinner. They were tired, to be sure, but like most exuberant kids of that age, they wouldn't know they were exhausted until they reached the dock and had to drag their equipment and their thoroughly waterlogged bodies off the boat. This was their first time diving on Coffin's Patch, and it wouldn't be their last as the boat's captain had decided this was a perfect playground for these intrepid young summer camp divers since it allowed him to stay on the boat and have a beer (he didn't think the divers knew he had a stash of the contraband aboard), while the little fish swam below within relative proximity and safety to the boat (he would watch their bubbles, if not even see them since the water was so clear, as they swam about).

Immediately upon entering the water, the four headed straight down to the reef and off to the side of some very high brain coral that reached to within ten feet of the surface. As the group formed into pairs, going two by two, they decided, in a group kind of way, to swim over the top of the upper reaches of the aforementioned brain coral. Just as the first pair scaled the heights, they immediately, and excitedly, turned about-face with feet kicking at high speed and arms going left and right, back and forth, up and down in an almost panicked assortment of gyrations. The second pair of aquanauts were almost to the top of the coral formation themselves as they met the first pair head-on. However, the second pair of divers were oblivious to the fact that a black-tipped reef shark with a remora attached to its belly was cresting said coral at the same time. Consequently, on that fateful day, and for a very brief period, four people, a shark, and a remora all occupied a very small section of the great blue ocean, and though man may be on top of the food chain, in this case, you were dealing with boys, and they figured they were dinner.

At the merging of the boys and the shark, the underwater fly-boys went brown smoke on and executed a fleur-de-lis of which only the navy Blue Angels aerobatic team would be proud. Each boy headed in a completely different direction from the other, and though much bravado was spoken at campfires of how they would protect each other in case of shark attack, each boy, when confronted with the actual possibility of being an hors d'oeuvre, quickly forgot such talk and sought to outdistance the others in a race that they all thought was for survival.

One boy headed to the northeast and didn't stop panic-kicking until coming upon the edge of the reef whereupon it seemed the seafloor abruptly dropped off into the abyss, but in reality, it was only twenty feet or so below the upper deck of the reef upon which he now swam. As he approached the edge, he finally managed a glance back, wondering if the shark had chased him this far or if it had decided to go after one of the others.

Relieved he was not being pursued, this boy now noticed the absolute beauty of the reef over which he was swimming. The drop-off he approached gave way to a much lower reef, but with an almost rectangular bit of sand in the middle, measuring about forty feet in length; it immediately reminded him of a runway.

He still had a lot of air remaining in his tank, despite his attempt at an undersea speed record, and though his buddies were nowhere to be found, save for the fact that he could see their bubbles in the distance, he decided to pretend to be an airplane. He "landed," his arms outstretched to each side, on the sandy runway, and stopped. Given the thickness of the water, versus air, his ground roll was re-markably short. He taxied back to the beginning of the runway, facing the end where the coral jutted the lowest upward and, kick-ing furiously, applied full power for takeoff. In a relatively short distance, he was airborne, the tilting of his head upward toward the surface providing a modicum of lift, but just enough to enable "flight." He climbed at full power until vertical clearance above the coral at the far end of the runway was assured, whereupon he began to level out and accelerate, the acceleration being announced by the backward movement of his arms to his side, in the same fashion as a swing wing fighter jet. With this takeoff complete, he banked hard to the right to come back around for another landing, though this next "pattern" was much more disciplined than the first. Remembering the flying lessons he had been getting prior to his coming to camp, he used the exact same procedures he had been taught and endeav-ored to hone his flying skills while in this underwater paradise and impromptu classroom of sorts.

Round and round for minutes on end he flew. Sometimes he immediately returned for another pattern, at other times he took a break in the routine to fly amongst the many varieties of coral and play as if he was fighter flying a low-level mission. Fish darted to and fro and dodged his "air-to-air" dogfighting attacks with innate ease and no doubt wondered what in Neptune's name had descended upon their secluded, and heretofore quiet, patch of heaven.

With his air-supply down to 500 psi, this land creature was now "minimum fuel" and had to return to his aircraft carrier. As he surfaced he took one last and long look upon his airfield and bid it adieu, not knowing if he would ever see it again but thanking God for this lovely playtime; once onboard the boat he learned that the shark had swum innocently away, ignoring all of the boys.

Thirty-five years hence this same boy had now grown into a man. His days of practicing flying, both underwater and in the actual air, had eventually taken him into many aircraft and airports around the world, but as much as he loved the sky, he was always drawn to the sea, and under it, for rehabilitation and rejuvenation.

On this particular day, he was diving off the coast of a small island located in the same sea where his first underwater flying began. He was in much deeper water, though, and equipped with much higher-tech scuba gear. He was also much more sophisticated in personality, the intervening years bestowing a dignified, maturing process to his persona.

Seventy feet down, he cruised a relatively deep underwater reef with his dive guide. It was akin to swimming in the Grand Canyon, with ledges and steep walls defining, if not dictating, their course and direction as they swam.

That day, on this dive, he had a déjà vu moment. The long-since-dormant memory of a past dalliance while under the same sea was just too great as he swam routinely along. Certain memories of a childhood dive long since passed flooded his immediate thoughts as the canyon walls tempted his undersea "aerial" acumen. He held his arms slightly out from his sides and pretended, once again, to be a fighter airplane, but now following a flight lead. Gliding under ledges and over ridges, dodging long-dead coral mounds and still living bits of new coral and following, at times, the contour of the very bottom itself when sand was most prevalent or cresting over coral ridges and then zooming back down into canyons was the theme of this wonderfully reincarnated game. After minutes of gleeful flying, he abruptly landed and stopped at the entrance to a cave; actually, it was one of many, made famous by Jacques Cousteau in the 1960s when he did a National Geographic special from this very spot—sleeping shark cave. It seemed like light years since this "boy" had seemingly swum for his life after sighting his first shark, now, on this day he was sticking his head into a cave, seeking them out and looking at them where they lay. The splendor of God's world is amazing.

CHAPTER 14

My first flight with Jack took place on August 16, 1974. I have no idea why he had called me the previous day and asked if I wanted to go flying, but I was happy he did. This was our second meeting since the first a couple of months earlier, and I was still a bit timid, but I was so hungry to go flying I thought, "Hell yeah, I want to go!" though I'm sure I was actually very quiet when I told Jack I'd love to go.

Jack picked me up at my house, and we rode out to Knocky's where both of his aircraft were based. I wasn't sure which aircraft we were flying that day, though I assumed it would be 2011Z, since that's the only plane I seemed to be allowed to fly. I assumed wrong.

Upon our arrival at the field, Jack walked smartly over to the Luscombe and began to untie her, and I eagerly helped. Hot damn, this was such a treat! I was so excited! She was so beautiful, and though she was small and a tail-dragger, I was overjoyed at the prospect of flying in such an icon (in my opinion) of an aircraft.

Once free of her bonds, I put my 140 pounds of skin and bones into the right seat of the Luscombe and waited for Jack to plop his well-fed body into the left. But unlike the 2011 Zulu, which I could start with the help of a starter motor initiated by the turn of a key, the Luscombe had to be "hand-propped." So, as I sat in the right seat, Jack remained outside the aircraft and reaching into the cockpit from the left side (he stood with the door open), he primed the engine with raw fuel, via the primer on the instrument panel, and then "cracked" the throttle open a bit. I was mystified as to why he was not getting into the aircraft, and I swear he had a smirk on his face as he was doing this because he knew I had no idea what he was up to. After all this pre-engine starting foreplay, he calmly walked to the front of the aircraft and told me to turn the mag. switch to "on" (the "mag" switch is a key in the instrument panel that, when turned to "both" allows the spark plugs to arc, igniting the fuel/air mixture in the cylinders) and put my feet on the brakes. I was supposed to say "Switch on!" in a loud, authoritative voice after which, Jack was to fling the propeller down to induce compression, ignition, and combustion in the 65 horsepower, four-cylinder engine. I am pretty certain, though, that I squeaked "Switch on," as I was sure Jack was going to be chewed up by the propeller during this whole process! But amazingly enough, after one good flip of the metal prop, the little four-banger popped to life and began to idle. Jack immediately ran to the side of the prop's spinning arc and, with surprising fluidity, flung himself into his side of the cockpit and pulled the throttle back to full idle.

I was in awe of this event because never before had I seen it with my own eyes, only on some World War I footage. And with age in mind, since I was speaking of old aircraft just now, never in my wildest dreams did I think I would be flying in an aircraft as rudimentary as this one. While not of World War I vintage, this Luscombe challenged and changed every notion of what I thought was basic for an aircraft. The generator for the electrical system was mounted right below the cockpit, in the open air, between the main wheels on a couple of support brackets with a little propeller attached to the front of it. The rushing of the propeller's slipstream caused the generator's propeller to spin and power up the electrical system. Hell, when I was eight, I had one of those on my bike! (Well, it ran off the spinning of my tire.) I felt I was certainly regressing in technology.

Once buckled in, Jack took over command of the brakes and added power to taxi us across the grass to the shorter of the airport's two runways. Since it was only 65 horsepower, the "little engine that could" must surely have cringed every time it saw Jack come to fly as the thought of accelerating and then elevating that mass of humanity, and whomever might be with him, must surely have caused "it" much anxiety.

Lining up with the runway, and after having checked the magnetos and doing a quick, short-radius 360-degree spin of the aircraft to check for traffic, Jack added full power, and over the grass we sped. Acceleration, while not head snapping, was brisker than I had thought it would be; and in a relatively short time we were airborne and climbing into a clear, blue, midmorning sky.

And while on that subject, climbing, it was not one of 28432's better attributes—at least not when loaded like we were that morning: fat man; skinny boy; full fuel (thirteen gallons); and a warm August temperature. I think the physics of Bernoulli decided to relax their laws a bit on that day, as we began to levitate well before the end of the runway.

Though Jack performed the takeoff, once safely airborne, he asked me if I wanted to fly, and to be sure I did but I was also very nervous about flying with someone other than my awesome instructor-pilot father. At the beginning of this flight, I had about forty-seven flying hours under my belt, all of it in 2011 Zulu and with the exception of my solo time, my father was the only person with whom I had flown, so, though Jack was a funny guy on the ground, I wondered what his instructional style was going to be like.

As I took control of 28432, I was in for another surprise . . . she had a stick for controlling the elevator and ailerons. I had flown in a Citabria when I turned thirteen, and that aircraft too had a stick, and I knew all fighter aircraft had one, but my forty-seven hours so far had been flown using a "control wheel," a.k.a. yoke. This stick business was a bit odd to me, as it seemed unnatural. However, once I gripped it, I liked it! It was so much easier, at least in my humble opinion, to control the aircraft than it was with the yoke; it was much easier to blend and combine the movements of the ailerons and the elevators together, and was just so much more natural with regard to aircraft control. I wondered why all aircraft didn't have one, and to this day I wish they all did.

After taking control of the aircraft, Jack directed me to fly southwest and climb to one thousand feet. We were bound for Cape May County Airport he said, where he had to go to take care of some personal business. It was only thirty miles or so away, and at 100 miles an hour cruising speed, we reached it relatively quickly.

Jack landed the aircraft but told me to keep my hands on the stick and feet on the rudder pedals and follow through with him as he landed. I did as he commanded.

After landing, we taxied on to the general aviation ramp and shut down next to a big and old World War II-type hangar.

After getting out of the aircraft, I asked Jack what he wanted me to do. "Follow me!" he boldly exclaimed, with a quick belly laugh acting as an exclamation mark to his words, and off he went with me in trail. I was desperately wanting to go explore the big ol' hangar next to us, but we headed to another building that looked like an old control tower.

As we entered the tower building, Jack asked if I was hungry, and of course what self-respecting sixteen-year-old male isn't?! So we went into the airport café for my first taste of the proverbial fifty-dollar hamburger! (I think back then, it was more like thirty bucks.)

As we ordered our food, Jack had some quick banter with the middle-aged waitress, causing her to laugh almost continuously as he very obviously flirted with her. Though married with two kids, I was to find out that though his looks weren't going to get him a spot as a Chippendale dancer, he was a firm believer in mind over matter and could be very charming. He was very jovial too and liked to joke around, a lot, particularly when he had an audience or when a woman was present; and the cuter the woman was, or the more plentiful the bystanders, the funnier and more animated he got. I laughed as much if not more than the audience he was "working," and yet I was so quiet; in retrospect, I must have seemed like Jack's stooge to others, but I couldn't have cared less because he made mine and others' days brighter.

After lunch, my secret prayers were answered, and we walked into that mysterious hangar we had parked next to when we first arrived.

We entered the old, wooden and very tall building from the north side, and immediately, I saw a P-51 being either rebuilt or refurbished. I had never been so close to such a beautiful flying machine, and to be sure, I was awestruck. Jack didn't slow down as we passed by the Mustang, so I was walking, turning my head, and looking back at the Mustang and then quickly looking forward again to see where I was walking and then looking back again at the P-51. I did this until we passed between two heavy tarpaulin curtains hanging down from the ceiling that separated the Mustang hangar floor space from that of the rest of the building.

On the other side of the curtains, the hangar seemed pretty boring. There were a couple of light aircraft, single-engine Cessnas, being worked on by the local FBO and there was another area that had some kids laying black nylon, five-foot-high letters, side by side, in a certain pattern on the floor, forming words. We walked past where these kids were working and into an office area that was embedded in the hangar's eastern side.

On the very southeast side of the hangar resided the offices of an aerial advertising company called Paramount Air Service. Andre Tomalino and his wife, Lois, had owned the business for the past thirty years. Jack wanted to talk to Andre and Lois, so after a brief introduction of them to me, and an awkward hello from me, I left the three of them in the office to chat while I stepped out into the entrance to the hangar, near where the boys were assembling a banner.

As I stood near them, I looked across the ramp at a very dilapidated DeHavilland Beaver. I was temporarily lost in thought, wishing my dad would want to buy that aircraft because even though there was no for sale sign on it, in my naivety about life, I figured since the owner obviously didn't take care it, he/she would surely sell it for a cheap price just to get it off their hands.

My short wishful gaze was rudely interrupted by a horrible looking flying contraption that suddenly appeared from around the hangar and had shut down and spun around as it rapidly approached me. It's occupant, a bearded, middle-aged gentleman with thin, black stringy hair, jumped from the aircraft as soon as it stopped and ran into the hangar offices.

I walked up to the obviously very neglected—aesthetically speaking—aircraft and inspected the cockpit; if I thought the Luscombe was primitive, this high-wing, canvas-covered, engine exposed, tail-dragger put me back to the days of Leonardo da Vinci. There was no real door—just a small, upward folding, trapezoidal-shaped, fabric-covered, metal-tubed affair that hinged at the bottom. This "vapor" barrier barely decreased the size of the hole on the right side of the pilot and no doubt it must get pretty breezy in the cockpit while flying. There was no window above this "door" on the right, nor was there a window on the left. The only real, and most effective, wind protection to the pilot was the front windscreen that sorta wrapped around on the left and right sides and trailed back about a foot or so on each side and then abruptly stopped. My thought, after the brief observation of this "thing," was that at least this aircraft had progressed from World War I standards in that it had a forward windscreen and only one wing. The engine was almost completely uncovered and open, and there was only one seat in the smallish cockpit in which to sit, and that seat looked like an aluminum beach chair that had been bolted into an empty space behind the instrument panel, if you could call rpm, airspeed, oil temp/press, and altimeter indications an "instrument" panel. There were no creature comforts in this aircraft at all, it just existed as basic as one of the erector set model aircraft I made as a boy, save for the fact that its wings and tail surfaces were covered with fabric that allowed for flight.

I was amazed that a person had the courage to sit in this contraption, let alone fly it, and for all I knew the pilot of this thing was

Baron von Richthofen, living out an alternate lifestyle because he had not really died in the "The Great War."

As I stood there, incredulous that this machine actually flew, let alone towed banners through the sky, the pilot said, "Excuse me," as I was blocking his way into the cockpit. I moved and then he jumped in, started her up, and taxied to a nearby runway about as quickly as he had arrived. I stood there looking at him takeoff and didn't know whether to give him last rites or to bow down in an "I am not worthy" praise to him, as if he was some sort of god.

I was upstairs, doing more exploring of Paramount's rooms, when Jack came out the office proper with a quick gait and barked, "C'mon! Let's go!"

I double-timed it to the stairs and ran to catch up to him as we exited the hangar in the same area in which we came in, and we both jumped into 28432.

After starting, taxiing, and taking off, this time with me in the left seat, Jack said we were going to stay in the pattern and do some touch and goes and that I was going to fly the aircraft while we did them. No doubt I was excited at the prospect for more flying time, but I almost had a cardiac when he told me he wanted me to fly the patterns myself while he instructed me.

"This is such a beautiful aircraft," I said to him. "Aren't you afraid I'll crash it?"

Jack's response was typical Jack. "Well, then don't!" whereupon he gave a big belly-laugh and patted me on the head.

So for the next thirty minutes, Jack proceeded to show me how to fly his beautiful little Luscombe. We did a few touch-and-go landings on runway 19, and after the fourth landing we slowed to a civilized taxi speed and he told me to pull onto the grass, that bordered both sides of the runway. I pulled off to the right side and stopped about twenty feet off the tarmac, and we sat there, the engine slowing, ticking over in a quiet, loafing idle. I wondered what in the heck was going to happen. Still, with that amazing fluid grace in which he always seemed to climb into his aircraft, he bid me adieu, jumped out of his mistress, and told me to go fly some patterns by myself.

As I type this and think back on that day, it's hard to convey the horror that filled me at that moment. As I've said before, I was an extremely insecure kid, and though flying was beginning to lift me out of my personal doldrums since I was now an "aviator," I still didn't have a lot of confidence in anything I did, except race a motocross motorcycle or scuba dive. Adding to my self-doubts about my own ability was the fact that I knew Jack loved this aircraft more than his wife, and quite possibly his kids too. So flying this man's pride and joy, after only four touch and goes, was not my idea of fun, and I can't say it inspired me. The irony of my deep-seated emotional turmoil then was that as much as I did not want to fly solo and given that I was scared to death, I was actually more afraid to say no to Jack and defy him than I was to heed my own insecurities.

So, even though I was aghast that he wanted me to solo this aircraft—and believe me, I made my feelings known to him—he said he was having none of my concerns and said, and I quote, "I wouldn't let you fly solo if I didn't think you could do it."

And it was that comment that actually gave me confidence in myself to do this.

Earlier I mentioned that I wondered what Jack would be like as an instructor, since I had only experienced my father's soothing words of encouragement. Well, in total contrast to my father, Jack's style of instruction was gruff at best, as I found this out on the flight down to Wildwood Airport and while we did our aforementioned practice patterns. I am pretty certain his street fighting upbringing and Navy experiences, combined with the personas of his own flight instructors when he learned to fly, caused him to believe that a certain measure of fear, sarcasm, and ridicule interspersed with mini bouts of compassion and humor, was the proper way to motivate his students. It was in his gruffness, I quickly learned, that unlike my father, who had an incredible eloquence and grace when he taught, Jack's manner was bluntly and blatantly honest; at times, I wondered if my father was lying to me when he said I was doing okay, but with Jack—wow—you got immediate feedback if you sucked; the man never candy-coated anything. And it was exactly because Jack was so brutally honest in his choice of words prior to this moment that when he said, "I wouldn't let you fly solo if I didn't think you could do it," that I found confidence in myself.

So, after pausing for a bit to look over the few instruments that adorned the panel, and waiting for my legs to stop shaking, I spun the "beauty" around and taxied a bit up toward the beginning of the runway. I checked the airspace around me by doing a quick 360, like Jack taught me, just to confirm no one was landing, taxied onto the runway from the grass, and took off.

Liberated from having to carry Jack and now piloted by a lightweight neophyte, 28432 leapt into the air with unbridled enthusiasm. I was not prepared for such sprightly performance, though I did like it. However, due to the reduction in gross weight (sans Jack), it did change the landing equation a bit when I came back around for my first touch and go as she wanted to float a bit above the runway before accepting the reality that we were actually going to have to touch down. Eventually, we did touch down and, to my amazement, relatively smoothly. But no sooner were we rolling on the mains with the tail in the air whereupon I added power and exited ground effect intent on another pattern.

In all, I did four touch and goes that afternoon with Jack patiently watching from the grass, about a third of the way down the 5000-foot runway. I was quite pleased with myself as I realized that once I started the first takeoff roll, nervousness was rapidly replaced by such an intense concentration that it naturally helped me to forget that I was scared. And in fact, I did not scare myself in the least during my orbits around the field and I began to actually enjoy the experience of flying 28432 without the weight of its owner.

Whether by design of chance, Jack's impromptu generosity of letting me fly his baby that afternoon was truly a life-changing experience that I have never forgotten.

To this day, I have no idea why he wanted me to solo on "that day," but I can tell you that because he did, I thought his cojones were definitely as big as his belly. He earned my total respect and admiration on what I thought was going out on a limb. I never knew if his actions were premeditated or impetuous, as he never once revealed any of his personal thoughts about that day to me. What I did begin to realize though was that I was a very blessed young man to have two very disparate, but uniquely wonderful, flying mentors . . . my father and Jack.

After picking up Jack with a smile occupying my entire face, at least according to him, he said he was going to fly the leg home as we left Wildwood Airport behind us.

CHAPTER 15

During the latter half of the 1974, the year in which I soloed, and while in the process of building time for my private pilot's license, I began to fret about what I should do for a living. At that time, in addition to flying, I was racing motorcycles and also actively scuba diving. I loved doing all three activities, and I was desperately trying to decide which one I should pursue as my career; why I felt the need to be so anxious about my future at that time I'll never know, but I did.

So, in search of wisdom, I took a chance and asked my dad for some advice. In all the time that I had known him—well, at least up until that point—he had never given me any deep introspective lessons about life. So after asking the question, I expected some shallow, sort of Doris Day "que sera, sera" ditty in response.

Instead, and totally out of character for him, he matter-of-factly said, "Do what you really like to do, whether it's the cycles, the flying, diving, or something else you may decide you like. Don't do it for the money, do it because you genuinely love it more than anything else. Money doesn't matter because if you really love what you do, you will become good at it and naturally rise to the top in pay. And even if you don't, because you love what you do, going to work will not seem like going to work, but more like going to play. If you take my advice, you will be happier than most of the working-class people."

I had to raise my dropped jaw with my hand. I had never, ever heard my father give such wisdom-laced, direct advice about life. When I was being bullied and asked him for advice, he was uncompassionate and indifferent; and then, when my expectations for any kind of career insight from him were at an all-time low, he spoke as if God was talking through him—and maybe He was.

I realized that indeed I should take his advice. Consequently, and almost immediately after his counsel was comprehended, I realized that becoming a professional pilot was my God-given calling, and I made a firm commitment to become one, though I had no idea how.

One impetus that pushed me over the edge and toward a winged career was the look in my Dad's and his colleagues' eyes as they talked about their mistress, the sky, and the aircraft that took them there. All the places they visited, all the people and characters they met, and all their fascinating stories therein are etched upon my memory and the fact that I never did hear a derogatory word about their career choice—that . . . that is what I wanted, a career without regrets.

Armed with beautiful words of wisdom from my dad and reinforced by his positive attitude and actions about his own career, and seeing also the same of his fellow aviators, did I too endeavor to embark upon an aviation-themed lifestyle a couple of years after he explained to me why some of the worker bees were so happy.

The official start to my career, to that of being a professional aviator, began on May 24, 1975; that was when I took and passed my private pilot practical flight test.

On that date, I gave up racing motorcycles, gave up on the idea of becoming a treasure diver and dive bum in general, and decided to concentrate solely on becoming an airline pilot.

Part of the agreement that I had with my father after I first soloed was that if I liked flying "that much" and if I wanted to get my private pilot's license, then I had to give up all my extracurricular activities, other than those I personally financed. And that is what I did. I sold both of my dirt bikes and bought a street bike instead, since I couldn't afford a car and my father wasn't going to buy me one.

I was never as aggressive as my father when it came to flying. After he got his private pilot's license, he was always getting into trouble for some mischievous act of daredevil flying. But not me, I was very conservative and approached flying more with a sense of awe and respect than a devil-may-care attitude like the old man.

One very funny little story about my dad's daredevil nature was when he flew west in a Waco UPF-7 to add to Wiggin's training aircraft fleet maintained in Springfield, Missouri. Shortly after his arrival, he saw Katherine, his future wife (the first one), walking on a sidewalk in the center of town. Being very shy and also new to the area, he had no idea how to meet her or make an introduction.

Since romantic desires of the heart can breed whimsical solutions to the complexities of courtship, the feisty Bostonian decided to highlight and announce himself to Katherine, if not the entire populace of Springfield, in what could truly be considered a novel and at the same time grand manner. Flying with a student in the Waco one Saturday morning, he decided to buzz Main Street, inverted, with his student. The Waco's engine could not run while the aircraft was flown upside down, so my father said he had to dive

quite steeply and from a fairly high altitude to get the speed necessary to carry them for a decent distance both above and along the
length of the street. They were having a small hometown parade at
the time of the impromptu air show, so needless to say, the inverted
low pass was a crowd pleaser to some, not so to others, especially the
police. The poor student was not really impressed with this seemingly random display of my father's flying acumen since that was
his first training flight and, consequently, his last since he quit right
after they landed. On a more positive note, the union of Katherine
and my father was assured, though I have no idea how they actually
did meet after that aerial advertisement of love.

As I said, I was a much more cautious and timid gosling. The
old man did encourage me to fly as much as I wanted and never put
any preconditions or rules on me as to where or when I could, or
couldn't, fly. Amazingly, the only rules I had were those under which
aviation itself is/was governed and structured. I had full access to a
few aircraft, and if I wanted to, I could've flown to California or anywhere in between; he never once complained to me about the cost
and indeed "encouraged" me to fly on days when birds were munch-
ing on chips and watching TV because the weather was so abysmal.

So, when I was a senior in high school and I told my dad that I
was flying 600 miles to the west in a Cherokee 180 to pick up a girl,
who was in my homeroom class and who was visiting her sister's
college, he didn't bat an eye. With a good buddy as my copilot, we
blasted off one Friday after school in high spirits, as we were told
we were going to be the guests of honor at a sorority party that
night. Unfortunately, this girl's knowledge of geography (and her
dad's also) was as bad as my judgment of their ability to understand a simple question. Needless to say, like my attempt with Dana

years before, it was a romance that never was as the laughter from about eighteen college girls sounding in unison when Carol (the girl) loudly told them, as I was talking to her on the phone, that I had flown to the wrong state, sealed any chance of aviation rock star hero status.

After high school, college followed, and I was lucky enough to break into the world of marketing.

Earlier, I mentioned the wisdom God infused in my father's asking of Jack to help train me to be a pilot. As a bonus to having him as an instructor and friend was the fact that Jack knew Andre Tomalino, and Andre owned Paramount Air Service. When I was six years old and saw an aircraft towing an aerial advertising sign, a.k.a. banner, over the beach, never in my wildest dreams did I think I would be doing the same. But at nineteen, and thanks to Jack, I began flying for none other than Paramount Air Service, in whose offices I had stood when I was sixteen. In all, I flew four summers with Paramount, as I worked my way through college.

I cannot thank the Lord enough for the deviation in my flying life with regard to becoming a banner tow pilot. I never, ever, gave a thought to towing banners, since my father kept saying to me, after I began flying, that I needed to get my instructor rating and start instructing students to build flying time, just like he did back "in the day." Make no mistake, I knew I was not as gifted an aviator as my father, and I felt that after I got my commercial license I still needed more polish before I would feel comfortable instructing students. And to be totally honest, at that time in my life, I had no desire to be an instructor, and God knew as much. So, instead of following in the old man's shoes, the Lord's will took charge, and to my relief,

I towed banners as I gained valuable flying time, learning so much in the process as well as enjoying every minute of the banner towing.

There was no better teacher for me than a beautiful 1957 orange and white Super Cub that Andre allowed me to fly while working at Paramount. While the very first banner aircraft I saw when I was sixteen was ratty-looking and dilapidated, 6897B, the N numbers of "my" Super Cub, was beautiful.

I flew her seven days a week, two to six hours a day, from Memorial Day weekend to Labor Day, for four summers. In those summers, I always went to work with a smile on my face and came home content; the wise words of my father's career advice were etching deeper into my soul with each flight in 97B.

As you have read, my father told me many tales about this or that flight of his, but as my summers progressed toward college graduation and my towing hours accumulated, I began to reciprocate with my father and told him of some of my own learning experiences. Those were some wonderful, summer-breeze-cooled evenings on the patio, or in a pub, as I told my dad of things I had done and learned while towing banners. I could see enthusiasm and approving twinkles in his eyes as he listened intently to me, and it was during such moments where the father/son love between him and me was the greatest.

Though I had many adventures in those summers, the one my dad laughed at the most was when I almost lost a banner due to flying into a thick fog.

I was headed northbound at 250 feet and 55 mph and just off the Atlantic City beaches. I was eating lunch and daydreaming of being on the beach with some of the bathing beauties below when I noticed that the view of the beach ahead was rapidly disappearing and that I could only see straight down upon the waves, and even that view was being obscured somewhat by fragmented wisps of clouds that were appearing below me. With Atlantic City's now unseen semi-high-rise buildings blocking a westward reversal of course and the lack of a discernible horizon, giving me pause to want to turn out over the water, I tried to climb above the ever-thickening mist while going straight ahead. No chance there either since the climb rate while towing a banner was anemic at best, and as soon as I began to go up, the waves disappeared, and I had no idea how high the top of this stuff was, so downward I dropped to 150 feet or so. A call on the CB radio to the banner kids at Bader Field Airport, which sits just off the beach and to the west of Atlantic City and from where I was towing my banners, told me the field was still clear, though the banner boys said they could see a fog bank mounting higher in the sky over the eastern edge of the city; no doubt it was massing for a final assault on the warm veil of air that separated the beach from the airport. I decided to follow the beach and turn inland as soon as I came upon the inlet that separated Atlantic City from Brigantine. The problem was that if I was at 150 feet or so AGL (above ground level), the tail of the banner was lower, maybe 10 to 20 feet (depending on airspeed), and as I flew farther north, the fog became even denser, and I had to go lower still.

Lord, my heart was beating like a hummingbird's as I kept one hand on the banner release handle, figuring, that if I had to, I would cut the banner loose over the waves of the beach and then I'd immediately, and rapidly, climb straight ahead, believing I could hold a reasonable wings level attitude until I popped above the stuff. As I reached the inlet, I turned ninety degrees left, went down to 100 feet, and had increased the airspeed to 70 mph to raise the tail of the banner as much as I could. I initially flew over the boardwalk on the Atlantic City side of the inlet, but the closeness of the people on the boardwalk gave me huge pause in keeping this flight path, so I elected to fly over the middle of Absecon inlet. While I initially patted myself on the back for this decision, which I thought was a good idea, it turned out to be poor execution on my part since there were so many boats rushing into the inlet that if I had to drop the banner there too, I'd probably conk someone on the head. However, the even greater folly of this change of flight path would soon be revealed in even finer detail a few moments after arriving over the middle of the inlet.

It soon became obvious to me as I flew ever lower over the water that it was a race between me and my aircraft and the distance the fog had gained in its advance down the inlet as to how low I was going to have to go to stay in visual contact with the boats and the water.

Unfortunately, I had forgotten about the new seventy-five-foot-high bridge that had been built across the inlet. In an instant of horror I saw the upper reaches of the bridge appear out of the opaqueness of the fog and now I was eyeball level with some seriously wide-eyed beachgoers in their cars as they crested the roadway above the inlet. The drivers rapidly stopped on the bridge in the same immediate reaction as I "popped" the airplane up to pass over them. Once clear of the bridge, I immediately nosed over, the letters of my sign following in suit with the tail of the banner, passing not more than ten feet above the roadway; there is no doubt the advertiser of that banner got his money's worth out of that tow, as I'm sure the words of that banner are indelibly etched upon the memories of some of those who observed their close passage in front, if not above, them.

As soon as the length of the banner cleared the bridge, the sky in front of me began to brighten, giving me hope that the fog would soon clear. As if on cue, after clearing the worst obstacle since I'd entered the fog, I flew into clear air—what a relief.

The summers of my college years were an odd existence. I loved the banner towing and going to the beach bars with my girlfriend, colleagues, and friends, particularly the one summer Jeff and I towed banners together. Those were wonderful times, and it was so refreshing to be flying for a summer job and not busing or waiting tables in a restaurant, which I had done for a few years in high school. Counter to the wonderful flying and socializing I was enjoying in those years were my father's continued random nightly attacks followed by acts of kindness and verbal praise. His bouts of rage, anger and mental abuse became even more extreme as I got older, for reasons unknown to me, but conversely, he became even more complimentary when sober. Maybe he saw that I was becoming my own person and that he was losing control over me . . . I don't know, I'm not a shrink. What I experienced firsthand, though, was a deepening in his rage, but oddly, his happy times seemed even happier, to the point that he would say that I could conquer the world or that it was my oyster. What caused his mood swings was never obvious to me, so I spent my life during those times either avoiding the old man or massaging his ego to keep him from blowing up on me.

On the nights where I got tired of his crap and challenged him, I had beer bottles thrown at me.

As an aside, once I entered college, very rarely did Ken come at me physically with his fists. Oh, he might throw something at me, but very rarely did he try to hit me with a punch or a slap once I got older. I've got to assume that because I grew from being shorter than him, to much taller (5 inches taller than him), in the span of 4 years, he was a bit intimidated by my physical size.

There were a few times in the summer, sultry nights with an ill-defined and warm breeze blowing, where he chased me 'round the house, throwing bottles my way since he could never catch me. If it were in a movie it could be seen as comical, and at times I do chuckle about the pure stupidity of it all, but back then, it was not fun. My father always made it known in those fights that everything I had was his to take back and that I had nothing and was nothing until he said otherwise.

On a few of those extreme nights, I escaped to Ocean City. I'd catch a bus, drive my motorcycle or car (when I got one) to Ocean City and walk the lovely boardwalk, feeling so alone though surrounded by thousands of tourists. On those nights when being alone was both a curse and a blessing, the God of the Lord's Prayer kept me company and made Himself known as He jumped into my heart and reasserted Himself as my newfound best friend and companion. We would stare at the waves, listen to the sound of the surf, stare at the stars and the flashing lights of the jets far above, or people-watch. Sometimes, I sat on the benches that lined the boardwalk, or, wanting more seclusion, I'd retire to the beach and sit near the water's edge, where the magical melding of three mediums occurred. With wanderlust, I would look endlessly to the east where the stars merged with the water, with God buoying my spirits about how wonderful my future would be. I told Him what I wanted to do with my life and asked Him if He could please somehow answer my silent and desperate prayers and see me through the hell I was living in and into the arms of my dreams.

After staring at the ocean, I'd make my way to the boardwalk and mope. A few times, I was offered a place to crash on the floor or couch of some young lady's apartment, someone whom I'd met and befriended while sitting on a boardwalk bench. However, after one encounter where a very nice young lady's boyfriend and she began to have sex on the floor right next to me after he came in from work . . . well, that kinda cured me of accepting offers of that kind. On occasion, I slept in the lifeguard booths that were on the beaches, but random police patrols might roust me from that slumber. Usually, around 3 or 4 a.m. I would arrive home as I knew my father would be sleeping off his stupor.

If he was there in the morning when I got up to go to work, he'd act like the fight never happened and was usually as happy as a lark. Like a puppy dog, I was always hopeful that the previous evening's fight would be our last and that he would change his ways, as he said he would many times during the mornings after. As odd as it is, I loved the old man when he was contrite and somewhat humble and particularly when the two of us were immersed in the realm of aviation. Flying was the one area where he and I could always relate, and it was also the one area, when I was actually flying in an aircraft, where he couldn't physically or emotionally hurt or harass me.

Pilots are very good at putting their feelings and emotions in a compartment when they fly so that the effects of those emotions, particularly if the pilot is going through a stressful time, do not affect their ability to perform their duties on that particular flight or series of flights. I had seen my father compartmentalize all my life, and I was amazed at how well he could live in such turmoil at home and yet still fly with aplomb. So, like father, like son, and I too began to realize as I lived amidst the turmoil of my emotion-filled college years, that I could live in a virtual hell on earth but, once I entered a cockpit I felt totally safe and isolated from my earthly issues. With each flight I found it so easy to leave all my cares and worries on the ground and looked forward to being reunited with the sky. It was a subliminal kind of déjà vu, because, though I didn't realize it at that time the cycle of being born again as a pilot and being totally in love with flying reoccurred over and over again in my college years, just as it did for me when I was in high school and first soloed. Flying was salvation for me back then and staved off the inevitable Armageddon that I was sure was to come one day between my father and me.

Though the majority of my flying during my college years was accomplished in the summer months, I did manage to maintain some flying proficiency, albeit at a minimum level, while away at college. I didn't fly a whole lot mostly due to the cost and lack of available aircraft, but on the odd occasion, I would bite the financial bullet and rent an aircraft at the local FBO or fly with a friend who had access to an aircraft.

Probably the oddest flight I had in college, if not my entire life (as of this writing), came on a late Saturday night in early February 1979, and to be honest, this is one of my most favorite flights too (so far).

While in college, I managed the Chalet. It was a school-owned bar/restaurant and activities center, centrally located on the college's small campus. It was around 11:30 p.m. and had been a slow business night, and there was no one else but me in the establishment at that time. The night before, we had an awesome blowout party I had helped to coordinate with the all-girls' college located across town, so tonight was pretty much a health night (no drinking) for most of the guys on campus, myself included (the drinking age at this time in the United States was eighteen in most states).

The dark wood-paneled bar area was warm and felt cozy as I listened to the rock music du jour blaring out of the jukebox while analyzing the sales numbers for the day. While busily counting money, lip-synching to the music, and making mental inventory/ ordering reminders, I occasionally glanced outside to look at the wilting snow piles on the wood deck, excited with the knowledge that a snowstorm was due to dump another eight to twelve inches the next day. As I was deep in multitasking thought, one of the college's few female students—a freshman, Tammy, who came from an exceptionally wealthy family and who was both facially and curvaceously beautiful—walked into the bar and sat with a purpose right in front of me.

Since Tammy and I breathed air from different universes— social, financial, and work ethic—we had a whole different idea of what we each wanted to get out of our college years. We rarely crossed paths except for when she was in the Chalet with one of her many suitors, girlfriends, or an entourage of both. If that sounds like an innuendo of dislike, not in the least—I did like her. However, I was very driven back then and Tammy was, well . . . not.

As I sat doing the books and counting money, Tammy asked me if I was sober. I said, "Yes."

She then said, "Well, what I mean is, have you had a drink at all today?"

"No," was my very simple response because I was counting money and didn't want to lose my place, nor did I look at her while answering her questions.

"Well," she continued, in an exasperated tone, "my sister is leaving her fiancé and wants to come visit me here on campus and stay with me for a couple of weeks."

"Well, I am very sorry for your sister, I guess, though I don't know her, but I guess staying with you would be a nice getaway. When is she coming and what the hell does any of this have to do with you asking me if I've been drinking?" I said out of breath.

"Because every boy on campus that I know that has a pilot's license is either drunk or drinking and headed that way and can't fly tonight, and my sister wants me to fly down now in my airplane and pick her up."

Collecting my composure and thinking there goes my theory on it being a health night for the roughly 400 guys on campus, or at least for whatever number of pilots Tammy approached, I said to her, "Tammy, we are under a winter storm warning, why in God's name would anyone want to fly tonight?"

"I checked the weather," she bluntly pointed out. "The weather guy said the snow is not supposed to start until around noon tomorrow, that's twelve hours from now. Right now, it's 5000 overcast, and it's gonna stay that way for another six hours at least and even then get slowly worse and the visibility is at least twenty miles and the winds are very light."

I then asked her the obvious question, "Tammy, are you, in a roundabout way asking me to fly you down to Martha's Vineyard to pick up your sister?"

"Yes."

I sat and looked at her for a few tense and long seconds. It was my thought that the truly rich have a different comprehension of life. From the side of the tracks I'm from, I'd suffer with my fiancé and try to work things out until the storm blew over . . . and take your pick on the storm—the emotional one or the winter one that was about to hit, or both. Because either way, there's no doubt they were both gonna pass . . .

So, after looking into Tammy's beautiful eyes, which I could see were desperately trying to seduce me into saying yes, I gave her a conditional yes. I said if the weather was as good as she said, then I was willing to pick up her sister, but I needed to check the actual conditions and the forecast myself. Also, I needed to go get a buddy in one of the dorms who had a current set of aviation approach charts and maps and wanted him to come along since I figured two pilots on a night like this would be better than one.

Having had another victory over coercing a male into doing what she wanted, Tammy happily skipped out of the bar and said she'd meet us at the aircraft, which was located just down the street from the campus.

Indeed, the weather was as Tammy said, and by a little after midnight and with legacy snow covering the ground in large patches, overcast skies, and calm winds, three college kids took off from Boire Field, in Nashua, New Hampshire, in a Cherokee Archer.

I always enjoyed flying at night because it was usually smoother, turbulence-wise, than during the day. Oddly enough, that flight was, in retrospect, a prelude to my future airline flying, which would generally see me flying at night in a sparkling, gem-sprinkled sky, dark cloud, or a combination of both.

As anticipated, it was creamy smooth as we climbed in the frigid winter air to our cruising altitude of 2,500 feet. Though the clouds were a little more than 2,500 feet above us as we leveled off, the visibility was almost unlimited, judging by the fact that I could easily see the glow from thousands of singular or merged lights emanating from the city of Boston and its many attendant towns, which were to the left of the aircraft. I called Boston Center and asked for radar flight following upon leveling off on this VFR flight since I wanted separation from any other idiot that might be stupid enough to be flying on one of Old Man Winter's Saturday midnights, and also for the security of having someone know where we were.

The "dark" of night on this flight took on a different hue than of those nights of my past. That previously mentioned layer of snow on the ground caused the residential and city lights to be reflected to the solid layer of clouds above me, and then from there it was re-reflected all around, thusly magnifying the intensity of the ambient lighting to the point that it was actually quite, and abnormally, bright, even though it was a little past the witching hour and no moonlight was available.

The shimmering of the lights from outside the aircraft and the subdued glow from the aircraft's instrument panel, combined with a warm cockpit, smooth air, the drone of the engine, and the occasional radio calls from ATC—made for an intoxicating cocktail of aviation character that never failed to seduce me into wanting to come back for more. On that night, the emotional rush from that previously mentioned blend of ingredients was quite exhilarating and surreal.

Since the island of Martha's Vineyard was only a hundred miles or so as the crow flies from our departure airport, and since we cruised at 130 mph, it didn't take long to get there since we were also flying as the crow flies . . . direct. The most dramatic part of the flight was the conscious disregard for the security and comfort of the bright lights of the city of New Bedford, Massachusetts, for the possibility that Martha's Vineyard lay beyond in the shrouding cloak of darkness that greeted the three of us as we headed offshore.

I'd never been to Martha's Vineyard before this flight, but I wasn't particularly worried about getting to or finding it since the island had a VOR that would electronically guide us to the field and the weather, upon flying over top of the airport, was good and the runway lights were all illuminated. The tower was closed due to the late hour and the time of the year, so I did one turn over the field, checking the lighted wind sock for the prevailing wind, and then set up for an uneventful landing on the runway most aligned into the wind.

After shutting down on the ramp, Tammy jumped out of the airplane and literally ran into the night and disappeared.

Being alone with each other now, my heretofore unnamed friend, Dan, and I walked up to the airport's main terminal building to see if we could get inside and stay warm. The moist sea air that surrounded us when combined with the freezing temperatures made it feel colder than Houdini's weenie, and we had no idea how long it would be before Tammy came back since she ran off without saying a word.

Since we had time to kill and were cold, Dan and I walked around the terminal looking for an open door. I chanced to peek into a windowed door that showed some promise of life, if only because I saw some light sneaking out between the shutters. I had my face pressed against the window, trying to look through slits in the shutter when I noticed a man inside looking back at me! Crap! I was so creeped out that I fell on my ass, and as I did, my buddy started laughing hysterically. The creepy man inside opened the door and asked if we had flown the aircraft that just landed. I said yes, rather cautiously, not sure if he wanted to make us a midnight snack or actually held some official capacity with the airport.

Being invited in to stay warm and answer some general questions, we sat on a sofa in his cozy little room while he sipped on what I believe was an Irish coffee. He watched TV in between glances at Dan and me while he was either talking or listening. Though not a whiskey or coffee drinker at that point in my life, I could seriously have used a belt right about then due to the still recent memory of that face staring back at me in the window. As the conversation warmed, and our bodies, too, this delightfully odd, old man explained that he was born and raised on the island and was the caretaker of the airport during the off hours of operation, though what his actual duties were I never could ascertain.

As the three of us were maintaining small talk, I saw car lights appear on the ramp and figured Tammy was back with her high-maintenance sister. Bidding the old man a courteous adieu while walking backward and promising to come back one day (I never have), I desperately tried to focus my attention on Tammy and our new passenger without being rude to this apparition in the window. Oddly, he stayed at the door to his cozy little nest and never ventured outside to see who drove their car onto the ramp and parked next to one of the aircraft.

It was kinda weird being on the island/airport at 2 a.m. in the dead of winter, and I really wanted to get out of there since I figured if anyplace would go down, weather-wise, first, it would be that island.

Dan was helping to expedite the loading of Tammy's luggage adorned sister so we could beat the snow while Tammy's mom went on a cute little conversational thread with me.

I had never met Mrs. Weaver before, and I have to say she was exceptionally beautiful—like mother, like daughter—and very nice too. But as we briefly chatted—actually, it being more like her talking to me—she mentioned how crazy kids could be.

Really? I was twenty, what the hell did I know about kids? I could tell her that I'd bet her a million bucks that her capricious daughter wouldn't last a week in the dorm with Tammy (I think it was four days) and I also could have told her that I'd never let my two daughters fly on a night such as the one we were getting ready to fly into with two boys of whose flying credentials I had no idea, let alone their personal morals and mental stability. I mean seriously? What idiot boy would be out flying at night, on a very early Sunday morning, during a winter storm warning, just so he could garner a couple of hours of free flying time? Yes, I qualify as being the village idiot, but I knew that I was a somewhat sane idiot, and I was confident of my judgment and ability. But how on earth would Mrs. Weaver know of my character unless she was a lot more probing in questioning me, which she was not? To this day, I still find that odd.

So, after Her Highness's bags were stowed, the proverbial preflight walkaround was performed and the emotional mother-to-daughter goodbyes expressed, the pilots and passengers boarded the aircraft and we started the engine. After a short taxi and a little after an hour since our arrival, we departed into the same black void from which we came.

The ladies were all cozy in the backseats and happily chatted away while Dan and I quietly enjoyed our own personal thoughts as the lights of Boston, now on the right, easterly, side of us, came into view.

The flight back was more uneventful than the one "down" because the weather was the same and the lights of the mainland could be seen as soon as we got above a hundred feet or so while climbing and turning toward the mainland.

We landed sometime around 3 a.m. in seemingly the same conditions as when we left; it was as if time and the weather, had stood still. Dan and I escorted the girls to Tammy's room and, upon arrival, literally dropped all her sister's crap on the floor and quietly left. Dan headed to his room to get some more sleep, and I, instead of heading to my room, headed back to the Chalet. I programmed the jukebox with a bunch of my favorite songs, poured myself a drink, started a wood fire in the huge fireplace that dominated one side of the bar's interior, and then lay down on an overstuffed couch that collected all the light and heat from that fire. I got into a cozy fetal position as the flames grew higher then proceeded to reminisce about what a weird night it had been while I waited for the morning, and the snow, to arrive.

Heading back home at the end of the school year was always bittersweet. I hated being in my parents' house, but I loved the summers on the Jersey shore and my summer job of towing banners. It was the same, summer after summer, during those college years and though I desperately wanted permanent separation from my parents, I loved the ambiance of the shore's environs.

As my years of college accumulated, my father became very worried about my future. I can't tell you how many times he wanted me to do this or that career and what follows is just a smattering of his "suggestions": (1) In my freshman year, he advocated that I take the air traffic controller's test and become an air traffic controller; (2) In my sophomore year, he thought I should join the Army—yes Army

. . . I have no idea why; (3) In my junior year, he said he could get me a job as a flight check pilot with the FAA, but also went back to "suggesting" I join the Army (he usually wanted me to join the Army when he was mad at me); and (4) In my senior year, he said he was willing to start an air taxi business with me after I graduated.

In each case, the old man was dead serious; and in each case, though I considered his thoughts, I discarded his "recommendations." However, he was very convinced about a couple of his ideas.

The only suggestion of his that I was actually excited about was in the forming of an air taxi service. I thought that would have been cool, but then again, I was extremely naive back then and in retrospect, he didn't have the money required to start such a business.

But unless I could have stretched college for another couple of years (neither mine nor my father's desire), my future was set on a course of flying; the fortunes of which would be dictated by God above, because I never could have charted the path He chose for me by myself.

As college came to an end, the eternal silver lining of providence used Mr. Grace's voice and wisdom to direct me onto a career path different to those constantly being thrust upon me by my father, and one that I never, ever remotely considered.

While I was on Christmas break of my senior year in college, Bob and I got into a conversation about my career aspirations. He asked me what I wanted to do for a living, and I told him I wanted to be an airline pilot but had no idea how to become one. He suggested that since the airlines like military guys, that I should consider going into the Air National Guard to fly fighters. I didn't even think they would take a young guy right out of college, but he said the Guard was really ramping up their hiring of young men right out of college.

So, on Mr. Grace's suggestion, I went to the F-105 unit at McGuire AFB, where I saw the Thunderbirds perform in F-4s years earlier, and applied for a pilot training slot. After a physical and an interview and some tough competition from a whole host of other guys who had the same goal, I got the one and only pilot training slot available that year. I was informed when I interviewed that they were going to convert to F-4s and was asked if I had a problem with that.

"No, sir! I just want to fly fighters! And if I have to, I'll go to every fighter unit in the country in my quest to get one, I will!" was my snappy reply. Maybe not a very eloquent response, but it did reflect the desire of my heart.

I was accepted into the 108th TFW (Tactical Fighter Wing) in the summer of 1980 and excitedly waited for mid-September and the start of officer's training school. My USAF pilot training class date was scheduled to begin in January, though I wouldn't be given the actual pilot training base and exact start date until I finished officer's school.

It all was a dream that, quite simply, I never, ever gave much thought to because I just never thought I was good enough to be a military pilot, let alone fly fighters. Yes, there is no question I had transitory thoughts about a military career and flying fighters, but the thoughts vaporized almost as soon as they existed. I dared not dwell on such hopes since I couldn't bear the disappointment of not seeing them answered. But in the area of my heart to which only God is privy, He knew of my hopes and dreams and, however brief those prayerful thoughts, amazingly, He answered them. And equally astounding is that no matter how many times my father tried to direct me into this or that vocation, his attempts were always thwarted by unforeseen circumstances. I have no doubt that though God used my father to kick-start my flying career, He enlisted the aid of others to more profoundly direct and shape it.

Since I had the summer of 1980 off, while I waited to enter the military, I was more than happy to give Andre and Lois one more season of banner towing while I milked the old man of one more glorious summer at the South Jersey shore.

As Labor Day of that summer approached, I can honestly say I was not prepared for the bittersweet moment that would shortly follow; after having flown the same banner tow aircraft for almost four complete summers, I would be leaving my mistress, N6897B.

Around the year 1992, I wrote the following short story in tribute to one of the finest aircraft I have ever flown.

LAST FLIGHT

The morning sky was cloudless and dark blue and the air cool, as I began untying Nine Seven Bravo (henceforth to be written 97B) in preparation for our flight to Cape May County Airport.

The length of the days was waning on this, the second week of September, slowly giving way to the coming equinox that marked the beginning of autumn. As it does every year, Labor Day sounded the unofficial end to summer a week ago. This seasonal passing of Labor Day weekend acts as a broom, "shushing" the tourists, en masse, back to the innards of America and back to their winter homes, from whence they came, and come, each and every summer.

This annual end-of-summer departure of the masses also brought an end to another season of banner towing. "Aerial advertising," as it is more eloquently called by people more refined than myself, is a summers-only business along the South Jersey shore. Paramount Air Service, which is located at Cape May County Airport in Cape May, New Jersey, owns eight aerial advertising, "banner towing" aircraft. Seven of these aircraft plied their trade towing banners out of Cape May from May to early September. The eighth aircraft, 97B, flew out of Bader Field, a small airport about thirty miles north of Cape May and at the back door to Atlantic City.

I had been towing banners in 97B for most of the past four summers while on summer break from college, but the flight today was to be my last in her, at least for the foreseeable future. I had graduated from college in May, and I was to start Officer's Candidate School in late September with USAF pilot training to follow. On that morning, I was going to fly 97B to Cape May where she was to roost until next summer's towing season, a routine to which she had been relegated for the past few years. So, like a connoisseur of fine food who chews each morsel more than the old wives' tale allotted twenty-first times, to savor each delicious bite, I too, as a connoisseur of the sky, intended to absorb and relish as much of this flight as I could.

Nine Seven Bravo, 97B. Those two numbers and that single letter are indelibly etched in my memory and my heart. That simple combination of human symbolism and communication represent the name, the "N" numbers, to be more specific, of the "lady" with whom I had a love affair. She was a 1956, orange and white, Piper Super Cub. Her official name was 6897B, so dedicated by the FAA bureaucrats, but to me she was simply 97B. We had a relationship that lasted for four years and almost 750 hours. In that time, I went from crawling to walking in as far as gaining "seat of the pants" flying experience. She taught me so much and gave so much and, with the exception of gas and oil, expected nothing in return. I am sure that she had seen more glorious days. In her prime, she may have crop-dusted or flown in the bush, or maybe she lived in the lap of luxury, sheltered in some cozy hangar, flown only on Sundays. But now, she was doing semiretired flying four months out of the year towing "Eat at Joe's" signs or some reasonable facsimile thereof; like a once-proud cutting horse, she was now relegated to pulling the equivalent of a plow. In spite of her years, to me, she was beautiful. Time and the elements had taken away her physical attractiveness, at least to the casual observer. However, as dull as she was in sheen, underneath, she still had spirit; and I always thought she looked like a high-spirited fighter aircraft.

No doubt that given her age, 97B had seen many a cocky young knight swagger up into her cockpit and then get humbled at her hands. But once the young would-be master of the skies realized that he didn't know it all, she began to teach. That's how it was with me. I knew all her idiosyncrasies, and she accepted mine. We were a singular machine once I got settled into her cockpit. My arms and legs, acting as neurons, and her flight controls melded into one another when we took flight, neither one of us separate from the other. I was the biological part of a living entity, part metal, part flesh—neither one of us capable of flight without the other.

And so it was, on this beautiful morning, that I found myself untying 97B in preparation for our last flight together.

The aroma of freshly ground coffee tantalized my nose as I performed my walk around. The source of this gloriously earthen smell, Ireland's Coffee, was right across the street from the airport and near the ramp. I had been smelling it for the past three years, and I never tired of its scent. It reminded me of my days as a very

young kid, going to the A&P food store with my mom and bury-
ing my head in the burlap bags of coffee that sat near the checkout
table. Also, because I smelled the coffee from Ireland's, it meant
that the winds were light, an unusual thing during the warm days
on the shore, considering there was an almost constant sea breeze.
Finally, the smell, particularly that day, brought back three years'
worth of memories, happy memories, of Atlantic City Airport and
banner towing and of 97B . . . the womb from whence I began my
aviation career.

Once all the preflight rituals were accomplished, I started 97B's
engine, and we taxied to the active runway. I always thought of her
as a P-51 Mustang, although the only similarity, albeit a weak one,
was that they are both tail-draggers. My mom always said I had an
active imagination, so where the truth ended, my delusional thinking took over. I imagined I was getting ready for the dawn patrol,
and my "Mustang" and I were the leaders of the pack. The morning
sun would glint off the propeller and create a stroboscopic effect
that, along with the rumble of the Lycoming engine, would seduce
me into believing that I was more than I really was.

In reality, 97B was not a Mustang, and I knew it. The instrument panel was about as rudimentary as you could get. It had indicators for airspeed, oil pressure and temperature, altitude, vertical
speed, rpm, and finally turn and slip . . . luxury for Jimmy Doolittle
maybe—but in today's world, definitely spartan. She had a split
door on the right side that allowed me to fly with the right window,
the top half of the door, folded out and up, against the bottom of
the wing. The lower half of the door could be left down during
flight. So, in essence, my entire right side, from the top of my head
to my knee was easily exposed to the elements; and if you had a fear

of heights, well, definitely not a good way to fly. The view, however, was fabulous! In the three years that I flew her, I always flew with both halves fully open . . . thank God for seat belts. On my left side, the Plexiglas windshield folded back to where it blended into what should have been a side window. That window, though, for at least a good two to three feet, was not there. Somewhere during her years of towing, the left side window was removed to afford better downward visibility. (When I went in for a banner pickup, I usually stuck my head out the left side, where the window had been, to look straight down and see if I caught the banner.) However, unlike my exposed right side, the fuselage, metal tubes, covered with fabric, around the window area protected my left lower flank from the elements; thusly, only my left shoulder and head were exposed to the swirling winds that visited me.

To say the least, it was a pretty breezy place and really noisy. Consequently, to protect my hearing from being damaged by the noise, I flew with earplugs and a snug-fitting ear-covering headset with a boom mic. There was no heater. Usually, it was hot enough, given the sultry summer days, and I flew low enough to stay warm; I usually flew in jeans, sneakers, T-shirt, ball cap, and aviator sunglasses (and this was before Top Gun . . . coolness knows no bounds). When the occasional summer "cold" front blasted through and the winds came from the north/northwest—chilly winds, relatively speaking—I would stick my left arm out the window and warm it in the exhaust . . . I figured the radiator effect of warming the blood in my left arm would warm the rest of me. In a psychosomatic sense, it worked!

With the sun still well below its zenith, I taxied 97B onto runway 16 for takeoff. There were a couple of ways in which she could be alighted from the tarmac. One was a rather boring three-point take-off. In it you kept the stick back in your lap to keep all three wheels on the runway (two mains and the tail wheel) and when flying speed was achieved she simply lifted off. The second way of elevating her was to perform a "wheels" takeoff. With this method, you lifted the tail up as soon as you applied full power and rolled only on your main wheels. The faster you went, the more nose-down stick you applied. In this manner the aircraft stayed on the runway until well past the point when flying speed was achieved and when the stick was pulled back, like a homesick angel she would leap into the air. And so it would be, today, in keeping with my imagined belief that 97B was descended from a World War II fighter and we were head-ing out on dawn patrol, that we would do a wheels takeoff. After all, I never saw a Mustang do a three-point takeoff! But more realisti-cally, I thought this type of takeoff was a more stately and dignified way for her to depart to her winter's roost.

As the throttle was moved to wide open, the airy cockpit con-veyed the exhilaration of the moment by allowing swirling air and raucous engine noise to envelope me. Initially, only my feet were busy. As the takeoff roll progressed, I would alternately feed in left and right rudder—sometimes rudely, sometimes gently—to keep her tracking straight down the runway. Since there was very little crosswind that morning the rhythm of the feet was kept to a minimum and 97B tracked as true as she ever had. But fancy footwork alone would not get this girl flying. As wise as she was, she still needed to have her ailerons and elevator tended to. At a speed I could only tell by feel through the stick and rudder pedals and not numbers on the airspeed indicator, I eased the tail up to get us on the mains. The faster we went, the sound of the engine slowly being drowned out by the rush of the wind swirling past at ever-increasing velocities. As a symphony increases in crescendo, as it nears its finale, each musical instrument adding to the whole, so too were all the elements of this takeoff, adding to the excitement—the breeze freshening, propeller spinning, fabric rustling, cylinders firing, control stick coming alive, rudder pedals dancing, heartbeats, breaths, glints of sunlight filtered by old aviator sunglasses, perspiration in the usual places, the seductive smell of burnt avgas, sea air, and roasted coffee. All were feeding this festival of sensation as we neared the climax that was liftoff. Adding more nose down elevator to hold her on the ground, I was enjoying the delayed takeoff, relishing in the emotion of the moment and in the feel of 97B. She wanted to fly, but I didn't—not yet. I was tasting, coming alive with feelings of nostalgia, four years' worth, and enjoying this last dance, not wanting it to end, knowing it would. This was my moment as a connoisseur. I was at the table with 97B, and this was to be our last supper together. Finally, at a speed well above which she could have lifted off, I gently pulled the stick back to slowly lift her off. I was enjoying being here, at this moment, as I had enjoyed all the past moments, when two distinctly different machines—one biological, one aeronautical—combined to take flight. In more than 750 hours of flying 97B, the thrill of flight was still as exciting as it had ever been.

Like an overladen Mustang, with a full load of fuel and ordnance, we slowly climbed away. However, only because I wanted to climb slow and not due to any lack of spirit from 97B. I elected to climb to a few hundred feet because once I was over the Atlantic Ocean, which was about half a mile from the departure end of the runway, I was going to descend to wave-top level for the initial part of my journey.

One of my first flight instructors, Jack, was occasionally exasperated while teaching me how to fly because I had a tendency, when I was flying VFR, to take a very circuitous route to my destination. It drove him nuts. After more than one very circuitous cross-country flight, Jack told me one of the reasons aircraft are better than cars is because they can go from point A to point B in straight lines. He said I reminded him of the kid in the Family Circus cartoon who, when sent on an errand, would visit every part of his cartoon's neighborhood while getting to his destination. My retort to his sternness was that that was why I liked to fly in the first place! I loved the view that the birds have and the freedom to flit about; getting to a destination was secondary to me, the journey was the gift.

Every Thursday morning in the summer, 97B and I would take off and fly to Cape May to pick up the paychecks for the ground crew and myself. That flight was my license to meander about "my neighborhood." I probably tripled the straight-line distance to Cape May as 97B, and I investigated all the nooks and crannies of the local area from above. I cherished those flights.

The first part of my neighborhood was the Atlantic Ocean off of Absecon Island (Atlantic City sits on top of Absecon Island, as do the cities—from north to south—after Atlantic City: Ventnor, Margate, and Longport). After crossing the beach, 97B and I swooped down to wave-top level, thirty feet or so, and headed southwest to parallel the beach about half a mile offshore. I always avoided flying directly over boats, and I avoided the beaches as there were too many people on them, even at 8 a.m. On this flight, 97B and I meandered about offshore, investigating buoys and lobster pot marker flags. There was no real reason for why I flew where I did over the ocean that day, or any other day for that matter. I simply enjoyed the moments spent flying my meandering path to whatever place struck my fancy. The ocean on this day was very flat with no perceptible swells, which may be the reason a lifeguard had rowed his rescue boat exceptionally far offshore. I decided to check out the boat; since it was so far offshore, I thought there might be a problem. That was my excuse anyway, playfulness was the real reason. I put the boat on my right side, about fifty feet out, thirty feet below and passed by at a hundred miles per hour. I waved to the lifeguard, and he waved back, each one of us surrounded by our mediums of choice and each enjoying this splendid morning while contemplating only what lay in the here and now.

After passing the boat, I stayed low and flew down the length of Absecon Island, just offshore, enjoying the calm air and the feeling of speed at thirty feet and 100 miles per hour. Because most of the summer residents had returned to their winter roosts, there were not many boats motoring about. The contrast between that moment and the week before was amazing. Normally, in the summer, these waters would be filled with dozens of boats, particularly on such a beautiful day. A lot of these vessels entered the ocean through the Little Egg harbor inlet between the southern end of Absecon Island and the northern end of Ocean City.

As I approached Ocean City, I turned in toward land and headed toward the inlet. Since there were so few boats, I decided to fly over the waves in the inlet. I have no idea why I did this. I would do it when I could, but I cannot give you a consciously good reason as to why I thought it was cool to do this, but I did think it was cool to fly over the waves. To be sure, if my engine quit, I'd be swimming, maybe even body-surfing to land. The inlet was about a mile or two wide, and I was about a half mile out to boot. What is really odd is that every time I flew over this area I always thought the exact same thing.

Once past the waves of the inlet, I was now flying near the Ocean City beaches. While there is only a mile or two physically separating the two barrier islands, in terms of culture, they were light-years apart. Atlantic City, with all the glitz and glamour of its casinos, gave way to the family-centered way of life that the residents of Ocean City cherished. Atlantic City's skyline was chiseled with skyscraper type buildings beckoning those with dreams of getting rich quick, while Ocean City's low-slung and rather sedate profile was more boring and less intimidating. The contrast between the cultures was as stark as the difference in skylines.

Ocean City is a mostly residential, summer resort with the main commercial district occupying a few blocks of real estate on the north end of this roughly seven-mile-long island. In the late 1970s, the winter population numbered around 20,000 people; however, in the summer it swelled to more than 200,000. It was, and still is, a dry town; no alcohol was/is served in any commercial business. Surfing, fishing, boating, and water sports in general were the major summer activities. As boring—or exciting, depending on your personal preferences—as this may sound, Ocean City did have one attraction that brought thousands of people to it year after year . . . the boardwalk.

The boardwalk stretched for two miles over the beaches of the north end. It was about 100 feet wide in the main, middle section, tapering to thirty feet or so at the ends. The boardwalk was, and still is, a world unto itself. Unless you've actually been to it, it's hard to imagine the attraction that wood planks laid above a beach can have to thousands of people who come back year after year to walk them. The "boards" was a microcosm of a world that had never gone bad. There were arcades and shops and restaurants upon restaurants and amusement rides and, of course, the never-ending procession of attendant hotels, all of which laid on or near the boards so as to disgorge their guests in steady streams onto the boardwalk to feed the never-ending parade of people. Whatever troubles existed in your life disappeared when you walked on the boardwalk. The surfer dudes and their groupies, the boy next door along with the girl across the street and their parents and siblings and friends, all seemed to come at some time in the summer to get away from the realities of life. During the day, Ocean City's beaches beckoned tourists by the thousands, but at night, the boardwalk was the cultural and to some, spiritual, center of the city. If you lay on the beach in the day, you walked on the boards at night. It was the happy days year after year for many thousands of people.

Earlier, I had said that Atlantic City Airport was the womb of my aviation career; well, now it can be said that the Ocean City boardwalk and its immediate environs was the womb of my pubescent teenage years. Because I had been so fortunate to live so near such a wonderful environment, I spent most of my teenage summer days and nights in, on and around the boardwalk. What my father couldn't teach me when we had that "father-son talk," my experiences in Ocean City did. With its beaches, surfing, movie theaters, arcades, amusement rides, and most important of all, girls, you had all of the ingredients necessary for endless summer romances. Yes, I had been hypnotized by Frankie Avalon's corny Beach Blanket Bingo movies. I fell in love more times than I can count, and out of love just as much, while socializing there . . . spurred on by hormones and in the hopes of finding my "Annette Funicello." I had under-the-boardwalk kisses and on-the-beach romances. I had entire relationships that started, endured and ended upon the boardwalk and its immediate surroundings. And throughout all those growing years, with all the relationships and all the neon nights on the boards and the sun-drenched days on the beach in front of the them, there always seemed to be aircraft flying by. From the simplest banner aircraft, towing its sign, to a military fighter slicing the air with its speed and noise, to the Coast Guard helicopter checking out the girls' tans, and everything in between, they all went by. Could it be that all these pilots (except the banner pilots of course!) were paying homage to some long past memories of some hot summer nights?

Considering this was quite possibly the last time I would fly 97B, I decided to pay my respects to both her and the boardwalk by flying the same route that the previous Romeos and/or Juliets flew before me and that had caused me to look up when I was immersed in my sea of love (almost six years after this flight I paid a tribute to 97B by flying a similar route, farther out to sea though, at 350 knots in an F-4 and then later in an F-16). I flew from the inlet to arrive just off the beach, outside the breaking waves, and abeam the boardwalk. I had large "N" numbers on the side of my aircraft, and I was worried about some double-chinned (one chin from God, the other from fat) FAA bureaucrat wrecking my career by telling me I was flying dangerously close to people, but on this day, I risked it. I owed it to 97B, all those memories of romance and friendships, and to myself. I flew along the entire length of the boardwalk at fifty feet, just outside the breaking surf, rocking my wings, saying hi to whoever was looking, and thinking about how I was going to miss my simple life of flights, nights, beach bars, beach babes, and buddies.

I contemplated going for a second run down the boardwalk, but I decided two runs was too much. One run was the dignified way to exit, and so I turned tail to the boardwalk's end and headed again for the open sea.

I frolicked about offshore, generally heading southwest as I flew the length of Ocean City Island; I was now contemplating the next act in my neighborhood journey. I had to cross from the sea to the land. I say "had to"—actually, that was BS. I didn't have to do any of this . . . I wanted to!

This was my "gift," this flight and every flight, and I was going to do what my mentor, Jack, hated most, and I was going to be pretty darned good at it too! That was my quest.

The reason I had to cross from the sea to the land was my desire to fly down the intracoastal waterway. This waterway lies between the mainland of New Jersey and its barrier islands, the islands of Absecon and Ocean City. (These islands are anywhere from two to three miles off the mainland and are much longer than they are wide, and they run from the southern-most tip of the state north to near Asbury Park.) There was a lot of water and marsh in between the two, and I loved to fly down a particular stretch of waterway that meandered like a snow skiing slalom course. I discovered it three years earlier, but because a lot of boats were usually on it in the summer, I couldn't fly low over it very much, except on the rare occasion, like that day!

The problem was, all the barrier islands were fairly densely in-habited. The homes and businesses on them created an invisible barrier to low-altitude flying because the regulations stated that you couldn't fly closer than 500 feet to any man-made object/dwelling (over thinly populated areas that is, 1000 for more heavily inhabited lands). A couple of islands up north had stretches of nature in their seemingly endless sea of homes, but down south, it was pretty packed. Except for one island . . .

God put the town of Strathmere where it was, for me, I am sure. The transition from crowded Ocean City to lightly colonized Strathmere was just too good to be true, so surely there had been divine intervention. Yes, there was an inlet, a water break between the islands where water flowed, a small inlet, maybe half a mile wide that I could have flown over to avoid people and buildings, but there was a bridge that crossed that narrow bit of water, and on that bridge was a toll booth. I did not want to have a toll booth collector get all worked up if I flew low over his/her bridge and then consequently call the "authorities"; discretion, I thought, was the better part of valor on this day.

So, I flew just off the beach, just outside of the breaking waves, looking for my moment to fly across. Only the northern end of this city, for about five blocks, had any sizable development; the rest of the city, until you got farther south toward Sea Isle, was very sparsely inhabited—probably because the island was quite narrow where I wanted to cross, only one north/south road being able to fit within the confines of the island at this narrow "waist" without the road encroaching on the sand dunes and beach or being swallowed by the marsh. The day was surreal in its brilliance and climate, and because of this, there were quite a few beachcombers walking about, scavenging for bits of driftwood or shells, or in search of charging up their spiritual batteries. I too was in a spiritual mood, and in this mood there was the matter of keeping a certain continuity to this flight . . . climbing above 100 feet was not a part of this continuity. So like a seagull flitting about looking for food, I was flitting about looking for a break in this human wall. I flew toward Sea Isle, which was very populated, and then backtracked up north again, cursing the people like my feathered friends surely must when they want to alight on a beach and humans are there. Finally, after turning once again southward, I saw a break and went for it. Staying low, but far enough away from the people to make me feel I was legal, I flew quickly over the thin strip of barrier island and out over the backwaters.

I must stop my story at this point and explain something to you, reader, which must be starting to become glaringly obvious . . . my seeming obsession with low-altitude flying. In the early days of my flying, I never flew lower than 800 feet, except when in the process of landing. I loved flying for the view and wasn't all that fussed about going back from whence I came. Then one day, Jack picked me up in the Florida Keys where I was attending summer camp and flew me back to New Jersey in his Luscombe. With 65 horsepower, she was not exactly a screaming banshee in climb, particularly since Jack was, to be polite, still carrying some baby fat. That trip is a story in and of itself, so too, for that matter, was my life with Jack; but to get on with this, we flew from Florida to New Jersey pretty much at 100 to 500 feet all the way. We flew along the coast, avoiding dwellings and people, and climbed up to 1000 feet only when we had to turn inland to land and get gas or lodging for the night. It was a wonderful trip. I was seventeen at the time, and when I started towing banners and got 97B as my "ride" I began my low-altitude forays. Also, banner towing itself is done at relatively low altitude, particularly when zooming in for the pickup, so I was kinda used to being down there, and Jack did teach me some principles so that I wouldn't bust my ass.

Continuing . . . once over the back bays and marshes, I flew to the entry spot of my slalom course. It wasn't hard to find as the beginning was marked with an out-of-service railroad bridge. I should add that it was exactly in the very waterways below me where my sister and I learned, thirteen years before this flight, how to water ski.

At 100 feet and 100 mph, it wasn't too hard to stay within the confines of the waterway. Marsh grass formed the lateral boundaries of the serpentine course and the channel was wide enough, and the meandering turns gentle enough to allow me to easily maneuver without any radical aerobatics or gyrations. Since my earliest days of flight instruction, I had been taught to be gentle on the yoke/control stick and flight controls in general, to include use of the throttle. Even when speed of flight control movement—be it the ailerons, elevator, or rudder, or a combination of all three—was of the utmost urgency, it was hammered into me to be fast but smooth. So, as I careened above the waterway, I practiced what Jack had been pounding into me. I was like a seagull looking for food, graceful in movement, however, quick, yet deliberate in direction. Yes, I know, I was supposed to be flying a P-51 Mustang, but I also loved to watch seagulls fly, so I was pretty flexible in my imagination.

I was really enjoying this union of man and machine. The winds were so light that nary a bump of turbulence was felt. I would start a turn and feed in rudder and ailerons and as soon as that turn was completed I would have to do just the opposite, I also increased and decreased power to maintain 100 mph. There were "straightaways"; however at 100 mph, and owing to the rambling nature of the water's course, the time spent wings level was brief indeed. I thought that this "course" should have been a mandatory flying lesson as it required sooo much continuous movement and coordination between the stick and rudder pedals. Finally, because of the waterway's serpentine flow, with the confines defined by the mainland and the outer islands, we flew a very circuitous, hence long, route that enabled 97B and I to do some heavy-duty bonding.

Soon, all too soon, the nature of the waterway changed, the turns becoming more angular and narrow; God was softly, gently, letting me know that I had to end this mischief. I was now down to where the Cape May Airport banner pilots picked up their banners.

Unlike my operation up north, where I picked up my banners within the confines of an airfield, the guys in Cape May had to fly a couple of miles from their aerodrome to drop off and pick up from a farmers' field that lay close to the marsh and very close to the Garden State Parkway. I had been to this field many times in the past three years. Usually, every couple of days in the summer, I would either tow a banner into this field or pick one up. And, as I previously mentioned, every Thursday I would fly down to Cape May to pick up the payroll checks. Of course, given my nature, before landing at the airport and after taking off for my return trip home, I had to investigate the early morning goings-on of the ground crew at the towing field! So, I usually flew a surreptitious approach to the field and would swoop down upon the place as if coming in for a banner pickup . . . it was my way of saying "Hi!" and "Good-bye!" You could definitely tell the seasoned ground crew kids from the newbies by the effect of my low-level passes. The veterans didn't miss a beat in their movement, save for turning toward me and waving. The greenhorns, however, usually dove for cover! Oh, I almost peed my pants many times during those wake-up calls! What can I say . . . I was abused as a kid . . .

Shedding feathers and changing back into Mustang colors, 97B and I headed for the towing field. I was sure it was devoid of banner kids and everything else except memories. I approached from the east-northeast. The barely diluted rays of the sun highlighted the marsh and trees ahead making them appear to be closer than they were. I used an old piling that long ago housed an object for water navigation of some sort as my marker for helping me find the field. I was flying at about twenty feet over the marsh, and since the towing field was on the far side of some thirty-foot-tall trees, I needed some landmarks to help me find it at low altitude. With the Air Force theme song playing in my head, I set up for my attack! I approached the old piling at 100 miles an hour when I saw a bird, a large bird, alight from what appeared to be a nest that had been built under the cover of some wood adorning the piling's top. What was odd was that this bird was not heading away from me, she (I assumed it was a she) was heading directly toward me. I was dumbfounded to think that this bird of prey—I took her to be a hawk—had the gumption to go beak to beak, no pun intended, with a much larger bird of prey . . . 97B.

I don't know the distance between us when I first spotted her, but what I do know is that we were now wrapped up in a proverbial game of chicken. I can only assume this bird was guarding a clutch and was going to fight to the death to protect it. I decided to see if she was going to back off from her intercept course on me, so I continued flying directly toward her, gritting my teeth and lowering my head. She did not waver in her determination and aim. I knew that if we collided, particularly if she hit me in the windscreen, we were both gonna' lose. If she hit me anywhere, it would not be good as I'd have to explain the damage to the owners, and anyway, I didn't want to damage either bird. I can only wonder what thoughts were going through her head . . . did she think I was the mother lode of all turkeys and that I was dinner? Whatever . . . I do know that what is supposed to separate man from animal is reasoning thought, so at about 100 feet from this recalcitrant creature, I reasoned that I didn't want to die, so I turned abruptly away.

It didn't bother my pride to be the first to flinch; I'm proud I did. I saved two birds, and now this duel of avians was over . . . the turkey lost!

Once the shock of the moment wore off, 97B and I collected ourselves and descended back into our role of the lead mustang on the invasion of the Normandy beaches during D-Day. As I said previously, finding the field was a little tricky from low altitude. Trees protected its eastern and northern flanks, making it mpossible for me to see the field from where I was, but there was a small pond with a prominent set of reeds just before the trees on the northern flank. Also, the trees on the northern flank of the field had been cut to half of their height to allow the banner aircraft to stay low on their approach for pickup.

I spotted the pond with its reeds and then picked up the lower cut trees, which are south of the pond. I was coming in on a forty-five-degree angle to the opening from the northeast and was in a good position for the attack. Approaching the parkway that parallels the taller trees on the eastern flank of the filed, I pulled up kinda quickly to gain some altitude so I could swoop down into the field . . . this was so exciting! I apexed at 100 feet in the climb and then began a left descending turn. About 100 feet before the low trees,

I was established on "final" and wings level. I cleared the low trees by ten feet or so as I continued down at 110 mph in a mock banner pickup. I pulled up into a twenty- to thirty-degree nose high climb after my low-level pass. I knew that I had no banner attached, so I immediately rolled left to begin a turn for another pass.

I always did two passes, and that day was no different. I flew a tighter-than-normal pattern rolling into sixty degrees of bank for my turn to final. I rolled out, as on the previous "attack," and proceeded to perform another mock banner pickup. I certainly didn't need the practice; I was just having fun.

Banner towing was fun. In the four years that I towed, I never got bored of the job, and for the most part, though it seemed the aircraft were frail and could break easily, they were actually very reliable.

I'd be lying if I said I didn't get the crap scared out of me a couple of times. The worst occurred when I accidently stalled and did a half turn spin right after picking up my first banner of the 1979 towing season. I was able to recover from the stall/spin with more than enough altitude to continue to fly and tow the banner on its run. But I have to admit, I knew I had nearly died, and my feet were shaking uncontrollably for at least fifteen minutes, as I towed the banner on its run. After landing, I sat for a long time in the cockpit, contemplating a different summer job. The banner kids thought I had done that "maneuver" on purpose and begged me to do it again.

What saved me was 97B. Oh sure, Jack and my father pounded some basics into me that no doubt allowed me to unconsciously react the way I did and keep from crashing, and I thank God for those guys and their instruction. However, on the flip side . . . I should have died. I stalled and spun at less than 300 feet. I should have been a statistic in the National Transportation Safety Board files. But I wasn't; I didn't crash and burn. God, knowing I could be a twit and wanting to protect his gosling as he left the nest, provided me with His hand for protection. His hand was in the shape of an aircraft 97B. In her, I could flit about here and there and do loops and rolls and spins and stalls and buzz barren beaches and tread near big thunderstorms all the while being protected and covered by His insurance policy for me. I should have died. Godless people can call it physics, I call it a divine 97B . . . don't try and change my mind.

Continuing with the flight at hand. With my second simulated strafing pass complete, my Mustang and I were ready to land. We were approaching the edge of the neighborhood, and the playground was empty. There were no banner kids to harass, no weekly paychecks to pick up, no banners to be towed. I didn't want to land at Cape May Airport. I didn't want to leave the womb, the cockpit of 97B, the comfort and security of which I had known for 750 hours. I was maturing, and even though I didn't want to grow up, the tide of nature, of life, was against me. Nothing lasts forever; if it did, it wouldn't be precious. My precious hours with 97B were almost at an end, and as sad as this sunset with 97B was, a dawn on new flying adventures was just beginning to break on a different horizon; 97B would be the mother of my instincts for all follow-on flying adventures. What she taught me, the aeronautical wisdom, would form the nucleus for everything I would do in subsequent aircraft, and for that knowledge alone, I thank God for the time He gave me with her.

We, 97B and I, landed at Cape May Airport to no fanfare, pomp or circumstance, and I taxied up to the other banner aircraft and shut down; I suspect 97B had a lot of gossip to catch up on with the other aircraft; such is the way in which I had personified her.

I said my goodbyes to the owners and their charges, people with whom I had worked for four years . . . good people.

After my goodbyes, I walked over to my father. He had flown in to pick me up in a light airplane and was waiting to fly me back home. I couldn't look back at 97B, and as I walked to the "other" airplane, I had tears in my eyes and a pain in my heart. I wanted sooo badly to take her with me, 97B, as I embarked upon my new horizon.

My dad asked me if I wanted to fly the other aircraft home . . . I said no. It is the only time in my life I have ever refused to fly. It was just too soon to try and meld with another aircraft.

It is inconceivable for anyone to understand how much I loved flying 97B. Not only did I fly her during the day, towing banners, but I would often fly her in the evening after dinner. There was a certain barrier island cut off from all the others and without any human habitation, save for an occasional boater who beached upon its shores. That island was my playground. I strafed it (pretend), bombed it (again, pretend), chased seagulls over it, and did touch and goes on it. After terrorizing the island's seagulls, I would fly over to the marshes near my house. My father was invariably outside, eating grilled chicken and drinking a beer—or two, or three, etc. Upon hearing the sound of my airplane, he would stand at the end of the street and watch while I performed aerobatics 3000 feet over-head. The whole neighborhood would watch at times . . . I thank the Lord I never ploughed into the ground doing some of the acro-batic maneuvers I did. While I did like to fly at the lower altitudes, one evening I decided to see how high I could get 97B. We climbed all evening it seemed. I flew long, lazy racetrack patterns over "the neighborhood" as we climbed . . . and climbed . . . and climbed. Finally, at 11,000 feet, I'd had enough of climbing. The sun was setting. When I looked about, I could see what I thought was all of the known world! The view was spectacular. When you live your days in the trenches, it's nice to stick your head up once in a while, but this was a little too much neck for me. I was feeling like I was out of my environment, particularly after seeing a couple of airliners pass a little above me on their way to New York. It took a long time for me to descend, and when I finally landed, it was after dark; that was the only time I flew 97B at night (she didn't have instrument panel lighting).

I have written this story twelve years after my last flight in 97B. I have flown many aircraft since her, and I have loved each type of aircraft flown since . . . F-4, F-16, and MD-11 to name a few. But what I have never achieved since flying 97B is the intimacy of flying one aircraft for 750 hours and four years. 97B was a school, a classroom, a dynamic learning environment that taught me the basic principles of flight. To some degree, everything I have learned while flying her I have applied to all of the aircraft that I have flown since, whether they were fighters, transports, jet engine, or turboprop. I will never know another aircraft as well as I know 97B. That is why I thank God for my hours in her.

In my four seasons towing banners I met a bunch of very unique and interesting pilots: the Grey Fox, an ex-WW II pilot of some sort and bartender at the local VFW who was usually found sleeping off his après work benders in his car outside of Paramount's offices almost every morning; or the most wonderful Allen, a black-beard-ed, hippie leftover from the Woodstock days who had more patience than Job when I asked him question after question about this or that mechanical and or aeronautical topic.

Beyond Allen and the Grey Fox, there were many other guys with whom I associated and flew. Some were fleeting images of men, pilots who lasted no more than a few days, probably scared off by the nature of the business and the rather dilapidated-looking aircraft. Conversely, there were a few others, swashbuckling characters with so many wonderful qualities who flew maybe a season or two and then moved on to another adventure.

But, and without question, the one person I miss and admire the most from my banner-towing days, and who has more flying ability in one finger than I do in my whole body, is Jeff Morris. He and I towed aerial advertising banners up and down the South Jersey beaches in the summer of 1977, which was both of our first season of towing; actually, I had begun working for Paramount, as ground crew, the summer before, but I didn't fly a banner aircraft until the following year. Jeff (with whom I flew that kite battle mentioned in the prologue) and I quickly became very good friends during our first summer of towing. He was twenty-two when I met him and came from extremely wealthy parents. Unlike his siblings, he "rejected" his father's wealth, as he said to me, and he was very independent, though he did live at his parents' house in Ocean City during the summer we towed together.

One of the most interesting moments of our friendship was when Jeff met my dad and Jack. The two (Jack and my father) had already had a few beers when the four of us met at the Rugby Inn.

As the "Hi, ya doin's" were expressed, Jack, in his typical very forthright manner, said to Jeff, and very loudly I might add, "I know you from somewhere!"

Jeff said, rather sheepishly, "Yeah, I remember you too. I was the guy who borrowed your Luscombe."

Jack's eyes got real big, and then he said, even louder this time, "Yeah that's it! Borrowed it my ass, you stole it!"

The rest of the story is this . . . Jeff was a lineman at a local airport, and he loved Jack's Luscombe. So, when Jeff got off work one day, he literally untied the aircraft, hand propped the aircraft himself (just like Jack did), and flew it around (he had never flown a Luscombe before this flight); it would not be the last time he took the aircraft for a spin. Every time he landed, he parked it in the same tie-down spot and filled it up with fuel equal to what he used. It took a while, but Jack began noting certain subtle differences in his aircraft upon his return and eventually caught Jeff in the act of tying it down after a flight. Jack was absolutely furious. Jeff said the eruption of Mt. Vesuvius, when it covered Pompeii, was probably a mere burp compared to Jack's emotional display that day. But Jack's temper quickly died down, and once composed, he said to Jeff, "Give me one good reason as to why I shouldn't call the cops and have you arrested!"

Jeff simply said, "I think your airplane is the neatest one on the airport and the only one I wanted to fly."

Jack was so taken aback by his answer that they both got in the Luscombe and Jack gave Jeff a proper checkout. Jack, too, said that Jeff was one of the most naturally gifted pilots with whom he had ever flown; needless to say, Jack and Jeff had a lot catching up to do that evening.

Of the four seasons I spent towing banners, I had more fun doing "flying circus" type aerial activities and mischief with Jeff than any other pilot I've ever flown with in my life.

The summer of 1977 was one of those magical summers of kite wars, playing follow the leader in our clipped-wing Cubs, looping small clouds, flirting with scantily clad girls at beach bars after flying, bar-talk about chasing dreams while downing beers, and all done on hot summer days and nights; it just didn't get any better. And like so many times in the aviation business, when it comes to meeting people, though I didn't know it then, I would never see or hear about Jeff again. I pray he is still showing the angels how to fly as they follow and hopefully protect him on his earthly adventures.

CHAPTER 16

With college completed and a Bachelor's of science degree in my drawer, I left the fogs of the Jersey shore and entered Clausewitz's fog of war. After attending officers' school through autumn of 1980, and much to my father's delight, I was ordered to report to Williams AFB, near Phoenix, Arizona, for forty-nine weeks of USAF pilot training. For a Jersey boy, that was quite a trek west, and I did it with a wife and horse in tow—well, the horse was in tow, the wife was next to me.

Once I had gotten selected for the pilot training slot in early summer, my father finally stopped trying to direct my professional life, and in fact, he was extremely happy that I was going to be flying a fighter aircraft in the military. I thought it was just out of personal pride for his son, but as I would find out many years later, there was a much more significant and deeply personal effect on him than I realized at that time in my getting the chance to fly the Phantom.

The drive west was an adventure if only because we broke down in Abilene, Texas, and spent two full days there as some shop rebuilt the blown transmission on my pickup truck. The shop guys said pulling so much weight (the horse, not the wife), for too tall of gearing, is what caused the smoking tranny.

My year in pilot training was and still remains one of the best years of my life. My wife was happy having her horse to ride while I learned to fly the USAF way, and I was exceedingly giddy to be learning to fly in the military; I never, ever thought I was good enough to be there. I loved my instructors—Sleaze (Lieutenant Silvestri) and Captain Palmgrin in the T-37, and then Kevin Hammond, my wonderful T-38 IP (instructor pilot). We worked hard, we students, during the week and on Friday evenings, the Officer's Club beckoned with the wonderful camaraderie we all shared as we talked of training blunders and accomplishments. Saturdays were an extension of Friday evening, but with the wives/girlfriends by our sides. We might go camping/water skiing on one of the "SCAR" lakes[17] or drive to the mountains or socialize as a big group as we drifted down the Salt River, which wasn't really salty, while drinking adult beverages and clowning around in the water; such wonderful times with so many amazingly wonderful people from around the country.

While I could write a short book about my pilot training weeks, the oddest and funniest thing that happened to me while I was learning to fly at "Willy" occurred on my second T-37 solo flight.

I was feeling pretty cocky, as I strapped in and started the jet that particular day. I had soloed a week earlier and did well on that pattern-only flight, so as I taxied from the T-37 ramp to the active runway, I was feeling like a smooth operator.

Shortly after I began taxiing, Willy Ground Control called and said, "Fourteen Solo, be advised that your aircraft is smoking," my flippant and very arrogant response, because I felt like I was a "smooth" operator, was, "Ah roger, Ground, jet engines do smoke."

---

17. SCAR lakes, Saguaro, Canyon, Apache, Roosevelt, four lakes in a row, from west to east, all east of Phoenix, AZ and all fed by the Salt River.

"Fourteen Solo, your aircraft is smoking much more than normal," was Ground's immediate response.

The next radio call I got was from one of the instructor pilots in my T-37 flight (my assigned flight was called Good Grief), "Hey, ace, I suggest you look over your left shoulder toward the back of the aircraft." (We taxied with our canopies up.)

Upon hearing the inflection of this instructor's voice, I knew I had either screwed something up or was about to, so I immediately looked behind me. To my horror, I saw a huge amount of "whitish" smoke emanating from the left engine on my little twin-engine jet trainer. From the pure thickness of the plume, I figured I had a serious fire and that the aircraft was about to explode. I immediately shut the engines down and did an emergency ground egress, stopping where I was.

The instructor who made the radio call to me was on the same taxiway, right behind my aircraft, and had been following me as we both taxied to the same runway, hence the reason he had full view of my smoking jet and was able to hear my arrogant radio call to ground.

I stood off to the side of my Tweet (nickname for the T-37), as the smoke slowly subsided and the firemen and maintenance folks tended to the matter. Upon seeing I had ground egressed, the instructor offset his taxiing to pass around me, and he and his student continued on their training flight.

The cause of all the smoke was a blown "pork chop" seal located near the aft end of the engine. The blown seal allowed engine oil to be sprayed directly into the hot exhaust, immediately aft of the turbine, thusly causing an unbelievable amount of smoke.

Some of my fellow students were laughing for weeks about the whole radio exchange and the smoking jet. The moral of the story for me was that I was determined to try and never get cocky again; sometimes, God teaches you little lessons in life in rather comical ways.

After flying approximately seventy hours in the T-37, my classmates and I progressed to the "White Rocket" T-38 Talon, and flew that for approximately 100 more hours. And finally, with the academic testing (which was spread between the Tweet and the T-38) complete, in late November 1981, with my wife, mother, and father present, I graduated from UPT. Class 82-02 graduated with sixty-two pilots, out of an initial eighty-four. I think I can safely say it was a wonderful day for all of us as we walked up on stage and received our coveted silver wings.

As excited as all of us graduates were, there was a wisp of black cloud that hung over our graduation. About a week before, a student on a solo flight crashed his Tweet in Butte MOA[18] and was killed. The student was not from our class, but it didn't matter, we were all for one and one for all while in training, so the loss of a member from one class was a loss to all the classes.

It took a couple of days to sink into my head and heart that I actually did graduate from United States Air Force Pilot Training. I just never, ever, thought that I was good enough to fly with the guys with whom I went through UPT let alone to even graduate from the program. I don't know if I'd ever felt happier in my life, maybe not quite as elated as when I soloed at sixteen, but the two experiences are neck and neck as significant milestones in shaping my character as a person and aviator, and in deepening my faith.

---

18. Butte MOA—Butte is the name of this Military Operations Area. A military operations area (MOA) is an airspace established outside Class A airspace to separate or segregate certain nonhazardous military activities from IFR Traffic and to identify for VFR traffic where these activities are conducted.

I gained supreme peace and a major shot of confidence after graduating from UPT, but not for what might seem obvious reasons.

I wanted to do well in UPT, so consequently I worked my arse off to achieve that goal. Let there be no doubt I was scared that I was not good or smart enough to be in pilot training in the first place and though most people would not have seen it externally, internally I was extremely insecure. I was particularly in awe of the USAF Academy people, because in my mind they were the best of the best and I never felt good enough to even be in the same UPT class as them.

However, though the written tests might have caused me concern as I progressed through those forty-nine weeks, I realized I could fly the USAF jets. My previous Zen/artistic form of aviating training that I'd received from Jack and my father served me well in the T-37 and T-38 as I found I could easily impart much knowledge and skill that I'd learned in my civilian training. Oddly, of all the phases of flying in the T-37 and T-38 programs—contact (acrobatics), instrument, navigation, and finally formation—the phase in which I had the highest grades (for me personally, not in relation to my classmates) was formation. I say "oddly" because I came with a stigma in my own heart, upon arriving at Williams AFB, that since I came to pilot training with almost 1,400 hours flying time and with a commercial license that it was only normal that I should do okay in most of the phases of flying. But since I never had flown or been trained in the art of formation flying in those 1,400 "civilian" hours prior to UPT, I was very happy when both my T-37 and T-38 instructors said they were quite pleased with my ability to fly formation, without question, that was answered prayer.

And then there was the broader scope of personal satisfaction that I did well in UPT without any help from my father or Jack. Yes, they had been extremely wonderful for my initial pilot development while I was young, but they had become like crutches to my learning, and I needed to break free from their sometimes-overreaching, though well-meaning, mentoring.

Finally, being away from the dysfunction of my father and mother was liberating beyond belief. Oh, my dad and I still talked on the phone quite frequently about aviation-related stuff in my time at Willy, and I admit I enjoyed immensely our talks, but the fact is that the old man couldn't reach out and touch me anymore, a.k.a. harass; nor did I have to endure listening to their fights—such an amazing amount of relief.

So, after eleven months of stressful, diligent, and dedicated hard work one of the greatest silver linings in my life was to receive my USAF silver wings and in being selected as a distinguished graduate; my smile had never been bigger.

It is not my intent to toot my own horn with my accomplishments while in pilot training, but I bring it up to illustrate that if a schmuck like me can get through USAF pilot training, anyone with ambition can too. Remember, for most of my young life I was a very unwelcome embryo to my mother and father. Given my parents' wonderfully warm way of boosting my ego before I began pilot training, I felt like a loser who would never accomplish much or amount to anything. So, the positive spin on this paragraph is to illustrate that if a low-rent like me could get through pilot training, anyone with drive, ambition, a strong work ethic, and a positive attitude can do the same. But—and without question—I shall never forget that the hand of God was always upon my shoulder, guiding my steps and coaching me through life, and in the end, it was God that got me through, I was just His very willing tool.

After UPT, both land and sea survival filled my weeks until I started fighter lead-in training at Holloman AFB, in Alamogordo, New Mexico. Where UPT taught its students how to fly the military way, fighter lead-in edified the prospective fighter pilot on how to maneuver a jet tactically. Since I was going to the F-4 after fighter lead-in, I got three phases of the course: navigation, air to air, and air to ground. I actually still have my gradebook.

The jet we flew in fighter lead-in was the AT-38. It was essentially the same aircraft as the T-38 flown in UPT, except they did a few mods on the fighter lead-in 38s that allowed them to carry and drop practice bombs and shoot a 7.62 caliber mini Gatling gun. Finally, it had a beautiful camouflage paint job that was supposed to make it harder to see in the sky. Other than those minor changes, the AT-38 was essentially the T-38 in a different shade of lipstick.

Unlike the super friendly and accommodating instructors in UPT, I thought a few of the instructors at fighter lead-in were jerks. I was told by another classmate, who felt the same, some of the instructors had a chip on their shoulder because they thought the powers that be in Tactical Air Command (TAC) were punishing them by assigning them to the lead-in school. All of the instructors that were at lead-in training had come from front line TAC aircraft, like the A-10, F-15, F-16, F-4, to name a few, prior to going to Holloman. Those guys (no women back then) did not want to leave their frontline fighter positions to teach students in a repainted T-38 while flying over the desert of New Mexico.

Most of the instructors I had in the air-to-air phase were not particularly pleasant. As I said, unlike UPT where the instructors were generally pretty upbeat, with almost every preflight at fighter lead-in I had to face an instructor with a scowl and an attitude. After a couple of weeks in the 3 to 4 month long course, and having interacted with quite a few attitude challenged instructors, I didn't have a high opinion of TAC. It seemed these guy's, the instructor's, feelings had migrated from their hearts to their faces, thusly distorting their expression . . . and not in a friendly manner. While flying, the instructor's scowls translated to impatience, as judged by their inflection when they spoke, with my flying performance as they tried to teach to me the concepts of BFM[19] which was, at least for me, difficult because it required thinking and flying and maneuvering in three (or four) dimensions, not to mention the very physically demanding nature of flying and fighting in a dogfight.

To say I was very naïve about the stress imposed upon the body while flying a fighter aircraft, particularly in an air to air fight, is an understatement. I saw a couple of old movies as a kid that dealt with flying jet fighters, such the "Bridges of Toko-Ri" or the very cheesy "Jet Pilot" featuring John Wayne. Those movies, nor any others that I saw that dealt with World War 1 or 2 flying, gave hint to the severe physical stresses imposed upon the upper body, neck in particular, while fighting in air to air; in the movie Top Gun when Goose tells Maverick, (when Jester is on their tail) to, "Do some of that pilot shit!"…it's much easier said than done…doing that "pilot shit."

I never expected flying a fighter to be so exhausting or hard, particularly if you were on the defensive; i.e. looking back over your shoulder at the bandit while "pulling" (pulling means pulling back on the control stick which usually translates into climbing or turn-

19. Basic Fighter Maneuvers—the beginning elements in learning how to maneuver a fighter aircraft against an opposing fighter. Three principles are taught: (1) Offensive BFM; (2) Defensive BFM; and (3) Neutral BFM.

ing, or both, and/or increasing the G force on the aircraft) 5, 7, or in some aircraft 9 Gs. The average human head weighs 10 pounds. If you are pulling 5 Gs, your head weighs 50lbs, if you're pulling 7.3 Gs (the AT-38's max G limit) it weighs over 70lbs. But, obviously, it's not just your head, it's your whole body that increases in perceived weight as the G force is increased. A 70lb head on a neck that is used to holding 10 is a big difference with regards to stress on the spine and neck muscles. Trust me, the relatively gentle nature of flight training in UPT never prepared me for the physical stress upon my upper body while looking over my shoulder at a bandit aircraft who was trying to kill me. In fighter lead-in we were normally pulling 5 to 7 Gs and moving our arms, head, neck, upper torso (to look around as far behind as I could), while maneuvering the aircraft in the process, in order to keep from dying (obviously simulated). It's quite a strain to be looking way back behind you, semi turned around, while pulling maximum structural Gs on the aircraft. In addition to looking back over your shoulder and trying to assess the bandit's position, movement, and relative threat (nose on you or pointed away), you are moving the throttles and flight controls as you look behind in an attempt to out fight the bandit. So, as you look back, straining against the G forces, you are attempting to maneuver your aircraft, relative to the bandit's and the ground (if you're low you don't want to pull into the ground and crash) and it just aint' that easy, as I found out in those early days of fighter lead-in. I cannot begin to tell you how much I huffed and puffed and sweated while working against the G forces as I learned to turn the aircraft at maximum G in order take a bandit who was at my deep six o'clock (behind me) and try and flush him to neutral or even go offensive in him.

In addition to the strain on the neck, the heart was also stressed because it had to beat harder in order to keep blood going to the brain. When you pulled high enough Gs (5 or more usually) the blood wants to pool in the lower extremities of the body, consequently lowering the blood flow and pressure in the brain, causing the pilot to either lose consciousness or "grey out" (where your vision is greatly reduced). In order to help the heart keep blood in the brain, we were taught a "G straining maneuver" (a modified form of holding your breath against the larynx for a few seconds, exhaling briefly, inhaling briefly, and then holding your breath again, repeat) which was used to try and keep you from passing out; there are many cases where fighter pilots have passed out while turning hard, with a lot of Gs on the aircraft, and they have either died, because of hitting the ground, or had the crap scared out of them as they recovered from an unusual attitude once they "woke up" after passing out. In addition to the G straining maneuver we wore "G suits" which were a kind of outer pants that went over our flight suit and inflated with air, as the G levels increased, so as to squeeze your legs and lower abdomen in order to keep blood from pooling in your lower body. The G suit was fairly effective at keeping you from losing consciousness, but when combined with the G straining maneuver, loss of consciousness was much less of a threat.

In the same manner as the shock of the physical stresses incurred on the body while turning under high G, another huge surprise was how much you needed to max perform the jet through the use of energy "addition" (using the afterburner and/or "unloading," reducing the G on the aircraft) or energy subtraction (pulling max G and depleting your airspeed but while increasing your turn rate, or momentarily pulling the throttles to military power, or less), combined with the use of geometry (invisible planes and angles in the air) to successfully attack or defeat an opponent. Fighter lead-in taught you to pull massive Gs while either in an offensive or defensive training setup and, in the process, to maneuver aggressively enough to either not get shot (defensive setup) or go kill the opponent (offensive setup). Contrary to the rather sedate and graceful maneuvering we did in UPT, in fighter lead-in some of the guys you would try to "shoot down" (the instructors) would radically maneuver their jet to try and reverse roles on you (from defensive to offensive). I'm here to tell you, I thought some of those guys were nuts and that I'd never be good enough to be a true fighter pilot. There are times you might be pulling 7 Gs, straining, looking way behind you, to the limits of your semi-turned upper torso and neck with your head turned insanely back in order to see the guy attacking you; in fact, many times I would use a free arm to pull on the canopy rail so as to help me look back even further (my other arm would be on the flight control stick, since the throttles were usually locked in afterburner). In my maneuvering, I would often switch which hand/arm was manipulating the flight control (stick) depending on what the direction of turn was. Thusly if I was doing a break turn to the left, to defend against a bandit way behind me, on the left side, I would use my right arm/hand to pull the stick back and use my left arm/hand to help pull my upper torso further around to the left; conversely if the bandit was deep on the right side I would lock the throttles in afterburner with my left arm and once locked, I would move my left hand to stick and use my right arm to help my turn further right. Your head weighs 70 pounds in those turns, assuming you're pulling 7 Gs and your heart is thumping, trying to keep the blood moving through a body that weighs 7 X its normal weight. As you strain to look back, and think, and maneuver, and try to defeat the bandit, he may then "flush out" (goes to the side or even in front of you) or he tries to run by unloading his jet (meaning he is greatly reducing the Gs he is pulling), so you unload your aircraft too, from 7 Gs to maybe minus 1 G in a second, bouncing your head against the top of the canopy as you suddenly get light in the seat as you push the stick abruptly forward. With full afterburners, you roll the aircraft while still holding zero or negative 1 G and accelerate and then once you've gained enough energy and/or a positional advantage on the bandit, you bring your nose on him to shoot, or you reposition your aircraft rapidly in some horizontal or vertical plane, in order to gain or maintain an offensive advantage. It was not easy at first, this harsh flying environment. The instructors were trying to teach us that in order to defeat your opponent you had to really move the jet quickly into or out of a turn and then dive and roll or loop and unload and then get back into pulling Gs . . . it was so contrary to my father's, Jack's, and UPT's training of being smooth and treating the aircraft well.

So, trust me, when Goose said, "Mav, do some of that pilot shit," if you want to do it well and survive, it's damn hard work.

I did manage to make it through fighter lead in, I am happy to say, and though I don't have a lot of affection for some of the more negative instructors, there was one A-10 pilot with whom I flew on most of my surface attack/low-level training sorties with whom I developed a wonderful rapport. Mike "Mad Dog" Madelin was awesome. I left the air-to-air phase of fighter lead-in shell-shocked, thinking I was going to suck as a fighter pilot, and then I got to fly with Captain Sunshine (Mad Dog was his call sign, but he is one of the most happy-go-lucky guys I've ever known in my life). We had a blast flying low levels around the New Mexico landscape and then dropping bombs or shooting the mini-gun. Because of Mad Dog, I had a whole new respect for TAC pilots that I didn't have when I left the air-to-air phase.

I began F-4 training pretty much right after fighter lead-in. With the nag (horse, not wife) still in tow, we left Holloman in the early morning hours for the long drive east to Wichita, Kansas. I was pretty abusive as a driver back then, and we drove without a hotel stop until we reached our destination . . . and let there be no doubt, I was also very chauvinistic too, since I would not relent and let my wife drive, I felt it was the man's job; in all of my years driving with both my mother and father in the car, from New Jersey to California, or Maine, or anywhere in between, my mother never touched the wheel.

Where my introduction to the Tactical Air Command at Holloman was somewhat caustic, it was the reverse at McConnell AFB. Entering the 184th Tactical Fighter Group's premises with its subordinate 127th Tactical Fighter and 177th Tactical Fighter Training Squadrons, plus a complement of seventy-six F-4s on the ramp, was like being in a different universe. Unlike the drab desert scenery of Holloman AFB, McConnell was surrounded with the greenery of the Kansas plains, and everyone was so nice and pleasant. The whole city, it seemed, was embellished with good ol' Midwestern charm and manners, and I immediately loved the area though it lacked the scenic and lovely mountains of the far west.

Laughingly, the F-4 instructor I was assigned to, Major Gary Haseloh, upon our first meeting said that his motto was, "I never met a student I liked." In contradiction to the cheeriness of most of the other instructors in the fighter group, Gary always seemed unhappy and gruff. When we met for our first preflight brief, he never smiled, and I swear he must've had nails for breakfast, causing his sourpuss attitude; he reminded me of the scowl-faced air-to-air instructors I'd just left at fighter lead-in.

Great. What joy, I thought, having Major Marvelous as my instructor . . . this was gonna' be a long six months.

The F-4 had two seats and Gary would be in the back for the first six or seven rides whereupon, when I soloed on the eighth flight, I would fly with a WSO who was also in training (the backseater in the F-4 was called a WSO, Weapons System Operator).

In a surprise turnaround of emotion, Major Grumpy morphed into a phenomenal instructor when he arrived at the aircraft in preparation for flight. It was like the "other" Gary stayed in the ops building and a new and improved model met me at the jet. It was a serious déjà vu moment, as I felt like I was getting instruction from my father again, although this time in the Phantom. Like my dad, Gary was almost angelic in nature when dealing with my screwups, as I learned to fly and fight in the F-4. He was calm, collected, and soothing when he talked me through the required training maneuvers and then even calmer when helping me correct mistakes I made on my first set of maneuvers.

There is no doubt that Gary and I had a complicated relationship, as I progressed through RTU, because like he said, he never met a student he liked.

As a funny example of the interesting dynamic that he and I shared as instructor-student, I offer you the following exchange that we had as he was grading me after one of my first transition rides, but before my first solo:

"Gary, has anyone ever told you that you are an excellent instructor?" I said as Major Grumpy was writing in my gradebook after our flight.

"Grrr," was about all he said as he continued to write, never looking up, with a frown on his face.

"But boy you sure are an asshole on the ground."

I have no idea why I was so blunt to him, but I guess my Jersey attitude and arrogant nature overrode any chance of better judgment. Gary stopped grading me upon hearing that last comment of mine, got a big smile on his face, and laughed! As his laughter tailed off and he went back to grading me he said, "That was shit-hot."

I was very blessed to have an instructor who inspired so much confidence in me. I loved flying with Hooter (Gary's call sign) either in my backseat giving me hands-on training or being on his wing with him as my flight lead when I was flying with a student WSO. His positive attitude with regard to how he instructed his students had such a profound effect on me that when I got to the air-to-air phase of my F-4 training, which I had been dreading because of my experiences at fighter lead-in, I made it through with relative ease.

I can never thank Gary enough for his patience and kindness with me while being my instructor. I greatly admire and respect the man, not only for his instructional and flying skills, but also because Gary was, and is, a great husband and father in spite of work-worn scowls. And he has improved with age, I am happy to say, because now he smiles when I see him! He is deeply involved with his lovely family and in the Wounded Warrior Program, helping vets learn to ski on the snow-covered slopes of Colorado. Gary "Hooter" Haseloh is a class act, in spite of his call sign, and he will always represent a wonderful cornerstone of my aviation career and life.

I finished my F-4 training in early autumn 1982. My six months at McConnell, like UPT at Willy, are some of the best months of my life. My wife and I left a lot of wonderful people in the rearview mirror as we headed east.

In prayers only God could hear, since I never spoke of my deepest feelings to either my wife or her horse, a funny thing happened once I got back to New Jersey. Gary called and said that the 184th was looking for a young pilot to check out as an instructor since they had so many old farts on their payroll. "Are you interested in the position?," he asked.

In a New York second, I said yes, bypassing the thought of even asking for my wife's opinion. (though she was all for it too) While the paperwork and orders were cut, and the transfer of my fighter soul from the 108th TFW to the 184th TFG was being processed, a waiver had to be requested from the USAF to allow me to become an instructor with so little F-4 flying time. I was given permission to fly sorties at McGuire while I waited for word as to when all the formalities would be done and I could report to Kansas.

As I waited for orders allowing me into the 184th, I was extremely excited about my life and my future. I loved flying the F-4, and no matter what type of sortie I flew—air to air, air to ground, intercept, or low-level—no matter what the mission, I was always exuberant when strapping into the Phantom in preparation for flight.

In the seven months I would eventually spend flying with the 108th TFW as the slow shuffle of official paperwork made its way across a multitude of desks, I made flying the F-4 a priority and volunteered to fly as many local sorties as they could give me, in addition to volunteering for every deployment that came up. By the wonderful grace of God, in addition to getting lots of local sorties, I did get to go on two awesome deployments.

The first unforgettable, though I probably should forget it since I flew so disastrously poorly, was a two-week trip to MacDill AFB, in Tampa, Florida. Winter weather was fully embracing the northeast as my squadron and I alighted into snow flurries and landed on a runway at MacDill AFB warmed by the Florida sunshine. We were there to fight against the famous USAF Aggressors[20] and the F-16 training units based there.

The aggressors' main job, as they flew to the various fighter bases throughout the States, was to show American fighter pilots the tactics that the Soviet Air Forces may employ, if we ever fought against them, as knowing their weaknesses would help us to defeat them. I am here to say that after two weeks' worth of one-versus-one or two-versus-two fighting, the biggest weakness was me. I "died" a lot in those two weeks. Ugh. I was depressed all over again about how poor I was in air-to-air combat. I vowed to God and myself that I would improve.

For their part, the aggressor pilots were all a really great group of pilots who were extremely skilled yet very humble and whose only desire was to improve the dogfighting skills of the pilots with whom they fought. They were patient during the debriefs after each flight, showing the "trainees" where they made their tactical errors and how to improve on the next fight. It was awesome to fly with

---

20. Aggressors—in the aftermath of Vietnam, the USAF formed a traveling group of specially trained fighter pilots, flying the F-5, who were trained to emulate Soviet Fighter Pilots' tactics. The belief was that if you could expose USAF Fighter Pilots to the tactics the Soviets would use in combat, the USAF pilots would stand a better chance of success in combat. It was an excellent training tool and still in use today.

them, and in spite of me being the poster boy for how not to fight in air-to-air combat, I learned much in my two weeks.

After returning to McGuire, and again volunteering for any flying time I could garner in the 141st TFS, Tactical Fighter Squadron, a component of the 108th Tactical Fighter Wing (TFW), I was asked if I wanted to go to an up-and-coming Red Flag[21] exercise.

Red Flag was known back then as the ultimate in flying training and wartime realism, so I was very excited about getting the chance to go. I had sleepless nights leading up to our deployment and was excited about flying an F-4 into Nellis AFB, the hottest fighter base in the USAF back then. Colonel Ockerhausen, busted my bubble however, when he said that since I was the most junior guy going I had to escort the mode 4 keys,[22] which were being shipped along with other support equipment aboard a C-130. Drat. The upside was that the view of the Colorado Rockies out the front of a C-130 is breathtakingly spectacular.

Rick Kertz was the flight lead of the four-ship of Phantoms in which I was assigned for our two weeks of flying, and I was number two in that four-ship; we flew every day except Saturday and Sunday.

---

21. Red Flag is an advanced aerial combat training exercise hosted at Nellis Air Force Base, Nevada. Since 1975, air crews from the U.S. Air Force, Navy, Marine Corps, and Army, and numerous NATO or other allied nations' air forces take part in one of several Red Flag exercises held during the year, each of which is two weeks in duration.
Under the aegis of the United States Air Force Warfare Center (USAFWC) at Nellis, the Red Flag exercises are very realistic aerial war games. The purpose is to train pilots and other flight crew members from the United States, NATO and other allied countries for real air combat situations. This includes the use of "enemy" hardware and live ammunition for bombing exercises within the adjacent Nevada Test and Training Range.
22. Mode 4 keys—the "keys" are an electronic device that codes in a discrete Mode 4 code for the IFF of the respective fighter. It allows that fighter to be identified as a friendly aircraft on coalition radars.

Rick was an outstanding flight lead and a really good guy, and he helped to keep me out of trouble while we bombed the various targets located throughout the Nellis Range Complex.[23] There must have been more than 100 aircraft involved in each of the morning and afternoon mass air wars, as roughly sixty or more "blue force" aircraft would go against forty or more "red force" aircraft; the red forces were protecting the target areas in the central and west areas of the range complex while the blue forces were intent on bombing certain targets without being "shot down" by air-to-air missiles from the red force aircraft or from surface-to-air missiles (SAMs).

Each day, the war plan was changed to enhance learning for the crews so new tactics could be developed and tested. Every aircraft was equipped with an instrumentation pod, which allowed computers to track all the aircraft as they flew about in the ranges to record bombs dropped, simulated air-to-air missiles shot, and to just give an overall situational awareness and prospective of the entire battle as it progressed across that vast airspace.

The massive morning and afternoon battles were debriefed with the aid of a computer-generated video of the air war, with a God's-eye view, played on a theater size screen in a big auditorium while all the pilots got to see the esoteric nuances of all the flights and fights. As the battle progressed on the big screen, each pilot looked for their aircraft/flight to see what red force, or blue force, aircraft were around them and to find out if they had been targeted and/or shot

23. Nellis Range Complex or The Nevada Test and Training Range (NTTR) is one of two military training areas used by the United States Air Force Warfare Center at Nellis Air Force Base in Nevada. The NTTR land area includes a "simulated Integrated Air Defense System," several individual ranges with 1200 targets, and four remote communication sites. [1] The current NTTR area and the range's former areas have been used for aerial gunnery and bombing, for nuclear tests, as a proving ground and flight test area, for aircraft control and warning, and for Blue Flag, Green Flag, and Red Flag exercises.

by a missile(s). (It wasn't uncommon for the blue force fighters to shoot down the red force bandits since we flew with self-protection missiles on our Phantoms, as did other types of fighter-bombers too.) Taken as a whole, it was amazing technology that I never knew existed until I saw it for myself and it was, to me, very Star Wars-esque.

In addition to the red force aircraft trying to shoot down the blue force guys, manned surface-to-air missile sites dotted the Nellis Range Complex. Those sites sent back videos of certain aircraft and/or flights that they had engaged that day with their active radar emissions but simulated missile launches to show either good or bad defensive maneuvering with regard to surface-to-air missile launches.

It was all so very surreal, the actual flying environment and the daily battles, and I was overwhelmed and in awe with the enormity of the sensory input while flying the missions, not to mention the mass air war debriefs. The big video screen could be zoomed in on a particular aircraft or group of aircraft, located anywhere in the range complex so as to see how one's tactics helped or hurt in their objective to accomplish their mission.

I was feeling more invincible with each sortie flown and target bombed, and that was the intent of Red Flag from the beginning—to give fighter pilots as real an experience in actual battle as you can get, without actually shooting real missiles or ordnance at other guys, etc. The USAF motto back then was to train like you were going to fight, and the Red Flags did a great job of taking training to a whole new, realistic level.

On day three of the exercise, Rick and I were "movie stars." We were debriefing that day's air war in the almost full Red Flag auditorium when they showed a video (remember, this is a movie theater–sized screen) of Chard 21 and Chard 22 (that was our call sign for the day), on the screen. The video was from one of the SAM (surface-to-air missile) sites in the western area of the Nellis Range, and it showed two Phantoms, in a widespread tactical formation, flying at insanely low altitudes, as we tried to get by that SAM site without being shot. The missile for that particular site had an effective altitude down to 100 feet and through the use of indirect terrain masking, chaff, and aircraft maneuvering, we figured we could defeat that SAM's missiles. The video of our Phantoms maneuvering, as taken from the offending SAM site as it tried to get an effective shot, was impressive to watch. In the end, the audio portion of the video announced that our tactics were effective, and the site said they could not get a valid shot.

"Whew," was what Rick and I said as we looked at each other after the video was played. We were all smiles, feeling as if we cheated death.

Smiles turned to tears on day four however. As our four-ship approached the entry point for the beginning of our low level into the range—student gap it was called—a radio call announced that there was a Red Flag knock-it-off, all aircraft were to safe up (safe up means de-arm, flip a switch in the cockpit that prevents missiles, bombs, rockets, or guns to be fired/expended), stop their attacks, low levels, etc., and return to Nellis, or whatever base they had come from. (A lot of participants to Red Flag flew into the ranges from other fighter bases in the country, usually utilizing air-to-air refueling to perform their missions and then flying back to those bases.)

The cause of the Red Flag knock-it-off, we were later told, was due to an A-10 that had crashed somewhere on the range. The pilot never attempted to eject and was killed; suddenly, this simulated war got real and claimed its first victim.

All in all, during my two weeks flying at Nellis AFB, an A-10 and its pilot were lost; an F-111 crashed somewhere near the ranges after having flown a sortie into them (the crew ejected successfully but sustained injuries); a B-52 hit a ridge, ingressing into the range complex killing all seven; and then an F-16 crashed right in front of my eyes—it went tumbling off the runway unable to stop due to brake failure. I was sitting on the top of my F-4, in the live ordnance area, when the Viper met its demise. I am happy to say the pilot survived with only minor injuries.

Then the tragedies became very personal.

As spring turned to summer, I got word that my orders were ready and I was supposed to report to the 184th in the middle of July. I was given permission to fly one last flight with the 108th before heading west and couldn't wait to fly the mission since it was going to be a four-ship surface attack sortie on a derelict ship in the Chesapeake Bay being defended by some A-10s. It was a hot, humid, and hazy day when we headed southwest for the Chesapeake after taking off from McGuire AFB, with my aircraft carrying six Mark 84 inert (concrete-filled and won't explode) bombs and two external fuel tanks. The lead F-4, as he approached the run-in to the target area and while I and number 3 were still about three miles in trail, engaged an A-10 and began a rather short aerial dogfight, which resulted in the lead F-4 impacting into the Chesapeake Bay at 500-plus knots. Both of the guys in the Phantom died as the airplane exploded in a spray of both water and bits of Phantom.

The pilot, Jack Preston—may he rest in peace—I didn't know well, but I heard he was a great guy and had a wonderful wife and children.

The WSO, Jim Flood, was relatively new to the unit, having just come off active duty in the USAF with his last duty station being Clark AFB in the Philippines. He was recently married, with a petite and lovely Filipino bride by his side when he arrived stateside to begin flying with us. I had flown with Jim quite a bit in my short time at McGuire, and he and I gelled quickly as a team and in respect for each other. He was always very complimentary about my flying, as I was when it came to him working the radar, the bombing computers, or backing me up in air-to-air battles or on low levels. Jim's passing really, really stung and showed me that on any given day, you could lose a friend, or your own life, in an instant.

As naïve as it sounds, I never really looked at flying fighters as being dangerous until the day that Jim died. Maybe that was a wake-up call from God . . . I don't know. The one peace I have from Jim's passing is that I know he was a devout Christian, so I know that one day he and I will be toasting to our careers while in heaven . . . there is always a silver lining to every dark cloud.

I arrived in Wichita at the end of July 1983, after delaying a couple of weeks in New Jersey to attend the funerals of Jack and Jim.

I had to get a few more hours in the Phantom before I could begin my instructor checkout, so I flew a bunch of local sorties over the maturing Kansas wheat as summer faded into the harvest season. It was nice to get the flying time because it allowed me to mentally, physically and spiritually prepare myself for my up-and-coming instructor pilot training,

As a young second lieutenant, it was an honor to be asked to become an instructor in the F-4 right after finishing RTU, especially since I had never actually flown in an operational squadron; but it was that fact, that I had no operational experience, that secretly bothered me. Yes, I did fly a few months with the 108th TFW and got some wonderful sorties with some very experienced guys, but I was still a few years short of the kind of operational experience a normal RTU instructor would have under his belt prior to getting checked out as an instructor. The USAF waiver that had to be requested to allow me to instruct said that I needed to get at least 200 hours in the Phantom before I could begin my instructor pilot checkout. But just because a waiver says you can do something with this or that amount of time doesn't mean you'll be good at doing "it," or even should be. The fact that Gary asked me if I wanted to become an instructor with so little time and operational experience was an amazing honor, of which, in my heart, I wasn't sure I deserved.

Once I set foot in Kansas, the enormity of what I was there to do started to weigh heavily on my heart. Yeah, I was excited as hell to get the chance to be an instructor in the aircraft and to be able to hobnob with some of the finest fighter pilots in the world, but I didn't want to "screw the pooch" on the road to becoming an instructor, or even once I became an instructor. Trust me when I tell you I never said the Lord's Prayer with as much zeal and additional pleas tacked on to the end of it as I did during that time.

Most of the instructors at McConnell had at least one tour in Vietnam flying the F-4, F-105, F-100, or A-7. Some guys did two tours, each tour in a different fighter/bomber, and I think a couple guys had three tours. All those Vietnam guys were certified heroes, in my humble opinion, and I was just a pipsqueak; what right did I have in being their colleague? So, consequently, given the talent pool of the instructors in the 184th, I was generally very stressed during all my instructor training and felt immense pressure to perform to the standards my ex-Vietnam fighter pilot instructors expected.

Imagine, if you can, that you are a second lieutenant, not even a real flight lead yet, and you have only 220 hours in the F-4 and you are briefing "the students" (when I trained to be an instructor, all the "students" were captains, majors, a few lieutenant colonels, and occasionally a full colonel, and were actually instructors pretending to be students) on performing an air refueling followed by a low level, which would lead us to attacks on the bombing range, with tactical deliveries, and then the return to base in a tactical formation. The actual instructor in such a training flight of four F-4s was number 2, and he may have flown 280 missions in Vietnam, with the number 3 pilot being the "low man" with 100 missions "up north" in the Thud (F-105), and the number 4 guy might have somewhere in between numbers 2's and 3's mission count. Bloody hell, as I briefed and then flew with those guys, I kept thinking over and over, "God please don't let me screw up." Because of the stress, there were many nights before a training mission when I was so nervous I couldn't sleep, or woke up after sleeping just a couple of hours. Instead of popping a sleeping pill, drinking a glass of milk or a scotch, my solution was to go run a couple of miles to burn off nervous energy. Oddly, for me it worked, and I slept like a baby after getting back to bed.

When I was finally given the title F-4 instructor, I prayed to God to help me be like my father as both an instructor and pilot. I didn't have his natural aviating skills or his bravado, but I did have my faith as my unseen wings, and I can say that God was my copilot with every flight I flew in the F-4, whether on a training or proficiency flight.[24] And as much as I was afraid I'd hate being an instructor, once I was immersed in the role, I can truly say I was a very happy worker bee . . . just like my father said I'd be those many years before.

When my dad recommended, years before, that I should become an instructor, I was secretly aghast and thought, "No way!" I hated the thought of teaching another person to fly while I watched. I was selfish and wanted to do all the flying myself, not to mention the unwanted responsibility of teaching someone a skill that could have potentially deadly consequences to them, or others, if taught wrong. However, once immersed in it, I realized the reward there actually is in training someone in an aircraft, particularly if the student has a great attitude and is willing to learn.

There were three phases in the F-4 training course: transition, where you taught the guy how to fly the aircraft; air to air, where you taught him how to employ the Phantom as a fighter to shoot down enemy aircraft; and finally, air to ground, where the students were taught how to drop bombs and execute complex bombing attacks with multiple aircraft on one target.

When assigned a student, you were his instructor through all the phases. You and another instructor might switch students for a ride or two every so often to give your student a chance to learn different techniques, etc., but for the most part and for continuity's sake, you and your student were welded together for six months, like it or not.

---

24. Proficiency Flight—occasionally Instructor Pilots and Instructor WSOs are scheduled for flights that only have instructors in the aircraft. These can be bombing sorties, air to air combat sorties, or more involved dissimilar air to air combat sorties involving other types of fighter aircraft. The flights are meant to help the instructors maintain their own war fighting proficiency.

In my two-and-a-half years as an instructor in the 177th TFTS, I had five "B" course students. The B course designation was the longest course we had, six months in length, and it was the same syllabus under which I was trained when I was a student.

To this day, I can clearly remember each of those five students, and I am amazed at how different each was with regard to flying ability, attitude, personality, and desire to excel. I got along well with four of them—the fifth, not so much (although the fifth was actually my third B course student). Three of the five were distinguished graduates, which says more about their character and ability than my prowess as an instructor.

Let me briefly digress about one of the students that came to McConnell AFB to train in either the latter half of 1984 or early 1985. In addition to instructing in the actual aircraft, I also taught a ground school course called aircraft general. On the first day of the roll call for the "kids" in this particular B course class and their first day of ground school, I called a name, "Vihlen," that immediately took me back many years to my summer of '74 and Camp Hugo in the Florida Keys. I looked up at the young lieutenant and asked him If he was related to Hugo Vihlen, a Delta Airlines captain and the owner of Camp Hugo. With his emphatic "yes" I then began to mention to Dana, this son of Hugo, that I attended his dad's camp in July, 1974. From that beginning conversation, Dana and I had much to talk about on the class breaks and beyond. It was so nice to meet him, and I remembered seeing him when I was at camp, though he rarely ever talked to the campers. Little did I realize that Dana and I would be roommates after he graduated from his training and went back to the "Makos," the nickname of the Air Force Reserve unit that he was attached to, based in Homestead AFB near Miami, Florida.

Imagine me, meeting, at F-4 RTU, the son of the owner of the camp that changed my life for the better. What a small world it is.

As I said, most students came to F-4 training with a desire in their hearts to be the best fighter pilots their skills would allow, and because of their enthusiasm they listened well to my preflight briefs and inflight instruction. To some degree, since I myself was so young and close to their ages and so junior in rank, I generally had a good rapport with all the students. Like my father, I found I could usually talk them into flying the aircraft the way it needed to be flown through the use of inflection, concise phrases, and timing of instruction. And unlike Jack, but like my father, I wanted my words of instruction to be calm, soothing and positive, not harsh, demeaning or critical. It was a very, very rare occasion when I had to take control of the aircraft from a student to avoid some of their natural tendencies to try and kill their instructor and/or themselves. (About 60 to 70 percent of a student's sorties, while in training, were done with an instructor WSO in their backseats and not an instructor pilot. When the syllabus called for it, a student pilot would be crewed with a student WSO.)

Two situations do come to mind, though, that I'd like to share, when I did take control of the aircraft due to unforeseen circumstances that might have caused us harm.

In the first case, I was flying with an excellent student pilot, Pat McGinn; he and I really got along well as student-instructor. We were in Eureka MOA, a big parcel of airspace that started about thirty miles east of the base and were on an advanced handling ride. I had briefed Pat to zoom straight up, and as the aircraft ran out of airspeed, I wanted him to feed in left or right rudder to get the nose to fall left or right just as we were running out of airspeed. We were reaching 31,000 feet and going through 150 knots, and Pat had not fed in the rudder as I had briefed. Since the airspeed was dropping so fast, as we neared 100 knots, I said to just keep the rudders straight and try to push the nose over (we were still pointed straight up). The nose didn't budge, and we continued in a pure vertical climb as the airspeed rapidly went to zero.

As the airspeed zeroed out, I pulled the engines out of afterburner and left them at military power[25] while I took the aircraft from Pat and watched the altimeter. We had stopped in our upward trajectory, but the nose continued to point straight up. I was a bit baffled, as I thought the aircraft's nose would fall in some direction prior to a total loss in the airspeed, but it didn't. I looked in the mirror above me, a mirror that allows the backseater in the F-4 to see directly behind the aircraft, and I was shocked to see that we were conning[26] and falling backwards into it. The white misty vapor was enveloping us as we slid, tail first, earthward, and I could see eddies and swirls in the vapor as it moved by the airframe. Though I'd never ever tail slid any aircraft, I figured if I kept the stick fully back, the air loads would eventually cause the aircraft to swap ends, and it did. I have no idea of the actual altitude, but while still above 20,000 feet, the aircraft rather quickly pitched nose down, and as it did, I neutralized the stick, and we were now pointed straight down and admiring the scenic Flint Hills, some four miles below.

---

25. Military (power)—combat aircraft usually have two maximum power settings: (1) Afterburner, which is the most power you can get from the engine, and that's when you see a large flame come from the back of the engine; and (2) Military power, which means the engine, the turbine, is spinning as fast as it can go, but wherein the afterburner is not being used. Usually afterburner increases the engine's thrust, above military, by 30 to 40 percent.

26. Conning—there are times when jet engines leave a white condensation trail, composed of water vapor, behind them normally called contrails. It usually occurs at higher altitudes, above 25,000 feet. It is harmless.

We leveled off at around 18,000 feet; whoa . . . that's an experience you don't soon forget.

Probably the most memorable part of that messed-up maneuver, and what I remember most, was Pat saying, as we slid backward, that he wanted to go home. In a way, he was headed there; and if we couldn't have recovered, he might've arrived home in a body bag. (In fact, a friend of Pat's, who was in a different B course class altogether died on July 1, 1985, impacting the ground while coming off of the Smoky Hill bombing range. The student pilot was flying with another student, a WSO, when the accident occurred and though an ejection for both was initiated, it was done at too low of an altitude and they both died. Chuck Fuller, the pilot, was a good kid, full of life, and an excellent pilot. He and I used to ride our dirt bikes [motorcycles] together on the weekends down by the Arkansas riverbanks. It was a bitter loss for all of the 184th.)

The second time I grabbed the controls from a student, more like violently pushed, was when I was in the backseat of a student who was being considered for elimination from the training program due to his inadequate flying skills. He was a very nice gentleman but just too genteel to be a fighter pilot in my opinion. I was asked to fly with him to assess his skills and give my thoughts to the training board to aid in their final determination of his fate as a future fighter pilot.

We were in Bison MOA in a flight of four Phantoms and were practicing lost wingman[27] procedures at the time of this near calamity. My student (I was instructing from the backseat) and I were

---

27. Lost wingman—when two or more fighter aircraft are flying in very close formation, particularly in the clouds, it is possible for the wingman to lose sight of their lead aircraft and if they do there are established procedures for the wingman to follow in order to ensure getting separation from the other aircraft in order to keep from colliding.

number 4 in the formation and on number 3's right side and in fingertip[28] formation. The pilot of number 3 was an instructor with a student WSO in his backseat, and they were on the right side of number 1's aircraft. At some point, lead, in the number 1 Phantom said, "Lost wingman demo now!" With that command, number 3—and for the life of me I don't know why—rolled very rapidly to the right, to almost ninety degrees of bank, and pulled very "hard" into a right turn, towards me and my student; we were only ten feet or so off his right wingtip when he did this.

Why he did what he did I'll never know because, in fact, he was supposed to wait for us, in our aircraft, to turn/bank first. We were turning to the right, since we were flying off of 3's right wing and it was supposed to be a gentle bank/turn to about thirty degrees off the heading we were on; after thirty seconds on the new heading, we were supposed to turn back to the original heading.

As soon as I saw number 3 start his very rapid roll to the right, I knew that if we didn't move, we'd die, all four of us. So, consequently it was by instinct and without hesitation, and though the young lieutenant up front had his hands on the stick and throttles, I overrode him and shoved the stick forward and slammed my student and myself against the canopy as we experienced about three negative Gs in the pushover. We could hear number 3's jet engines' roar above us in his steeply banked turn with his right wingtip only inches above our canopy as it passed quickly on by and to our right.

There was no time to be scared and take an emotional pause, since we had to finish the ride. So, without anything being men-

---

28. Fingertip—USAF term to describe two or more fighter aircraft flying in very close formation. One aircraft is the lead and the other aircraft (usually a maximum of four aircraft in the formation) will fly off of their lead, watching his aircraft as they fly in close formation.

tioned on the radio, or between me and my student via the intercom, of the near catastrophe we reformed in fingertip formation to set up again for the lost wingman demo. This time lead was very explicit in stating that this was not a pitchout and rejoin.[29]

I can say to this day that number 3 and I never talked about why he did what he did, all he could muster when I saw him on the ground, after the flight, was, "I'm sorry."

"Shit happens," I dryly retorted . . . what else could I say?

Like UPT, the flying at McConnell was generally conducted Monday through Friday with Friday nights being reserved for blowing off steam at the Officers' Club or another local honky-tonk type of bar after we were kicked out of the Officers' Club (long story). It was the one time during the week where the students and instructors could meet, on an informal basis, and bond while discussing the week's flying or listening to the old guard tell war stories of their Vietnam days. I have to say those were some very wonderful social evenings, and a lot of the instructors, and most of the students and some support folks, looked forward to those wild and crazy nights. The music was cranked up to decibels that matched the roar of our fighters while our hands visually told the stories of how we maneuvered against our instructor to shoot him down . . . or how he shot us. Many stories of the past week's training escapades were no doubt embellished by "jet fuel" that was consumed in almost the same quantities as it was by the jets we flew; this was déjà vu for me all over again, but this time, I was involved in the stories, not my father and his colleagues.

---

29. Pitchout and rejoin—generally, a training exercise used to teach fighter pilots how to widely separate from each other and then rejoin into fingertip formation.

As a transition from being an RTU instructor, in the summer of 1986 I entered F-4 Fighter Weapons School. Prior to entering the military, I'd never heard of Fighter Weapons School. When I flew against the aggressors and then went to Nellis AFB for that previously mentioned Red Flag exercise, I learned that the crème de la crème of fighter pilots went to Fighter Weapons School to further hone their skills at flying whatever missions their respective combat aircraft was designed to perform. Since the F-4 was both a fighter and bomber, the weapons school for the Phantom was four months in length, contained both an air-to-air and an air-to-ground syllabus, and was a notoriously difficult flying school with very stern instructors. Though the unpleasant memory of the fighter lead-in instructors came to mind when I heard about the hard-ass reputation of the FWS instructors, I also heard the actual flying performed was the best and most challenging flying in the military, so I was hooked, and secretly prayed that one day I could attend the school.

As providence would have it, the F-4 Fighter Weapons School was relocated from Nellis AFB to McConnell in 1984-85 and placed under the banner of the 127th TFS. Since I was instructing B course students in the 177th TFTS, I would talk to some of the Fighter Weapons School instructors at the bar on Friday nights and pick their brains about tactics, techniques, etc. Most of the FWS instructors were nice but standoffish, and they all carried a distinctive fighter pilot swagger uniquely their own; some of those swaggers, as I would find out later, were genuine and earned through superior flying skill, and some were merely facades.

The squadron commander of the Fighter Weapons School, Chuck "Quisto" Younquist, displayed rugged good looks with deep blue eyes and topped by blonde hair. His voice matched his looks being deep and husky from which emanated much cowboy-fighter pilot bravado; his character exuded, if not personified, the Fighter Weapons School mystique. I must say I really admired him as a fighter pilot. Since I was the youngest instructor in the 184th (and always would be), Quisto loved to give me good-natured ribbing when we passed in the hall or chanced to briefly share pleasantries on a Friday evening at the Officers' Club. Because I was so young in the 184th, I always kinda felt like I was the mascot, so it was not unusual for most of the other instructors to give me good-natured grief too. But I loved talking to Chuck at length about war-fighting tactics and admired him greatly for his patience with my youthful exuberance when it came to talking about flying fighters. On the odd occasion when I got a chance to pick his brain about the latest tactics being taught in the Fighter Weapons course, I would lay hints that I'd love to one day attend his school. He usually smiled and, with his husky voice and a twinkle in his deep blue eyes, said I needed to prove myself first. And that was what I set out to do as I endeavored to be the best instructor and fighter pilot that I could possibly become to earn Quisto's professional respect.

In early summer 1986, I was walking past Chuck in the hallway; he was just coming from a flight and I was heading to suit up to go fly. As we passed, he said to me, "Jedi, when are you going to come train in the Weapons School?"

Continuing with the ribbing he and I always shared, I said, "Whenever you can admit that I can kick your ass in air-to-air!"

We both had a hearty laugh, as we each continued walking in different directions.

In the next hallway, I saw my squadron commander, Sammy Small, and he asked me if I had a moment to chat. Looking at my watch briefly, I said, "Yes, sir, I've got a few moments . . . uhhhh, am I in trouble?"

Sammy, one of those amazing ex-Vietnam-era guys with like 288 F-4 missions, chuckled and said, "No, not that I know of, are you?! I just talked to Quist, and he said they have an open slot in the next Weapons School class, and he wondered if you wanted to go."

My jaw dropped. I was honored and scared at the same moment, if only because I had an instant flood of all the cocky comments I'd made in jest to Quisto in the previous months about how I could kick his ass in either bombing or air-to-air—whoa . . . now I may have to back that up, and I seriously didn't think I could, no matter how hard I trained.

But it was my dream shot since I'd learned of the school, and in a New York second, after the previous New York second spent regretting my flippant comments about kicking Chuck's ass in flying, I said, "Hell yeah! Uhhhh . . . sir!"

Sammy smiled and said, "I figured you'd want to go. Now go fly, and we'll get the orders worked up to get you in the class."

I was flying before I even got to the aircraft I was so happy at the thought of going to Fighter Weapons School.

If F-4 RTU was like getting a college degree in military flying, Weapons School was like getting a master's or more, but with extremely critical professors. I knew the flying could be tough at times, but the debriefs, they were insane. It was not uncommon to fly a forty-five-minute, two-aircraft, air-to-air BFM training sortie and then debrief for four hours—yup . . . four hours. The most we'd ever debrief on the RTU side might have been an hour or slightly longer, and that was if four aircraft were involved in the sortie.

When we flew our FWS training flights, both pilot and WSO carried cassette recorders[30] (within a few months of my starting

30. Cassette recorder—now relegated to museums, cassette recorders were small, magnetic tape players/recorders that we used to record our inter cockpit and inter flight, ATC, GCI radio transmissions.

Weapons School, we got VHS tape players installed in the aircraft so we could record the radar screen in addition to all of the other communications) in our G suits, which we could patch into our communications cord that carried all the external and internal communications into our helmet's headphones. We would turn on the recorders just as we began a training maneuver—let's say an air-to-air defensive BFM setup—and we would record all the communications that occurred as we fought, periodically saying, to be recorded on the tape, that we were turning right, climbing, descending, nose-in lag, unloading, etc., and then shut the recorder off after the maneuvering for that fight was stopped, whereupon you might set up again for another engagement. The comments made on the tape—turning, climbing, descending, etc.—were made to enhance SA[31] in the debrief so as to be able to accurately recreate the fight on a whiteboard later. You also could, as I did, draw on a piece of paper strapped to your thigh, short little diagrams, after you stopped your maneuvering of course, so as to further aid in the debrief. Unlike Red Flag, we didn't have the luxury of aircraft instrumentation pods and ACMI[32] ranges with their computer-generated images to aid us in debriefing our air-to-air, or air-to-ground training fights. Nope, after the flight and after freshening up all the pilots and WSOs in the sortie, with the lead instructor standing at the whiteboard and

---

31. SA—without question the cornerstone concept in air combat. Situational Awareness, SA, is succinctly defined as "What has happened, what is happening now, what is going to happen." Without good SA your life expectancy in air combat is very short.

32. ACMI Range—Air Combat Maneuvering Instrumentation (ACMI) systems record an aircraft's in-flight data. They are often used by the military for aerial combat training and analysis. This enables real-time and very complex air-to-air or air to ground, or both, exercises to be carried out with detailed and accurate ground debriefs. Such debriefs involve the use of modern graphics and display techniques that can bring out important training insights for aircrew and supporting assets.

everyone else seated (the pilot instructor being in the number 1 aircraft for the BFM sorties, or numbers 1 and 3 aircraft or numbers 2 and 4 aircraft, depending on what the training syllabus required), we would debrief, aided by the recordings on our cassette recorders, every turn; every radio call; every time afterburner was used or not used, and why, when and why chaff or flares were dispensed; where we were looking, both individually and as a crew and why; what we were thinking, etc. Everything that occurred between the fight's on call to the knock it off was discussed in excruciating detail—four hours of everything, and sometimes more. We ordered pizzas one time, we went so long. And this went on for almost seventeen weeks, Monday through Friday, flying three to four sorties a week on average, weather permitting; Weapons School was certainly not for the faint of heart.

Every ride was meticulously and critically graded, and it felt as if each training flight was a checkride, which in a way it was. The pressure from the instructors never let up, even on Friday nights. When we socialized at the bar, it always seemed there was a distinct social barrier between the students and the instructors that kept a true rapport from developing; that barrier did not exist on the RTU side of the house.

On the first Friday of the beginning of Weapons School, it was tradition, and mandatory, that each student eat a raw egg—shell and all—and that had to be chased by a shot of Jeremiah Weed. I compressor-stalled my first attempt at eating the egg (blew it out of my mouth), so I had to down another—yeechh, raw eggs do not taste good. You had to really crunch the shell too so as to pulverize it so it wouldn't get stuck in your throat when you swallowed it; three shots of Weed was my preferred method of getting the taste of the egg out of my mouth. And let it be said, Jeremiah Weed isn't exactly a gourmet libation.

In a few pages, I give a detailed account of what it's like to fly in a twelve-ship surface attack sortie into the Nellis Range, so I'll save the detail of tactical flying for that story. For now, I'll just give a snippet of a few interesting things that occurred while training to get my "patch." (Fighter Weapons School guys were sometimes called target arms or patch wearers because of the distinct nature of the patch they wore after graduating.)

Probably my proudest moment while going through FWS was when Quisto and I flew in the same four-ship, air-to-air fight against my old nemesis, the Aggressors. While I was immersed in the advanced threat phase of the FWS's air-to-air phase of training, Chuck told me that I needed to get a Tac Qual Check.[33] It didn't matter, he said, that I was going through FWS, I still needed to get the annual checkride that all fighter pilots got once a year to maintain currency. The only difference this year, and for me, was that my Tac Qual Check was going to be combined with one of my FWS training missions, since by nature they were tactical missions. In that same vein, Quist was the only person in the FWS qualified to give me the checkride, so he decided he'd administer the evaluation on a four ship versus four ship, FWS DACT scenario. YGBSM. (Ya' gotta' be shitting me.)

I sighed deeply when he said he had to give me the checkride. All the cocky comments I'd slung at him over the past months about how I'd kick his butt in air-to-air and now he is giving me a checkride on an air-to-air sortie on a FWS scenario and with the F-5

---

33. Tac Qual Check—once a year a USAF fighter pilot is required to receive an operational evaluation, administered by a Standards Pilot, that tests their fitness for their assigned duty with-in the squadron and as a competent fighter pilot.

Aggressors as my adversaries . . . wonderful. I made a vow to really try and tone it down with my pithy remarks in the future.

The mission was a four vs. four, F-4s against F-5s, and I was nervous as hell going into the brief because the last time I flew against the aggressors, that time at McDill AFB, they ate me alive. I was the flight lead for this ride, and Quisto was my number 2. My backseater was an awesome ex-Vietnam vet and instructor WSO, Jim Bell. I lost my crewed WSO a few rides earlier; he busted out, and they crewed Jim with me every now and then as I went through the various phases in the school.

At around 9 a.m. and flying in tactical formation,[34] I claimed home field advantage and led my flight of four Phantoms to the east side of Eureka MOA. I stuck the aggressors on the west side since the sun was fairly low on the easterly horizon, which might make seeing us more difficult as we approached them for attack.

With the fight's on call and Jim sorting all of the radar contacts, I briefed the flight earlier that we would faint slightly to south to isolate the aggressors to the north and try and keep the sun in their eyes. Unfortunately, as I maneuvered my flight, not all of the WSOs could locate, on radar, all four of the aggressors, and my targeting/sorting plan fell apart. Consequently, though I didn't want it to happen, we wound up in a fur ball.[35]

All eight aircraft merged in one very small area of a great big blue sea of sky, some aircraft turning sharply while others floated

---

34. Unlike fingertip, Tactical Formation is the normal formation fighter aircraft operate when in combat. The aircraft are spread 1 to 2 miles wide, and stacked at different altitudes. This enhances threat lookout and maneuverability. The minimum number in a formation is 2, but many flights of two can be operated together to form a very large formation of aircraft.

35. Fur Ball—military slang term for many combat aircraft in very close proximity, maneuvering/fighting against each other.

in easy turns, looking for an advantage. My number 3 man, also a FWS student, who had been at my nine o'clock was now at my two o'clock position and slightly low. He was maneuvering against an aggressor that was high and to my right. Bob, the pilot of number 3, was intent on shooting the aggressor, who evidently did not see him as he converted from low to high in an almost vertical climb. The aircraft Bob was chasing was of no immediate threat to Jim and me, so as we turned level and to the right to keep an eye on Bob and his target, Jim and I kept a lookout for other aggressors. Almost immediately after I turned right to cover Bob and my wingman, number 2 (Quisto and Shag), who was still to my right, I recognized that another aggressor that was low and to Bob's deep six was going to attempt to shoot Bob since I could see him changing his lift vector to convert on Bob. Seeing that number 3 was in immediate danger of getting shot, I immediately rolled very rapidly right and began a max G pull, putting my lift vector above the bandit, who was slightly low and across the circle from me. The aggressor was beginning to climb rapidly to put his nose on Bob to shoot just as I was continuing with an energy-depleting rolling and climbing turn to get my nose on the aggressor as soon as I could. There was urgency on my part as I didn't want number 3 to get shot (even if it was simulated). There is no doubt the aggressor I was attacking did not see me as he seemed intent, when based upon his projected flight path, on attacking my number 3. As I was concentrating on number 3 and the aggressor, who was converting on him, Jim continued his lookout for other aggressors and also checking number 2's six o'clock; my intent was shoot the guy I was converting on with a missile if I could, to kill him faster; but if I had to, I was prepared to use my 20 MM canon if I got too close for a missile launch.

Honestly though, to describe how number 3, me, and the bandits maneuvered would be a waste of words as it's always confusing to try to describe a three-dimensional, fluid air-to-air fight with two-dimensional words on paper. The bottom line is just as Bob, number 3, was shooting the F-5 he was chasing, I shot the F-5 attempting to shoot Bob; we both used AIM-9s for our kills.

The attacks, Bob's and mine, were successful. After I called a kill on the aggressor attacking Bob, he called a kill over the radio on his bandit. The radio-called kills were relayed to the aggressors (they operated on a different frequency) by GCI[36] to kill remove[37] them. After the kills, I called for a disengagement of our F-4s from the fight and to bug out* north, with a slow turn to the east to follow.

In spite of the fact that my battle plan did not go according to my brief, not one F-4 was shot in that engagement . . . thank God.

In the next fight, which had the same ROE[38] as the first flight, I pointed my four-ship more aggressively at the F-5s, instead of trying to isolate them, and in short order, all the F-5s were identified, sorted, and targeted on the radars' of all of the F-4s and all four Aggressors were killed by AIM 7s prior to merging.

After that second engagement, and with fuel running low (we were flying clean aircraft), I called for a total knock-it-off and all the

---

36. Ground Control Intercept—fighter aircraft can be directed to hostile aircraft by air combat radar controllers who use their radar to direct the fighter aircraft to threats.

37. Kill remove—in peacetime air combat training, simulated "kills" are called by one fighter on another involved in the fights. If one aircraft believes he shot down another aircraft, as based upon a certain set of ROE (Rules of Engagement), the attacking aircraft then tells GCI who they killed and GCI informs the killed aircraft to either leave the battle temporarily or permanently, depending upon the scenario.

38. ROE—the rules under which all simulated and real battles/engagements/wars operate. Sometimes it's a fine line and/or grey area in which ROE dictates how the "good guys" must operate, often times to their disadvantage. Depending upon which ROE is violated can mean the difference between living or dying, being grounded, or court marshaled.

aircraft returned to McConnell for an exhausting, and somewhat heated, four-hour debrief. Even though they were "training aids," the Aggressors were not happy with the results on this flight since, when flying against the weapon schools, they really wanted to win and not necessarily act like impotent targets.

The long, marathon debrief was grueling since the aggressors' flight lead, a previous F-15 pilot, was not used to being hammered by Phantoms. He argued from the untenable premise that there was no way his flight of four aggressors could have been so badly beaten. The facts of each engagement were brought out before every pilot in excruciating—and I mean excruciating—detail as I went through and diagramed on a big whiteboard what each and every aircraft did in each of the two engagements, to include each turn, climb, descent, radio call, chaff and/or flare discharge, afterburner use/or not, where each pilot/WSO was looking, and finally when/where each shot was taken.

There's a saying that when flying training missions, the fight is not won in the air but in the debrief. I have to say, I battled the aggressor flight lead in that debrief more than I'd ever battled anyone in the air, and I knew what I knew and I had to pound that guy's ego to the point that he had to admit defeat; by the end of the debrief, he did just that, and he congratulated my flight of four on an excellent performance.

After the debrief, I began to erase the whiteboard of its elegantly drawn, four color swirls of both intertwining and disengaging geometric lines and loops. All of the boys walked out of the room while I went into my own little world as I erased. I was deeply pleased, with both the flying and the debrief, and I was so hoping I had finally proven myself worthy to Chuck. It was rare in FWS for an instructor to give you a pat on the back, you had to be internally happy with your performance. As I erased the whiteboard's memory of the air-to-air battles, out of the corner of my eye I saw Quisto standing at the door, getting ready to walk out. I looked at him in a puzzled kind of way, wondering if I was in trouble for something when he said, "Jedi . . . six and oh" (meaning a Phantom-to-Aggressor kill ratio of six kills to zero losses). He then smiled, gave a short nod of his head with a twinkle from his blue eyes, and walked out; that was my longed-for pat on the back (I have the grade sheet from that Tac Qual Check mounted in a plaque with my FWS patch and a picture of my FWS classmates).

After the air-to-air phase of FWS training was complete, we entered the air-to-ground syllabus. Air-to-air flying is, to some degree, subjective in nature because unless real missiles and bullets were coming off the aircraft and real kills happening, who shot whom and when, i.e. who would survive and who would die, was all somewhat subjective. But the air-to-ground phase yielded more definitive results, at least when it came to hitting a target. A bomb dropped from an aircraft, whether it's practice or live bomb,[39] was going to land somewhere, either near or far from the target, and you could certainly measure that distance. Obviously, the closer the bomb to the target, the better. Now, I will allow, getting to the target alive to deliver that ordnance was the problem during this Cold War era of the 1970s and 1980s due to the self-defense network deployed by the Warsaw Pact nations. I learned a few years before at red flag that Soviet SAMs could reach out and touch you at almost all altitudes and getting through the SAM belt was hazardous to your health. It was believed, back in the 1980s, that flying very low, avoiding the

---

39. Live bomb—it actually will blow up when dropped, a real bomb.

concentrated SAM areas, and using other tactics could afford a modicum of success in getting through to the target and then back home.

So, fast-forward to a surface attack mission that I was flying as my FWS training neared its end.

Since almost every surface-attack sortie was flown at low altitude, it was, like, never that we climbed above 500 feet while flying a low level, hence the reason it was called a "low level"; the lower you were the fewer the SAM envelopes you were exposed to, so the better your chances of survival; at least that was the thinking back then. So, with that in mind, probably, the most difficult situation I have ever had to face, with regard to an unusual flying situation in my life, let alone while going through the FWS, came on the low-level segment of a surface-attack training mission in the latter stages of my seventeen weeks at FWS.

Again, I was leading a flight of 4 Phantoms with my instructor in the number 2 aircraft and about 7,000 feet to my right, while numbers 3 and 4, in the same spread as me and 2, were 9000 feet behind. We approached the target area at 480 knots ground speed on the second to last leg of a low level, this low level leading us to the target area. We were about 200 to 400 feet above the rather flat Kansas farmland as we zoomed, looking for potential bandits and mentally preparing ourselves for the up-and-coming bomb deliveries. At some point on that second to last low level leg, my backseater, a rather hard-ass and gruff FWS instructor WSO, said he had a radar contact and that we were going to have to shoot the bandit. At first I was like, "OK, let's do it!" But when I looked at my radar scope, which showed the same information as the WSO's scope, I saw that the bandit he wanted to shoot was really high, like above 30,000 feet, and relatively far away and I said, "Dude, let's blow it off, he's no threat."

Nope, I was the student; and though I voiced my opinion to not prosecute his radar contact, the IWSO said he ID'd it as hostile and we had to shoot it down. YGBSM.[40]

To get in parameters for the kill, I had to pull up very steeply, initiating full afterburner as I did, needing the 36,000 pounds combined thrust of both J-79s to maintain the steep climb angle, while also maintaining our airspeed, as we climbed to get into missile range. Also, I needed all the thrust I could get so as to get our aircraft's nose way up and on an intercept course in the vertical that would allow our missile a chance to get to the target (simulated; no live missile was ever carried on ANY of our training flights, nor were any ever actually launched). So, from 200 feet above the ground, we zoomed to 18,000 to shoot down some innocent airliner that my FWIC IWSO was pretending to be a bad guy; if only the passengers knew (Just FYI... we passed at least 13,000 feet below the target and I had a visual on it, so it wasn't dangerous in a real world sense, but we did get a simulated kill).

Once we timed the missile out and fulfilled the ROE for a valid kill, I had a huge problem. Unless you've actually done this, gone from 200 feet to 18,000 and then looked down upon a flat Kansas plain, and this may be hard to imagine—but holy crap—from that vantage point, everything looks the same. There was so much homogeny between the farmland and the towns and the roads and the railroad tracks and the grain silos. I was crapping gold bricks because I had zero clue where the low level route, let alone my formation, was. Somewhere, three miles below, were three Phantoms at low altitude heading to bomb a target, and I had absolutely no idea

---

40. A mostly military slang term meaning, "You've Gotta Be Shiting Me." It's usually said, or thought (depending upon the decorum) by a person, usually a fighter pilot, out shock or surprise.

where they were. Number 2, Jabba (one of the FWS instructors), said he lost sight of me as we climbed through 15,000 feet, which is actually pretty remarkable in itself (if you're wondering, I looked at my altimeter when he called lost visual). To my benefit that day, it was very clear, and as I rolled the aircraft almost inverted while at 18,000 feet to get an unobstructed view of the area in front of and below me, I happened to see the one rather prominent geographic feature that differed from most of the other scenery of the Kansas plains, which bathed my vision. The lake was obvious, even from three miles high, and I knew that the last turn point of the low level we were flying was located on a bend in a river/stream that exited the lake on its east side. So, with no idea where the boys were, I decided to head for the general area of that last turn point as I figured I might be able to rejoin my lost flight near there. So, now armed with a plan, I pulled my nose down and dropped rapidly from 18,000 feet to re-enter the low-level structure, and sped up in the descent because I knew I had lost time in that wicked steep climb.

Now, you are probably wondering . . . why didn't my backseater use our radar to look for my wingman while we descended back to the low level? It would have been difficult at best for the WSO to find the wingman on the radar as I descended because our aircraft had an early generation pulse radar.[41] With my steep descent back to

---

41. Pulse radar—all fighter aircraft radars now have sophisticated electronics that allow these radars to reject, not see, the ground and to only see an airborne target. The old pulse radars, on the early generation fighters, saw "everything" and displayed the ground, mountains, buildings, flocks of birds, as well as aircraft on the radar scope. The radar operator in these early generation radars, be it the pilot (F-86D, F-102/104/106) or WSO (F-89, F-101/111, F-4) had to be able to tweak both the gain and elevation control knobs on the radar set in order to breakout the bandit aircraft from all the clutter displayed on the radar scope. While looking up, from low to high was relatively easy, or while over water (Looking up or down), looking from high to low while flying over land could be very difficult. Pilots/WSO's who were good at finding bandits in clutter were worth their weight in gold, or jet fuel, as the saying goes.

low level, the ground return on the radar scope would have been so overwhelming it would have taken all of the WSO's concentration and skill to discern the F-4s from the state of Kansas; it's not impossible, but the WSO's main job during this point was to find bandits, not my wingman. We had no clue where the other guys were, and even though I asked them for their location as I started my descent back down, it was like looking for three needles in a haystack, both visually and with our onboard radar.

Now, we did have an electronic feature on the aircraft called an APX 76, which would have helped display the mode 1 or 2[42] position of the guys, but the WSO I was flying with—well, let's just say he was from the Deep South (and a redneck), and I'm from Jersey; he and I just didn't play well together. When I asked him to use the APX 76 to give me a "paint" (as displayed on the radar scope) of the other aircraft, he made it known that I had to do "that pilot shit" on my own and without his help to rejoin and reform the formation; I expected as much.

Finally, in FWS it was hammered upon us to keep our radio calls short, clear and concise. In the school, we had been taught a standard vocabulary of often-used words that had much meaning when spoken, so if you got verbose on the radio it normally brought a certain amount of retribution in the debrief from the instructors. As I just said, I had actually asked the flight where they were when I began my descent, and the response from number 2 was something like, "We're flying over a road that has railroad tracks next to it and a

42. APX-76 and IFF modes—all fighters are equipped with an IFF (Identification Friend or Foe) interrogator that when activated "paints" (displays) one of 4 possible, 1, 2, 3, or 4, modes of IFF channels. What mode is interrogated is easily selectable in flight and each mode, and the code that mode displays on the radar scope, means something to the operator with regards to type of aircraft returning the code and/of if it is a hostile.

grain silo to the west about three miles." Uhhhmmm okay, that narrows it down to about 3000 places I can see from where I am. After that worthless inquiry on my part, I decided it was best to drop down to a much lower altitude before I began to search for the lost formation in earnest while continuing to head for that previously mentioned turn point.

Amazingly, as I descended below 5000 feet I spotted one, then two, then all three aircraft of my missing formation. I was behind them a couple of miles but pretty much going in the same direction and offset to their right. I pushed it up to military power (100 percent rpm on the engines) to overtake them more rapidly and gave a quick radio call saying I had a visual and was dropping in to retake the lead on number 2's left side, where I had left him a few minutes earlier. There was no skill on my part in me finding those guys, it was absolutely by the grace of God.

The rest of the flight was typical FWS dogma—we flew, we debriefed for a couple of hours (at least, though not as long as we did on some of the air-to-air missions), we were told that we had passed the ride (huge relief), and then we planned for the next day's surface attack mission, usually staying up until midnight and briefing at seven the next morning. It was a grind, but I did love the flying nonetheless.

The third very interesting event that happened to me while navigating between the joy and heartbreak flights at FWS was on a "live drop" mission. I have to state that I guess I'm a psycho, because I used to love to drop real bombs (ya know, ones that go BOOM), fire the twenty-millimeter cannon, or shoot air to air missiles. I thought that stuff was neat and maybe my lead-in to that excitement was due to my teenage years. A very good friend of mine and I used to launch

Estes model rockets and make homemade bombs. The rockets we launched off the high school athletic fields, and the homemade bombs we'd blow up in various locales. We never harmed human or fowl in our experimenting with different ways to make bombs; however, there was some collateral damage to certain abandoned buildings located deep in the woods. I never said I was normal.

On this particular four-ship bombing ride, we flew south by southwest of McConnell to Fort Sill, Oklahoma, where they had a live ordnance bombing range. The army fired their cannon and rocket rounds into the large, very beat up, and undulating impact area and the bomber aircraft from above peppered the Oklahoma countryside with their 500- to 2000-pound bombs, CBU[43], or strafed soft targets with their cannons.

On this day, we had a USAF FAC[44] who was directing us to drop our bombs on whatever target he assigned and he had a bunch of army enlisted guys with him who were getting an education on how close air support operations were conducted. I was number 2 in the formation and was crewed with a student FWS WSO named Joe.

After checking in with the FAC and setting up in a wide orbit over the target area, the FAC tried to direct our eyes onto the first target he wanted us to bomb. Though I know the FAC thought his description of the area below, and more specifically of the target he wanted us to bomb was effective, it was not. I'll be blunt and tell you the surface of the ground below was so featureless, with no veg-

---

43. Cluster Bomb Unit is a big bomb canister that contains tens to hundreds of small bombs. The canister is dropped in flight and at a predetermined time or altitude it breaks open and disgorges the little bomblets that then spread out and cover a large area.

44. Forward Air Controller (FACs) can be either on the ground or airborne. They are specially trained to direct bombing operations in combat. Specifically, they direct and control fighter aircraft in the successful completion of destroying whatever target needs to be attacked in that specific area of operation.

etation to speak of from years of being blown up that I had no clue what target we were supposed to bomb. There were so many objects in the debris field below I had zero clue, which object fit his description. It's one thing to be on the ground, looking through binoculars at a target two miles away that doesn't move in perspective, but quite another to be flying overhead in a large racetrack orbit, as the four of us circled, at 5000 feet and 350 knots, with the potential targets changing continuously in perspective and distance.

So, as we orbited, I told Joe I had a target in sight, well within the confines of the live drop area, and that I had no clue if it was or wasn't the target being described by the FAC, but it was the only one that I could truly keep and maintain my eyes on as we orbited. I talked Joe's eyes onto the same vehicle I saw, and he agreed that we should go for that, but we had to wait for lead to have a go first.

The FAC was not marking the target with white phosphorous rounds (either a rocket or an artillery round), as they usually do in the real war, so it was everybody's guess, as I found out later in the mission debrief, what the actual target was.

We were told to roll in from the west, using an easterly attack heading. Lead, number 1, rolled in first—as expected—and as he settled on his attack heading, he was cleared to drop his bombs; we were dropping doubles, two 500-pound Mk 82 bombs per pass.

Of note, was that in the brief, prior to going out to our aircraft, lead told us to use a certain "intervolometer" setting, in milliseconds, that would cause the bombs to be spaced a certain distance apart when they impacted the ground. I am not certain of the setting he wanted us to use, but it was not the shortest time setting that our weapons selector panel offered as an option.

So, lead rolls in on his twenty-degree dive and drops. His bombs are nowhere near the target I'm looking at, and I thought about going through dry[45] on my bombing pass, worried that I might get in trouble if I dropped on the wrong target. But reason quickly overtook fear of a berating in the mission debrief simply because I couldn't see anything that remotely looked like a target near where lead's bombs impacted. Since my target was in the "general area" of his (like in the state of Oklahoma), I thought, To hell with it, I'm going to go for what I could actually see, and I could easily justify my decision later.

As lead was pulling up and off his bombing pass, I was calling "in" from the west and given clearance by the FAC to drop. I did change, just before I rolled in, the intervalometer setting on my weapons panel to the shortest delay possible because I wanted the bombs to be as close as possible to each other when they hit the ground. I had no real reason for this other than if my bombs were close to the target, I thought two bombs closer would be better than one close and the other farther away. I must make it a point to say that I was a worse bomber than I was an air-to-air pilot, so I was happy when we starting dropping multiple bombs in one pass in this phase of the air-to-ground syllabus. (You started out dropping one bomb at a time and then progressed to dropping all six in one bombing pass.) I knew the more bombs I dropped, the better the chance of me hitting the target with at least one bomb.

As I went down the chute on my bombing pass, I was extremely intent on meeting the parameters that would make for an accurate bomb drop—and oh, by the way, no computers were used in the bombing of targets back then, at least not in the F-4. We dropped bombs manually. We flew as exact a profile as we could, actually flying the aircraft to a certain airspeed, dive angle, aim point, and

---

45. Going through dry—not dropping a bomb.

altitude until release; it took practice to be okay at it. Some guys were Zen bombers,[46] most were not.

At the release altitude for the bombs, my pipper[47] was right on the target and airspeed was perfect so, I hit the pickle button and away went two live, 500-pound bombs spaced about thirty feet or so apart. As soon as I dropped, I smartly pulled the nose up to climb back to the orbiting altitude, and I rolled almost ninety degrees right because I wanted to see where my bombs hit. Looking down and back at the target, a derelict APC,[48] Joe and I saw each bomb visually just before they hit the ground. The first bomb literally hit right at the front of the vehicle and the second at the end and then the ground exploded, covering the target in a cloud of dirt. Joe and I instinctively yelled in joy as the APC disappeared in the earthen turmoil, and by the time we had leveled at 5000 feet, the smoke and dust had cleared, and the APC ceased to exist.

To confirm the serendipity that Joe and I had bombed the correct target, as number 3 was about to roll in on his bombing pass, the FAC said that he had to get a new target since the first target was just obliterated. I will admit I was relieved that I hadn't bombed the

---

46. Zen bomber—a pilot with the natural ability to bomb. Just like there are natural pilots, there were bombers who, and this in the old days when bombing was done manually and not with computers, were extremely good at getting the bombs on the target in even the most difficult of circumstances.

47. Pipper—a little red dot superimposed on the glass in the front of pilot and used to aid in bombing, shooting the cannon, or firing a missile. The entire displayed gunsight was called a reticle with the pipper being in the center of the reticle. Newer gunsights are free floating and lead computing for more accurate air to air gunnery.

48. Armored Personnel Carrier is a fairly heavily armored vehicle used to protect soldiers while transporting them from one location to another, generally on the battlefield.

wrong target, as I'm sure I would have no doubt heard about it in the debrief; to this day I still have the bomb clips[49] from those Mk 82s.

A little over four months after we started Fighter Weapons School, six of us out of an original class of eight graduated with an S prefix in our military records, telling the powers that be that we were certified "patch wearers." In conversations in the bar that followed our graduation ceremony, my fellow classmates said they would not want to go back through the school again, if for some reason they were told they had to, as they said it was a very tough seventeen weeks. For me, I was kind of ambivalent. There is no doubt the school took a lot out of you mentally and physically, and some, if not most, of the instructors were hard asses in a flying sense and demanded excellence in flying skills that a couple of them did not actually possess themselves. I can also tell you none of the instructors beat around the bush when it came to telling you if you did poorly on a particular flight. But, for me personally, it was an honor to have survived the gauntlet and I have some very fond memories of most of my classmates and our instructors with whom I trained and flew.

RICK HENRY

The story that follows was written over a period of many weeks back in the mid-1990s. Admittedly, it is long. I wrote it with the intention of

---

49. Bomb clips are specially designed wires that are attached to the fuses of bombs that are carried on fighters. When the bomb is released/dropped one end of the clip (wire) stays attached to the aircraft and the other end releases from the fuse on the bomb as it falls away. This allows the fuse to arm after it falls a predetermined amount of time. Some fuses are G sensitive and will detonate when suddenly slowing upon impact while others will detonate upon frontal impact with an object due to a small initiator charge in the fuse itself igniting the main explosive in the bomb; still other bombs are detonated by a radar fuse that causes them to explode at a preset height above the ground. Regardless of the fuse type, when loaded on the aircraft they are safetied with clips until pulled after being dropped.

describing to the layperson what it was like flying the F-4 on a ground
attack mission in the Nellis AFB bombing ranges during the mid-1980s.

Many years ago, I received F-16 flight training in Klamath Falls,
Oregon. One day my mates and I were attending a classroom lecture
on how to do no-lock intercepts using the F-16's radar. The instructor
giving the brief was named Rick Henry, and at that time, Rick was
one of a very few number of IWSOs remaining in the USAF. (IWSO:
instructor weapons system officer. If a U.S. Air Force fighter aircraft
had two seats, the front or left seat, if the aircraft was an F-111, was
occupied by a pilot. The backseat or right seat, if it was in the F-111,
was occupied by a weapons system officer. The WSO, "whizo," operated the radar and bombing computers. IWSOs "eye whizzes" were
instructors to WSOs and, in my case, fledgling F-16 pilots.)

IWSOs and WSOs were an endangered species of sorts back
then. The USAF was converting its two-seat F-4 and F-101B squadrons (Rick used to fly as an IWSO on the F-4) to single-seat F-16s,
and this transition was leaving a lot of WSOs and IWSOs scrambling to find jobs within the military structure. It was heartbreaking
to see these men's lives and families so disrupted by this moderniza-
tion of the force structure. Many guys (it was a males' only business
then) went into "desk" jobs in either the maintenance or personnel
departments, many more got out of the USAF "proper" and went
into the Guard or Reserve, and still others left the military altogether. The "lucky few," IWSOs that is, were given instructor opportunities in positions in which they were well-acquainted. They
would most likely spend their remaining military life teaching fledgling F-16 pilots how to employ their weapon's system radar. Far too
many good men were put out to pasture when their squadron went
to single-seat fighters, and Rick was one of them.

As I listened to Rick that day, I could detect a sadness and a longing in his voice. He missed flying. He missed what he did best, and a very part of his soul was lost when the F-4s left. He had devoted his career to perfecting a profession that technology was able to surpass before he was able to fully express his own capabilities. It is believed that technology is able to detect, receive, process, diagnose, warn, display, direct, and defeat just about anything to allow the pilot to be free to fly the aircraft . . . but is that flying?

While Rick continued with his lecture, my mind daydreamed of the old days . . .

I could see the days when Rick and I both flew F-4s. They were hot jets to us, a waning pinnacle of leading-edge technology. When I began to fly the F-4, it was the old man in the sky. It didn't turn tighter than the newer F-16s or F-15s, it wasn't quicker, it burned more fuel, and it "broke" more often. And according to some, the F-4 wasn't exactly the best-looking fighter on the ramp. But for what the "Phantom," nickname for the F-4, may have lacked in technical attributes, its shortcomings were balanced by the "street-smart" crews that flew it. Many a tired F-4 equipped with outdated and aging gadgets would kick the tar out of the wonder jets; wisdom has a way of balancing the scales.

There was a distinction about the F-4 that went beyond sheer technical numbers when compared to the latest "Mattel" toys (F-16/15). It had an aura, an ambiance that permeated the whole community of Phantom personnel, from the crew chiefs to the pilots to the admin clerks. The Phantom was beautiful, in an ugly sense, such as a Mack truck is aesthetically appealing to a truck driver, for the form bestows the function. Through the years, the Phantom fought in many conflicts around the world and was a proud veteran with a noble spirit that, on many occasions, flew beyond its designed abilities to bring its biological masters back to safety.

The cockpit smelled of fuel, ionized air, and sweat. Unlike the super efficiently cooled cockpit of the F-16, the F-4's air conditioner was just a placebo, intended to psychologically fool the aircrew into thinking that it served a useful purpose. In the winter, you did not lack for heat, and temperatures were mild. But in the summer—on a hot summer day, you were drenched in sweat twenty minutes after strapping into the cockpit. While airborne and flying a low-level, drops of sweat beaded down your face and onto your oxygen mask. Sometimes your eyes would take a drop or two, and you would lift your visor and take a quick wipe of your brow with your gloved hand, cursing that damned air conditioner and its old, impotent plumbing.

Unlike the automated systems in the newer fighters, flying the F-4 took a lot of manual labor and deliberate, calculated thought. At 500 knots, it took a relatively strong pull on the stick to turn it and the G forces, while turning at 500 knots, tried to keep you glued to your seat. You huffed and puffed, straining with your arms, neck, chest, and stomach muscles, using each group to either pull your head and upper body off the seat back so as to perform your requisite duties, or to keep your arms in place to operate the stick and throttles; conversely at 100 knots, it took a sensitive, delicate feel to keep it from going out of control. The ailerons and rudder demanded special attention in the F-4. At low angles of attack (AOA[50]),

---

50. Angle of Attack is the difference in angle between the relative wind passing over the wing and the chord line of that wing. All aircraft lose a gross amount of lift if flown at too high of an angle of attack. Such a large loss of lift is called stalling, whereas the lift generated can no longer support the aircraft for flight and the aircraft descends. There are many interrelating factors between, AOA, lift, and, airspeed and an aircraft that stalls isn't necessarily out of control or always in danger of crashing.

the ailerons were used to roll and "turn" the aircraft and the rudder was somewhat ignored. But as the angle of attack increased, the ailerons were used less and the rudder took center stage as the flight control of choice. The ailerons, if used with reckless abandon at higher AOAs, could cause the Phantom to, quite violently at times, depart controlled flight; therefore, they had to be left alone as much as possible. But even the rudder, if used without respect for your current flight envelope, could impart an out-of-control situation, so its input, too, was not abused unless you were certain of its affect upon your flight path. On the flip side, the engines (there were two of them) were always willing to be abused and were as reliable as the watch on your wrist; the military issued one, of course! Finally, flying a low-level, like the flight controls previously mentioned, demanded much of the rest of your "undivided" attention to remain on course and on time.

Unlike the super accurate inertial navigation systems of the newer fighters, the F-4's INS would usually fix your position within the state or country (depending on size) over which you were flying. The Phantom's INS was only accurate on rare occasions. The INSs of the newer fighters allowed those pilots to confidently fly to their targets, thusly freeing the crews from a lot of map reading and also allowing them to concentrate more on threat detection (both visually and with the radar).

The "INS," Inertial Navigation System, uses a gyroscope, either mechanical or ring laser, to measure movement and position of the aircraft. In its most basic form, it tells the crew where they are and the distance and ground track to a manually selected latitude and longitude, corrected for wind. It literally can guide you to any point in the world. It also tells the crew their ground speed and their magnetic ground track, as they fly over the ground. Finally, the system can be tied to the aircraft's weapons system to more accurately drop either conventional or nuclear weapons. In older fighters, the INS was reliable but tended to drift in position. It was not uncommon in the F-4 for the INS to be two miles off after forty-five minutes of flight. In the F-16s that I flew after the F-4, after two hours you might be off by a tenth of a mile, but, in either aircraft you could manually update the INS's actual position whenever you wished. An accurate INS helped to relieve pilots and WSOs of the stress of accurate map reading while flying at very low altitude.

No such luck in the Phantom. Since the F-4's INS wasn't the most precise, we rarely used it as our primary reference for navigation along the low level routes. Instead we "Phantom Phlyers" preferred (prepherred?) to navigate in much the same way as Lindbergh did on his flight to Paris in 1927, using dead reckoning (dead reckoning, a.k.a. DR. Where the dreadful name came from, I do not know, but I suspect from the early pioneers of aviation, some of whom did die trying to get from A to B using the following procedure. To "DR" in aviation speak means to navigate with reference to the aforementioned tools. You preplanned your intended route of flight on a map. You figured out the headings you needed to fly, from turn point to turn point—you rarely flew a straight course to your target—the times to each turn point, based upon a ground speed that you intended to fly, and the overall time of the low-level. Also, you studied the route of flight to learn its terrain features and to look for prominent landmarks that may help you to stay on/get on course. More often than not, "DR"-ing worked, but you had to have faith that it would.).

In fact, we used the same tools—a map, a clock, and a compass (we didn't really use a compass, per se, for everyday flying, instead we used an HSI . . . horizontal situation indicator).

However, unlike "Lucky Lindy," who just needed to hit a continent on his trip over the "pond" and wasn't too worried about a time schedule, save for his fuel, when we flew our low-levels, we had to be accurate and on time, particularly when it came to finding and bombing a target. (Usually, you were given a time "window" in which you had to hit your target.) Low-level navigation could be very difficult, particularly if flying over featureless terrain. Nature wasn't always cooperative when it came to positioning landmarks where you wanted them, particularly when the visibility was poor, hence trying to find some low-level turn points demanded most of the pilot's attention.

Because so much had to be considered by the pilot, flying the aircraft had to be done by unconscious thought, and while the WSOs/IWSOs did help with some navigation, normally you wanted him "in the radar" searching for possible threats, or in concert with checking the radar, he would "be outside," visually checking the flight's "six o'clock" for bandits. In all fighters, new and old, you had to learn how to multitask; but in the Phantom, you had to learn how to prioritize the many tasks required and, in essence, you really had to learn how to prioritize the multitasking of multitasking! In any jet, it's an adrenaline-producing environment; in the F-4 however, since so many things had to be done either physically or mentally in a short amount of time, and done accurately, it was sweat-producing and gut-wrenching work!

But it was satisfying "work," particularly if it was a hard mission. One time, while on a TDY (Temporary DutY) to George AFB, in California, I was tasked to lead a strike package of twelve F-4s against targets in southwestern Nevada.

The challenge was formidable. I was leading "my" four-ship of F-4s from my home squadron, plus an additional eight F-4s that belonged to the Luftwaffe Fighter Weapons School (because the weather was so good in Southern California, the West German Air Force [at that time, there were still two Germanys] based its Fighter Weapons School at George AFB, in Victorville, California). My four ship's target was an airfield in the Nellis AFB Range Complex.

The Nellis Range Complex, where the Red Flag air wars are fought, also contains "Area 51," of alien spacecraft and top-secret USAF aircraft fame. It is about 150 miles wide, east/west, and fifty miles or so "high," north/south, and starts about sixty miles north of Las Vegas, Nevada. The area contains many bombing targets such as airfields, industrial complexes, air defense sites, and railroad-type facilities and it also has "very active" and realistic manned air defenses that "simulate" shooting surface-to-air missiles at ingressing/egressing participants. Not only does your aircraft indicate that a missile has been launched at you or is about to be launched, via the electronic displays in your cockpit, but "Smokey SAMs," real, unguided, but very visible rockets, are launched to add even more realism. Aircraft have crashed and crews died trying to evade detection from these sites, or, if detected, the crews have crashed trying to break the radar lock from the offending SAM site. At the end of a day's Red Flag mission, the sites would send video footage of aircraft that they tracked and the countermeasures that that aircraft used to try and defeat either radar lock or missile tracking guidance. It was an excellent training experience, but it was pretty embarrassing to be a "movie star" at the end of the day's mass debrief where about 300 fighter pilots and support personnel might see your aircraft, on a huge movie theater type screen, doing the "funky chicken," jinking up and down and left and right very deliberately and abruptly, very close to the ground, trying to evade a "simulated" SAM (surface-to-air missile). You really worked hard to avoid "stardom"; peer pressure can be hell as a fighter pilot!

The mission frag (a frag is an order from the upper echelons of the command structure detailing which targets are to be hit, at what time, with what ordnance, and by what aircraft (squadron and or wings). Other restrictions pertinent to the mission will be put on the frag, such as other assets in the area and possible ingress/egress restrictions) ordered us to destroy aircraft on the airfield ramp, cut the main runway, and destroy ops buildings as well as other targets in the immediate area of the airfield. Also, because of mission tasking, we had to fly a circuitous route to the target that was at least 300 nautical miles in length. Another constraint was the target defenses; the surface-to-air threat surrounding the target was the most advanced anywhere in the world, particularly the SAMs. Finally, to make things that much more difficult, F-16s and F-15s from Nellis AFB were trying to intercept us, either en route to the target, at the target, or while on egress from the target area.

The terrain over which we were to fly was typical Southwestern desert—distinct, prominent mountains and their associated ranges, their features still chiseled and sharp in appearance, gave way to equally distinct, owing to how flat they were, sagebrush-covered valleys. There were no major population centers anywhere along the route of flight, and any smaller towns that could have posed a problem were avoided during the planning of the low-level. The weather was forecast to be sunny with the temperature in the mid-nineties.

After planning the mission the previous afternoon, we took off from George AFB about three hours after sunrise the following morning. We lined up on the runway, all twelve of us, in groups of four, with 500 feet between the groups, and with my four-ship being the farthest down the runway. We were loaded with six 500-pound nonexplosive practice bombs, three under each wing, and two 2,500-pound external fuel tanks, one on each wing. Because we were carrying bombs (actually cement-filled bombs, which we used to simulate the real thing), I briefed the flight of twelve to take off single ship, in twenty-second intervals, hence with twelve aircraft, it took three minutes and forty seconds before we were all airborne.

Once I was airborne (I took off first), I turned my aircraft to the north and proceeded to climb to twenty-six thousand feet (FL 260). I kept my speed in the climb at 300 knots (normally it's 350) to allow the trailing aircraft to join up.

By the time we reached 26,000 feet, all twelve aircraft had "joined" up . . . if you could say seven to ten miles between the lead two aircraft and the trailing two aircraft being joined up; some things in life are relative. From takeoff to landing, I had briefed that we were to fly in "tactical formation" (to allow fighter aircraft more survivability and maneuverability in high threat areas, we flew our aircraft pretty far from one another; in the ensuing paragraphs I will describe the distances and positions of each aircraft involved when "flying tactical"). Normally, this meant we flew two by two by two, each two-ship behind and slightly offset from the other two in front. (In a world without air traffic controllers and their control, we would have been flying at grossly different altitudes whilst en route to the low-level start point so as to make the formation harder to see, but the realities of flying in civilian airspace necessitated that we fly, all twelve of us, at exactly 26,000 feet.)

The first 100 nautical miles of the trip were flown at medium altitude to conserve fuel, and it was also considered "friendly" territory. Our route of flight took us over Edwards AFB and to the eastern border of the Sierra Nevada mountains. From just abeam Mount Whitney, in the Sierra Nevadas, I turned more north and east to fly to the northeast shore of a dry lake bed called Owens Lake; this is where the low-level portion of the flight was to begin.

The weather that day was beautiful, and since it was so clear and there were no pressing duties while cruising to the start of the low-level point, I chanced to glance at the world around me . . . I was not disappointed. To the left, west, and just immediately below me was Mount Whitney, California's highest peak. The morning sun's golden rays cascaded onto the mountain's eastern flank, causing the snow-crested mountain to appear to stretch to the heavens as if it was just waking up and performing a morning yawn. The lesser mountains, west of this imposing granite monolith, and in its shadow, were still enjoying their slumber, nestled up with white blankets of low-lying clouds. Beyond the mountains, and still farther west, I could see the blueness of the world's largest ocean, the Pacific. In direct contrast, to the wetness of the Pacific and the snow adorning the mountains immediately below me, the view to the east afforded me the opportunity to see Death Valley and the bleakness of the Mojave Desert beyond. And in front of me, as if meant to separate the two extremes, was the eastern side of the uprising Sierra Nevada mountain chain. This imposing wall of mountains, all sporting crowns of snow and, in their lower evaluations green wraps of pine, seemed to be nature's sentinels, standing guard against any intruders from the east. It was on mornings such as that, with views such as the one I just described, that I can understand the reason why birds sing the sweet melodies they do, as I caught myself many times whistling some unknown tune while cruising the skies.

As we approached Owens Lake, it was time to descend into the low-altitude environment in preparation for the start of the low-level portion of the mission. So I asked Los Angeles Center for a descent to an altitude below 18,000 feet. Once below FL180 I cancelled my IFR[51] clearance and sent the flight of twelve aircraft to our tactical radio frequency for the rest of the mission's ingress and egress. Once we began the low level we would never really climb above 500 feet above ground level, except to enter the traffic pattern at George AFB upon our return.

To descend to low altitude is not as simple as it might seem. Firstly, you don't want to go into a screaming dive because your ground speed has to be kept to the speed at which you planned to fly the mission ingress, which included the medium altitude segment (to include the takeoff and climb to altitude), the descent to the low-altitude structure, and finally the low-level itself. Starting the low-level at the correct time was critically important. Secondly, you don't want to be sixty degrees nose low 2000 feet above the

---

51. IFR—instrument flight rules. In the world of air traffic control and controllers and airliners, and airplanes in general, in order to keep separation between aircraft most airliners fly on an IFR clearance, on this type of clearance, air traffic control keeps continuous watch over the IFR aircraft and maintains a minimum separation between them. Also, the controllers are more directive in their control: aircraft cannot go where they want; they can ask for this route or that direction, but ATC, unless the aircraft is having an emergency, decides where the IFR traffic can go. Flying IFR is mandatory anytime an aircraft flies above FL 180 (18,000 feet) and when the weather is below certain cloud heights and visibility minimums. If an aircraft is not on an IFR clearance, then they are flying VFR, visual flight rules. Flying VFR means that you can fly without talking to a controller and have more freedom to maneuver at will. There are certain rules that apply, but in general when flying VFR you are much less restricted in where and how you fly.

ground because your turn radius is so high that you would impact the ground trying to pull out. So you descend in stages, starting at sixty degrees of dive angle, while at the higher altitudes, and as you got lower, you shallowed out to forty degrees and then twenty degrees and then ten degrees and then level flight.

While Rick Henry wasn't in my aircraft on that day, I knew that he'd flown on many missions like it. The heart pounds and sweat soaks you as you get closer to the target. As you near the start of the low-level, the backseaters stood by to update their old INS in the hope that it may help its accuracy. As previously discussed, the pilots in the newer fighters rarely worried about their INS being off course or in error, and even though F-4 crews viewed their INS with a healthy distrust, WSOs would still update the INS's position over the low-level start point in the hope that it might guide pilots unfailingly along their low-level route.

Since you didn't trust your INS's accuracy, you navigated, as previously stated, with a custom-made low level map, clock, and compass. Whereas an F-16 pilot's INS automatically tells him/her when they'll get to the next turn point and what ground speed to fly to get there and at what time they will arrive at that point, we F-4 guys had to calculate it ourselves. Assuming you were on time at the start of the low-level point, the lead aircraft adjusted his ground speed to match the flight-planned ground speed. The ground speed planned for low levels varied from mission to mission, based on a multitude of factors, but on today's mission we planned on flying at 480 knots until two turn points before the target whereupon we would accelerate to 540 knots for the target run and then go as fast as we could after we dropped the bombs. In between all this navigating and map reading and calculating time, you were visually checking all around you for bandits (usually you are looking inside the flight toward your wingman or lead, depending upon whom you are). And while you are map reading and navigating and checking for bandit aircraft, you are flying your aircraft and dodging rocks and hills and valley floors and trees and generally trying to fit the F-4s flight profile to match that of the terrain. At times you'll fly for minutes not really knowing where, exactly, you are, and, at eight to nine miles a minute, that can be a lot of uncertain ground. You learned early in the F-4 to become proficient in dead reckoning. Because of route study before the mission you know which "get well" points to look for, landmarks that are like sirens in the night, guiding you to your turn point. At each turn point you checked your actual time there, versus when you were supposed to be there and adjusted your speed to either gain or lose important seconds.

Before I move on I would like to make one thing perfectly clear with regards to flying at low level . . . when I say you are looking at the map and checking your ground speed or doing anything that involved looking in the cockpit, you usually looked very quickly at whatever it is you wanted to look at and then you looked back out again. You memorized what you looked at and then comprehended it as you were looking back outside. Hitting the ground was a serious consideration at 100 feet and 500 knots, and looking too long in the cockpit (we're talking one to two seconds) was the absolute max, down that low. You might have to take several glances to accomplish a task, but so be it. The PK, probability of kill, after hitting the ground was about 99.5 percent (I know of three guys who brought that down from 100).

While the pilots are reading their maps and calculating the times and doing "that pilot stuff," the WSOs are "tweaking" their radars, adjusting the electronics and manually fine tuning their old equipment to better search for hostile aircraft. The F-4's pulse radar didn't have the ground clutter rejection capability that the F-16 and 15 have. It showed everything that was "solid," be it a mountain or airplane or thick flock of birds. So the WSOs must finesse and cajole their antiquated black boxes to get the most from them and to be able to decipher the difference between geese migrating to a summer home or bandit aircraft intent upon shooting us down. They must also know the strengths and weaknesses of their own equipment, and the enemy's, to capitalize on the situation. And when they do suspect they have acquired an enemy aircraft on their radar, they will direct the flight to either turn left or right, off the center of the low-level corridor, to avoid that threat, thus compounding the pilot's navigational problem. The WSOs, too, in addition to checking their radars and visually checking six, are also helping to navigate and keep abreast of the flight's progress.

Because each aircraft had its own radar and pilot and WSO and bombs and air-to-air missiles and twenty-millimeter, cannon it was its own military arsenal with pilot and WSO trusting that the other would perform their respective duties with 110 percent of their ability. If either guy lets his performance slip, it could mean the difference between life or death. We were a team that was so finely honed that one word could have much meaning. We listened to the radio, and each other, with prejudice and spoke only for the express purpose of accomplishing a specific task.

And beginning with this single aircraft, you add two and then four, or more, and you now have a machine, a formidable war machine, in the singular, that is moving en masse to its destination. And if attacked, this machine can defend itself and if it loses a part of itself, it can still continue and it can split up and divide to survive to continue to its target. Like a column of ants on a mission, you can step on some, but their independent nature allows the others to doggedly continue on their quest, undaunted, deviating if need be, but unstoppable. However, unlike an ant, the F-4, now being more like a bee, had a sting to it; trying to swat it could extract a certain measure of pain.

The goal of this "machine" was to destroy whatever it was ordered to destroy, and the sheer beauty of the land that we were flying over went unnoticed in our singular design to accomplish our goal. The mountains were noticed, not because of their beauty, but by the question, "Is that my turn point?" Or, is there an enemy aircraft lurking behind that mountain? Old ghost towns passed underneath, the sounds of the spirits in them drowned out by the scream of afterburning wagons and the voices of still living souls in them, urging their fire-propelled chariots on to distant lands.

As hard as it may seem for the lead aircraft, in this case today my WSO and me, who were navigating for the whole flight of twelve, the trailing fighters, spaced every one and a half to two miles behind each other in pairs of two, have the difficult task of trying to maintain a "visual" on the aircraft in front of them. They curse the purple mountains' majesties, as they compound their problem of trying to keep track of the preceding fighter, as well as possibly hiding a bandit aircraft or two. As the lead aircraft flies a sinewy flight path through the mountains trying to terrain mask, so too do the trailing aircraft try to fly the same terrain-matching profile. But at times the visual between the leaders and the trailers is lost and the trailing aircraft "DRs" where he thinks the preceding aircraft is. It could be a nerve-wracking wait, guessing, hoping, and sometimes praying your leader would come into sight. In the meantime, the pilots and WSOs in the trailing aircraft are assessing their maps and compasses and clocks and radar and the sky and the ground to check on their progress to the target and for any sign of hostile aircraft.

It must be understood that all the pilots in all the aircraft had the innate responsibility (innate because it was in a pilot's personal code of ethics, or should have been) to know where he was on the low level so that if his lead should either crash or have to abort the mission, then each aircraft could continue to the target. Also, if the lead had a system failure of some kind, he may pass the navigation lead to another aircraft, his wingman for example, so knowing where you were, at all times was essential for your situational awareness. However, if you were over hostile territory and your wingman aborted, had to go back to base, then you went with him. In the USAF, the basic, or minimum, fighting force consisted of two aircraft, which was called an element; formations of twenty to 100 fighter aircraft or more were built upon this two-aircraft concept. Visual mutual support was of paramount importance in those days, and having each aircraft flying a line abreast formation, even as a two-ship, offered both aircraft the ability to maneuver and visually watch over each other. As the Ice Man said in Top Gun, "You never leave your wingman."

Wingmen, who are flying abreast of their leaders,[52] flew on one side, or the other, of their leader, and would try to maintain a

---

52. Leaders—even in a two-ship, one aircraft was designated as a lead aircraft, and one as a wingman. This lead-wingman designation pertained to four-ship flights of aircraft as well, with the overall lead aircraft being designated as number 1 and the wingmen were numbers 2, 3, and 4. But since you flew with only two aircraft in a line-abreast formation, the other two aircraft, in trail of numbers 1 and 2, aircraft numbers 3 and 4, flew in trail of the "leaders." This was called a "box" formation, and the number 3 aircraft was designated the "element" lead. If the number 1 aircraft was shot down, then the number 3 aircraft (usually) picked up the overall lead of the flight, delegating either number 2 or number 4 as an element lead, and then they flew in trail of the number three aircraft; this was called a "vic" formation. This "ranking" stopped with four aircraft, i.e., you did not count 1, 2, 3, 4, 5, 6 . . . and so on. It was always 1 and 2, or maybe 1, 2, 3, 4, and then back to 1, 2, 3, 4, etc. Each four-ship, to eliminate confusion, was given its own call sign, hence the reason for all fighter pilots having their own personal call-sign.

6000- to 12,000-foot line-abreast position. As their lead maneuvers through a canyon or mountainous area, he/she might "close it up," bring their aircraft closer than normal to their leader, to maintain better mutual support. If the flight was approaching a ridgeline running perpendicular, or almost so, to its flight-path, the wingman would look for a low-point, or saddleback, as would lead, to fly through. Just before reaching the top of the opening of the ridge, each aircraft would roll inverted, and the pilots would begin to pull the aircraft down so as to conform to the mountain(s) and not fly too excessively high above the surrounding terrain. There are times where you are "pulling" through a notch and all that you can see to the left, right and "above" (remember . . . you are upside down) are hard, impact-resistant boulders, and maybe you are fifty feet away from them as you flash by at 500 knots . . . all the time "pulling" the aircraft "down" to conform to the mountain's contour. Over a wide alkaline valley or above a plateau, or any expanse of flat earth, assuming good visibility, the wingman will fly wide of their lead, spreading the formation out, so as to not highlight both aircraft if there is an enemy lurking about looking for wing flashes of glint off of canopies. The wingman has a tough job, for he is literally trying to "hang on" to his lead, and in the process of "hanging on," he is also navigating and visually checking the formation for enemy aircraft and trying to spot any aircraft flying low level in front of him, so as to avoid a collision within the formation, and in general, the wingman is trying to maintain mutual support. In the purest form of flight lead-wingman covenants, his sole job is to keep a visual with his lead and fly off that lead while trying to have a clue as to where he is on the low level. Often the inexperienced pilot's situational awareness was so out to lunch (screwed up!) that he didn't realize he was at the target area until lead was popping up in preparation to drop his bombs or was dropping them!

Approaching the target, the WSOs search their radar with even more conviction and the pilots readied their bombs for release by selecting switches that tell the aircraft which bombs you want to drop, in what millisecond interval, and then setting the master arm switch to "arm." Additionally, in-between performing all the afore-mentioned navigation and formation maintaining and bandit look-out duties, the crews rechecked the attack plan with its associated headings, times, airspeeds and bomb delivery parameters, as well as reminding oneself of what the specific target is. (When a large target area, such as an airfield, is to be bombed, individual targets on the airfield are singled out, such as aircraft parked on the ramp or fuel storage tanks. The mission frag is what identifies the target complex and the DMPIs on it (desired mean point of impact... the individual targets), but it is up to the mission commander to determine who bombs what, and in certain cases, special ordnance is requested for specific targets, such as cratering bombs when bombing a runway.)

On this particular day, my twelve-ship was attacked from behind by two F-16s, which caused the four trailing aircraft in my flight to perform a 180-degree turn to defend themselves and to try and bring some weapons to bear on the attackers. And then two more F-16s "tapped," pounced upon, the other four German aircraft! In short order, it was like a mini Battle of Britain with aircraft everywhere! Break turn calls[53] were heard on the radio, aircraft were calling shots

---

53. Break turn—if an enemy aircraft was behind you, naturally you wanted to protect your rear and turn to bring weapons to bear on him. So, if you saw an aircraft behind you and threatening you in particular, or your wingman, then you turn as fast as you needed, depending on how threatened you felt. Men have "broken", over G'd, the Phantom per-forming life-or-death break turns. But it must also be said that there were times when not turning, increasing your speed, and maybe decreasing your altitude were better options; it was a judgment call. Going faster and lower would shrink a missile's engagement range.

on the bandits, and the bandits were calling kills on the good guys. And as if this wasn't enough excitement, the surface-to-air missile sites were locking their radars onto the F-4s with the intent to shoot them down. So, in addition to the constant radio chatter of the other aircraft and the intercom communications between you and your WSO, you also had the "bell and whistle" sounds emanating from the radar, warning receivers telling you that enemy radars, either from an aircraft or surface-to-air missile site, were looking at you.

Through all the chaos and mayhem that occurred as we neared the target, my wingman and I made it, seemingly unscathed, so far.

Because I had been turning so much en route to the target, due to the hard reality of the bandits behind me and the paranoid calls from the WSOs in my lead four-ship who were seeing "mirages" with every sweep of the radar, I had gotten considerably off course. Believing the enemy behind me was either dead or satisfied with its meal of German F-4s and not coming after my four-ship, and ignoring the delusions of WSOs calling for turns when my WSO had no target in sight, I made a sharp left turn to a rather prominent mountain that was at my ten o'clock position and about twenty miles away. This mountain was a get-well point for me and immediately gave me total SA[54] as to where I was. Believing that no more F-16s existed in the world, but still not sure about the F-15s' whereabouts, I increased our speed to make up for lost time. In a little over two minutes, I was in a right turn, rounding the north side of this rather tall mountain, when my WSO said he had a radar contact on a possible bandit!

---

54. Situational Awareness is a recognition of where you've been, where you are, where you are going, and what you believe has happened, is happening now, and will happen in the future. It is influenced and made more astute by your total knowledge and comprehension of the situation and events that have happened and are presently happening when combined with the successful application of previous experiences and keen intuition.

We had been flying at an uneven 100 feet above the ground due to undulating terrain and were zipping along at 500 knots. We were about halfway through the turn when the WSO said he had a radar contact. We were pretty low to the ground and turning at fairly high G, so I can't say I was looking too far in front of me since I really didn't want to hit the ground, so my bandit lookout wasn't as detailed as it should have been at that point. We were also about two minutes from our target, and I was getting ready for the bomb run, so you can imagine that the bandit call from my WSO as we were turning around the mountain really caught my attention!

I briefly looked inside the cockpit at the radar (normally, the WSO tells you where the bandit is verbally, so all you have to do is look to the position where he is directing your eyes, but since I had been looking in the cockpit, briefly, to check my map, as I was going outside with my eyes, I glanced at the radar scope to save the WSO some words) for the relative position of the target—the front cockpit of the F-4 has a radar scope—and then looked outside to where I thought the bandit was. Sure enough, there was another F-16 . . . Man, the USAF sure bought a lot of them! He was about three miles away, a thousand feet or so higher than us, and in a fairly hard (turning rapidly but not at the maximum capability of the aircraft) right-hand turn, but his turn was taking him through a nose-on position where he was about to go belly up to me! My WSO was screaming for me to shoot a missile, particularly since he was locked on to the "Viper" (nickname of the F-16). We were loaded with two radar-guided AIM-7Es and two heat-seeking AIM-9Ps. (AIM-9Ps—in reality, we had "simulated ordnance." In place of the AIM-7 missiles were AIM-7 plugs that told the aircraft's weapons system an AIM-7[s] was loaded in one of four AIM-7 weapons stations. The AIM-9s were a bit different. We had four AIM-9 stations, two on each wing, but we did carry a full-size AIM-9P missile, sans warhead and rocket motor. The seeker, though, which gave guidance commands to the missile's autopilot, was there. That was required because we needed to know if the missile was "seeing" the heat source of the intended target and the only way to know that was to have an actual seeker on a dummy missile; the seeker head, when it saw the heat source, would emit a growl-type noise that we heard through our intercom), so when you armed up the system, you saw, via your weapons panel, two AIM-7s—we had two "plugs" on this aircraft—and one AIM-9P [we limited ourselves to two AIM-9P shots]. When you "fired" your missile, the system "stepped" automatically to the next loaded AIM-7 station, or went right back to the AIM-9 if that missile had been selected.)

My missile of choice while flying that low was the heat-seeking AIM-9P, but the F-16 was coming straight at me, and the AIM-9s we had were not all aspect; meaning I couldn't shoot him while he was nose on to me. I needed more of a tail aspect; however, the more he turned, the sweeter the shot got. I was very low, so I had to climb a bit to fire the AIM-7. (An AIM-7 is kicked off the bottom of the aircraft and drops a bit before the rocket motor fires, about forty-eight inches. While it doesn't need more than twenty-five feet for this whole process, I always felt that a couple of hundred feet was better than 100.)

I "fired" (I pulled the trigger, but obviously, no actual missile came off!) one AIM-7 and waited as the F-16 continued his right-hand turn. My WSO and I continued to close in and with about a mile separating us, and with him heading away from me,

I switched to "heat" on the weapons control panel. With a good look-up angle—his aircraft was framed by only the blue sky—I put the AIM-9's seeker head aiming reticle, which is illuminated on the front windscreen of the F-4, on the target. The growl from the AIM-9 was instantaneous, like a wild child being held back by a parent. I waited a second, there was no warbling of the tone, and then squeezed the trigger to let the little varmint loose. The hunted had killed the hunter. (Hunter—there were rules of thumb that we used to determine if we had killed this or that bandit, based upon the distance, altitude, and speed. On the F-4 we didn't have a heads-up display [HUD] or any VCR tape recording the actual shot. We could record, using an onboard VCR recorder, the radar scope image, to verify the radar lock-on, and the VCR tape also recorded the intercom communications as well as transmissions from the UHF radio and the RHAW's audio emissions. In addition, the VCR tape recorded the sound of the AIM-9's seeker head growl as it tracked the heat source from the target. Finally, in some cases, like in Red Flag wars, when an aircraft took a missile shot, a signal was sent to the Red Flag computers, and they computed, based upon actual archived missile shots and the parameters of the aircraft and their weapons systems and the missiles they were shooting, as to whether or not the shot was a kill. In the end, though, nothing was absolute, and unless the missiles really started flying, you had no idea if your missile shot[s] would have been good or not.)

There was no time for a victory roll or a celebration yell because just as the missiles had timed out and my backseater and I called a kill, to record on the tapes and also to let GCI[55] know of the kill, our RHAW lit up with video and audio

RHAW—radar homing and warning. Ever since the latter stages of the Vietnam War, and due to the widespread use of SAMs, fighter aircraft were being fitted with onboard receivers that told the pilot and WSO if a SAM radar was either tracking them and/or had shot a missile at them. The early RHAW gear was very basic but quickly became very sophisticated and included the ability to detect airborne radar from other fighter aircraft in its "sniffing" abilities. On my F-4 that day, we had an ALR-46 RHAW set. When a new/different ground radar began to track us it gave what we called "new guy" audio, beeping about three times to say, "Hey, someone new is looking at you!" You'd check the RHAW gear to see what the beeping was about and from what direction the radar was located. To find this direction, you looked on a smallish, round CRT visual display mounted, on the F-4, just on the forward, upper right of both cockpits. A symbol for the type

---

55. GCI—ground control intercept. They monitored our frequency for safety and gave bandit bulls-eye information as we flew through the Nellis Range Complex. Bulls-eye information is not specific in nature, but general. The "frag" may specify a certain landmark that is called "bulls-eye," and GCI will broadcast to whoever's on the frequency that bandits are detected XX (xx meaning whatever distance at the time) miles west, east, north, south, etc., of bulls-eye. While I would listen to it, I also took it with a grain of salt as many times I got to where the "bandits" were, and they had disappeared. In the Red Flag Operations, building these air wars could be seen real time as they occurred. Each aircraft carried an AIS pod on its wing that transmitted a multitude of aircraft information to the many antennas that sat on the barren and isolated mountaintops throughout the military airspace. This data was sent to a main computer that (1) correlated the aircraft and their movement/position relative to each other and the geographic area they were flying over, (2) generated a computer icon of the aircraft, (3) displayed all of the aircraft that were involved in the battle on a huge movie theatre screen in the auditorium. You literally could be like one of the angels watching from above as the battle unfolds. Tapes were made of the battle to be replayed at the debrief for training/learning.

of SAM, SA-2, 3, 4, 6, 8, etc., would illuminate at that position on the scope relative to the actual o'clock position of the missile site, and the distance that the symbol was from the center of the scope was the "black box's" best guess on its relative range. What would really get your attention with the RHAW system was a missile launch. When a missile was launched, that bad boy (ALR-46) would detect it and start howling! There was no doubt when a missile was launched, unless you had the volume for the system turned down; and even then, your backseater would be screaming at you to maneuver to either break the radar's lock or cause the missile to miss. Additionally, the system, as I said earlier, could detect the radars from other fighter aircraft, as well as our own. So if an F-16 locked on to you, you knew it! The F-15 was different. In certain modes, the explanation of which exceeds what I want to convey in this book, you could not tell if they were locked on to you, and when you could, it usually meant that they had already shot a missile . . . not good.

Since I had highlighted myself by coming out of the low altitude environment (if you can call 300 feet above the ground highlighting yourself), a SAM site had locked us up and was about to fire! The "new guy" audio yell in my ears of the SAM site's missile tracking radar locking us up was unmistakable, as was the symbol indicating what type of missile it was on my radar warning receiver's scope. In addition to the type of SAM, its relative position, and estimate of range were also indicated on the radar warning display. The RHAW showed the offending site was at my twelve o'clock. I immediately asked the backseater to "drop"—actually it is ejected—chaff,[56] and I started a very hard left-hand descending turn. At 300 feet above the ground, I can't say I descended too rapidly, but I had to turn to put the missile site at my three or nine o'clock; in this case I turned left to put it on my right side, and I wanted to get low to try and terrain mask. (Terrain Masking—there are two types of terrain masking: direct and indirect. Besides dispensing chaff, another way to try and defeat a missile tracking radar, or, well any radar site that was trying to find or track you, was to hide behind the ground, or buildings . . . if there were any big ones nearby. Usually, mountains were the best, as they were the highest; hills would work, too, anything with vertical development that you could put between your aircraft and the radar. Indirect terrain masking was the opposite; you put vertical development "behind/next-to" you, but you wanted to be close to it. In other words, you put yourself on the nearside of the mountain but still used the mountain as a "noisy" backdrop to camouflage your aircraft from the radar. With newer radar sites, which have pulse Doppler radar or have moving target indicators, indirect terrain masking is not nearly as effective as direct.)

I wanted to get the missile to the beam (beam, meaning put the missile directly at my three or nine o'clock position) so I could see it and then maneuver against it. As I got the missile site on my beam, I saw a "Smokey Sam" going up in the air; it looked to be about four

---

56. Chaff is as old as radar itself. The F-4 carried a normal load of sixty chaff cartridges and thirty flares. The chaff cartridges were about the size of 12-gauge shotgun shells and held thousands of bits of very thin fiberglass rods, cut of different lengths, and coated with aluminum. When ejected by an explosive charge these cartridges disgorged their aluminum rods in a "puff" and created a "blob" that only radar could see, certain radars anyway. The F-16's and F-15's radar rejected the blobs as they immediately slowed after being dispensed and these fighters' radar rejected any targets that slowed down to a speed close to zero. But the surface-to-air missile sites' radars, particularly the older systems, were more susceptible to this deception.

miles away. I headed for the dirt when I saw the missile as I knew the SA-3 was good down to 100 feet, and I intended to "blend" with the local vegetation . . . of which, seeing that I was flying over a desert, there wasn't much. There was a fundamental rule when flying near the ground though, that I never forgot as I neared it. The "PK"—probability of kill—of hitting the ground at 500 knots was almost 100 percent. As I said earlier, I know a couple of guys who had brought that statistic down to 99.5 or so, but I was never one to want to screw with trying to change a statistical model. Also, the odds of the missile not hitting me, based upon my maneuvering and other factors, was a much safer bet, so I wasn't going to kill myself for the sake of worrying about being on the "evening news," however you looked at it.

Beam —the idea was to "beam" the missile, put it on your left of right wing's side, pop chaff to confuse the tracking radar, and then start maneuvering up or down—fighter pilots call it using the vertical—to try and get the missile to miss your aircraft. Your goal was to get the missile to miss your aircraft . . . the farther the better since the warheads in some missiles were pretty big. The earlier missiles, SA-2, 3, 4, were fairly easy to out-maneuver . . . assuming you saw them. However, the older missiles were big, relatively speaking, and their booster motors [for initial launch] and sustainer rocket motors [to give them range] made a lot of flame and smoke. The SA-6 and 8 were newer missiles and were more difficult to both see and deceive. But as I was saying, if you could get the missile going up, and then you go down, or vice versa, and you did this a couple of times, you got the missile out of sync with your movements and sometimes the missile would tumble out of control, or the radar, because of chaff, may break lock and the missile "went stupid." At the least, you hoped the missile would miss you by A LOT, and then you could be on your way. However, the enemy usually shot more than one missile and then may shoot from more than one missile site! You could have your hands full if you were the target of a couple of SAM sites! Sometimes, you carried a jamming pod that would jam either the enemy's tracking radar, acquisition radar, or missile guidance uplink. When they worked they worked well, these jammers, but they weren't a panacea, and they had their limitations.

As I neared the ground, I turned my tail away from the missile site and continued in a hard left turn.

Non-pilots have often asked me how I turn at so low an altitude . . . do I look at the instruments, the VVI (vertical velocity indicator), the artificial horizon indicator—what? At very low altitude, where hitting any obstacle is a very real and immediate threat, my eyes are glued to the outside world, specifically in the direction in which I am turning. I judged altitude based upon experience, occasional looks at the radar altimeter, relative motion of the ground (going by the size of vegetation/dwellings, which in itself can be dangerous). When you're pulling five Gs at low altitude and turning, and covering three football fields in a second, you need to look into your turn to make sure you will clear any terrain you might be turning into, so it is imperative to keep your eyes outside. Also, you need to clear the sky in front of you to make sure you don't hit another aircraft, be it your wingman, another friendly, or a bandit, smacking any of the aforementioned could definitely ruin your day. Finally, while turning, you had to be very careful where you put your lift vector. In a turn, you could easily develop very high descent rates, so you had to be careful to not overbank for too long, or else that too could ruin your day.

It is hard to imagine, as you read this, the environment that you are in when all of this is going on. My WSO and I were turning at five times the force of gravity, 5 Gs, all the while as the ground was moving by in a blur at 840 feet per second about 100 feet below. While turning at such a low altitude and trying to avoid the rocks so as to not make spam out of the WSO and me, I was looking for landmarks so as to get us back on course and get to the target; and adding even more stress, I was looking for enemy aircraft and other SAM sites, not to mention looking for my wingman. I could have pulled more than 5Gs if I needed to, but with the bombs and fuel, etc., pulling more could have over-G'd the aircraft, depleted my air-speed/energy state, or both. Nope, 5Gs was the norm for that kind of maneuvering, unless of course you had to do what it took to save yourself/aircraft/both.

The WSO too was looking for the wingman and visually check-ing for bandit aircraft in addition to using his radar to scan the area ahead and to the left and right as we turned.

Sweat was dripping from the top of my helmet, just above my eyes and I raised my visor to wipe the saline solution before it stung my eyes and made seeing more difficult; however, the eyes are not the only sense that was being assaulted.

My ears were acutely aware of any audio emanations from the earphones built into my helmet. I remember hearing my second ele-ment, numbers 3 and 4, call "split" over the radio as I maneuvered against the SAM site, meaning they are not being attacked and are continuing on the low level to the target, thusly leaving my number 2 man and myself to fight our own way out—that's a "standard" for most missions, nothing cowardly about that, and I expected his call as soon as I started fighting against the missile. I was definitely spring-loaded for any new guy audio sounds from the RHAW gear . . . not wanting any! Also, I heard GCI broadcasting in the blind that there were bandits just west of bull's eye and moving east. Finally, as if the previous "decibel deluge" wasn't enough, my WSO was telling me the SA-3 site's radar had broken lock and that the "IP"—initial point, the last point on the low-level from which the bomb run begins—was in the INS.

I didn't consciously notice the extra weight of five bodies on me as I held my head slightly forward and tilted so as to look in the direction in which I was turning; after flying fighters for a couple of years, you get used to pulling Gs. In fact, I kinda missed the "feeling" when I hadn't flown in a while.

I continued my turn to head toward the south, toward where I thought the IP was located. The SA-3 site was now at my six o'clock, moving to seven, and we were still at very low altitude, since I didn't want to become the poster boy for the SAM missile sites in the area. And all the while, as I continued this turn, I was dodging small hills and big rocks at almost 600 mph. I continued the turn to aim where I visually "thought" we should be heading and as I rolled wings level, to my surprise, I saw my wingman in perfect line abreast tactical formation!

After 200 miles of flying a twisty low level and flying in valleys and canyons; over mountains and hills; after performing defensive break turns to avoid being shot by surface to air missiles; after speeding up to 600 knots and then slowing down to 400 knots; with all of this maneuvering being done with very little consideration for my wingman and without a single whine from him over the radio, there he was, my number 2 man, in a perfect line abreast position for the attack. Awesome.

I just needed to make sure I was headed in the right direction for the attack! Quickly checking my map, I confirmed that the edge of the small hill, next to the dry lake bed with a dirt road coming from its northern "shore" was indeed the IP. I then looked at the clock in the aircraft to make sure we weren't too early or late for the attack. I had hacked the clock at the start of the low level and was referencing it for total time on the low level. If we were too early we would have done a big 360-degree orbit to kill time and if too late, well, we had a "dump target"—a backup target that was more lightly defended than the primary . . . a.k.a. desert—and we would have proceeded to bomb it.

Amazingly enough, as we overflew the IP, I glanced at the INS distance-to-go window and it showed us two miles off, which wasn't too shabby given the older technology.

With my wingman in position for the attack, about a mile to my immediate right, I proceeded to stabilize our ground speed at 540 knots, the speed planned for our bomb release. We also had to "climb" to 200 feet above the ground, as this was our delivery altitude: we were dropping six parachute-retarded bombs, military designation BSU-49, from a level delivery (The BSU-49/Mk-82 drag unit/bomb combination was used to deliver 500-pound bombs from very low altitude. When the bomb is released, a wire on the aircraft pulls an arming wire on the bomb fuse, arming it, and another one pulls a release for the "drag chute" [ballute]. This ballute quickly slows the bomb to provide safe separation between the delivery aircraft and the exploding bomb). A quick glance at my thigh, upon which sat a piece of paper—in fighter pilot lingo we called it a "lineup" card—which had, among other things, my bombing parameters and target info. Looking at the card reaffirmed my own memory of our targets (aircraft parked on the airfield ramp) and re-assured me that my flight was indeed heading for the correct target area, and, lastly, was in the proper position for the attack.

Once on the target run, a lot of attention is paid to being exactly on parameters, which requires flying the correct airspeed, radar altitude, and drift angle. You want to destroy the target on the first pass so you do not have to come back tomorrow, or worse yet, not get your bombs off on the first pass and have to reattack (if a reattack was briefed). Reattacks were "bad" as the enemy now was wide awake, if they weren't on your first pass, and if one of your wingmen got some bombs off, they were most likely pretty pissed off that you were bombing them, and I am pretty certain they would want a piece of you and your WSO's butts. WSOs were of supreme help during those vulnerable seconds on the bomb run as they kept a visual lookout for enemy aircraft and SAM launches. Up until the actual release of the bombs, if you had to save your aircraft, or flight, from attack, you would do so . . . you had to stay vigilant!

That day, the actual IP to target run was almost uneventful, given the hell we had to fly through just to get here. Flying as well as I could to maintain the aforementioned bombing parameters, I would alternately look at the airspeed, radar altimeter, and bombing reticle, which is a red illuminated circle with a little dot (pipper) in the middle of it. This reticle is projected onto a slanted piece of thick glass, "combining glass," and is directly in front of your face, but over the instrument panel, and right behind/below the front part of the canopy. Looking out the front windscreen/canopy I could see both the pipper and the ground beyond it. I let the pipper run along the ground, and when it touched the target, assuming my airspeed, altitude and aircraft pitch attitude are correct, I released the bombs via a "pickle" button on the flight control stick. On the weapons release panel, before takeoff, I set the bomb fall interval so as to allow fifty feet spacing between each bomb impact. Thusly, when I "hit" the pickle button I needed to hold it for a couple of seconds as the bombs release in microsecond intervals and if you release the pickle button too early then all of your bombs my not drop-off (you can actually feel the bombs as they thunk off the bomb carrying ejector racks).

Between my wingman and I, we dropped twelve bombs on an "enemy" airfield. My bombs landed on an airfield ramp loaded with aircraft, and number 2's bombs were dropped on some ops buildings. According to my timing, all the bombs were released within our TOT window (Time Over Target). There was not another aircraft or Smokey SAM in sight as we screamed along at 200 feet and 600 mph over the targets, disgorging our venom.

Once the bombs were released though, we weren't home free yet!

I went into "min" afterburner—that's when you see flames coming out the back of the jet engine's tailpipe, purposeful flames that is, not your "Holy crap, I'm on fire!" flames—accelerated to six hundred knots plus, so as to quickly exit the immediate target area, and turned the flight to the egress heading.

We were now only a two ship. As crowded as the skies had just been, they were now empty, but listening to the number of bandit calls on the radio, it was obvious to my WSO and I that there were still plenty of bandit aircraft in the area.

We had exited the target area to the southeast, initially, and were still in the western areas of the Nellis range complex. I had Beatty VORTAC tuned into the TACAN receiver and was headed for it when we caught up to a lone RF-4 from who knows where. (The RF-4 was built for one purpose—to take pictures of potential targets, take after-strike photos of targets that should have been bombed, and snap pictures of various other things that the higher ups wanted photographed. They were generally faster than bomber F-4s because they were more aerodynamically sleek and they were lighter.) We were flying at about 300 feet AGL and the RF-4 was slightly higher and about three miles in front of us. My WSO locked onto the aircraft with our radar and with that, the "RF" lit his afterburners, dropped down to less than 100 feet AGL, and literally left us in the dust! Garry, my heretofore unnamed backseater, and I were laughing our butts off, thinking how much we must have scared that guy when an F-15 locked onto us from our six o'clock; now it was who were scared!

After my call to the wingman to push it up due to a bandit RHAW strobe at our six o'clock, Garry spotted an F-15 about two miles or so behind us, quite a bit higher and not closing which wasn't surprising since we were accelerating past 650 knots and low enough to scorch the desert cacti with the heat from our afterburners. In conjunction with increasing our speed and descending, number 2 spread out even wider on me in order to make the bandit commit to just one of us.

We were only chased for a minute or so when the Eagle pulled up and turned away and since we did not hear a shot or kill call from GCI we figured we had not been shot. As before, after the initial flurry of activity it got quiet on the radios and once again we, our flight of two was alone.

After the Eagle left us I switched our flight to a different working frequency so we could talk, if we had to, in private.

With 140 miles to go to the base, according to the INS, we were back in "good guy" territory and since I didn't expect any more threats attacking us I told my wingman to go chase and with that call he dropped into a one mile trail position. We had some extra fuel to burn so I decided to enjoy the morning and told number 2 we were going to do some sightseeing.

A southeast-northwest running set of mountains stood tall, as we approached them rapidly from the north, their chiseled crests illuminated by the undiluted rays of a desert sun still well below its zenith. As soon as I cleared the mountains I turned hard right, flew for a few miles and then cranked in a hard left turn and entered Death Valley.

I was favoring the west side of the valley and had slowed the formation to a rather sedate 400 knots indicated when I spotted a couple of large RVs a few miles ahead. I decided to give them a close visual inspection so I pushed the throttles up to military power as we approached at very low altitude As I got right over top of them I rolled on a knife edge and looked down. I saw four people standing side by side, looking up and waving! We, were smoking along at close to 600 mph so even though my F-4 passed overhead in relative silence, just a short distance behind me, and furiously trying to catch up, was the absolute shrill scream of a Phantom in near full grunt! As my wingman passed over the same two couples he said they had their hands over their ears but were smiling!

After the RV encounter we flew over "Skidoo," an abandoned gold mine and from where the term "23 Skidoo" comes (twenty-three miles was the length of the aqueduct that brought water to this old desert ghost town and mine area).

From Skidoo we continued south with the Panamint mountains just to our right. Before crossing into Panamint Valley, I decided to fly near the tops of the mountains just for the heck of it. As I cruised along, admiring the view all around me, I would occasionally see a little spot of trees and plants, nestled in tight little rock folds near the peaks. In contrast to the aridity of the valley floor, these mountain redoubts were like little ecological islands unto themselves. With their green vegetation and tiny streams, they looked so inviting and cozy and yet, owing to their remoteness above the valley floor, I suspect the only visitors to these sanctuaries were less than human. I have always been fascinated by these nature hideouts, and I swear that one day, I will visit one of these "castle keeps" of nature.

After admiring the Panamint Mountains, I took us into the same named valley barely clearing the mountain peaks as we dropped into the narrow and very flat valley. What number 2 did behind us as we were sightseeing I have no idea. Occasionally I would glimpse him in the mirrors, or Garry would make mention of his position as he maneuvered from side to side.

Eventually the valley played out and with fuel now getting low, I climbed the formation to a few thousand feet and slowed down to 300 knots so my wingman could join up in preparation for recovery at George AFB. Coming up initial, we pitched out over the numbers and flew as tight an overhead pattern as we dared; my wingman and I were the first of the twelve to return.

During the mission debrief, we learned that six F-4s had been killed and that four F-16s had been shot; though in reality, unless real missiles are flying those "electronic" kills are always taken with a grain of salt. The one F-15 that chased me, after coming off the target, couldn't get close enough to shoot before his fuel supply got too low. The optical scorers, who scored the bombing accuracy, indicated that 60 percent of the bombs were on target and all bombs were dropped within the TOT window. As for the lone RF-4, no one knows who he was or where he came from. Finally, the SA-3 site that engaged me as I approached the target said that between my maneuvering, chaff, and indirect terrain masking, the odds were less than 10 percent of a successful guide by the missile.

That night at the bar the Germans were buying. They had passed their fighter weapons course, and they were going back to the fatherland. All in all, it was a good mission, a great mission in fact. We went in, hit the target, and yeah, we "lost" a few airplanes, but considering the difference in technology between the F-4 and the wonder jets, we should have been decimated. Instead, we "shot down" a few of the F-16s and due to the wisdom of deviating "a bit" when coming off the target, the F-15s were hard pressed to catch us.

I'll never forget that flight. It represented what flying the F-4 was all about—tough, macho (this was the '80s and "macho" was still in vogue), and with a street fighting mentality. We busted our butts to fly well, and we loved every minute of it. As much as I sweated, I'd sweat some more, and I loved it more. The Phantom was the last of the stick-and-rudder airplanes, and the kinship that I had with my backseaters will never be replaced. At 500 knots and 100 feet, he trusted me with his life, and I trusted him when he would tell me my "six" was clear or scan the area ahead with his radar.

I often wonder, "What is the measure of a man?" Is it by what he does? What he did? Or is it by what he thinks and feels, or what is in his spirit or soul? Everyone has his own answer. One of my favorite sayings about this is from Martin Luther King Jr., who said, "The ultimate measure of a man is not where he stands in moments of comfort and convenience, but where he stands at times of challenge and controversy."

There is no doubt that Rick Henry had faced many difficult trials and challenges while flying fighters. And though time's march and life's unpredictable erosions have taken Rick out of the cockpit, the memory of his valor and devotion in those trying times didn't go unnoticed by me and no matter what distance we may be from "where we have been," in both time and/or geographical miles, what the heart holds dear is never very far from us and the examples we have set.

. . .

Besides the absolute wonder of flying fighters over some amazingly beautiful scenery, another joy for me during my time in the military, particularly the early years, were all the great fighter pilots with whom I flew and socialized.

I was very fortunate to meet speed-of-sound-buster Chuck Yeager when he came to the fighter group's dining in as the guest of honor.

With Chuck was another aviation great, Joe Engle. Joe flew many missions in the iconic X-15 and then flew as commander on the second space shuttle flight, Columbia, in 1981. To top off Joe's laurels, he is a recipient of the USAF Distinguished Flying Cross.

The dining in[57] Yeager and Engle attended was one for the record books. I was Mr. Vice, military jargon for master of ceremonies, and as such I was tasked with helping the evening to flow in an orderly fashion as cocktails, dinner, speeches, and dessert were served up. In the world of fighter pilots, at least back in the 1980s, there was no such thing as proper decorum at a dining in since it was assumed that things would get a bit rowdy. Nobody was disappointed at this

---

57. Dining in—a formal military dinner that includes only military personnel, not friends, dates, or spouses.

event, of that I can assure you. I think the crowning moment was when I had to drink grog from the "grog bowl" (a toilet bowl, which I think they cleaned beforehand, that was brought in and which held some seriously alcoholic and putrid drink). Upon me downing the "grog," and then facing and saluting the mess (all the guys attending, except the head table guests, were the mess), and after putting the drinking glass upon my head in traditional dining-in fashion, I found myself the target for hundreds of objects being thrown at me from the mess. Dropping to the floor in quick fashion, I managed to dodge most of the arsenal the men had saved during dinner . . . but there was this one huge slab of roast beef I saw fly over my head; it was medium rare and wafted end over end, and it would have slammed me right in the chest had I not ducked. Unfortunately for the mess and me, General Chuck Yeager was directly in the line of fire after I dropped to the floor. He was seated at the head table, which was on the other side of the grog bowl, opposite the mess. A student (I do know his name but won't mention it) was the launcher of said weapon, and his throw would have been a thing of beauty had it hit me, but it didn't, and General Yeager was collateral damage. Given that the General had been a fighter pilot for all of his career, I assumed he would have laughed off such fighter pilot shenanigans as a "boys will be boys," but . . .ahhhh, no. He was pretty pissed. Once I collected myself and was properly seated at my own table, which was apart from everyone and where I was conspicuously visible to all, Colonel McMurdy signaled to me, very prematurely I might add, that the smoking lamp was to be lit so we could all take a pee break. Upon our return from the break the whole mess was informed in a very stern talking-to from the colonel (he was the group commander) that our behavior was uncouth and disrespectful to General Yeager. The colonel then informed the mess and me that no more pranks were to be done, nor was food to be thrown, and that we were to act like officers and gentlemen. As we all sat there solemnly, listening to General Yeager talk, his speech coming after our ass chewing, it suddenly dawned on me that I had taped a very loud alarm clock underneath General Yeager's chair, and it was due to go off, soon . . .

Shortly after that dining in I got to instruct Joe Engle in the F-4. I was actually his flight lead as he checked out in the F-4, and I relished those few flights. I was his BFM, basic fighter maneuvers, instructor, and I must say, though he hadn't flown a fighter in many years, he was awesome, and I let him think he was beating me every time we flew. Seriously though, I can't say enough good things about Joe; he is a man's man and about as classy, gracious, and nice as they come.

And finally, the icing on the cake was when Robin Olds came to visit for a few days to talk to us about flying and fighting. General Olds is probably the most quintessential and iconic fighter pilot of the Vietnam War. He was the commander of the Triple Nickel, 555th, Tactical Fighter Squadron, which flew the F-4, and he was credited with at least four MIG kills while in Vietnam, though it's believed he had more but didn't claim them because he didn't want to be pulled from combat duty. To add even more feather's in his cap, Robin was a triple ace in World War II flying P-38s and then the P-51. Having personally chatted with him and hearing him speak to all the pilots in the 184th, General Olds was very charismatic, charming and a maverick with swagger few fighter pilots in the world could match. Unfortunately, Robin passed away before I finished this book; throw a nickel on the grass.

All three of those aforementioned and amazing aviators were unique in their own way with regards to their field of expertise and left awe-inspiring aviation legacies in their passage through time. But, I shall not ever forget the men of the 184th and 108th with whom I trained and flew as a colleague and friend. They are all great aviators and men: Preston T. Duke, Col. Bobby Ockerhausen, Sammy Small, Pat Carter, Ed Sykes, "Dirty" Dirks, Roland Smith, Jim Bell, Gary Haseloh, Larry Kavouras, Joe T Short, Frank Romaglia, Vince Putze, "Quido", "DT", Darryl Hannah, Darryl "Waldo" Emerson, "Cowboy," Jeff "Viking" Danner; WSOs such as Jim Bell, AJ Pinkley, "Crash" Cassiday, Jon Baxt, Steve "Fiwacs" Filo, Pat Ayers, Don Janke, Jim Flood, Rich Buckley, Ron Harbist, et al.—so many incredible and wonderful fighter pilots who deserve to be mentioned as heroes. I am so blessed to have had the chance to fly fighters and socialize with all of them.

CHAPTER 17

I was once told by a very devout Christian that if you want to increase your faith, then look at your past. Continuing, she said that God's positive influence, His silver linings, can clearly be seen by gazing backward in time and seeing where He has intervened on your behalf and in your favor. There is no doubt, with regards to my career, that God's direction has been very evident, and considering where I was emotionally and in spirit in my sophomore year of high school, to me personally, my achievements through God's grace have been nothing short of miraculous. The funny thing is, just when I thought I had it all figured out, my career path, and got a little cocky, God pulled an amazing sleight of hand upon my dreams as my days in the 184th came to an end toward the latter half of the 1980s. It would take twenty-five years for me to realize the blessing, silver lining, upon which I was bestowed, since I initially felt God had cursed me.

When it comes to matters of faith, patience and trust in God's process are a must.

If it sounds like I am promoting my faith, I am. If God can take a wretch like me and bring good into my life, then He will do it for anyone, you just have to reach out to Him with a humble heart and believe. As you have read, before I began to take flying lessons I hated myself and my life and never thought I'd amount to anything, at least that was my father's war cry against me when he was drunk and in one of those all too familiar dark moods. If you tell a child thousands of times words of negativity during visceral personal attacks on them, those words will begin to take hold in their heart and mind; I couldn't have gotten any lower in self-esteem as I was when I began to fly. And though, even after I began to fly and my father continued his attacks on me, becoming an aviator slowly began to elevate me above the detritus of his words.

Prior to getting into the military, I had no idea how to proceed to achieve my dreams of flying around the world. I have no doubt that my prayers to God while languishing on the beach so many times after a depressing day at home due to another emotional beat down and berating by a once again drunken father were the catalyst that began God's connecting the dots to my career, eventually bringing me into the left seat of a B-777, in spite of my father's continued attempts to misdirect my career.

CHAPTER 18

After being on active duty in Kansas for almost three years, airline fever started burning through the pilot ranks. The airlines, because of a booming economy, were hiring in huge numbers, and no longer was thirty-two years the age cap for getting hired. The airlines began hiring all age groups, and classes of sixty new-hire pilots a month were being sent through all of the major airline training pipelines . . . American, Continental, Delta, Eastern, TWA, United, USAir; even the regionals were hiring and growing, the brightest being Southwest and Piedmont.

Many of the guys with whom I was a colleague and friend when I began to instruct in the 184th TFG in 1983 were hired and gone by 1985/86 only to be replaced by others who eventually were hired and left. Not all of the guys got airline fever, some of the more senior guys, nearing retirement, stayed on active duty orders to get their retirement, and then they too eventually were hired by one airline or another. Only a relatively small sample of the fighter pilots I knew at McConnell never entered into the airlines, such was/is the draw of being an airline pilot.

In 1985 I didn't want to be left behind, so like everyone else I sent out applications to most of the major airlines, and the first responder was Eastern. Eastern was my first choice because I had ridden them almost exclusively when I was growing up—twice down and back to Miami for summer camp and then up to Boston many times. I knew a couple of guys, Jack Distefano's friends, who flew with Eastern, and they told Jack to tell me that they would help get me domiciled in Philadelphia if I were to get hired.

In June 1985, I went through the interview process in Miami, and I must say I thoroughly enjoyed it. Right off the bat I flew a DC-9 simulator with a retired Eastern captain, and he and I hit it off so well' I didn't feel nervous at all while he evaluated my flying skills. From the physical exam, to human resources' mind-probing questions, to the testing—it was all a very nice experience.

I was offered employment about two weeks later and was initially ecstatic, but then reality began to sink in.

Eastern was doing very well at that point in time, but they also had just gone through a bad spell financially, and were struggling against all of the other airlines in the wake of airline deregulation that occurred in 1978. Though the U.S. economy was doing well, and Eastern with it, there was still a lot of animosity between the employees and management at the same time as Eastern was fighting for a bigger niche in the world market.

My single biggest goal back then was to get hired by a financially sound airline, and I never wanted to get furloughed—or worse, have the airline go out of business, like what happened to my father. So, as I read up on the financials on Eastern, I began to have serious nagging doubts about taking a position there. I worried about them going out of business. I floated my feelings with my wife, dad, friends, colleagues, everyone, everyone but God that is. I never thought about going into prayer and giving this to God, as odd as

ROGER BLAIR JOHNSON 277

it sounds given the fact that I continued to pray the Lord's Prayer every day and went to church almost every Sunday.

After delaying my decision by a month while I fretted about their future prospects, I finally gave in to others' advice, which stated the following: (1) "You have to go with the first airline that hires you"; (2) "No major airline has ever gone out of business" (actually not true at that point in time); and (3) "Eastern was a great airline and was going to do well." In spite of those pep talks, my gut continued to nag me to the point that on some days I felt like I was going to vomit.

With bittersweet thoughts in my heart and a continuously rumbling tummy, I drove to Miami in mid-August to start my training with Eastern, leaving my wife, dog, cat and seventy-two F-4s on the ramp at McConnell AFB. I couldn't help but think that I wasn't quite finished with my life in Kansas, as I drove southeast.

Once in training in Miami, my gut—and I mean literally my physical gut—continued to gnaw at me, and my instincts told me to run away from the company. Unless you've been there yourself, like the way I was feeling in Miami at this time, it's hard to describe the anxiety I was feeling, particularly when everyone in my new-hire class was so happy about being there. While in basic indoctrination, I was excited to hear of the company's future plans, and I was somewhat motivated hearing the excited talk of those with whom I was just hired. I was hoping all this positive feedback would quell the whispering in my head and heart that said to run, not to mention reduce the nausea in my stomach.

In an odd twist in my life, while in Miami, I was rooming with the son of Hugo Vihlen, the F-4 student whom I mentioned earlier, Dana. Dana's father, as I said, was a Delta Airlines captain, L-1011s, and at one point had the record for sailing the smallest boat across the Atlantic; a very small vessel indeed, something like six feet long. Hugo and his wife lived in the Miami area, Homestead I believe, near their son and his one-bedroom apartment, which Dana graciously offered to share with me; I got the couch, for which I was very appreciative.

After two weeks at Eastern, on a Friday, I called my old squadron commander, Sammy Small, and asked if I could get my job in the 184th back. Sammy said, "Sure, c'mon back, the airlines aren't for everyone. You won't even have a break in your active duty orders since you're still on terminal leave." I cannot begin to tell you what a relief I felt with his words and in the space of fifteen minutes, the nagging in my stomach ceased and I could breathe again.

I told Dana that evening that I had resigned from Eastern and was heading back to my old F-4 position. I must admit I told him with some trepidation, fearing his response. His laughing at my confession caught me off guard, but then he explained that his laughter was not meant out of sarcasm or ridicule. He said it was ironic, me leaving Eastern, because his dad told him, after the four of us had dinner one night, that he was very happy one of the campers from his Camp Hugo days became an airline pilot. No doubt, Hugo Vihlen's joy was short-lived, because I know in fact, he vilified me a few days later after Dana told him I quit.

That vilification continued, though in a much more subtle manner, when I returned to fly at McConnell. There were those that could not comprehend why I left Eastern when the airline was doing so well. I could only tell them that it just didn't feel right being there and I needed to leave. Eventually, the low-key "vilifiers" got airline jobs of their own and no longer had to worry about me, and I got a break from their snide comments.

Looking back, had I stayed with Eastern I never would have gone to Fighter Weapons School, nor would I have been brought back as an instructor to the same F-4 Fighter Weapons School. It was the penultimate position which I never thought, in my wildest dreams, I could ever achieve. I was instructing the USAF's "best of the best" F-4 pilots and the flying just didn't get any better as I thoroughly enjoyed the challenges of instructing so many wonderfully talented fighter pilots.

Sadly, Eastern Airlines went out of business in 1989 so had I stayed I would have been on the street within a couple of years. I have no doubt God was using a knotted stomach to get my attention.

CHAPTER 19

As I just alluded I wound up going back into the Fighter Weapons School, but this time as an instructor. It was toward the summer of 1987 when I began my training to become a FWIC IP and though my military flying career was peaking, internally I was falling apart. The years of living with the dysfunction of my parents were finally catching up with my psyche. During that period of time, my dad and I talked on the phone about once every two weeks with the topic always being aviation related; rarely did we deviate to anything personal in nature. With regard to my mother, she and I rarely ever spoke, other than a quick hello and a gratuitous how are you doing; it was a mutual indifference. In spite of this seeming peace with my father and not having had an argument or berating from him for a few years, the latent effects of having lived with his alcoholism and rage, my mother's parental indifference, and the regular harsh fights between my parents and me were revealing themselves as I began to enter the black hole of "the failing aviator" syndrome.

I have no idea who coined that term "the failing aviator syndrome," but in retrospect, at that time, I was the poster boy for it. The good news is that, like my father, I could compartmentalize the extremes of my daily life, fighting with my wife one moment but flying glorious F-4 missions the next, and all washed down with alcohol on the regular Friday nights with the boys at the Officers' Club.

I knew something was wrong "with me," since you don't live with fires of deep emotional rage without suspecting you've got "issues." But I rationalized that being married to my wife, Kim, was the problem, since my father had been the one who "pushed" us together, and I'd only married her to get him off of my ass while I was a junior in college (more on that later). With every marital breakup between Kim and me, and we'd had a couple by that time in our short marriage, I sought the affections of other women. Poor them (the other women and Kim). I had such high expectations for every woman I met back then and expected each of them to give me total fulfillment, both emotionally and sexually. I was literally like a vampire demanding they give all of themselves to me—heart, mind, and body—and I sucked them dry until I was no longer fulfilled and then I'd move on. I had totally unrealistic expectations, hugely unrealistic, of what a real relationship was supposed to do for me… let alone the woman I was seeing. I just wanted more sex, more emotional affection, and a total commitment on their part to me. I wanted so badly to form a deep bond with every sexual partner I had, yet try as I might I could never achieve any lasting fulfillment in my heart or head with anyone. In fact, with each intensely sexual and deeply emotional relationship, my desires were increased, not decreased and I just never felt I was achieving the true intimacy that I desired; I felt more empty with each new partner.

As I said earlier, you can't grow up in emotional hell, the kind with which my siblings and I were raised, and not expect the seeds of dysfunction to germinate in one form or another in each of the kids. As we aged Linda, Gail, and I each manifested psychological and emotional injury with Linda exhibiting the least damage, Gail the most, and me somewhere in between.

Linda, being the oldest and having had to mature at an early age due to my mother's negligence, became angry and very rebellious as she aged. She had the unwelcome chore of having to care for Gail and I in Iowa after my father left his family upon seeing his wife in bed with another man. Linda was barely 8 years old when our mother decided she needed more time alone with her boyfriend. Since she couldn't afford a babysitter, Linda was unceremoniously left with the responsibility to feed and watch over Gail and I all day Saturday, sometimes into Sunday, and on the occasional weeknight; I was 3 years old at the time, Gail 6. After my parents remarried and we moved to New Jersey, and in spite of the hell created by my father, Linda began to develop into a great daughter. She played clarinet in the high school marching band, earned good grades, had nice girlfriends, and never dabbled in drugs. As her brother, I did notice a very deep undercurrent of anger in her while she was home and I can say without equivocation it got much worse as she entered high school. What angered my parents about Linda, and after she'd entered high school, was when she began dating her first boyfriend, an African American, who was the star fullback of the high school's football team. (This was circa 1968, interracial relationships were very much frowned upon then). My mother had disdain for two types of people in her life: Southern Baptist ministers and blacks; I have no idea why the negative feelings for each, but without question Southern Baptist preachers were her mortal enemy and blacks just a group with whom she preferred not to associate. My father, on the other hand showed no bias against any race or creed other than the Japanese, his reason being their absolute brutality during World

War 2. In my parent's attempt to keep Linda from seeing her boy-friend, they sent her to an all-girls boarding school in the Blue Ridge mountains of Eastern Pennsylvania. Linda had absolutely no desire to be stuck in that school and away from the love of her life and consequently she ran away from the school so much she was eventually expelled. But, getting expelled didn't matter much because she promptly became pregnant and, in order to hide her from the rest of the world, she was placed into a home for unwed mothers until her baby, which was given up for adoption, was born. Linda never came to live with us after giving birth. She lived in Atlantic City, eventually graduating from high school and promptly got married. Her husband, Richard, was another wonderful African American and he went into the army relatively soon after they spoke their vows. My father and I visited Linda and Richard quite a few times before he was shipped out on his first assignment. By the grace of God that was Schofield Barracks, on Oahu island, Hawaii and that is where she, Linda, lived for 13 years. (Richard and she divorced after a few years in paradise).

Gail, poor Gail, was the most affected by my parent's life of hate. Early on, while still in grade school, she too showed great promise, like Linda. She took piano and tap dancing lessons and was a cheerleader for the Jersey Devils city football league. She and I loved to swim and she was an excellent swimmer and diver and she and I spent a lot of time at the beach in the summer months of our grade school days. But, for some reason after entering high school she left the tracks and became very promiscuous and a drug addict. What might have pushed her over the edge, besides the frequent domestic battles of our parent's, was the horrific automobile accident she was involved in with two of her friends, and the fact that another good friend of hers was murdered by her father; the father actually killed the entire family to include their dog and himself. The automobile accident was horrible in the sense Gail was unconscious for 2 days, one of her friends had the right side of her face sliced completely open, losing sight in one eye, and the other friend lost her spleen. The Dodge Charger Gail and her friends were riding in flipped 3 ½ times, landing on its roof. I came upon the accident by chance while collecting for my newspaper route and being curious I watched as they pulled the girls out of the wreckage; I was horrified when I saw that Gail was one of the young ladies. I don't think Gail ever recovered from all of the trauma of those years. She over dosed on drugs more times than I can count, my father picking her up in New York City on a few occasions after she'd run away with some guy offering her the promise of lifelong love, only to be dumped on the streets after he got his sexual fill. Usually it was the police who found her on some sidewalk, overdosed, maybe with the intention of killing herself. She was raped in high school, never telling my parents, and in fact was raped many times after moving to Los Angeles, and while living on the street there or in Las Vegas when she decided to be homeless there. She eventually moved-in with Linda, in Hawaii, where she was institutionalized for a bit of time, her diagnoses being she was paranoid schizophrenic (due to all of the drugs and over-doses affecting her brain's chemistry). She would never get better.

As for me, I was luckier than my two older siblings in one sense, but worse off in another, the cause of the paradox…I was the male child.

More than my sisters, when I was young I used to love to hang out with my father, whether it was on the odd occasion that he took me flying, or when he went to his favorite bar on Saturday afternoons. When we lived in Absecon, Mickey and Minnie's was his bar of choice. We'd spend hours in there with him drinking and me playing pool with some of the old timers as they showed me their trick shots and gave me pointers in the art of playing. I have to admit those were actually some nice times with my father, he never got angry or belligerent and he seemed to like having me with him.

In the same vain as being with my father, for a short time after my mother came back to us, after their remarriage, my mother actually paid attention to me. Because Linda and Gail were in school and my mother didn't work (My father was worried about her having another affair so he forbade her to work after they remarried) my mother and I spent a lot of time together, going to the beach, parks, or just at home with her playing the music she loved. For my mother and I, except for the weekly fight nights between my parent's, those were the golden times, lasting maybe a couple of years.

Conversely, the curse of being a male in my family was the fact that as I aged my father would viciously attack me, in addition to his wife, while he was drinking. He never attacked Linda or Gail, but I guess being a male, I was a threat to him in some perverse way that I could never figure out, at least that was my simple-minded thinking back then.

In the final analysis, all of us siblings were greatly affected by the continually emotionally charged environment in which we lived and due to our parent's inability to truly love and emotionally care for their offspring. There were moments of affection, but far too few to change the nature of Linda, Gail, and I as we aged.

CHAPTER 20

With regard to my faith, I chose to shut God out my heart when it came to my personal life, if only because I knew what I was doing was wrong. I was actually angry with Him. God was "out there," somewhere, but since He wasn't quenching the emotional hell within me, and oh Lord how I prayed for His help, I held a grudge against Him. I never wanted to be married so young, and I was extremely bitter at getting married to a woman whom my father forced upon me. I blamed God, my father, My mother, my wife, everyone, for everything bad. I refused to look with any depth into the man staring back at me in the mirror.

Without a doubt, I was a ticking emotional time bomb. I was an ass to my wife, and some other ladies, and honestly not a very good friend to my friends. In my defense, I'd never been taught, nor had I seen by example from my parents, how to be a friend or even carry on in a relationship. What I learned from my parents, or didn't learn, I carried forward into my adult life, though try as I might, I wanted to change almost every aspect of myself. Mistakenly, I sought that "one" person, that one perfect woman with whom I believed I could have my happily ever after, my Hollywood ending. My own heart yearned so much for some kind of deep connection with a woman who could quell my emotional anxiousness. Most times I was able to keep a lid on the flames but sometimes not. And it was during those brief periods of time where I let my heart reign over my actions that caused me to do some rather impulsive and stupid things which, at times, bordered on self-destructiveness.

One example of the "things I did for love," occurred in early 1988, just before a Fighter Weapons School deployment when I was out on the town with my old UPT pilot training buddy, Bill, who was now going through Fighter Weapons School. At this time, I was separated from my wife, this being the second separation in our rather short marriage, and I was wanting to make up for "lost time" on the dating scene since I'd gotten married so young. I was going to be Bill's instructor for the next morning's one versus one BFM sortie. The evening before that flight, he and I decided to go to Harry's Uptown Bar and Grill and have a few drinks before heading to our respective abodes. In the bar that evening, I met an absolute treasure in the form of a cute little, five-foot-four blonde with a pair of 36 Ds. She and I hit it off like we were made for each other; she loved seeing the F-4s blast through the sky, and the pilots in them, and I loved the fact that she loved that. She said she loved to watch the aircraft takeoff and land and that she sat at the end of runway 19 on many mornings watching the fighters take off (there was a little public observation/parking area that was just off the southern end of the Air Force Base's two north/south oriented runways). I told her that Bill and I were going to fly a sortie in the morning, and if she happened to be sitting in the observation area I'd give her a little, personal fly-by. She asked me how'd she know it was me who was taking off, since we had so many flights of Phantoms coming and going; my parting words to her were, "You'll know."

The next morning, the sky was clear and blue as I initiated the after-burners on my twin J-79 powered F-4. We were flying clean jets (no external ordnance or fuel tank[s]) and in the cold air my Phantom lifted off in about 3000 feet. I climbed just high enough to let the gear raise without being hindered by the runway and kept the jet on the deck, accelerating rapidly; Bill was doing the same thing only he was following ten seconds behind me. At the end of the runway, instead of pulling out of burner and climbing rather rapidly, which was normal procedure, I held about fifteen feet of altitude (above the runway), knowing the observation area where this femme fatale would be sitting was about a quarter mile ahead and about ten to fifteen feet lower than the runway's surface. As I approached the car park area I rolled into a knife-edge, rolling ninety degrees to the left, while kicking top rudder and waved to my future date, as we sped by at 350 knots and thirty feet or so above her. I cannot imagine what the noise was like as she sat on the top of her Jeep and waved.

I was grounded for two weeks because of that public display of affection, missing my squadron's advanced threat deployment, but on the upside, I was afforded quite a bit of time to become acquainted with this lovely young lady.

Humor aside, though, and as much as the aforementioned story of mine about buzzing that young lady could be a "boys will be boys" stunt, there was something missing in me, a fundamental need that should have been acquired while I was very young. That I would continue to struggle in relationships because I was incomplete in a psychological sense was a forgone conclusion. I wouldn't realize I was truly "broken" until a horrible personal tragedy befell me in the latter half of the 1990s whereupon I sought professional help in order to better cope with the calamity.

However, at this point in my life, 1987, I didn't see that I was failing. But, God did and He took steps to help, although at first I thought He was cursing me.

As spring 1987 rolled into summer, I felt I needed a change of my surroundings. My marriage was deteriorating at a rapid rate, and I was determined to do a life makeover and once again felt the urge to become an airline pilot, since I thought it would allow me a bit more freedom in living my life.

All the airlines were still hiring in 1987, but I only applied to three when I happily sent in my applications, expecting a quick reply. I figured since Eastern took me so readily, I was a shoo-in for the others.

I was rejected by American, USAir, and Delta, and in that order. I have to admit, just to write about that rejection is painful. However, to God be the glory, because there is a wonderful reason for those rejections as you shall soon read, though at the time being rejected was a huge hit to the ego. Delta was an especially bitter rejection since I'd thought, besides Eastern, they would be a cool airline for whom to work, and they were my second pick when I initially began my job search in the mid-1980s.

Dejected, bitter and angry are but a few impotent adjectives I could use to describe how I really felt after all three of the airlines coldly turned me away.

The flurry of rejections caused me to rethink my career, and I resigned myself to retiring at McConnell and then looking for an airline position after I retired. I was twenty-nine years old by the time Delta gave me their rejection letter; that was sometime in the fall of 1987.

I was furiously angry at God because I felt He should have gotten me hired with at least one of those airlines, and I will tell you, my faith was severely—and I mean severely—tested. Consequently, along with my marriage failing, so too was my faith, and I lived my days looking for emotional painkillers in the form of women, booze, and flying.

And then the oddest of things happened. I was sitting at the SOF[58] desk for the Fighter Weapons School one early morning in January 1988 when a voice from my recent past spoke to me. Preston T. Duke, an ex-Vietnam F-105/F-4 fighter pilot and a past instructor in the 184th, called. PT knew I was still flying in the 184th, and he pointedly asked me why I hadn't updated the resume I had on file with the airline for which he now flew. To be honest, I told him, I forgot about it, since I had never received a response when I sent it in three years ago. In the 1980s the only way in which you could get an interview with PT's airline was through a sponsor, someone whom already flew with the airline, and unbeknownst to me PT had been checking on my resume's progress every so often, since he was a very attentive sponsor. Eventually my application was discovered and dusted off and when Cargo Service Express (CSE, and not the real name) tried to call to tell me I was wanted for an interview, they were told by Ma Bell that my number was disconnected (this was when we actually had house telephones and no cell phones). I had never updated my resume and had changed residences so the number on the application was out of date. PT

---

58. SOF (Supervisor of Flying) Desk—when aircrafts were airborne a pilot was always on duty and immediately available in the squadron building in case of an emergency.

was told by the human resources person who tried to call me of the incorrect phone number and asked if he knew how to contact me. Hence, PT's call to the SOF desk that early morning was in reaction to HR's request. In addition to the good news of the interview request, PT dryly added that I was a dumb shit for not telling his airline I had moved and in not updating my resume because my jet-flying time had increased substantially in those three years, and they might have called me sooner than they did (the more the jet time, the better the resume).

I must take a brief moment to expand upon my sponsor, Preston T. Duke. If ever there is a more dignified southern name, other than Rhett Butler, I don't know of it. Preston grew up in Collierville, Tennessee, where his father had hundreds of acres of land that he either farmed or raised cattle on or both. Preston lived in a house not quite as dramatic as Tara of Gone with the Wind fame, but it was close. He flew F-105s in the Vietnam War and then, after coming back stateside and instructing students in UPT at Willy in the T-38, he went back to Vietnam for another tour in the F-4; he was an amazingly gifted pilot.

My first meeting with him was on an early Saturday morning when he had flown in to fly a sortie in the F-4. I was in RTU at that time, and Preston was one of the few "part-timers" we had instructing in the 184th. At the time I first met him he was a new captain with CSE, besides being in the military part-time.

I had been at home when Cheryl Ballway called and asked if I was interested in flying a local single-ship sortie, not a training one, but a freebie, but I would be sitting in the backseat of the Phantom. Since I was always looking for flying time, I said sure, I'd love to go, and I'll be right there (I lived like five minutes from the base).

Upon showing up and meeting PT (his nickname), I found him to have one of the driest senses of humor I'd ever experienced. As he briefed me on our flight I swear he was nodding off, and I even joked that if he wanted to fly in the back and sleep, that I've "got this." He deadpan looked at me and continued to brief, no chuckle, no smile, not even a retort. If I thought Hooter (Gary Haseloh) was grumpy, PT was stoic with an attitude. I immediately became reserved, as I saw he wasn't in a comical mood, and I just vowed to shut up, unless spoken to.

The morning was amazingly beautiful with no clouds, light easterly wind and skies that give the definition of deep blue its meaning. The sun immediately blinded and bathed PT and me as he opened the door which took us to the flight line. A KC-135 had taken off as PT and I exited the OPS building, and you could smell the burned jet fuel from the tanker's engines, as we crossed the flight line. We were halfway to the Phantom in our walk and the silence between PT and me was killing me. Losing my senses and not enjoying the quiet as we walked together, I asked him what it was that caused him to want to fly fighters in the Air Force.

Initially, there was no response, and I was wondering if he'd heard me. Then he stopped, took a deep breath, and I am not lying about this, he said, "Do you smell that?"

Uhmmm . . . "What?" was my very weak response, now regretting I had asked the question.

"The smell of burned kerosene. I love the smell of burned jet fuel."

Right . . . okay, note to self, no more stupid questions with PT.

After taking off, with me in the backseat, where I had never sat before, and where PT expertly taught me how to operate the INS and radar, we enjoyed the smooth morning air, and for the better part of one hour and thirty minutes, flew around the state of Kansas with PT as my personal guide. He showed me this farm and that farm and who owned each, and interspersed with his agricultural tidbits, he pointed out where this or that F-105 had crashed over the years (a total of forty-eight in the state alone; McConnell used to be the main F-105 training base during the Vietnam years). As we neared the base, nearing the end of the most agriculturally educational flight I've ever flown, PT asked me if I wanted to fly an ILS into Hutchinson Airport, a small airport twenty miles or so northwest of Wichita. I about crapped as he hadn't asked me if I wanted to fly the whole flight and now he was asking me if I wanted to fly an ILS from the back-seat of the Phantom with an ILS indicator that seemed like it came from the days of Lindbergh. Since I did love to fly though, I said, "Sure."

Giving me control of the aircraft PT asked approach control for vectors for the ILS and that is what we did, flew the ILS. Asking PT for the gear and flaps as appropriate, since I didn't have those controls in the back, I intercepted the localizer then the glide slope, and concurrently slowed the aircraft to on speed AOA, using the audible tone generated by the aircraft and sent to the crew's headphones in their helmets to signal what the optimum AOA was for the approach. (We obviously had an airspeed indicator, but on approach we always flew by AOA and not airspeed. To this day, I couldn't tell you what the normal approach speed in the F-4 was since I was always looking outside, if flying visually, or looking at the attitude indicator and other instruments if flying in the clouds and on approach.) Using the antiquated ILS indicator on the upper part of canopy bow and referencing the heading on the RMI and the attitude on the AN/AJB7 artificial horizon, I flew an approach to minimums. I can't say I impressed anyone with my skill in flying that approach, but at least I got us near the runway (and yes, it was severe clear and PT no doubt saw the runway from miles away, but for me in the backseat, my visibility was severely restricted). Upon reaching minimums, PT said he had the aircraft and initiated a missed/low approach down the full length of the runway, no doubt the noise of our jet causing those in their rocking chairs to fall over backward to the ground; not many Phantoms did approaches into sleepy ol' Hutchinson on a Saturday morning.

Directly from that low approach, we rapidly climbed to about 5000 feet and flew back to McConnell and landed, quiet once again taking over the morning.

There were a few other, more formal training flights in my RTU days where I either flew with PT or flew in a flight he was leading. He was a "Zen" bomber, and no doubt his forte was surface attack and dropping bombs. I had much respect for him and though his sense of humor seemed to get drier the more I got to know him, I liked him very much.

At some point in my RTU days in the F-4, PT asked me if I ever considered applying to Cargo Service Express. I really hadn't, and told him as much, but I also didn't think I could get hired there because I knew they only hired those that who had a sponsor. PT then looked at me in that all familiar are-you-a-dumb-shit-and-not-understanding-what-I'm-saying look and said, "I'll sponsor you, just fill out these forms and give me your resume, and I'll see what I can do."

And that was that. I gave him my employment package a couple of weeks later and, to be honest, completely forgot that I did, until that blessed day when Preston T. Duke personally called me to tell me again, what a dumb shit I was. There were very few people that could call me that, dumb shit, where I considered it a compliment. PT had such privilege and Jack DiStefano, the other.

While I have mentioned emotional reasons for pursuing the change in employers there was always the core, lifelong, dream of becoming an airline pilot. Every so often the Holy Spirit would whisper to me in my dreams and remind me of my heartfelt pleas to God about discovering those exotic places over the eastern horizon when I prayed on the beaches of my youth. So, with my personal life going to hell (my wife left me and moved back to New Jersey in the latter half of 1987) and really wanting to leave the land of Oz and get back to the sea, I saw no reason to dally, and I interviewed with PT's employer.

Like the Eastern interview, CSE was a class operation. In an amazingly small world kind of way, the gentleman who gave me my simulator checkride, Fred Johnson, knew my father quite well because CSE and the FAA had done some sort of joint project. Passing the simulator at CSE was the biggest showstopper to getting hired, so it stands to reason I was nervous as hell while I flew the DC-10. Fred kept asking me questions about my father while I flew the checkride profile, and I wasn't sure if this was part of the test or not—i.e. seeing if I could manage both talking, thinking, and flying. After we got into holding, and being there for at least fifteen minutes, I was soaked with sweat and believed I had tubed the ride. I timidly asked Captain Johnson (Fred) if I was doing something wrong since we'd done like ten turns in holding. He laughed and said, "Relax, you did fine, I just needed a break and wanted to know how things were going with your dad." I was hired three weeks later and started class the last week in February 1988.

CHAPTER 21

Earlier I wrote that if you look back over a period of time in your life you can see how the hand of God has worked upon it. Sometimes the clarity of God's influence can be realized by reflecting upon only a few days or months, at other times it may take years for the Lord to shape your destiny and fulfill your dreams.

As the end of 1987 rolled around, I was in the depths of despair and convinced that God was punishing me for all of my personal misdeeds. I thought no airline would hire me because I'd angered God to the point that he was fed up with me, and then, out of the blue, Cargo Service Express called and hired me.

As of this writing, I am still flying for them, that's twenty-nine years and change.

While that may not seem extraordinary, what is amazing is that since I've been with CSE, every major carrier that existed in 1988 has either gone out of business (Eastern, Pan Am), has been absorbed/ merged with another carrier and then filed for bankruptcy (except Southwest) or has been through bankruptcy and then merged with another legacy carrier. In those bankruptcies, most, if not all, of the pilots' accrued retirement monies that were managed by their airline were lost and then, to add insult to injury, the salaries of most of the pilot groups were dramatically cut while the airlines that went into bankruptcies reorganized. In addition, there were many thousands of pilots furloughed and lost their retirement plans. To date, CSE has not experienced a bankruptcy, and though I've seen some ups and downs in our business and revenue, and though we pilots took a temporary cut in pay after the 2008 economic crash, we've never had a furlough, and we've long since recovered from those financially stressful times right after the market crash of 2008.

I will be very honest and admit I did not think flying cargo would be glamorous, but over the years, the expansion of the company's service, to include "the world," has allowed me to see so many wonderful sights around this planet of ours so as to far exceed the prayers of years earlier when I ran to the beach for emotional and spiritual rejuvenation. As of this writing, I've been an airline pilot for twenty-nine years with the same amazingly wonderful and great airline, and I cannot thank God enough; whatever plans I or anyone else had to get me here, or not, were inconsequential because in the end, only God's will for my life prevailed.

Besides the amazing worldwide flying, and probably the most important of my answered prayers, was the "bottom line," the financial aspect of the airline. Over the years, CSE has done well, and that was the one major prerequisite I had in getting with any company in the first place. I never could have known how well they would do so as to keep my retirement intact and my salary on a never-ending ascent. It was never my desire to work for the highest paying airline, just the one that was the most financially stable, and so far, that dream has been well experienced at CSE.

I cannot thank Preston T. Duke enough for his perseverance in doggedly checking on my application as it gathered dust in the corporate offices. Were he not persistent in following up with me, I never would have gotten in the door and begun working for such a remarkable company and allowing my passion to become my career.

But ultimately, as I said before, I never really planned any of my steps in the first place, and I believe PT was a willing person in God's plan for my life; had it not been PT, I believe it most assuredly would have been someone else. For my part, I just went with either the whispers of the Holy Spirit or a kick in the butt from God . . . one much gentler than the other, but both effective in motivating and moving me toward God's plans for me.

CHAPTER 22

My arrival into the world of commercial aviation, the airlines, was not near as embracing nor felt as intrinsic, both in men and machine, as it did when I entered the USAF. There are a few reasons for this.

In spite of what Lieutenant Schenk said when I was in Officer Candidate School, and I quote, "Officer Candidate Johnson, you are the worst officer candidate I've ever seen graduate from here," I felt the military was a natural fit for me. It taught me discipline, a certain amount of attention to detail, and introduced me to a cohesive and welcoming group of people. My military years are one of, if not the most wonderful flying times in my life and I couldn't have asked for a better "family" of people with whom to work and socialize. The esprit de corps and camaraderie of every one of the units in which I flew would never be matched, nor would the aircraft be as exciting once I entered the civilian side of aviation.

The airlines, on the other hand, were/are the "real" world, at least in a Wall Street/free market kind of way, they don't print their own money (like the government), so they must rely on making a profit. The people, employees, don't necessarily socialize with each other in the same breadth and depth to which I was used to in the military, and the attitudes of the folks so much less uniform and not near as cohesive. Management expects results and wants a return on their investment, whether that investment is in a pilot or an aircraft. The training, too, personified the profit motive, at least when compared to the laid-back military style of syllabus flow. In the airlines, the training was fast-paced, fire hose they told us, and more time sensitive than what I ever got in the USAF; but, to aid in that transition, the instructors that I had were all top-notch and knew how to instruct in their aircraft well.

My father's reaction to me becoming an airline pilot was not exactly enthusiastic, hence the reason I guess he continually tried to steer me away from getting an airline position in the first place.

When I began taking flying lessons, my dad and I talked almost every day, or at the very least once a week about the goings on in the aviation world, and it was quite simply the only area of peace between us. Once I entered the military, our regular conversations took place on Sunday and became almost sacrosanct. As I've already said, my dad was a flight ops test pilot with the FAA and was on the cutting edge of what was going on in the civilian side of the business, and when I got in the military he loved to hear about my fighter pilot adventures and the advances being made in aeronautical warfare. Every now and then when we talked, particularly if I dominated that particular Sunday's conversation with some wildly cool military escapade, like flying the Red Flags and other very cool deployments, I could feel a hugely deep undercurrent of jealousy in him. He lived so vicariously through me while I flew in the military I felt I was fulfilling his dreams and not mine, and there is no doubt that many times during those father-son mind-meld conversations with me, it dawned on him, like cold water in his face, the limitations of using me and my career as a surrogate for his fantasies.

Since my father needed me to fulfill dreams that he'd never personally see, sometimes it was hard (I'm assuming), given his narcissism, for him to separate his own self from his son. So, I think it came as a huge shock to him when I left the military, full-time, in order to fly in the airlines. This is something he would not have done, at least not since losing his job at Meteor. It was an airline and its union that killed my parents' Camelot lifestyle in northern New Jersey. Why in the hell would anyone want to leave the relative safety of a government job and go into the private sector? My father had the experience of losing his shirt in the private sector, so as soon as he could he joined the ranks of the federal government nine-to-fivers, generally guaranteeing him that his weekends would be free to eat barbecue chicken and watch football from the comfort of his well-worn Barcalounger. (My father said he had many chances to go to other airlines after leaving Meteor but declined for job security reasons.)

All I could do when I left the military full-time was tell my parents that I felt it was the right thing to do, and I needed to fulfill an innate desire that I'd had since long before I thought of being a fighter pilot. The only saving grace for my parents' broken spirits was my announcement, which came as a kind of addendum after I told them that I was leaving the active duty, that I'd be rejoining the original F-4 Guard unit that hired me in the first place and which I had so rudely left (for Kansas) before spending any real time there.

Airline pilots, unlike military pilots, were from all corners of the aviation world and wildly different in personality, drive, attitude, and ambition. As a fighter pilot, we, the group of guys with whom I flew, were generally very homogenous in persona, if not psyche, and most likely it was that persona that motivated us to want to get into the fighter business in the first place; we really were like a tight knit family. Not so in the airlines, at least not at first blush. But it wasn't necessarily a bad thing, just different, and I really had a blast asking this guy or that gal where he/she learned to fly and picked their brain about their flying experiences; there are so many different and fascinating people!

Right out of the chute, that is to say right after my initial airline training and on one of my first airline trips, I met a captain who had flown B-58 Hustlers in the USAF. To say that I tipped my hat to him in a Wayne's World kind of bow is an understatement as the B-58 Hustler was and is, to me, one the neatest aircraft the world has ever produced. The good news is that I had several flights with this man, and though I know he was probably puking in his lay-over hotel room after my nonstop interrogatories related to his B-58 flying, I felt privileged just to have met him.

As I progressed rather quickly from the short-ranged and domestic 727 to the internationally flown DC-10-30, my layover venues changed dramatically. I had begun cavorting about the world, and I loved it! And, with the change in scenery and cockpits, the disposition of the captains seemed to change too. I met so many worldly, wonderful and colorful captains in my new international adventures. It would take volumes just to describe them all, but by far the best of the best I met at the dawn of my aeronautical renaissance, thanks to CSE.

The magnificent captain of whom I speak is Mike Peterson, and he is not the previously mentioned ex-B-58 Hustler pilot. I wouldn't know Mike was so amazing as a captain until almost twenty years later because I hadn't flown with enough captains at the time to realize just how much providence had blessed him with so much poise, talent, charm and leadership. (more to follow on him later)

One perk to being an airline pilot is the ability to pretty much live where you want and then commute to your domicile. After getting hired by CSE I, decided to move to Ocean City, New Jersey, leaving Kansas and Dorothy and Toto behind. I also reunited with my estranged wife in the hopes we could make things work. I was praying that being near the beaches of my youth with their invigorating sea breezes would breathe new life into and rejuvenate a very stale marriage.

I had a wonderful son borne to me a couple of years after returning to the shore, so I guess the sea air did rejuvenate a couple of things in my wife and me, so that was a wonderful positive about moving back home. Kyle, my second child, was born in August 1990 and followed Christina, his older sister, by three years.

In addition to flying with CSE, I was back flying in the 108th TFW on a part-time, traditional Guardsman basis. Since I had trained a few of the 108th's young pilots while I was in the 184th, going back to the unit that gave me my start in the military was a nice reunion and I thoroughly enjoyed flying sorties without being encumbered by having to brief/train a student.

As I settled into my new career path, that of being an airline pilot, I was really, really trying to calm down emotionally and settle into what a wonderful life that God had provided for me; but some things are easier said than done. What I didn't count on was, once again, my father's meddling into the life of Kim and me, and the realization that the old man was living vicariously through me, and the fact that he was in love with my wife and not his own.

My parents' horribly dysfunctional marriage was once again causing collateral damage in my life, so moving back was both a blessing and a curse.

There was a wonderful silver lining in being near the dark clouds of my youth (my parents) which was being near my kids, the beach, and the wonderful flying, whether it was with my airline or in the Phantom.

The following story was written many years ago. I wrote it for posterity, desiring one day to have a book full of some of my more memorable flights of fancy, daring and drama, such as my father used to tell me on those many wonderful storytelling nights of his.

This story describes the only time in all of my F-4 flying where I fully departed a Phantom and thought I may have to eject.

Out-of-Control Phantom

I was just a "Butter Bar" (Second Lieutenant) in 1981 and going through USAF Pilot Training when I read an article in a military safety magazine, written by some colonel, about how he almost died one night while flying an aircraft. After all these years I can't remember what type of aircraft the man was flying or, for that matter, what actually happened other than the moral of his story was that he got complacent and this complacency almost killed him. Since I read a lot of aviation magazines back then, and they all had their share of safety talk, I always found it odd that his one story seemed to always make its way into my brain when I went flying. I'm not sure if it's because back then, when I was brand new and an impressionable military internee, that when a colonel spoke I listened and obeyed, or because the title of the story was "Complacency Kills," and that really made me sit up and take notice or, maybe both of the above.

Now, fast-forward to the end of the summer of '89 . . . I'm living in Ocean City and am an airline pilot in addition to flying F-4s in the Air National Guard. I'm listening to Don Henley's song, "The End of the Innocence," a song he wrote to sum up the decade, or at least so the DJ says, as I drive to work on a beautiful late summer morning.

The drive from Ocean City to McGuire AFB, where my Guard unit was located, was fairly long, but I didn't really care since much of it was through fields or forests penetrated by a whimsically meandering two lane road. It's certainly a really nice way to start the day, particularly if you drive a sports car.

I'm thinking about my upcoming F-4 flight as I carve my way through the road's twists and turns. My flight that morning should've been fun. I had volunteered to take a military leave of absence from my full-time airline job so I could train the newest member of our squadron pilot ranks. Steve O'Neal was just a butter bar himself and was trying to get fully qualified in the F-4 before we transitioned to F-16s. Since most F-4 units had been converting to the Viper, the school that trained F-4 pilots closed while Steve was in his last few weeks of a six-month F-4 training course. Since I had been an instructor in the F-4 RTU that Steve just left, I figured I was a natural candidate to finish his training and volunteered my services to do such. Evidently, the group commander thought the same since he was more than willing to cut six weeks of active duty orders for me to bring our young "Weedhopper" up to war fighting standards. I was really looking forward to taking a break from my airline's monthly schedule of international flying, and doing some hard core, full-time fighter flying again. I was living the best of both worlds, aviation-wise, and knew it. I really felt God had blessed me greatly in my career and on that morning I was singing praises to Him with each change in guitar riff, from rock song to rock song, as the music powered me from curve to straightaway and back on those wonderfully forested country lanes.

I was also looking forward to Steve's and my first flight together, particularly since today's flight, our first, had been one of my favorites in the F-4 training syllabus . . . advanced handling. Normally, a green F-4 student would get this Advanced Handling ride relatively early in his F-4 transition, but since I had not flown with him before and he needed a couple of warm-up rides to "get his hands back" (he'd been out of the cockpit a couple of weeks shuffling between units and moving) I thought I'd give him a "fun" first ride as a way of saying, "Welcome to the world of fighters!"; as you will see . . . Steve got a weeeeee bit more than either he, or I, expected!

I arrived in the squadron parking lot fully refreshed and invigorated from my splendid morning drive and by coincidence Steve had arrived at the same time. Since we had met a couple of weeks earlier at a Phantom "Pharewell" party at McConnell AFB in Kansas, our greeting in the parking lot was pretty casual. After attending the morning's mass brief, Steve and I moved to a briefing room to review the flight.

Since Steve had never flown out of McGuire AFB, I thoroughly briefed him on the standard stuff first: ground ops, start, taxi, take-off, departure, and arrival procedures, divert fields, and local area orientation. After that, we talked about the meat of the mission, advanced handling, F-4 style.

It had been a while since I had actually briefed a green F-4 pilot, so I can't say my brief was as smooth as I think it used to be when I was a seasoned RTU instructor. However, since I was more concerned with what he actually saw in the aircraft, then how I briefed per se, I considered the brief a mere formality at this point as the real learning was to take place in the wild blue yonder. And with that said, I briefed the young Weedhopper on how to do loops (both high and low speed), pitch backs and slice backs, hard turns, gun breaks, slow speed flying and finally, the pièce de résistance . . . my patented vertical zoom climb from 10,000 feet and 500 knots to 30,000 feet and zero knots; it was a real confidence builder!

From the briefing room to the "classroom" we moved and in no time we were sixty miles off the coast of New Jersey, 15,000 feet up, in "Whiskey 107" (a so designated chunk of military airspace off the Jersey coast in which military aircraft did maneuvers) on an absolutely glorious morning.

Once we entered the "working area" (W-107), we had to get right to work as the F-4 wasn't exactly the most fuel efficient of aircraft and we would be using "gas" at a pretty high rate because most of the maneuvers required high power settings. I was instructing Steve from the backseat of the Phantom, as we performed the laundry list of aerobatic maneuvers fairly quickly to cover them all before our fuel ran too low. I wasn't looking for perfection in Weedhopper's flying skill since this was more or less a demo and gee whiz ride than anything else. Real learning for every pilot comes when the instructor is out of the aircraft and you are solo, with a "real" backseater, not an instructor. There were many esoteric nuances when it came to maneuvering the Phantom well in battle; trial, experimentation, and failure were required to learn, and that usually occurred without the instructor onboard.

As our total fuel on board registered 6,000 lbs., we had done everything I wanted Steve to do, at least up to this point. If we were at cruise altitude and "cruising," 6,000 lbs. of fuel would have equated to roughly one hour of flight, but, since the throttle was usually in military power (100 percent rpm) or in afterburner (A/B), we were using up "dinosaurs" (we usually called fossil fuels "dinosaurs") pretty quickly. Also, I waited until 6,000 lbs. before the zoom climb demo on purpose. I wanted the CG fairly forward as it helps in bringing the nose down with more authority. Finally, with six grand of fuel in the tanks the F-4 weighed about 40,000 lbs. Since the engines put out 36,000 lbs. total thrust in full A/B, we were fairly close to a one-to-one thrust-to-weight ratio, which helped to get that lovely beast up to 30,000 feet while going pure vertical.

With Steve flying, we accelerated to 500 knots IAS at 10,000 feet, about thirty miles off the coast. I quickly reviewed to him what we were going to do to set up for this last advanced handling maneuver—accelerate to 500 knots in military power, at 500 knots pull the nose up in an airspeed/energy conserving pull (light "tickle" in airframe buffet, about five Gs on the G meter), and as you are pulling go into full A/B, all the while continuing the pull. Once you reach ninety degrees nose high, vertical, hold the nose there while maintaining full A/B.

For most students, the hard part of this maneuver was holding the nose in the pure vertical . . . you actually had to push the stick forward slightly to keep the aircraft tracking straight up, and this was counterintuitive to most guy's instincts; I usually had to give a continuous "dialogue" as we climbed to get the guys to keep the aircraft going straight up as they kept wanting to pull over into a loop. Having said that, on today's flight my young charge seemed to defy the conventional wisdom of most students and was pretty fearless in this part of the maneuver, as he held a pure vertical climb without much coaxing. As we approached 200 knots indicated airspeed, I told him to get ready to apply left or right rudder and deselect A/B, as I had briefed earlier, so as to get the nose moving one way or the other as we apexed and afterburner was not needed since we had all the altitude required.

What was "supposed" to happen was for the student to apply this rudder input gently, feed it in deliberately, and not all at once, for to do so, kick in full left or right rudder immediately, could cause the aircraft to depart controlled flight; feeding the rudder in over a period of time also would cause the nose to begin to fall from the vertical as the airspeed went to zero gravity then doing the rest, both with the nose and aircraft trajectory. With the engines now in military power and the airspeed at zero, the nose would fall slowly earthward and as it did you went weightless, though it never really seemed you went fully zero G for too long. The altitude obviously stopped increasing, and as long as the controls were then neutralized, and you weren't asking the Phantom to do anything—like fly!—via the flight controls, it was a really nice transition from going straight up to straight down, and a very gentle maneuver. Once the airspeed increased to 300 knots, while going straight down, I would have the guys pull the aircraft to level flight and level off. Altitude loss was usually around 10,000 feet; hence, if you topped out at thirty thousand you'd be level at twenty thousand on the recovery. I'm telling ya, it was a real confidence builder with the guys. Now remember, what I just said is what was supposed to happen.

On this day, as we dropped through 150 knots, I asked Weedhopper to "kick" in left or right rudder—and he did as I asked—he kicked in full left rudder, and without hesitation!

"Rhut, roh," (deciphered as, "Oh crap") I instinctively blurted.

I will tell you, my heart leapt out of my chest when I felt the rudder go full left and the aircraft responding. Having flown about 1,500 hours in the F-4 at that point, I knew this was not good, and as soon as he put in the flight control input I told him to take it out—the rudder deflection—and I also directed him to push the stick forward (a lot of times a rudder input, a big one, will increase your AOA, so pushing the stick forward will counteract this increased AOA); I did not want an increase in AOA at this point, given the rudder input, and we were entering a gray area in my knowledge of F-4 flight characteristics with regard to this attitude/airspeed/flight control combination.

Now, this leads me to another article I once read in a safety magazine, and it was called "Temporal Distortions." It went into some pretty deep theory about how, under times of stress, the body/brain goes into a kind of hyper awareness state and time seems to slow down because the senses become more aware...a second seems like a minute, etc. I don't remember the body's biological cascade of hormonal production that causes this time warp, other than it happens, as identified by many accident victims' testimonies.

So, after the aircraft lurched to the left, I launched into a "temporal distortion" of my own. My first thought was to take the aircraft from Steve and fly it myself, but since the airspeed was now dropping through 100 knots and rather rapidly, I thought, "What's the use?" We were approaching thirty thousand feet, the throttles were back to military power, airspeed was rapidly bleeding off, and, so far the aircraft was just yawed to the left, what could happen? In fact, I even said to myself that we were too slow for anything bad to happen! I am telling you, these thoughts went through my head and as they did, it seemed to me that we had been going straight up forever, like in super-slow motion.

So, there we were, yawed to the left, still going up, and I was thinking, "This is a nonevent, the nose is just going to drop any second."

Though my wait for something dramatic to happen seemed long, in actuality I'm sure it wasn't, because in short order I was rewarded with the ride of my aeronautical life.

What the aircraft actually did, as best as I can figure, and to try and give you a visual perspective is this: Think of a springboard diver in the Olympics as he leaps off the board and into the air. As he goes up, he starts a twist—roll—and then starts to flip. Very shortly after beginning this upward vector, he apexes and then starts down toward the water, and all the while he is still twisting and flipping. In short, that is what Steve, the aircraft, and I did on that day . . . had we done it at low altitude during an air show, I'm sure it would have been a real crowd pleaser.

But whereas the diver is in control of his/her motion, we weren't. (One thing I didn't tell you is that the F-4 has an "aural" AOA indicator, in addition to a gauge and chevron lights. As you approach "on speed" optimum AOA, it beeps; the closer you get to optimum, the faster the beep, until you get to "on speed" and then it is a steady, medium pitched tone. But, if you go slower than on speed, higher AOA, it begins a higher pitched, faster beeping that is really irritating, no doubt to get your attention. The volume is controllable though so you can turn it way down, but most guys kept it at least at some audible level as it was a nice way to know your AOA without looking inside the cockpit.)

So, the AOA tone was screaming as we began our gyrations, adding to the dramatic way in which the aircraft departed controlled flight, and giving a sense of urgency to get things back under control. As the aircraft rolled rapidly to the left, and the nose fell through the horizon, I thought it, the nose, would stay "down" once it passed ninety degrees nose low. It didn't. I also thought the rolling would stop. Wrong again. The nose sliced through nose low and up again, as we continued rolling, and then went back to a nose high slice, still rolling. I must add, at this point, that none of this rolling and slicing/pitching was violent in as far as physical discomfort. Visually, it was interesting, and no doubt a weaker stomach would have launched its breakfast from the pathway in which it got there; but for the most part, it was a very smooth and fluid ride.

Up to this point, in all of my years flying the F-4, every time I have unloaded, reduced AOA (pushed the stick forward), the jet responded immediately; and whatever out of control gyrations it was beginning to do, once unloaded, it stopped. Not this time; I was now in virgin territory and had to resort to the F-4's Boldface procedures for help. (The USAF taught you to commit certain time sensitive procedures to memory for instant recall if the need arose; they called them Boldface maneuvers. I'd say this was pretty much one of those times.)

The out of control Bold Face Maneuver for the F-4 was as follows: Stick forward, rudder and ailerons neutral, if not recovered, maintain full forward stick and deploy the drag chute; there was also a note in the manual, which said that unless at low altitude, the throttles should be brought back to idle. (As a note here, if the throttles were left in A/B and you deployed the drag chute, you would instantly burn it off!).

I can't say I wanted to deploy the drag chute . . . not yet, so I didn't tell Steve to pop the chute; that was akin to admitting failure, and I wasn't ready to do that! I had done the out-of-control boldface a lot in the F-4, save for deploying the chute, because if you wanted to win dogfights in the F-4, particularly against F-16s or F-15s, you had to max perform the jet, and a lot of times you departed controlled flight. But, in every case in the past where I departed, popping the stick forward and neutralizing the ailerons and rudder brought me back into controlled flight. As Steve went through these memory items to confirm that he had the flight controls where they should be, the aircraft continued to roll, and the nose traced an unpredictable arc through the morning sky.

It was pretty evident that the out-of-control procedure wasn't hacking it, so we quickly moved onto the next series of boldface maneuvers, those for the "Aircraft in a Spin." This directed you to the following: maintain full forward stick; aileron full with spin/turn needle; (when/if) aircraft unloaded, (put) ailerons neutral. (That's not a misprint with regard to "aileron" in the singular. The F-4's ailerons only went "down," not up; so in a spin, only one aileron was being deflected.) As we spun and flipped from the wild blue yonder toward the deep blue sea, which was now 25,000 feet below us, and getting much closer with each complete gyration, Steve applied the spin recovery controls in an attempt to stop this madness. I can't say I was worried at this point as I was sitting on a zero-zero (zero altitude/zero airspeed needed for safe ejection) Martin Baker ejection seat with a fantastic survival record, and I had no qualms about giving the aircraft back to the taxpayers, albeit not exactly in same condition in which we received it, in exchange for my life.

Since we were not under any real physical discomfort during all this, other than maybe some visual disorientation, I talked to Steve a bit as we descended.

He asked if this was a normal result of "the maneuver," and I said, "No. I expect the airspeed to increase at any second and for the aircraft to pop into something more 'normal' with regards to aircraft control and flight path orientation."

What I didn't say was how screwed up this was and that we may be swimming home, but I didn't want to scare him anymore than he already was. I also told him that once the airspeed did increase, it was firmly planted at zero at this point, but once it did increase, not to be too hasty to pull the nose up as it was really easy to enter a secondary stall/out of control situation at that point and we most likely wouldn't have enough altitude to recover from another out of control situation.

As we passed 18,000 feet, the roll rate rapidly slowed, but the AOA was still way high and audibly screaming; much too high for a recovery, and the nose still wasn't dropping like it should, thusly leading me to the third and final boldface for situations like this.

The final memory item with regards to being out of control was thus, passing 10,000 feet AGL, if still out of control—eject! Because of this edict in the F-4 Flight Manual I told Steve that we were going to have to eject if the aircraft was still uncontrollable passing ten grand. Almost on cue though, as if the aircraft was listening and didn't want to be abandoned, the nose stopped its 360-degree slicing, the wings fully stopped their rolling and the tail pointed itself directly skyward with the opposite end going seaward. The airspeed went from almost zero to 250 knots about as fast as you are reading this sentence and at 300 knots IAS (indicated airspeed) I told Steve to begin a smooth pull on the stick and recover, which he did, leveling at around 10,000 feet AGL.

Whoa.

The cockpit was now very quiet. We were headed south, 180 degrees out from our initial heading, and cruised for a few long and silent seconds. Steve broke the silence first with his announcement that he wanted to "Go home." Without hesitation I concurred, and told him to RTB (return to base). The rest of the flight was uneventful.

In the mission's debrief, I learned that Steve never realized he was supposed to slowly feed in the rudder. He said he thought, as he listened to my very inadequate brief, that he was supposed to go full left or right rudder passing 150 knots and this thought process was actually reinforced as we passed 200 knots when I said to him, "Standby to 'kick in' left or right rudder!"

So, what happened? Why did a maneuver that I had done so many times before get so screwed up on this flight, almost causing us to lose an aircraft and possibly die? I'm sure you've figured it out already . . . complacency of course! The "voice of Sybil" that I'd heard so many times before as I was about to fly a mission, or was actually flying one, about how complacency kills, had abandoned me while I briefed and flew that day.

I can only think that all the elements that led up to this wicked departure from controlled flight, the proverbial links in the chain, had started with my lovely morning drive to work and my carefree, life is great, I can do anything attitude. This fed into every part of the day's events. When I briefed Steve, I was so full of myself! I had been an F-4 Fighter Weapons School instructor pilot, and Steve was just a new guy; I had been at the pinnacle of F-4 flying, and Steve had barely scratched the surface, I was going to show him how to really fly the F-4! At that point in my career, I considered the brief a mere formality. Most guys I had been briefing for flights, since I had left the Fighter Weapons School environment for the airlines and my part-time guard unit, were so used to the "standard" stuff, the same ol' missions, that they barely listened to the brief and were experienced enough to catch whatever might be different and ask questions if they weren't sure about something. Because of this, Steve was collateral damage in as far as my brief was concerned. I had glossed over the most important part of the flight believing that he would know what I was talking about and figuring that I was good enough anyway to catch whatever errors he might make in flight and then instantly correct them.

Which leads me to the second area of my complacency . . . the actual flying. I had 1,500 hours in the F-4, as we alighted from the runway that day, and I had done so much in the Phantom that I considered myself bulletproof and figured that I had seen it all. I mean I had instructed green F-4 students for three years and had dealt with all of their self-destructive tendencies and survived.

As I drove through the forests and cranberry bogs of south central New Jersey that evening, heading home, I was enjoying the breeze upon my face, the dimming of a late day's sun and the tunes emanating from the car's stereo. Amazingly, Don Henley's raspy rancor, once again, pulled me out of my trance and reminded me, very bluntly, that for me, that day's out of control departure was truly the end of my innocence.

CHAPTER 23

I really tried to become content being married to Kim, but it didn't work and, in fact, moving to the shore actually seemed to exacerbate my angst. So, in late spring 1991, and in what is the second most painful emotional experience of my life, I left Kim for good. I was scared to death in doing so, and it took every ounce of courage to make the decision and then follow through with it, particularly since I was a professing Christian, but my own furtive, emotional demons were demanding the change.

I must lay it on the line and say that in no way did Kim deserve the emotional burdens I put on her because of my personal issues. The years of emotional trauma that my sisters and I endured during our youth, and its consequent psychological damage to us, was now rearing its ugly head in a very destructive manner with my wife and the children we had; it simply was not right on my part to be so selfish, yet I felt I had no other recourse. Kim had always been very attentive to me, was an outstanding mother, and to this day, I am so sorry for all of the BS I put her and my kids through. If anything, she was a blessing I couldn't see because I was so blinded by dark clouds of emotion continuously stirring up ghosts from my past.

I was single-minded in the belief that there was a better life "out there," and I needed to find it.

The actual act of leaving Kim, Christina and Kyle is the hardest thing I have ever voluntarily done in my life . . . my God, it was horribly gut wrenching and the thought of it as I type this still causes me pain, particularly in leaving my children. By the time we actually separated, we had moved slightly inland, into a beautiful little neighborhood near the airport from which I first began flying, and realistically, Kim and I had a great life, I only wish I could have convinced my psyche of how good God had been to me then and how truly blessed I was.

I won't say that I felt relieved after I left her, I did not. I felt all alone and worried about how I would provide, financially, for my future ex-wife, the kids, and myself. The fact that God didn't strike me dead with lightning right away was a bit of a relief, and I have to be honest and tell you I was horrible at handling money and spent as much as I took in, sometimes more, so I had a lot to learn there. I was a basket case in every area of my life except when it came to flying an aircraft. That was the only aspect of living where I felt I had complete control and where I felt most comfortable and confident.

My leaving Kim, as expected, caused my father and mother to question my sanity, and as expected, my father disowned me, wouldn't acknowledge my existence, and cut off all ties with me to include the regular aviation themed chats we'd ritualized for the past twelve years.

I can't say I blamed anyone for questioning my mental state, as I had been questioning it myself, daily in fact. But, I was committed to finding a life without my father's influence since the only reason I married Kim in the first place was to get him off my ass. I now realized he absolutely adored Kim, to the point he controlled and manipulated me, and her, to carry on a weird relationship with her; Dr. Phil would need a whole season of TV episodes to work out that whole relationship mess.

Almost immediately after divorce proceedings had begun, my mother began a crusade to have me stop the divorce.

My mother was on my case because my father was devoting so much attention to Kim that she (my mother) felt like the odd woman out and was also concerned about the amount of money Ken was spending on a horse business in which my father and Kim had embarked. My suddenly attentive mother did a full court press on me at every chance she could get, when she knew I was home, but I wouldn't budge with regard to reconciling with Kim. I was amazed at my mother's gall, particularly when she would come over, sit at my kitchen table, smoking cigarette after cigarette, and then selfishly recant all the stories of her broken dreams. Most of them I'd heard many times before, but one day, during her pressuring me to reconcile with Kim, she said she wished she could've aborted all her children, because according to her, she never wanted kids in the first place and that we ruined her life.

How? How can a well-into-her-middle-ages woman and mother of three children casually sit with her own son and tell him she wished he'd never been born and that the three children she bore ruined her life? She said it so casually it was as if she was confessing to a friend of her sins while not really believing there was anything wrong with her thinking. I was in such shock when she first told me that I had to go to the bathroom to collect myself as it cut so deeply I thought I was going to emotionally vomit; while in the restroom I gave myself emotional triage just so I could re-enter the realm of my mother's version of the Twilight Zone. To this day I can't comprehend anyone, however dysfunctional, ever telling their own child they'd wished they could've killed them by means of abortion and that their very existence (that child's) made their life miserable, yet that's what my mother did with me and she said it as calmly as if having a nice Sunday chat.

After a few months, June gave up with her designs of reuniting Kim and me, and I was finally getting a well-deserved respite from her constant harassment.

However, just when I figured the fires of hell had burned out with them (my parents) and I could finally live in peace, one evening, I got a call on my house phone. I hastily answered, thinking it might be work calling, but nope, it was Ken.

No matter how my mother and father treated me, I was always willing to talk to them in the hopes that maybe, just maybe, we could become a "normal" family . . . I cannot express to you the pain I felt with the separation between my father and me, and I was still reeling with the thought that my mother wished my sisters and I never existed. It all hurt so badly, and as much as I tried to bury it in my head somewhere, shards of emotional pain stuck me at the most inopportune of times.

Answering the phone that night, my heart leapt because for the first time in a few months, my father was talking to me. He was very drunk, I could tell, and he asked me if I could pick him up from a bar at the local airport and take him home.

"Sure," was my shaky reply.

About twenty minutes later, my father was in the passenger seat of my car. I was cautiously optimistic as I met him as I had hopes of mending the rift between us. Yet again, though, my seemingly ridiculous eternal hopes of having a "normal" and loving father-son relationship with him were quickly dashed as we drove. Shortly after leaving the curb behind, my father said that the only reason he called me was because he couldn't reach my mother on the phone and he didn't want to pay a cab for a ride home. To be honest, I felt used, and I was severely brokenhearted. But his slurred comments didn't stop there. As in the past, he began to rant and verbally abuse me with a loud volley of compound, X-rated epithets meant—no doubt—to try and put me on the defensive and under his control. Try as I might to contain myself and stay calm, I was quickly reaching a climax of anger that was going to cause me to kick him out of the car. As one verbal assault from him was followed by another, I snapped and started yelling back. It was at that point that I guess my father, too, was at his breaking point and he began to punch me in the face.

I have to say I wasn't expecting it, and the first punch almost caused me to crash. I was on Fire Road, appropriately enough, and I began to pull into a local business to keep from crashing and to defend myself. I was trying to block punches and slaps with my right hand while steering with my left, and considering he was horribly drunk, he was not really connecting too well. I stopped very abruptly once in the empty parking lot and with that my father briefly fell forward, and as he collected himself and then looked at me to start punching anew, I ploughed him in the face with my right fist. I tried to pull the punch because, I mean, he was kinda old, and I was pretty strong. The punch landed right between his eyes and slightly above them. At the time, I was wearing a college graduation ring. The punch pretty much went through the ring and into his skin and left an enormous red mark, much as if he was from a certain caste system in India. I have to be honest, I kinda laughed to myself as we drove home as the red mark became more prominent and inflamed; maybe the laughter was an emotional self-defense mechanism or black humor on my part, as I began to separate from the reality of what had just happened. The positive aspect of the punch was that my father totally calmed down and just sat quietly in the seat after asking me to take him home. That was the first and only time I ever hit him.

The wheels of my car had barely stopped turning when "Rocky" flew out of the car and headed for the front door of his house. Upon gaining some distance between us he started up again with his verbally abusive tirade. My Lord, he was obstinate. But he carried the mark of a rajah upon his forehead, so I had the distinct satisfaction of knowing that, for the foreseeable future, every time he looked in the mirror he would be reminded that he was owned by one punch.

The Armageddon that I had feared would come between my father and me climaxed on that night so many years ago. It would be a year or so before he and I would speak again, and when we did, it was only because of a quantum shift in my father's relationship with Kim; providence was continually hard at work in my life.

The pain of the divorce, losing my children, fighting with my future ex-wife, mother, and father was only made bearable by the silver linings in the clouds through which I continued to fly. Like my father did before me, I could leave my troubles on the ground and elevate myself into another realm, compartmentalizing all my troubles, preferring to ignore the issues that never left me no matter how high or far I flew, instead believing that my youth would allow me to eventually distance myself from my troubled past and present; the apple didn't fall far at all from the tree with my father and me.

If I could ever doubt in God's existence at this point in my life, it might be because of the relationship hell and emotional turmoil in which I was raised and continued to experience as an adult. Conversely, if I should ever doubt in God, I would be crazy, for He had laid the most wonderful career path before me and bestowed upon me 2 wonderful kids. And so it was at this point in my life that there existed inside of me a paradox of faith of epic proportions, and though it would eventually go from boil to simmer, my crisis of faith, it would take many, many years to rectify the conundrum.

CHAPTER 24

At the time of my break-up with Kim I had transferred to the fighter squadron where Bob Grace flew F-84s, F-100s, and F-105s. The 119th FIS, one of the oldest squadrons in the USAF, was based at Atlantic City International Airport and when we lived in Absecon, New Jersey, before we moved to Linwood, I'd seen Bob and others flying fighters directly over my house. I loved to see the jets fly and always paused to watch them, being in awe of their beauty and power. Never did I ever think that the Lord would allow me to live dreams never dreamt when circumstances unfolded in my favor so as to allow me to fly F-16s from the same airport, and fighter unit, in which Bob Grace flew . . . how cool is that?

I transferred from the F-4 to the Viper in mid to late 1990. A call from Colonel Ockerhausen, the group commander of the F-16 unit, caused me to leave McGuire and come under Ock's command. Ock was a fighter pilot's fighter pilot, and I'd known him for quite a few years. He visited McConnell when I was an RTU instructor and asked me if I'd watch over the lieutenants he sent from the 108th TFW and help them when they needed it; he added that a Christmas card sent to him every year could go a long way in helping me in the future. So, taking him at his word, every time

Christmas rolled around, he got a card. My loyalty in both watching out for his young aviators while they learned to fly the Phantom and in my Christmas card sending landed me an F-16 when God felt the time was right.

Without question, flying the F-16 was an amazing aviation gift, which I never would have realized had I not actually flown the jet. Truly, God meant for man to fly because He allowed men to build the Viper. It is the most beautiful aircraft I have ever flown and I miss flying it, even as I type this. It was like a magic carpet ride, but with much more thrust and wind protection.

I only flew the jet for four years, far too short of a time, but still I thank God for even those four years. To be honest, I damn near never got any years in it because I was messing around one evening on a severely cloudy night mission and almost bought the farm.

I was flying a single-seat (A model) F-16 on a night air intercept sortie against a two seat (B model) Viper. The guys in the two-seater Viper were using NVGs (night vision goggles—they are light amplifying binoculars that are mounted on your flying helmet and allow you to "see" in the dark) and we were practicing for an up-and-coming deployment to Howard AFB in the country of Panama.

Since we never used NVGs in our normal daily flying while at home station in Atlantic City, we had to requalify in NVG use prior to our deployment. All training sorties with the NVGs were flown at night (for obvious reasons).

On this night, I was acting as a "target" for the B model. We would separate by thirty miles and then I would fly a profile dictated by our training procedures and the two-seat Viper, using its radar and then the NVGs, would perform an intercept on me. Each sortie could last ninety minutes to two and half hours, the longer flights being enabled by air-to-air refueling.

The weather that night was pretty crummy. There was a solid layer of clouds from 500 feet above the runway to 29,000 feet. Because we liked to "train" in the clear air (free of clouds), we were flying above 29,000 feet in the warning areas (airspace) which lie all along, and offshore of, the eastern side of the United States, and in which many military aircraft training operations are flown daily.

After an hour or so of being intercepted (we did not air refuel on this evening), the two-seat Viper said they were low on fuel and needed to head back to base.

I had more gas than they did and said I'd follow them. They departed the training area first while I did a couple of orbits in the working area to separate the two of us. Approach control gave me a clearance to return a few minutes after the other Viper left, so I began a descent to the recovery altitude as I talked to the guys on our VHF radio (we used our UHF radio to talk to ATC), as they were being vectored in. We agreed we'd meet in a local pub after I landed for the flight's debrief. It was still late winter and pretty cold outside, so having a beer by a fire seemed like a great idea as I began my recovery.

I was cleared direct to a fix called "APPLE," which was the beginning point for the arrival into the Atlantic City Airport. I had descended to 14,000 feet and was heading direct to "apple," using the aircraft's navigation computer. As I sat in the dark, at 14,000 feet and in very cold and thick clouds, I got to thinking how weird it was to be flying out over the ocean in such lousy weather and the only sensation I had of flying was through my eyes/brain interpretation of the instruments and HUD (Heads-Up Display) symbology in front of me and the vestibular (vestibular—the feedback about motion/movement/balance your brain gets from the semi-circular canals in your inner ear) sensations from the actual movement of the aircraft due to changing airspeed, attitude, etc.

In order to accomplish the night intercepts while working with the two-seat Viper I had to fly with my flight instruments completely dark (i.e. lights out) and with a screen over my radar display to darken its glow. I was given a glow stick to use to see my instruments as we performed the high-altitude intercepts. Once the training intercept work was complete I was not to use the glow stick for instrument illumination but instead go back to the standard, installed aircraft lighting system. But me, being weird—and in this case really stupid (if you knew me you might consider that a redundant statement)—I decided to try a vestibular sensation experiment. Instead of turning on the electrical lighting system, I kept it off and once level at 14,000 feet and headed for "APPLE," I engaged the autopilot and put my glow stick beneath my left thigh. I wanted to see what it would "feel" like with absolutely no light coming to my eyes while being in a fighter flying at 300 knots in the clouds. I was also curious as to what the vestibular sensations would feel like.

Well, I can tell you . . . it was what you'd expect . . . somewhat anticlimactic actually; it was very dark. I could hear the muffled wind noise from the 300-knot slipstream passing by the canopy and filtered through the earplugs I wore in my ears, which were surrounded (my ears) by padded headphones, which in turn were embedded in the helmet I wore. Since I was steady at 300 knots and neither accelerating/decelerating nor climbing/descending, there was really no vestibular sensation. I could feel the subtle vibrations transmitted from the aircraft through the seat and onto my body, but it was the normal feelings I'd been accustomed to since I first began flying the F-16.

As I cruised along toward the beginning of the recovery fix, I began to notice changes in the cockpit noise; it was getting louder. I still had no vestibular changes and the aircraft vibration was the same, but the cockpit noise definitely was increasing. At first, I ignored this subtle decibel increase thinking it was my hearing that was getting sharper due to my brain increasing my sensory perception due to the lack of light. But after an unknown number of seconds flying in absolute darkness, my gut feeling said to pull the glow stick out of hiding and shine it on the instruments…

To my utter horror—and I mean horror!—I was sixty degrees nose low, almost inverted, passing through 6000 feet and accelerating through 400 knots!

Without any thought process at all, I rolled the aircraft level and initiated a max G pull to bring the nose above the horizon and away from the ocean, while doing so I also increased thrust on the engine, a lot, as I knew I'd bleed a bunch of knots (airspeed) in the high G pull and in the consequent climb back to 14,000 feet. There was a chance I could have blacked myself out in the rapid pull, but I had begun a grunt as I rolled to level wings and was prepared for the G onset.

Words cannot express, to this day, the shock I had in seeing the attitude of the aircraft when I saw the instruments. Why I didn't have a bowel movement then I don't know, but I can tell you my heartbeat must have exceeded 1,000 bpm when I perceived the danger I was in.

Approach control saw the decrease in my altitude and asked what I was doing, as I climbed back to 14,000 feet. I was still not technically in their airspace yet, so I had not violated any regulations but, I am sure they wondered why I descended. I didn't acknowledge them with a full description of my incredibly stupid stunt, other than to say I was climbing back to 14,000 feet.

The rest of the recovery into base was uneventful.

The aircraft got into that attitude because I am sure I had actually never engaged the autopilot in the first place. The F-16 is very sensitive in roll, and since a lot of the Vipers we flew were hand-me-downs from the active duty USAF, they had been "bent" by the previous operators, and if your hand is off the side stick controller the jet would start a very slow roll left or right. Also, the Viper is unique in that you normally don't have to trim the elevator when flying straight and level. The fly-by-wire system would always trim for one G flight. If you were wings level, nose on the horizon, this was fine, and the nose of the aircraft would stay level. But if you rolled over, the flight control system would try and achieve one G and consequently begin a very slow "pull" to maintain that one G. If you were rolling inverted, as I did, the auto trimming system essentially began pulling me into a split S, which never would have happened since the water would have interrupted us, and rather dramatically as you can imagine.

I have no doubt had I crashed that night the accident board would never have surmised what I had been doing and no doubt would have ruled I crashed due to spatial disorientation and not the real reason . . . incredible stupidity; I guess God had other plans for my life and saved me.

In addition to the beauty and wonder of flying the Viper, some of the guys in the F-16 unit were awesome and became my family as I suffered through my separation and divorce from Kim. God's timing couldn't have been more perfect as aviator extraordinaire Slim; Charlie Ohrel, one of my life's dearest friends; Boltz; Kristine (a lady); and a few others, became wonderful anchors to reality and without them even knowing it they helped to keep me sane. We spent some very nice times at the various local pub type bars laughing and telling flying stories and socializing; it was really nice actually and it was a welcome respite from sitting in my rather spartanly furnished house. I actually took Christina and Kyle with me on some of the evenings out, in particular to a place that did karaoke since Christina loved to sing to the crowd about "two little apples being way up high in an apple tree."

In addition to the wonderful friends I had made while flying the Viper, I had started dating a British flight attendant whom I met while on a layover in Anchorage, Alaska. Liza was much younger than me and the youngest of two girls raised by her wonderful mother and father. Liza was my Achilles heel with regards to women: English (the accent and my romanticism of English ladies due to all of the James Bond movies I'd seen); beautiful in the face; and she had an amazing body. I won't lie I overlooked all the reasons we shouldn't be together—totally different morals, philosophies, and faith, and instead I just concentrated on the aforementioned three "positive" attributes because quite simply I was pretty shallow at this point in my life and as I said before, broken. In Liza, I had the vision of my dream girl, at least in physical terms and in lifestyle. However, in fact the only thing Liza and I had in common at that time was working out in the gym, beyond that we were very opposite. But, I was immediately overtaken with passion for her after our first meeting. I loved going over to the UK to visit her when I had some time off, and we also met on our airline-financed trips all over the world as we were pretty good at coordinating our schedules to get the same layover cities. Oh, let me emphatically say, it was a wonderful, jet-set kind of lifestyle that added an incredible romanticism to our repeated reunions around the world, but, the thought of what life would be like beyond those years of being on fire with passion never entered my mind; in many ways Liza had become an idol who displaced God in my life. The consequences of my turning to her and away from God would have horrible consequences later in my life.

. . .

After five years with my airline, and while first flying as a flight engineer on the B-727 for a year and four months, and then as a flight engineer on the DC-10 for the remainder, I was awarded a bid to fly as a first officer (copilot) on the MD-11.

The Mad Dog, as the MD-11 would soon be nicknamed, was a brand new, wide-body aircraft when my airline bought it for cargo hauling, and it was a kind of derivative of the DC-10 produced by the McDonnell Douglas Aircraft Corporation. It was bigger and longer-ranged than its incestuous brethren, the DC-10-10 and DC-10-30, with CRT displays, FMS computers, and adorned with winglets to accentuate its trendy aerodynamic styling. The MD-11 was beautiful to me in every way and was supposed to be the epitome in commercial aircraft systems and flying automation.

The largest aircraft I'd flown, with any regularity, prior to going to training on the MD-11 was the F-4E (The F-16, which I was flying in the Air Guard, at the time when I went to the MD-11 is smaller than the F-4). The Phantom was sixty-two feet long, thirty-eight feet from wing tip to wing tip, and had a max gross takeoff weight of 62,000 lbs. and was pushed along by two GE (General Electric) J-79 engines that produced 36,000 lbs. of TOTAL thrust. In contrast, the MD-11 is 201 feet long, has a wingspan of 170 feet, can take off weighing 630,500 lbs. and is propelled by three engines that produce 62,500 lbs. of thrust each—yup, there was a significant size difference between the two.

My training on the MD-11 began in August 1993, and to say I was excited is an understatement . . . mere mortal words couldn't express my glee at the thought of being a first officer on such a beautiful new jet. Though I had been flying around the world as a flight engineer, I wasn't actually a pilot, I was just an aircraft monitor for the fuel, air, hydraulic and electrical systems we had on the aircraft. I flew behind the pilots and managed the back end of the jet while the captain and first officer actually flew. It was nice initially, just being an airline crewmember, and being a pilot in the Air Guard helped me to keep my aviator skills honed and my actual hands-on flying addiction appeased. I always wanted a "window seat" with my airline, but I didn't want it flying the diminutive and domestic only B-727. So, I bided my time, waiting a couple of years until the day when I could get an MD-11 first officer (F/O) slot. Fulfilling the dream that I had held very near and dear to my heart for so long a time in my life was such a wonderful gift from God. After so many nights listening to the old man's wonderful wanderlust-tainted stories and after so many years, concurrently, of putting up with the hell of his mental, psycho bullshit and my mother's eternal self-pity . . . the dream, my dream, and its fruition was with-in my grasp...I just had to make it through training.

During my MD-11 training, I had been staying at a very good friend's house. Darryl and Sylvia were very devout Christians and went to the biggest church I'd ever been to in my life. Whoa . . . it must seat 5000 people, and its size blew me away every time I went into it, particularly on the last Sunday in which I would be attending prior to leaving for my company's new domicile in Anchorage, Alaska, from where I would be based while flying the MD-11.

Since God hadn't destroyed my life in the years since I left Kim with the intention of divorce, and in fact my fortunes had improved with the transition to the MD-11, I felt a debt of gratitude to Him and decided to get baptized in that humongous church prior to going to Alaska. But, that baptism was really the public affirmation of a spiritual rebirth and growth I'd had in my faith since separating from my estranged wife.

A couple of years earlier, and about six months after leaving Kim, I had started going, in earnest, to a very nice nondenominational church. Kim and I used to go to Catholic church almost every Sunday when we were together, but after we split I distanced myself from my faith and the God of the Lord's Prayer, although I did continue to pray the prayer, though more out of compunction than zeal.

However, as odd as it sounds, given my fear that God was going to punish me for divorcing Kim, I began to read the Bible every day. It had always been one of my life's goals, to completely read it, so with vigor and enthusiasm I read history's bestselling book every chance I could get.

During my spiritual renaissance, and when I first began attending that nondenominational church in South Jersey, I sought the advice of the church's pastor on how to deal with a deep-seated pain in my heart that just would not go away. What my mother had told me a few months before, about wishing she had aborted all of her kids, and the total disintegration and dysfunction of my life was haunting me daily. I needed help in reintegrating all the disassociated parts of me—mental, spiritual, emotional—into a person that was pleasing to God, others, and in which I could be at peace within myself.

So many questions! The poor pastor was bombarded by my horribly emotionally burdened pleas, not only for answers to my questions but also for relief from the persistent and incredible guilt of leaving Kim, which still haunted me almost every day since we had split. Though this wonderfully patient, wise and loving man couldn't give me a definitive analysis of God's reasons for the whys and ways of the universe, let alone my life, he did assure me that God loved me beyond all measure of my understanding and to continue to read the Bible and seek Him in prayer and in practice. Also, he gave me some very soothing words of wisdom that freed me from my guilt in leaving Kim; I was at last free of the emotional chains that had bound me for so long to her and the relationship my father forced upon us and my weakness in not standing up to the old man when I should have. And finally, I was able to differentiate and understand the difference in the unconditional love of the Christian God, to the very conditional and debilitating, "love" of my mother and father.

It was liberating, this pastor's wisdom, but, it would take many more years and many extreme emotional adventures before I was finally free from the burdens of my parents' sins.

So, taking me back to the one Sunday just before I finished my MD-11 training, and feeling very appreciative to God for blessing me with my wonderful aviation career and friends, in front of three or four thousand people, I was fully immersed in water and baptized. The choice between the God of my faith and the demigod of my previous life (my father) had been made and I was borne anew; never again would my father, directly, influence the choices I made in my life (though the lingering effects of being raised in his shadow will persist all of my life).

Liza and I were still together at that point in my life. When I had returned with vigor to my faith, which was after Liza and I had begun dating, it caused a fairly big rift in our relationship. In addition to reading the Bible from cover to cover, which had always been a bucket list item of mine, I also started going to church in earnest and with enthusiasm. Liza wasn't into anything spiritual at that point in her life, except on the odd occasion when she consulted either a mystic or fortune teller. But, for the most part, with regards to Christianity, she had no leaning or understanding. Because I realized what an idol her body had become, the sexual aspect dominating us as a couple, and also because she was not interested in becoming a Christian, I abruptly ended our relationship. Without question, it was our sex life that bonded and kept us together during this period in our life, and nothing else. We were very disparate in personality, and Liza even admitted several times to me that she had trouble and felt uncomfortable carrying on deep or meaningful conversations with men and therefore used her physical beauty as a way to attract and hold men; she was very insecure back then, as was I, so for both of us sex is what drove us together and initially sustained us. Sex, for Liza, was a tool for her and a way to get men to bond and commit without her actually having to become truly intimate and emotionally close. For my part Liza was the perfect emotional storm that dovetailed nicely into my dysfunction. She was extremely giving of her amazingly beautiful body and because of her insecurity she was very attentive, in a shallow sort of way, which caused me to believe she truly loved me (and I think she actually did, in her own way). Unfortunately, everything about our relationship was so physical I needed a break, to breathe, and to get a grip on my emotions so I could concentrate on God and get back, realistically, to my faith. Liza was not happy about the break-up. But, in time and during our separation she said she had come to know the Christian faith and was wanting to get back together. I took her for her word, as I had gone to church with her in the UK and also she began to go to church with me in the states. I honestly felt that God had breathed new life into each of us and that we had a chance for success at a long-term relationship. But to prove to God my choice of Him over Liza, I told Liza we were not to sleep together until as such time that we married... I am pretty certain she had to inject herself with epinephrine to get her heart started after I made that proclamation; hell, it was hard enough for me to get the words out of my mouth let alone hold that vow to God. And, on that note, though I would like to say that we remained celibate until we married, I did back slide at some point and caved, so for the most part the only change in our relationship was the fact that I continued to pursue God while also pursuing Liza; the eventual outcome wasn't pleasant for Liza and me.

In December 1993, after passing my simulator check-ride, I progressed to the actual line-flying segment of my MD-11 training. My company called this final phase of training, before being released to the line, IOE (Initial Operating Experience). For IOE, I was crewed with an instructor (IP) who would teach me how to fly the real aircraft while operating on revenue trips which spanned the globe; to say I was excited is an understatement!

FLIGHT JOURNAL

I had decided before I began my IOE that for a full year I would journal my MD-11 flights. Selected portions of that journal follow:

4 December '93

ANC to NRT, Capt. Mike Danosky

First flight in the MD-11. I got my MD-11 type rating and ATP checkride in the simulator about three weeks ago. Captain Mike Danosky is checking me out in the actual aircraft, in preparation for being released to the line. We flew from ANC (Anchorage International Airport in Anchorage, Alaska) to NRT (New Tokyo International Airport in Narita City, Chiba Prefecture, Japan; about forty miles northeast of Tokyo City). The weather at both ends, and in the middle, was perfect. I had a real nice first landing in Narita after a hand flown ILS/Visual to Rwy. 34. (Runway 34; 34 designating the magnetic heading, roughly, of the runway. So 34 meant 340 degrees magnetic. If it was runway 05 it meant 050 degrees magnetic . . . or close to it. If there are two, or three runways that are parallel, which is the case at many international airports, they designate the runways with an L or C or R after the number. For example, DFW airport, in Dallas, has runways 35L, 35C, and 35R—left, center, and right. Obviously, it takes the confusion out of which runway you are supposed to take off from or land on.)

■ ■ ■

6 December '93

NRT to MNL, Capt. Danosky

Second flight; 9:30 p.m. T/O out of Narita bound for MNL (Manila International Airport, Manila, Philippines). Manila is straddled by two typhoons. Lola passed over Luzon twelve hours earlier, and Manny was about 200 miles east of Manila moving westerly. Because of the first typhoon we were delayed about six hours to let the leaves and branches settle to the earth after the maelstrom's passage. We followed a Northwest 747 cargo flight out of Narita, each of us with the same destination. We leveled at FL330, Northwest at FL 370, and we passed "him" about an hour out of Narita (we were cruising at point 83 Mach). The arrival into Manila was anticlimactic. We could see the city lights from ninety miles out. We over flew the airport on vectors for a VOR Rwy. 06 approach. Once on final, I clicked the autopilot off and hand flew for a visual approach and landing. The wind was from 060–070 degrees at twelve to twenty knots. Again, if I do say so myself, as did the captain, a nice landing was accomplished.

I have a distinct tendency, however, much to the captain's chagrin, to land at least twenty to thirty feet right of centerline. I think it's due to me thinking the airplane is so wide that I need to offset to the right to put the left side of the cockpit on the left side of the runway; weird, but, I believe true. The Northwest flight landed ten minutes behind us. Manila, well at least the airport, was very wet.

■ ■ ■

7 December '93
MNL to TPE, Capt. Danosky

After a three-hour wait in Manila we headed for TPE (Taipei International Airport, Taipei, Taiwan or Chiang Kai-shek Airport). This was a very uneventful flight of one hour and thirty minutes' duration. We flew an autoland Cat III B approach. The weather was clear; I just needed an autoland demo to fill my IOE squares. The wind was 070 at 22 kts. and we landed on Rwy. 05 Left. The jet landed a little left of centerline, rather firmly, and then immediately corrected back to the centerline; with the auto brakes on medium we stopped rather quickly. It was a really nice demo and a good way to give a new guy confidence that the "system" really works. (I'd done a million auto lands in the simulator during training, but, let's face it . . . a simulator is just that, a "simulator," and not the real thing, no matter how well they are made.)

. . .

7 December '93

TPE to ANC, Capt. Danosky

After a brief twelve-hour layover, we were off again. This time we were bound for Anchorage. We also had a third crewmember, an RFO, Ron Davis. (RFO—relief first officer. Anytime scheduled block time for a flight exceeded eight hours, on a two crew aircraft, a third crewmember was/is required. It could be a captain or a first officer. My company usually schedules first officers as RFO's for these longer flights.) I alighted the aircraft from Rwy. 05L in Taipei at 7 p.m. local time. After thirty minutes at the controls, and shortly after leveling off, I let the RFO take my seat and I went to the back for a two-hour nap.

For the most part the flight was pretty "routine" and boring. However, we did pass directly over Shemya Island, in the far western Aleutian Island chain, and for the second time in my life I was able to see the island. Actually, since it was dark all I could see were the lights of the airport. While I've never been there, Shemya, I can't imagine it's a wonderful place and I have absolutely no desire to ever do anything other than fly over it en route to more hospitable places.

The midmorning sunrise while flying over the mountains west of Anchorage was breathtaking! With the wide expanse of cockpit glass, "windows," with which the MD-11 is designed, the views can be positively superb, as they were this morning! With nary a cloud in the sky, save for the certain white blankets lying upon a still resting valley or two, the mountains seemed higher than ever. Oh, what a glorious way to arrive at our destination!

Beyond the mountains came ice-filled Cook Inlet and a bit further on Anchorage.

While Anchorage—indeed all of Alaska, it appeared—was clear, in seeming defiance of God's own laws of nature, a ground hugging bit of cloud enveloped the approach end of runways 06 right and left. Actually, the recalcitrant little puff of white was camped out with its western edge over the shore (the Anchorage runways, 6R/L, are about a third of a mile from the waters of Cook Inlet) and its eastern edge halfway down the aforementioned runways. We could have broken off the ILS approach to runway 6R, fly a visual to runway 14, which was wide open, but, I elected to continue hand flying the ILS. At 400 feet above the runway, we entered this obstinate freak of nature and at Cat I Mins, 200 feet above the runway threshold, Mike called, "minimums," and said the runway was in sight . . . whew! I seriously thought we were going to go missed approach. Amazingly enough, I proceeded to land very, very smoothly (even blind squirrels find a nut every now and then . . . meaning they get lucky) and as we rolled out, to add a nice finishing touch on this flight, we broke out into full sunshine leaving the odd little puffball behind us.

After blocking in Ron offered me his MD-11 tie tack as a memento of my IOE experience and of course I refused it, but he insisted so I humbly accepted; what a thoughtful and generous gift from someone I barely knew.

Two things of note here: (1) We landed before we took off... one of the idiosyncrasies of crossing the international dateline going eastbound is that you get to "relive" (depending on your departure time) a good part of your day again; and (2) Mike, my instructor, is without question one of the most laidback instructors with whom I've ever flown. I am not sure if his heartbeat rate ever goes above "resting" no matter what kind of faux pas I make or in whatever phase of flight we are in. He is truly amazing. I am convinced I could accidently roll the airplane inverted on an ILS (if that's even possible to accidently do) and he'd speak in the very soothing, sage-type voice he has and talk me into righting the aircraft and recovering . . . amazing man.

■ ■ ■

10 December '93
ANC to ORD, Capt. Danosky

We left at 2:30 p.m. in clear weather bound for ORD (Chicago O'Hare International Airport, Chicago, Illinois). We had a jump-seater who was on his first flight, hence he was reading his Bible (I'm serious) while we were loading; though I'm not sure if he was reading it because it was his first jumpseat flight, or because I was going to be at the controls (Editor's note: During this time, before 9/11, the company allowed all employees, whether a secretary or cargo handler or whomever, to fly on its aircraft in the jumpseats, extra seats, besides the crew that were located in the cockpit, or in courier seats which are immediately aft of the cockpit). Ground ops and takeoff were normal. Okay, well, about as normal as you can get with four flights under your belt, and the view, climbing southeast-ward, over the mountains east of Anchorage was almost as glorious as was the view a few days ago when we arrived.

The arrival into O'Hare was, for the most part, uneventful. I flew a visual approach, backed up by the ILS, to runway 27L. I landed, right wheel down, in a 22–25 kts. right crosswind. The landing itself wasn't hard, but then again, I've had better ones. I'm still tending to land to the right of the centerline and I still have yet to let the auto brakes do their stuff; I'm on the brakes before the auto-brakes themselves have really begun to activate.

■ ■ ■

12 December '93

ORD to MSP, Capt. Danosky

Mike and I took off at midnight, from O'Hare, bound for MSP (Minneapolis International Airport in Minneapolis). We departed runway 14R. I hand flew the aircraft to 18,000 feet. The weather was perfect, not a cloud in the sky and no moon. The aircraft was quite sensitive in pitch once the tail fuel management got the CG back to 31.5 percent MAC; just two fingers was all you needed to fly her, or quick bursts of trim, to control the altitude/attitude. We were on vectors until we reached FL 350 whereupon we were cleared direct to MSP.

I hand-flew a visual approach to runway 11R at MSP. It was a bit of a mistake to accept the visual while level at 6000 feet though. I was close in, near the airport and heading away (west). I lost sight of the runway as we flew westward and consequently I was asshole and elbows trying to get slowed down, descended down, and turned around. I finally turned myself onto final, with the aid of the NAV display, but the lights of the runway were lost amidst a sea of city lights. Again, with the aid of the FMS NAV display, oh what a wonderful device! I was able "self-vector" myself onto final for the runway. The wind was a sixty-degree cross at ten knots. The landing wasn't pretty, but I just wanted to get my IOE over with.

And it is! AHA! As I write in this journal, I am doing what I have dreamt since I can remember! I am now one of those fast-moving stars that I've stared up at so many nights in my past when I was just a kid in my backyard. I would listen to my dad tell his stories of ocean crossings, European cities, and his escapades all over the world and dream of doing the same. Yes, I am taking the torch from my father and am one of those distant blinking lights immersed in the starred night sky and leaving a trail of short-lived, whispering jet streams across this world of ours, causing people to look up and wonder to what distant and exotic place is that light bound. Oh, I thank God for fulfilling this dream! I've got many more miles to fly, Lord willing, and many things to learn. But now, it's time to enjoy flying, enjoy my new life, and devote time to writing about the good fortunes of my aviation life!

. . .

5 February '94

SFO to ANC, Capt. Jamieson

My leg; I took off on runway 10L in San Francisco. The sky was clear as we turned to a 340-degree heading right after takeoff, which put us flying right down the bay. Shortly thereafter we were cleared direct to "KATCH" and to climb to FL 310.

En route, the northern lights were spectacular, particularly in the vicinity of Mount Logan (far northwestern British Columbia).

The lights were to the northeast, how far I don't really know. You could actually see, since it was so clear, how the entire northern lights curved around the Earth's magnetic lines of force. It must have been a huge curve, 200 to 300 miles in radius at least, but it was very apparent; an absolutely beautiful sight.

The weather in ANC precluded me from landing the jet—2,400 RVR (the captain must land the aircraft, as per company procedures, when the visibility is less than 4000 feet RVR [runway visual range] or three-quarters of mile), so "Hal" (I say "Hal" because of the errant computer from the movie 2001: A Space Odyssey, but it is the autopilot to which I am referring.) was going to do it with the captain as the final authority. The descent went well, except for an attempted level off at 1,600 feet as we neared the airport. For some reason, the aircraft didn't want to stop descending when it should have. "Hold" appeared on the FMA for altitude, supposedly giving us a visual indication of what the autopilot was going to do, but at 1,700 feet, 100 feet above the selected level off altitude, the aircraft's rate of descent was still 1,500-2,000 feet per minute (it should have been more like 100 feet per minute). As on Dec. 22, I had to disconnect the autopilot and level the aircraft manually. As I was doing this, leveling off, the GPWS (ground proximity warning system) was sounding its alarm, due to rate of closure and proximity to the ground, and then, to add even more wonderful sounds to this already distracting environment, the autopilot disconnect warning was whining, as was the captain. Finally, to add to this assault on the senses, the air was turbulent, causing an uncomfortable series of gyrations as I tried to attain level flight, and the snow was attacking the windscreen with such vengeance that I swore it was angry at the captain and I for disturbing it. So, what started off as a simple autopilot glitch was turning into a very busy and stressful arrival! However, "Hal" did redeem himself and did a real nice job landing the aircraft. I guess computers have bad days/nights too; who said they aren't human?

. . .

25 August '94

SEL to NRT, Capt. Rick Gattis

Rick's leg. Nothing of note. Rainy and drizzly in SEL though. However, on top we had a beautiful sunset and one-hundred-mile viz going into NRT. Nice flight.

THE WILD WEST SHOW

I'd like to pause here in the flow of these selected journal entries to discuss layovers. Most non-airline people have wildly preconceived notions about the glamour of flying around the world and that our flights are just vehicles to take us from one party to the next; the party being the layover. Maybe that's true with certain airlines, and I won't lie, when I was dating Liza, who I eventually married, we would meet around the world and have a blast in this city or that one (she was a flight attendant with Japan Airlines and based in London). There was no finer dating life than that, unrealistic as hell on which to base a marriage maybe, but so intoxicating was the actual glamour of the romanticism and jet-set lifestyle!

But the reality is, I flew for a cargo airline. We flew with tons of stuff, and yes possibly even some highly valuable rubber dog shit from Hong Kong, but it was cargo, "stuff," not people in the back, so usually, the only humans on the aircraft were just me and another pilot (unless the flight was over eight hours and we had another crewmember or if we had one or more jumpseaters who usually sat in the courier cabin which was right behind the cockpit). Our cargo didn't clap if we landed well and we didn't have beautiful flight attendants feeding us grapes, bringing us our meals, or fanning us as we watched the autopilot work. Nor could we whine to the flight attendant about what a jerk the "other" pilot may be, if indeed they were one; nope, we served our own food, got our own coffee, dropped grapes into our own mouths, and suffered in silence, sometimes, the two of us in that big ol' MD-11, preferring to read a book rather than to talk to the other person if one of us was being PMSy (ya know, bitchy).

It's funny, but the fact that cargo flying could seem "lonely" never occurred to me before I got with my airline. I actually never thought of being a cargo airline pilot and I must say that when I got hired and started flying the line I was like, "Wow, this is kinda lonely."

So I endeavored to make up for the loneliness on the layovers, like a lot of guys did. Usually the same guy with whom you flew you met for dinner, lunch, etc., and/or you may plan on going to a sporting event, museum, library (no, not really a library) or other tourist site that was germane to that city/area.

A lot of foreign cities had expat restaurants, bars, pubs, etc., that catered to, or were draws for, airline crews or other non-indigenous people. One such place in Narita was called "the Cage."

The Cage was a small karaoke bar, which was right next door to our layover hotel. I had been going to the Cage since I first began flying to Narita, late 1989, being led there by word of mouth from other airline crews. Sometimes I had one drink and then left, other times I closed the place down.

With regard to our layover hotel, "the Lets" (yes . . . "the Lets Hotel"), it was not exactly the Ritz, but it was right in town and there were quite a few expat places to frequent in that area since Narita was a huge layover destination for thousands of airline crews. The company changed hotels a few years after 1993, moving closer to the airport, but a hotel shuttle bus still runs regularly throughout the day to take hotel guests to downtown Narita and the local mall.

As I said, the Cage was small, maybe fifty by thirty-five feet, and it had extremely steep steps leading up to its second-floor entrance. Rumor has it an airline crewmember fell down them and died; as steep as they were I believed it. You seriously had to watch your step when leaving if either inebriated or tired, or both. Stepping inside, the bar was immediately on your left and there was a metal grate kinda thing separating the immediate bar area from the main seating area. The karaoke stage was against the opposite wall from the bar and in between there was booth type seating on the left and right sides and some couch seating in the middle. You could easily see through the grating to the stage so people often sat "on the bar" to look over the heads of others who might be standing near the bar or closer to the front. The bathroom was novel in that it was very small, located on the right side of the room, yet it could accept one male at the open urinal and a female sheltered in an enclosed stall; modesty, for the guys, was not optional when using the loo.

The Cage could get amazingly crowded, yet there seemed to be no rhyme or reason as to what sparked a standing-room-only crowd one evening, and then an almost patron-free evening the next. During the times when it was packed I felt like a sardine in a can, but the mood was always festive because when elbow-to-elbow, the multinational airline crews were forced to interact and alcohol-fueled détente reigned supreme.

Let there be no doubt, I could not and cannot sing. I did not go in there to break glass with my screeching but more to hear others who actually were quite good. The two times I did sing were because I had had too much to drink and someone dared me; the modest applause I got after singing was no doubt due to the fact that the song was finished, and I was leaving the stage; I had no delusions of quitting my day job with dreams of being a rock star.

But the Cage was a place of entertainment and camaraderie for all crews, and it was certainly a melting pot of cultures and a draw for people lonely for home and friendly company.

On one layover in Narita, I had gone in relatively early to the Cage to wait for my captain to arrive. The place was half full when I got there so I went to my usual hangout spot, the bar, ordered a drink and sat upon it (the bar) and right next to another guy. I had just gotten new cowboy boots and the guy next to me remarked about my boots and how he liked them. He was a United F/O, he said, and he was in almost constant communication with two very beautiful Filipino ladies who were standing, one in front, and the other to his right, next to him. After downing a drink, the United guy heard the beginning intro to a song, said "This is my song!" then jumped down from the bar and took the mic from the previous singer and sang a very well-sung song. Wow, I was impressed!

A couple of hours into my stay the bar had gotten a little more crowded, but still well less than what you would call packed. I still sat on my perch in the back talking to this or that pilot from either my airline or another while minimally talented, none at all, or amazingly gifted singers aired their notes. At one point in those two hours, a group of five American Samoan men entered the establishment and sat all the way in the front left of the room. They looked like junior sumo wrestlers, except without the flab, and didn't exactly look happy.

My United friend had moved to some seats, closer to the stage, since he was a frequent singer and his female entourage now flanked either side of him. At some point that evening, and after the Samoans had been there for a certain amount of time, a song began to play. It is a song that I loathed (then, and to this day) when it first came out on the radio and even more so when sung by the karaoke artists who usually butchered its vocals—"To All the Girls I've Loved Before," sung by Julio Iglesias and Willie Nelson. Ugh.

So, the music for the song begins and the United guy jumps onto to the stage and is getting ready to sing when two of the Samoans walk up to the stage and start talking to him. You could not hear what was being said since the mic was being held away from their faces, but it looked like a heated conversation judging by the body language and the looks on the faces. I was watching intently, as was everyone in the room, since this kind of display just never happened.

Then one of the Samoans very quickly put his arm around the neck of the United guy, pulled his head low, and started punching him in the face.

There is a line in Animal House where Dean Wormer says to Flounder, when chastising the pledges for their poor grades, "Fat, drunk, and stupid is no way to go through life, son." Well, at the time of this fight, I was two of those three . . . fat not being either of the two.

Whether it was the cowboy boots that caused me to have no fear of the repercussions of taking on two American Samoans, or the fact that I was indeed drunk and stupid, I don't know. What I do know is that as soon as I saw the punching start I jumped from the bar, ran to the stage, pushed one Samoan out of the way and grabbed the other, the guy who was punching, and held him tightly to keep him from doing more harm to the American.

I need to add that I was very physically fit back then and worked out with weights a lot. Though not a body builder wannabe, nor displaying an Arnold Schwarzenegger physique, I was still strong and muscular. But, my strength was no match for all five of those guys.

What I thought would happen, when I jumped to the rescue of the hapless singer, was that all the other guys in the place would rush up to help too. But, alas, they—the other male patrons—were thinking men, endowed with brains from their creator that they actually used. I, being, well, me, was not thinking. I was not thinking about the three other Samoans sitting quietly to the left of the stage either. Upon my triumphant arrival and pulling the Samoans from the now bloodied pilot laying on the stage, I felt certain the other guys in the crowd would rush up to help.

So, when I felt a lot of pushing and shoving behind me as I held a bear hug on the Samoan who started the punching, I thought it was a few of the other male crews dealing with the Samoans behind me; nope, it wasn't. It was actually them, the other three Samoans, taking turns punching me in the back, trying to get me to release their buddy. I turned to look behind me since I was getting some serious hits to my back, and I was wondering what the hell was going on. It was a pretty inopportune time to glance over my shoulder because as I turned to my right I got a fist right in my face. It was then, as I got turned around, that I realized I was solo in this fight: It was one American versus five from one of America's protectorates.

I was bound to be DOA if this kept up. As I got turned around, the Samoans were trying to grab my arms and wanted to use me as a punching bag. Somehow, as they tried to hold my arms, I went to the ground, fighting to keep from being killed, and when I did hit the floor, that seemed to be the trigger for all the other guys in the place to come to my aid, and a good ol'-fashioned barroom brawl broke out with a fair bit of punching going on by others.

The fight broke up fairly quickly after a few of the other male patrons jumped in to help. Seeing they were outnumbered, the Samoans deftly extricated themselves and left, leaving many in the bar shell-shocked at the whole event.

After the chairs, drinking glasses, and beer bottles were picked up and with adrenalin returning to more normal levels, I sat at a table with the two Filipino ladies tending to my injuries. Besides a bruised ego from feeling dejected that I should have defended myself better, I was bleeding from my mouth and nose, and my ribs on the right side hurt like a son of a bitch. As the ladies wiped blood from my face and thanked me for coming to the aid of their friend, a Qantas pilot came up to me and dropped a beer in front of me and told me to drink up. I said, "What is that for?" and he said "Mate, that beer is for you, and if you want more it's all on me."

Again, I said, "Why?"

He said, "That was the best entertainment I've had all month, it's the least I can do!"

I had to laugh.

An odd twist to this tale is the après-fight conversation I had with the two Filipino ladies. After tending to me and wiping the blood from my mouth and nose the ladies left the bar, though I stayed for a bit, trying to wind down. It wasn't until the adrenalin subsided and the alcohol had been pissed away that I realized I was really hurting in my ribs and wanted to go back to my room. It hurt like hell just walking, and going down the stairs of the karaoke bar was an exercise in masochism.

I walked the short distance to the hotel and headed for the elevators when I saw the two Filipino ladies sitting in the lobby. They called me over and again thanked me for helping their friend. I said it's okay, and then they said the oddest thing. They said they were going to make sure that the Samoans would not be back at the bar, nor would they be allowed to stay within the confines of the city of Narita, in any hotel located there. I was incredulous at their declaration, and to be honest I thought they were full of crap.

However, as it turned out the Samoans were employees of an airline, the name of which I can't remember, and the ladies that I had been casually talking to all evening were employees of the Japanese Mafia—working ladies, if ya catch my drift. They had contacts in their little black books that would have made many high-level politicians or prominent businessmen run for cover if exposed. So, on this night, right after the fight, the ladies called in on a few favors from their clientele. Both of them, evidently, had the connections to get the Samoans thrown out of the hotel they used in Narita and the karaoke bar forbid any employees of that airline from entering for the foreseeable future. I really thought the ladies were bluffing until the owner of the karaoke bar told me that, indeed, they were two very well-connected, and not to be messed with, women. Now, how the United guy knew them, I don't know since I never asked, but, I have no regrets for my impulsive nature in helping the United guy and I have a great story to tell my kids.

In reality, fights rarely occurred on layovers. In fact, in my entire flying career that was only the second fight I'd ever personally seen and the first in which I was physically involved.

. . .

28 August '94

PEN to TPE, Capt. Rick Gattis

The flight from hell, or more accurately, the flight through hell—it was my leg. We took off from beautiful, sunshiny Penang and headed north toward a huge convective area (actually this whole equator area is convective country, but today there was a huge area of instability that was giving birth [it is "Mother" Nature, ya know] to a lot of thunderstorms). We started encountering these storms about an hour out of Penang and it didn't stop until 100 miles from Taipei.

We initially cruised at FL330, due to traffic, and flying at that altitude really bugged me. The problem with being at that altitude was the fact that we were always in the clouds, and I had to totally rely on our radar for weather lookout. I say that not as if that's a bad thing, per se, using the radar, but down around the equator on most days you will usually be in relatively clear air and see a storm or storms, or suspicious looking clouds, with your eyes and then confirm their nefarious nature with your radar and consequently deviate around them, if need be, or if they aren't bad, fly through them (actually, even light green, as shown on the radar when looking at a towering cumulus, can kick your ass, turbulence-wise, so you still want to avoid it). For some reason, I liked this division of responsibility between my God-given, "Mark I eyeballs" and the Collins Radio-built radar. Looking outside and actually seeing those behemoths, for some reason, gave me a warm fuzzy feeling, as I could actually see that they were there and then use the radar to "X-ray" those "puppies" and either confirm their ferocity or dismiss them as just a shadow of their former selves, which gave me great comfort; why this gave me comfort I don't know . . . maybe because you have two ways of identifying them, maybe I'm not a trusting person, who knows. (PEN to TPE is always a day flight; it usually departs PEN at noon so you usually had the ability to look pretty far in front of you.) We didn't reach clear air, and I mean severe clear, until we were 200 miles south of Taipei and then Mother Nature, as if to say, "Yo, buckaroos, I'm not finished with you yet!" placed the biggest thunderstorm I've ever seen in my life right over southwestern Taiwan, on our proposed route of flight, near Kaohsiung (a major industrial city on Taiwan's southern end).

Digressing a bit here . . . The problem with being in clouds is that you can't see the buildups that won't paint on radar but which also will still bounce you around. Rick showed me a trick of keeping both of the ND (navigation display) maps at the same range so the radar updates the ND with every sweep (if the ranges are different it only updates "your" nav display every other sweep). There were sooooo many thunderstorms we deviated at will, usually never more than seven to eight miles left or right of track; asking for clearance to deviate would have been hopeless, given the number of times we would have had to ask. We eventually climbed to FL370, at my urging, and yet we were still in clouds and we still couldn't top some of the storms.

Twice we actually flew through some of the painted weather. When I say flew through it, I mean on the radar it wasn't painting as yellow or red stuff, but spotty green; however, I know from personal experience, after a brief encounter with a seemingly benign looking green dot at FL350 while flying from Tokyo to Singapore some months ago, that green stuff at FL350 can beat the crap out of you. Finally, green at FL370 can be red at the lesser altitudes as ice reflects less than water. So, it was with great trepidation that we penetrated the area of storms where we did. However, we did do a vertical profile of the area we planned to penetrate with the radar and though there was some yellow down below, it was mostly green. Before we entered this visually unconfirmed (with our own eyes that is) tempest up ahead, we cinched down on the seatbelt straps, slowed to our turbulence penetration speed (.80 to .82 Mach) and turned on the continuous ignition. (My dad said that back in the old airline days, when he flew DC-3s, they used to lower their seats, turn on the cockpit lights to full bright, drop the landing gear, go to METO (maximum except T/O) power and just plough through the storm.) In the MD-11 the autopilot was left to handle the flying duties as it was believed it could do a better job of flying, and I have to say it did a really nice job. On the other hand, you did have to override the auto throttles almost continuously when it got turbu-lent as you would get some pretty wicked swings in power advances and declines as the airspeed either radically decreased or increased in or out of tempo with the bumps; it was not uncommon to go from the low-speed "foot" to the high-speed "zipper" (low-speed foot is the speed at which the aircraft is very near stalling, loss of lift to sup-port its weight, and high-speed zipper is the speed which the aircraft was designed not to exceed) in the space of a couple of bounces if you were flying above the FMS-computed optimum altitude.

I could tell we were entering the storm as the fabric of the sky changed from a hazy, incredibly bright whiteness to a very forebod-ing darkening and thickening of the air mass; also, my nose was immediately assaulted by the sharp smell of ionized air flowing into the cockpit. Those two sensory changes, the visual and the smell, because of past experiences, have turned me into a sort of Pavlov's dog, automatically causing my heart to beat faster and my senses to heighten; even if the radar doesn't show anything bad, I always wonder if I'm getting myself into something worse than what I've bargained for. (More on this at the end of this journal.)

As expected, it was bumpy . . . mostly moderate turbulence; however, there was the occasional worse-than-moderate bump, the type that makes your heart leap and you think, "Oh God, have I made a serious error in judgment here . . .?" (That's a rhetorical question I mumble to myself.)

In addition to the off-road, four-wheelin' type of ride that a "mild" thunderstorm gives, all the other elements were present too. The light show was very entertaining. You could see lightning flashes all around, most being suffused in the clouds below. But on the odd occasion, a very thin but erratic streak of white light could be seen jumping from cloud to cloud as we transitioned from one storm cell, into a clear pocket of air between these cloud massifs, and then right back into another. Though most of these lightning flashes appeared to be thankfully distant, we did have ol' St. Elmo up close and personal, continuously entertaining us with a seemingly never-repeated and variable display of electrical arcs across the front windscreen. Conversely, and in total contrast to the electrons trying to fry us, the precipitation—rain, snow, ice, whatever—seemed determined to drown the fire in the engines; at times, this aquatic assault on the aircraft was deafening and I wondered if we would need a new paint job upon arrival in Taipei.

Though it seemed like an eternity, because of the heightened senses, it was only for a few minutes, at best, that we were in this aggressive massing of the elements. The delineation between psychotic clouds and the more benign type was indicated by an immediate brightening, if not blinding, of the diffused light in the sky around us, and though we were still immersed in visible moisture, it was much thinner than the ocean we had just penetrated.

Once the radar indicated that the coast was clear—of thunderstorms—Rick went back to reading his book, me looking at and playing with the radar, and the flight in general back to its previous routine of deviating around the more defined buildups; whether by luck, skill, or providence we didn't encounter either hail or severe turbulence; "All in a day's work!" my dad would have said, rather matter-of-factly.

As I said earlier, about 200 miles south of Taipei we burst from solid cloud into solid clear with the Mount Everest of thunderstorms up ahead, showing us the way to the island of Taiwan. Our original routing, as we closed on Taipei, was from TNN to HLG, via the W4 airway and then from HLG direct to TPE (actually you are always given a STAR by ATC as you get close to TNN). Out of habit I had always put in an arrival STAR, named "Sierra Foxtrot," and then the appropriate ILS approach.

Closing in on the airport, I asked for, and received, clearance to descend to FL150 since it seemed like the controller was keeping us abnormally high. Eventually, we were given the clearance to descend so down I screamed at 355 knots (the aircraft's normal descent/arrival speed) and four thousand FPM. I knew there was an aircraft in front of us, but Rick, in a moment of acute awareness, asked Taipei control at what altitude was the aircraft in front of us? With that, Taipei said, "Nineteen five"; we were at FL 220 and descending fast. Suddenly the light shone on Taipei and concurrently, as I arrested our descent rate to 1,000 FPM, the controller turned us thirty degrees left. Lo and behold, there, appearing from my one o'clock low, and 3000 feet lower, was a Mandarin MD-11! Would we have hit him? I don't know, but it would have been close. So now, with us being vectored to mainland China for separation, I slowed to 250, and eventually, we found our way into Taipei. The weather was beautiful.

■ ■ ■

3 September '94

SIN to PEN, Capt. P

Initially Capt. P didn't know how to get to the Penang Rwy. 04, 15 DME ARC approach into the FMS (it's stored in the Rwy. 04 ILS file as there are three ILS's to Rwy. 04 and it must be called up under the "WMKP" lateral revision). Also, he had a bit of trouble putting in the flight plan. The RFO was still with us, obnoxious as ever, and today he started to really irritate the captain and me. He would just stand behind us, watching and giving his little-listened-to input. I must say I think the captain was a weeee bit overwhelmed on this flight, short as it was. (I also need to say that he was going through a rather bitter divorce and on the flight from ANC to Narita, mentioned earlier, I got an earful of his travails. This is the first time I've ever flown with someone visibly affected by marital issues and on the way to the airport this morning he did say that his future ex called and told him she had maxed out one of his credit cards.) Takeoff, climb and en route were routine enough, and the weather in Singapore was nice. But about two-thirds of the way to Penang, it was thunderstorm hell.

Capt. P was holding 350 knots in the descent, which was normal, but we were heading for a rather ominous-looking bunch of clouds, both in a visual sense and when scrutinized by the radar. I asked "El Captano" if we were going to deviate around a really big buildup showing solid red on the radar, and at first there was no response. He was just staring straight ahead, outside, and not acknowledging my inquiries. Finally, after asking him a couple more times and pointing to the really big red spot on the nav display, he agreed that we needed to deviate to the left. I requested such from Kuala Lumpur (the controlling ATC sector), but they must have taken a coffee break, as they were not answering my requests. Since we were hauling ass in the descent and with no sign of the captain slowing down, I was fidgeting in my seat big time, and I asked him to turn anyway, as I was thinking we were going to die if we didn't. He said he wouldn't turn unless we were cleared by ATC, and for some reason he wouldn't slow down. I tried with my best New Jersey tact to get him to slow to turbulence penetration speed because we were now visually entering a very black looking mass of moisture and, I will tell you, I was shitting gold bricks. I was working the radar more than he was at this point, tilting and gaining, hoping the radar was lying to us. It wasn't, but there was one good surprise . . . though I would've sworn we had flown into a lake suspended in midair, I mean it was that heavy with rain, there was almost zero turbulence. Thank you, God! We entered the black mass at 20,000 feet and at 350 knots. After a second or two of about ninety-plus decibels of "rain hammering an aircraft noise," it seemed to snap my fearless leader back to reality, and he immediately slowed the aircraft and turned in the shortest direction out of the mess (which was to the left); about that time too ATC cleared us to deviate at will . . . gee thanks. We didn't see any lightning during all this, nor did we get St. Elmo's fire . . . just lots and lots of rain . . . how those engines continued to run is beyond me. We did have continuous ignition selected, but still, I am amazed the water didn't quench the fires in the burner cans.

So, now I have some more food for thought in the radar interpretation file of my brain. I still have yet to fly with any captain that I find knowledgeable on the subject and I still think the F-4 and F-16 radars were much better than the MD-11's in weather avoidance due to their power output and their ability to "see" through heavy rain and thunderstorms. I also think the captain was seriously behind on this flight, but I also fault myself for not being more proactive and letting him fly us into a potentially serious situation.

■   ■   ■

11 October '94
KIX to ANC, Capt. Bob Duncan

My leg. Nice evening! We flew with a "dark cockpit" (no dome/overhead light on) for the whole leg; I personally like it that way as I can see traffic storms, etc., and I also like the ambiance, but, most guys fly with the dome/overhead lights on once you get to top of climb. About fifty minutes east of SYA, inbound to it (Shemya), Bob and I saw what at first appeared to be a very slow-moving shooting star. We were headed 070 and the red object came from our upper right side, three o'clock position, and was heading roughly 090. We watched it disappear over the easterly horizon; you could actually see a kind of vapor trail remaining after it passed. Now you have to get into the mood of the moment when we saw this aberration . . . Bob and I were talking about UFOs; Bob totally believes in them, but I don't. He was trying to convince me of how wrong I was in my belief when we saw this slow-motion meteorite. He was so happy that this happened, and said to me, "What do you think that is?" pointing over my shoulder and out the window. I have to admit I thought it was perfect timing, but I said, not wanting to concede anything that would bolster his argument that "it" had to be something that could be logically explained! We came up with all of these theories on what it could have been, from the new Air Force spy plane "Aurora," an SR-71, or a satellite in a decaying orbit. As we passed over SYA ,and I called ATC on VHF to report our position, I bluntly asked them if they had had any reports of a UFO. Oddly enough, I must have been the first person to fess up that I saw something as all of a sudden a bazillion guys are chiming in with an "I saw it too!" radio call . . . actually, it was pretty amazing how many aircraft were on frequency. Anchorage Center said that the UFO was the space shuttle on re-entry for a landing at Edwards forty-five minutes ago . . . how cool is that? The rest of the flight was pretty easy and uneventful . . . though Bob's pride was a bit hurt when the UFO turned out to be an IFO—identified flying object.

■ ■ ■

NAKED IN NARITA

Again, I'm going to take a break in the journal entries and tell you of another story that happened while on one of my layovers in Narita. I'm not sure why Narita saw so much drama in my layover life, but it did, and the following story, though maybe not as exciting to you, the reader, as it was to me, it is something, I never, ever want to repeat. (I wrote the story about ten years after the event.)

During the wee morning hours of one February day, during a year I don't remember, in a foreign country I barely remember being in, I entered my room in the "the Let's Hotel." I had flown in from Singapore, and my captain and I had been crisscrossing the Far East daily or nightly, depending on the flight schedule, for the previous eight days. My circadian rhythm was less rhythm and more mood swing due to this trip and some much-needed sleep was calling, nay, begging.

In addition to being ungodly tired, I was somewhat tipsy, too, since, after the flight my captain insisted I join him for a couple of drinks at the Cage to hear him sing. I had bid the captain an early adieu, after watching him pretend to be Frank Sinatra, or Alfalfa, that choice being based upon the singer versus the listener. Tired, I thought, is no way to end a trip, so I set off early, for my room in search of sleep and the brief sanctity it brings and hoping to be rejuvenated for tomorrow's night flight back to the States.

Since I was so tired, I began stripping to my primordial nakedness as I walked from the door to the bed; I didn't bother to turn on a room light as that would have required too much effort. As for the manner of dress in which I slept . . . I was young, early thirties, and in great physical shape, and I usually slept in the buff, so I make no apologies. The circumstances that you will soon read about, however, have helped to forever, well at least up until this writing, change my nocturnal dress code while in a hotel.

The room door had barely shut, and light from the hallway scarcely had time to scurry itself out of the room before I was off to la-la land and totally immersed in my dreams.

I have no idea how long I had slept when the Cokes I had drunk parted company from the rum they went down with and were persistently trying to wake me up so they could be released from my body. In a zombielike state, I walked from the bed to what I thought was the bathroom door; in fact, I had opened the door to hallway, and before I was awake enough to stop it, the door closed and locked behind me.

I was now on the sixth floor, in the hallway, of the Let's Hotel in Narita, Japan, and I was buck ass naked. Not good. My employer would no doubt frown on the type of publicity I could bring them if it got out that one of its crewmembers was escapading "in the raw" in a local hotel, particularly since they were trying to build brand name recognition and loyalty over there. But I digress . . .

I was still sooo tired I knocked lightly on my own room door for a minute or so until the realization came that there was no one in the room who could open it and the room key was on the inside. About this time, too, I realized that this was no dream.

It is amazing how fast you can wake up and sober up when faced with enormous quantities of adrenaline. After realizing I was indeed locked out of my room, and buck-ass naked, I put my back against the door and slid to the floor. I needed to think and I wanted to shrink my "profile" as much as I could so I pulled my knees up to my chest and put my arms around them.

Many thoughts were going through my head right about now: First and foremost, the word shit passed through my head about fifty times; then Maslow's hierarchy of needs popped into my semiconscious brain because I am pretty certain that the desire for clothes is right up there in the "basic needs" part of the pyramid . . . ya know, the bottom part, right along with food and water, heat, light and air. After my Psych 101 review, other less scholarly ideas wafted their way through my jet-lagged synapses. In no particular order, they were: (1) go knock on the captain's door and ask him for help, assuming he was in his room; (2) knock on any door and ask for help; or (3) just boldly "strut" (ya gotta have pride, dude) down to the front desk, au naturel, and ask them for help.

I evaluated each of the thoughts that offered a potential solution and in turn disregarded each because I thought that if I went to anyone's door, or the hotel counter while I was bare assed naked they'd think I was a looney toon and I'd be locked up and the proverbial key destroyed.

I needed to think "clearly" and I wanted to sober up. The adrenaline, which was still being produced in quantities my body had never seen before, helped to increase my heartbeats to something slightly below the speed of a humming bird's and was definitely helping me to metabolize the rum at an increased rate. I was trying to think of past events that could help me work this out, but, none came to mind immediately. No, I was in "virgin" territory with this predicament.

I'd had some interesting stuff happen in college and while in the USAF, stuff that would have opened eyes had I done it at the age of thirty-two. But in college you are almost bulletproof because whatever stupid things you do are chalked up to the exuberance of youth, and in the USAF, it was chalked up to the eternal immaturity of fighter pilots. In either case, back then I had a "get out of jail free" card. Not now. I was a full-fledged adult in a responsible position as an airline pilot and parading myself as Adam, of Adam and Eve fame, would not bode well for my career, particularly if the company for whom I flew was included in the press release.

I have no idea how long I sat in the corridor, back against my door, legs drawn up, face into my knees and arms around my legs. It seemed like an eternity, as I kept waiting for a door to open or someone to come off the elevator and head to his/her room. I finally did realize, in whatever amount of time it was, that that was that, I had no plan. So, being the incredibly bright person that I was, I decided to take a walk down the hall.

I cannot consciously tell you why I took this "stroll." No conscious thought told me that walking down the hall would be a good idea, but, I knew my door would not open by itself and I needed to do something. The two thoughts I do remember, though, as I moved down the hall, had more to do with the here and now than with any plan.

As I maneuvered down the corridor, in herky-jerky, squirrel crossing the road movements, I remembered as a kid, the educational school movies they showed of the prehistoric times and of the cavemen. They always showed those guys—now remember, they too were buck ass naked, (okay . . . they had a lot of hair and were wearing a skimpy little loincloth; like I'm sure in real life they really wore those loincloths)—anyway, they showed them running kind of bent over, like they were constipated. Well, I'm here to tell ya, it must be a natural thing when you are nude in public, because I thought of those movies as I ran down the hall and I felt like I was moving just like Cro-Magnon. Actually, I didn't really run. Like I said above, I would move, stop, look around, move again, stop, look. I jinked and jived as I went, hyper as all hell that someone would dart out of their room and I'd be discovered.

The other thought I had as I "e'd and e'd" (military term, means escape and evade) my way down the corridor was of an old Air Force buddy. He was a student of mine, and I was teaching him how to fly F-4s. On one particular mission, he did something so unscripted, off the wall, and unbriefed that I was sure he would not only fail in his objective that day but would kill us both. To my amazement, he actually succeeded and in the debrief I asked him what his thoughts were on how he did what he did. His response was, "Flexibility is the key to airpower, and indecision is the key to flexibility." In other words, he had no idea how he did what he did . . . he just lucked out! Well, as I made my way down the hall, I thought of John and his comment. Like a broken record, it played over and over in my head . . . how I wished I were back in my F-4.

It's said that death and taxes are inevitable; however, at this point in my life, a third inescapable fact became clear . . . the hallway was ending, and I still had no idea as to how I could extricate myself from this mess.

I was now at the end of the sixth-floor corridor, still searching for a clue. I put my back to the end of the hall wall. To my right was a guest room door, on which I had no intention of knocking. To my left was the exit door to the outside stairway. It was the middle of February. Earlier in the day, the temperature was about forty-five degrees, and it was now o' dark thirty—and, oh by the way, it was drizzling outside. Not a good night to be out with clothes on, let alone nude.

There have been times in my life when I have done things without thinking, or, with extremely little thought, and the outcome of these "blonde moments" has always been a positive in my life. By positive, I mean I didn't die, go to jail, lose my career or health, or anything else that had a lasting negative effect on me. I call it providence, some call it luck, still others fate. I was in a jam right now, and I was extremely aware of it . . . trust me on that. But whatever you call it, the unseen guiding hands that directed me in the past were, as I was to find out, still there.

Going outside on a night such as I just described was not something I would have believed to be a good idea, particularly with my current attire. I did want to wake up though and I thought going out for fresh air and escaping, if even for a minute, the limelight of the hallway might be a good idea. So I decided to scoot out the exit door and onto the emergency exit stairwell and into the night air. As the door closed I heard a distinct click . . .

Rhut roh . . . I was now locked out of the hotel.

I did not realize that the door would lock behind me. I sincerely thought that I would be able to get back in after taking a few breaths of fresh air. This was definitely one of those times when a little thought got me into a lot of trouble . . . see two paragraphs above.

Considering that I now had all the fresh, a.k.a. "cold," air I wanted, sobering up and waking up were pretty much not a problem.

I wanted to sit down, again, and rethink the stupid steps it took to get me here, in this stairway exit, an outside stairway exit, in February, in the Let's Hotel, in Narita, Japan, in the Far East, where I am a foreigner and they think Americans are murderers and rapists and overall bad people. Yup, I wanted to dwell on my bad points for a minute, because up 'til now, things were not going well, and being the masochist that I am, I wanted to beat myself up some more. However, sitting down was not an option. It was freezing outside, and the only thing I could sit on, the steps, were cement; and cement, which conducts cold very well, would have transferred that cold to certain body parts that don't take, with kind grace, that kind of direct contact with cold.

But at least I still had not been discovered.

The bad news was the fact that there was an apartment not more than fifty feet in front of me, with a full view of me, and I knew this because I had an almost unobstructed view of its living room. Normally, at twoish in the morning, this wouldn't have bothered me, clothes or no clothes, but a bright light was on in the room, and I thought maybe some night owl was up watching late night TV. There was no doubt in my military mind that if the occupant of that dwelling saw me in all my perceived glory that he/she would call the police and then in no time I'd be the bitch of some imprisoned, "gone bad" sumo wrestler.

The thought of my indecision, of running down the hall and then venturing outside, was still with me as I rounded the floors on my way down to the ground floor. I had decided to leave the lofty heights of the sixth floor and venture earthward. There was no conscious thought to this action, as it was, simply, the only option that was available to me. As I neared the ground floor, I came to the realization that I had only one option left. I was going to have to walk in the front door of the hotel and up to the front desk and confess my predicament . . . I simply had no other ideas or plans. Walking out the sixth floor exit door sealed my fate…or so I thought.

As I hit the ground floor, to my amazement, I saw some white boots. There were two pairs, lying on the ground, near the first-floor exit door. Since I was barefoot, I stopped to see if the boots would fit me. Now the Japanese are not the largest people in the world, and to be honest, I didn't give it a snowball's (it was cold outside) chance in hell that any of the boots would fit. But, to my joy, a pair did, quite well I might add. And, what was even more marvelous were the plastic trashcan bags I found next to the boots!

The bags were large bags, big thirty-two-gallon ones. It gave me an idea, the first solid idea I'd had since this whole ordeal began. I thought I could punch a hole in the bottom and opposite sides of a bag and then, like a raincoat, put it on. As fast as I thought it, I did it, and within thirty seconds of putting the boots on I was fully dressed.

I must take a moment to ask a question and possibly cause you to ponder what you may never have really thought about . . . clothes. Sure, we all wear 'em, most of the time, but the question to ponder is . . . do the clothes make the man, or does the man make the clothes? I can tell you, when you don't have them on, you feel pretty exposed, in more ways than one! When I put that bag on, I felt like a million bucks. I was suddenly full of confidence and had no problem with the thought of walking up to the night manager and getting my room door opened. The mere fact is that one moment, I had no clothes on, and the next, I was fully bagged and my confidence level shot up to astronomical heights. I started walking more upright, like I normally did.

Walking with a confident step, I left the security of the stairwell and headed around to the front of the hotel to get inside.

As I rounded the building I formed a story as to why I had a bag over my head. My story was… "I couldn't sleep and I wanted to take a walk. It was drizzling outside, and I didn't have a raincoat, so I improvised and put a bag over my head. Unfortunately, in my haste to leave the room, I had forgotten my key and therefore needed to be let in."

So could he let me in?

I must have actually still been a little tipsy and tired since I thought this was a great "cover"—that pun was intended—story and surely the night manger wouldn't give me a second look.

The hotel lobby was dark and devoid of any sign of life as I entered. I walked right up to the counter and rang the bell. After a few seconds a man, a slight man of smallish stature, appeared from a backroom. I half thought that I had awakened him. The counter that separated us came up to my lower chest so he could not see that I was not wearing any slacks or socks. I explained to the manger that I had taken a late-night walk because I couldn't sleep, but left my key and ID in the room and needed to be let in. He was very accommodating and without hesitation he said he would escort me up to my room to indeed verify that it was actually my room that he was letting me into.

The elevators that would lift us to the sixth floor were just to my left so I took a few steps in that direction and waited for the manager to come out from behind the reception desk. The lobby was fairly dark as it was 2:30 in the morning. I knew the exact time now as there was a clock above the check-in desk. The wait for the manager was very short. Moving with purpose, he came out of a door located next to one of the elevators, and without really glancing at me, he kept the right turn going after exiting the doorway and immediately headed for an already open elevator that was eagerly waiting for work. I entered the elevator right behind him.

At the check-in desk I had told him my name and room number, so as we entered the lift he selected the sixth floor button without asking me to which floor we were going. The entire actions of this man, so far, of coming out of his office and turning right and walking smartly into the open elevator and his sure steps gave me the impression that he had done this many times before and this was a common occurrence, people forgetting their room key.

As ridiculous as it seems, it was only by this man's automatic actions, the way he came out of the office and walked into the elevator, that I felt some other crewmember, somewhere in the past, had committed the same faux pas. The thought that some other poor idiot had done what I had done on this night was very comforting. No one likes to be an original idiot, because that means you really might be one. But if you have a predecessor(s), well, that gives them precedence as being the original village idiot; as if any of this mattered anyway. I had no real proof of anything. I was not, however, going to ask Mr. Night Manager if I was the "original" village idiot because at this point, I honestly felt like I was just another fully clothed person who had locked himself out of his room, I was not about to incriminate myself; not that wearing just a plastic trash bag like a poncho wasn't incriminating enough.

So, as we entered the elevator I was feeling pretty darn normal. I had almost completely forgotten that I was wearing white rubber boots, with no socks, and a whitish-colored plastic trash bag, that came down to mid-thigh, and absolutely nothing else underneath.

The elevator doors took a few seconds to close. Of course, Mr. Night Manager had hit the doors close button after selecting the floor, again indicating his efficiency and that he had done this a million times before. It wasn't until the doors had closed and the elevator began to rise that there was a period of time when there was nothing for this man to do. When we entered the elevator, I stood in the back right (from the perspective of looking in) and the floor select buttons were on the left, front. Turning off his "automatic pilot" for a second, as the elevator rose, the manager turned around and glanced at me. You could see it was a glance that he performed a million times, just like I had done before, in or out of an elevator.

God made the lovely Japanese people the way He did for whatever reasons He did. Without a doubt, the most identifying trait
of these wonderful people is their eyes. Being wider than "high" in
dimension they look more oval, just as Westerners' eyes look more
"round." However, for a brief period of time, after getting the full
view of me, Mr. Night Manager became transformed; he was no
longer Japanese, he was a Westerner . . . a very wide-eyed Westerner!
I don't think I saw eyes any rounder on anyone as I did on him that
night. In addition, he decided that the distance between us was a bit
too close, even though we were already on opposite ends of the elevator, and he proceeded to try and expand his corner of the lift. By
the time we reached the sixth floor he was so wedged into his corner
I was sure I was going to have to pull on his arm to get him out. My
instincts told me touching him would have given him cardiac arrest.

After he looked at me he didn't look again. Upon reaching my
floor, the doors couldn't open fast enough for him. As soon as the
spread between the doors was wide enough for him to pass through,
sideways I might add, he did, and with even greater urgency then
when he entered. He never looked back at me as he walked around a
corner into the sixth floor hallway and straight toward my room, increasing the distance from me with each step. As I got to my room,
he and I met 180 degrees out, him leaving and me still a couple of
steps from the door of my room. I reached the door as it was closing,
Mr. Night Manager obviously being pretty efficient in his assessment that indeed the room that I said was mine really was.

Because I was jet-lagged, tired, still a bit tipsy—or well, really
an idiot—I couldn't understand what this man's fuss was all about.

I entered my room and, for the first time since I had left it, I
realized what had gotten me into trouble in the first place . . . I had
to pee . . . and now I had to pee really, really bad. So, I turned on the

entry light for the room and proceeded to liberate the Coke and the rum. As I walked out of the bathroom, I chanced to glance at myself in the full-length mirror opposite the bathroom entrance. What I saw scared the hell out of me.

The reality is . . . I was nude. If I had had a mirror when I "got dressed" outside I would have known that I was not wearing Armani and would not have been so . . . hmmm—pardon the expression— "cocky," when I walked up to the counter. What I didn't realize was that that plastic bag was fully and unabashedly see-through. Why I didn't notice it when I was outside I don't know, but it was. Mr. Night Manager had carnal knowledge of me. All the time that I had that bag on, I felt so secure and confident . . . and for no reason. I was the "king" in new clothes and the night manager was the "boy."

I sat on my bed and wondered if the police were gonna' come knocking. But I was so tired and so relieved to be in the sanctity of my room that I didn't care; in fact, I kind of chuckled at what this man must have thought, what he may still be thinking. And, sweet mother of God, the expression on his face in the elevator! Oh, I had a really good laugh both in conscious thought and in the welcome escape of REM sleep.

Before nodding off to sleep, though, I did two things: (1) I made a mental note to avoid Narita layovers for the foreseeable future; and (2) I put on my workout shorts.

■ ■ ■

3 November '94
PEN to TPE, Capt. X

Interesting thing happened today on this flight. After leaving PEN the captain, and I got into a conversation as to whether or not you had to do a holding pattern that's depicted at the end of the

15 DME arc on the ILS to runway 04 at PEN. He said that you had to automatically perform the hold unless you asked for permission not to. I said that I was told you didn't have to do the hold; it was there to allow you to lose altitude on the approach and/or for spacing and that you had to tell tower if you were going to enter a hold for spacing/approach considerations, unless they told you first. Well hell, you would have thought I said the F-word in front of my mom when I disagreed with him! Lord he got really red in the face as I continued with my explanation as to what our MD-11 standards folks told me. I thought he was gonna have a stroke or a heart attack; his face got so red . . . I was absolutely shocked. He exploded into a tirade of barely understandable utterances about me not respecting him and his knowledge as a captain. After a few minutes of a very one-sided conversation...I can tell ya, it wasn't coming from my side . . . he then went quiet and, except for radio calls, he didn't speak to me until we neared Taipei. I finally got tired of this "cold war," and I looked over at him and, with a funny face (well funnier than normal . . . I had no choice in my gene pool) and said, "Are you still mad at me?!" He broke into a laugh, and at the bar that night he went into a dissertation as to all that he knew about being a pilot. I made no attempt to challenge him on any aspect of what I thought was bogus information . . . discretion is the better part of valor.

An interesting, in a relative sense I guess, thing here was the accident that this captain and I got in on the way to the hotel. It's a fairly long drive from the airport to the hotel, Grand Hyatt Taipei, and most of it is on interstate-type highways that can get quite crowded. Well, as we were approaching a tollbooth and almost at a stop behind a line that was forming at this one slot in the line of booths, I guess the guy behind us was in a bit of a hurry and didn't quite slow down fast enough . . . CRUNCH! We were nailed from behind pretty hard. I was actually looking at the captain, as we got hit, and it was kind of sickening to see his head slam into the headrest behind him only to bounce off. We were in a pretty sizable Mercedes-Benz, so the trunk absorbed a lot of the energy, as did our bags. I was fine and the rear-ender didn't do a thing to me, but the captain, who was a fairly sizable individual, was hurting.

As an editor's note: A month after this flight, I found out he went out on a medical for a few months.

. . .

20 November '94

ORD to ANC, Capt. John Dreier

I deadheaded to ORD.

My leg. The captain said he hadn't flown in a month, so he gave the leg to me. The actual flight to ANC was, in and of itself, uneventful. However, once we got there the weather was miserable. ATIS was calling the weather as thus: Indefinite/obscured ceiling, 500 overcast, one mile in snow, with winds from the north at ten to twelve knots. The NOTAMS said that all the runways and taxiways were covered with snow.

The only approach that was available was the localizer to runway 06 Left. Normally, you shoot the ILS to runway 06 Right but they were plowing that runway and were diverting arrivals to the Left side. The minimums for the approach were 379 feet above the threshold to 06 Left (500' MSL[59]) and three-fourths of a mile (4,000 RVR).

---

59. Mean Sea Level—altitude based upon the height above sea level and not above the actual ground.

There was a SIGMET out for severe turbulence below 10,000 feet . . . I must say it was shaping up to be a rather exciting morning!

I was vectored to a right downwind for runway 06 Left. Actually, when coming from the lower 48, you are usually cleared direct to YESKA (actual name of a navigational fix), to cross it at 10,000 feet, and then given vectors from there, which is usually a 240 heading, which puts you on a reciprocal to the runway and about five miles south of it. Below 10,000, it was pretty turbulent and, actually, it was frequently difficult to fly the aircraft with any precision due to the bouncing (and that was with the autopilot engaged). Due to that turbulence, I held a ten-knot pad above the "foot." (The "foot" is 1.3 times the stall speed at that current weight, and is always displayed on the airspeed tape in an amber color. The aircraft will fly, if the airspeed is left in "FMS speed mode," assuming no other restrictions, at foot plus five knots.)

The snow was about as heavy as I'd ever seen in flight by the time we got down to final approach altitude. We had entered the clouds at about 12,000 MSL and by 8000 feet it was snowing hard. I asked the captain if we could keep the extendable landing lights off once passing 10,000 feet due to their distraction with the snow and to allow my night vision to stay keen as I was concerned about being able to seen the runway lights. John agreed with my thoughts, although he did extend them without actually having them illuminated.

There was a fair bit of traffic as we arrived so we were put in a conga line that took us about fifteen miles from the field as we turned onto final. A JAL 747 was in front of us and reported the braking action as "good" as we crossed the FAF and began our descent to the MDA.

To digress, the actual localizer approach to 06L isn't in the FMS; you have to manually "build"/program it. It's a fairly easy procedure to perform, but I had to load it while on downwind since I had originally loaded the ILS to 06R (because it was snowing so heavily, tower was alternating between the Left and Right runways, plowing one, landing on the other, and vice versa). But, what really made loading the approach a royal pain in the ass was the turbulence. It was really rough, and I kept hitting the wrong CDU (control display unit) keys/buttons, as I was finger surfing over the keyboard. As per our flight ops manual, the captain was flying the aircraft while I built the localizer approach.

Now, continuing where I left off . . . at the FAF I selected a 1,300 FPM rate of descent (the autopilot was still flying the aircraft and we were in localizer track mode) and down we went into the visual dichotomy of swirling white snow and pitch-black sky. About two miles from the runway, we leveled at the MDA of 500 feet MSL, or about 360 feet above the threshold. At one mile from the runway, John said he saw the lights, so at that point I looked up and saw . . . a light. It was more of a faint glow than a distinctly focused dot. And now, suddenly, this dot became my world as I disconnected the autopilot and began my descent from the MDA. Though the nonflying pilot was supposed to give descent rate and altitude above the ground after leaving the MDA, the captain was completely silent as the dot rapidly grew into a discernable row of runway lights. The wind was pretty strong, even at 500 feet, according to the wind readout on our NAV display, but thankfully, the turbulence was fairly light. (Once we had gotten established on final, it lessened considerably.) One thing I had serious trouble with, once I had visual with the runway lights, was nailing the crab angle.

Because I couldn't actually see the whole runway, as I started out of the MDA, I initially put the lights I saw at my twelve o'clock (not a good thing to do) and due to the left to right crosswind, we began to drift south of the runway. As more of the runway came into view, I could see that we needed to correct back to the left so I had to cut it pretty hard to the left, while still descending, to line up with the runway. I did a couple of these left right deviations on final and by the time I reached 100 feet I was pretty well lined up and the wind was steadying out (ten to fifteen knots). I blew off any notion of a soft landing as I just wanted to get on the runway and stopped. One thing I did notice as I flared was just how hard it was actually snowing . . . harder than I had ever flown in! I flared just enough to break the rate of descent, and besides, the effect of ground effect on the MD-11 will help to somewhat soften the touchdown, and that alone actually made for a smoother touchdown than I had planned. After landing I quickly put the nose wheel on the runway and went to max—and I mean max . . . braking. The aircraft's autobrakes were set to max, but I use that to initiate braking, once I've got everything squared away landing wise, I like to come on the brakes myself with my own two feet. Today was the first time I'd ever put the brake pedals to the floor . . . to be honest, I didn't even know they'd go that far. Oddly enough, maybe because of my concern for runway alignment and getting stopped with the manual brakes, I didn't go into reverse with the engines. I didn't realize it until eighty knots whereupon the captain mentioned it as he gave me the eighty-knot call. Now . . . our flight ops manual does warn about loss of control on slippery runways when using reverse with the number 2 engine and with crosswinds present (the reverse from the number 2 engine can blank out the rudder's effectiveness), but I can honestly say that this didn't come up in my mind as I landed. As it was, the aircraft stopped surprisingly well given the completely snow-covered runway, and we easily turned off 2000 feet from the end of its 10,000-foot length. One thing I did think about with regards to using reverse, and this has been my experience so far in the MD-11, because I'd never flown an aircraft with reverse thrust before this one, I am more concerned with the brakes than getting into reverse. I believe that as I gain more time in the MD-11 reverse will be more on the forefront of my thinking once I've landed. But since old habit patterns take time to fade away during times of stress, I suspect it'll take some more time in the jet to get this chore in my habit pattern.

Taxiing in, as I alluded to earlier, was a chore due to the heavy snow and the very busy morning's traffic. But I have to admit, I rather enjoyed the slow pace once we landed. The cockpit was warm and cozy with a myriad of Christmas-colored lights and displays arrayed all about it and in absolute contrast to the cold and predominately white world just outside the cockpit windows. Christmas was approaching, and soon I'd be off to merry ol' England to see my wife and her family for the holidays, and I couldn't wait.

■ ■ ■

I was based in Anchorage for about two years. Somewhere during that time, another company wide MD-11 posting came out asking for more captains and first officers to be based in our main domicile and, in concert with that posting, the training department was looking for more instructors to augment those already on staff. The company was buying more MD-11s, and they needed more instructors to meet the increased training.

So, I put in my bid to change my domicile and also handed in a resume for an instructor position on the MD-11.

I had made the decision that if I got hired as an instructor I would move away from South Jersey. It was a hard decision to make, but I felt it was the best thing to do to break away from my father and mother and start a new life without my parents' meddling.

After dating the English flight attendant, Liza, for what seemed an eternity, we married. She lived in the United Kingdom and me in South Jersey, so we usually met while on respective layovers with our airlines, or during the odd times when we both had time off and one of us would visit the other. It was a wonderful dating life, but yet a curse, since each layover was more like a honeymoon and not the real world. The implications of our jet-set dating life, and the shallowness of it, would impact us shortly after marriage, as we settled down, but we had to settle down first, and I decided that would be far from my mother and father.

There were two emotional burdens directly related to relocating to the new domicile. And each caused me much stress in the ensuing months and years after the move.

Without question the greatest emotional grief was in leaving Christina and Kyle. While I was based in Anchorage (1993–95), I had been going back and forth between there and South Jersey to see them on most of my days off. But moving south meant less time seeing those two, so I vowed to myself that I would put aside one long weekend, three to five days, with them every month to maintain our relationship.

Another deeply emotional struggle was ending my F-16 flying with the 119th FIS. Beyond words, I loved flying the jet, but between the needs of Christina and Kyle, and the new wife, who was demanding much of my attention because of being in a new country with no friends or relatives and finally, my new instructor position, I was stretched pretty thin on all fronts. I can't begin to describe the pain of leaving that wonderful jet, but in addition to the personal stressors at home, Colonel Ockerhausen retired. I greatly respected Ock, and I was saddened at his sudden departure, particularly when he was replaced by another colonel of whom I had a less than sterling opinion, due to past experiences with him in the 108th TFW. There was no replacing Ock, as he was a true fighter pilot and a man's man, and the colonel that replaced him—let's call him LBW—was more of an administrator than a true fighter pilot and leader, though I'm sure LBW thought differently. In the end, the morale in the unit declined due to a vacuum of character and leadership after Ock retired.

As a parting shot, when I went in to formally resign, face-to-face, with LBW, he made me wait for about twenty minutes before he would meet with me, I guess his way of showing he was "the man." I am very certain he thought I came in to ask for forgiveness because I told the director of operations, about three weeks prior to this visit, to shove an F-16 up his ass, due to his mishandling of a scheduling issue with me. When the secretary finally said I could go into LBW's hallowed nest, he was sitting at his desk smirking and said, as I sat down and faced him, "Well, I guess you came to apologize and ask for your position back." (When I told the DO where to hangar the Viper, I said I quit as I hung up on him; not a very mature way to handle things, I know, but I got so mad because I knew I was right and the denser-than-lead DO didn't "get it"; eloquence went out the window that evening.)

As polite as I could be, and ignoring the smirk on LBW's face, I said, "No, I have come to formally resign. Having a few weeks off allowed me to see that there is a life outside of flying Vipers, and I am going to pursue that life."

To say that LBW's jaw dropped is an understatement. If there is one thing he knew, it was that I loved flying the Viper, and fighter aircraft in general, almost more than breathing, but I'll be damned if I was going to be held hostage by this putz and his ineptness. If anything, his last comment to me summed up everything that I knew was true about his character . . . He said, "Well I'm glad you're leaving. You Fighter Weapon's School guys fly too aggressively, and you were going to cause me to lose an aircraft. Also, you will never make major."

I walked away with a clear conscience, and he was fired about four years later after the unit had a midair collision, thankfully with no loss of life, but the subsequent investigation into the accident revealed LBW's lack of leadership skills.

As I just alluded, I did get the instructor position, and as my new wife, with a baby under construction inside of her, a dog, and I drove westward into a setting sun, I reflected upon my two action-packed years while based in Anchorage.

CHAPTER 25

Right after getting hired by my airline, they bought another, much older, worldlier, and certainly better known (internationally) cargo airline and began merging the two entities, to include the pilot seniority lists.

It's always an extremely touchy process when it comes to merging seniority lists due to the effect that seniority has upon bidding for positions within the company, promotions, and standard of living considerations, etc. While the merging of our two seniority lists might have appeared, to the casual observer, less arduous than in other historical airline mergers, on a "local" level and within the pilot groups, the whole process was very emotional and caused much angst and heartburn among the aviators.

As the merger progressed rumors and innuendo caused tempers on both sides of the pilot groups to flare so I asked my father for advice about how to deal with all of the dogma I was hearing. Once again, just like when I asked my father about how to choose a career, the old man came back quickly with some very profound and simple wisdom. I had asked for his thoughts while the evening was still young, so he was still sober and very lucid.

He looked at me, a beer one hand, a piece of chicken in the other, and with a very disarming smile upon his face, he very eloquently said, "What can you do? Can you change or affect anything? Buck, that's what you get when you sign up to be an airline pilot. You either let the drama and negative ramblings and rumors of others get to you or you just accept the whole package as part of the business, blow off all the seditious rumormongering, and when in uniform be as professional as you can; let the negotiators and union folks lose sleep."

After months and months of cross-table, boardroom, verbal-style battleship fighting, the two merger committees failed to correlate the two groups into one master seniority list that both could agree upon, so an arbitrator was called upon to settle the issue. The fact that just about every pilot was pissed off with the arbitrated list must have meant that it was a pretty fair merging of the two groups; and that is my humble opinion because for years after the merger there were/and are, still, some very bitter people.

The arbitrated pilot seniority list was published in black and white for all to see, and oddly this is a good metaphor for a comparison the two groups. There was a huge difference, black and white you could say, in attitudes and corporate culture between the respective groups that tended to keep them apart in terms of a true integration, at least initially. Hence, when a new domicile for CSE was announced, Anchorage, and a new aircraft to go with it, the MD-11, the pilots of the bought-out company, let's call them AVGers, immediately gravitated toward it (Anchorage) since it was far away from the headquarters of CSE.

Because of the reputation of the AVGers and the stories I heard about their animosity toward being bought out by CSE, it was with great trepidation that I embarked upon my "north to Alaska" career choice. As I said earlier, I wanted a window seat on the MD-11, and if it meant being a "bush pilot" so be it; life's an adventure, enjoy the ride, but I still had some angst about going up there.

As an aside . . . one day after an F-16 mission, while flying in the Air National Guard, I was standing at a urinal getting rid of my permission coffee. As I stood there, with my eyes closed, forehead leaning against the headboard above the urinal while thanking God for the invention of urinals and for getting me back without peeing in my flight suit (I'd had a lot of coffee) I heard the familiar, gravelly voice of Kirk, a squadron mate and American Airlines pilot, ask me if it was true that I was moving up to Anchorage to fly the MD-11. I should add that Kirk had violated the unwritten rule of male bathroom protocol that says when there are more than two urinals open in the men's room you do not pick the one right next to the "other" guy. Anyway, I said, "Yeah, it's true, but I'll still be flying in the guard down here." With that answer, Kirk took a seriously long, and I might add, given the fact that we were both still standing at the urinals peeing, uncomfortable look into my eyes. This seriously deep kind of staring, eye-to-eye contact, made me feel pretty uncomfortable, given "the intimacy" of going to the bathroom. The fact that Kirk didn't break his gaze made the whole moment kinda surreal and caused me to instinctively look away. After a fairly long and tense silence Kirk took his hand, put it on my shoulder (which, by the way, was another huge and major violation of the unwritten rules of male restroom etiquette), and said, "Dude, you can't go up there . . . people go up there and . . . well . . . like disappear!" If I hadn't been peeing at that moment, I would have!! This bit of concern coming from Kirk was so out of character because Kirk was, in a good way, kinda badass and it made me laugh since he was so concerned about me! To this day, I still chuckle over his seriousness and the timing of his gaze, touch, and remark.

Getting back to my Anchorage bid.

I was pretty concerned about how I was going to fit in with these hell's angels of airline pilots (as they were called by a psychologist who was hired by the company to help with the merger) because, though I may have thought myself a rebel as a fighter pilot, I was about as straitlaced and conservative as they come in my airline flying and attitude toward my company. There is no doubt that many of the captains with whom I flew while based "up north" were caustic, cynical, and militant as compared to the comparatively laid back and mostly southern CSE pilots.

In retrospect though, my time in Alaska was actually a bit anticlimactic with regard to getting into philosophical and heated discussions about various topics, particularly with regard to "the merger." That's not to say I didn't have those conversations, but I usually let discretion be the better part of valor and chose my battles only when I knew it wouldn't affect the flight. If I saw things were heating up, I just swallowed my pride and dropped the argument or agreed to disagree, depending on the individual and/or the situation.

Without a doubt, one huge difference between the two pilot groups was in the area of smoking . . . bloody hell, quite a few of the old timer AVGers smoked as much as the engines propelling us. Though they couldn't smoke in the aircraft, as per our company regulations, they tried to be "sneaky" and go into the toilet and fulfill their nicotine addictions there. God forbid you go take a leak after one of their "potty breaks" since you'd be asphyxiated by the leftover haze. There was no way I was ever going to report their insubordination to anyone, as my mom smoked and I saw how hard it was for a smoker to break the addiction, if they even could. I just resigned myself to waiting a while after one of these guys had to relieve himself before I ventured into that ashtray. Also, I'd rather have these guys smoke in the toilet and get their relief that way than to have to deal with someone going through nicotine withdrawals, particularly if it was a long flight . . . I mean, seriously? Some of these guys were nuts enough, you take away their cigarettes and Lord knows what kind of chemical imbalance that would have created in their brains.

As implied by their smoking vice, many of the captains with whom I flew in Anchorage were hard-charging, old timers, fully permeated with a certain measure of mystique and swagger earned through their international, worldwide flying into both modern airports and bare bones, Third World destinations. In addition, the Wolrd War II, AVG[60] heritage of their airline (hence me calling them AVGers) added a certain type of swashbuckling aviation aroma and charm that few airline crews could claim. Being couth was a challenge to some and though the electronic gadgetry of the MD-11 gave them pause more often than not their ability to hand fly the aircraft was inspiring and they taught me a lot. In fact, one of the finest aviators with whom I've ever flown was, and as of this writing, still is, based up there (Anchorage).

Now mind you, it must be understood that there were other dudes, AVGers or CSE, since neither side cornered the market on stupidity, that concerned the hell out of me, and I watched them like a hawk. I'd voice my concerns about their decisions, or lack

---

60. All Volunteer Group—during WW2 China needed pilots to help fight the Japanese. A large group of American pilots volunteered to fly P-40s in support of the Chinese. Eventually the US Army Air Corps expanded into China and absorbed these amazing, swashbuckling heroes.

thereof, loud enough for the cockpit voice recorder to hear so my possible "last words" might at least be words of defiance against whatever stupid thing they insisted upon doing before the tape abruptly stopped. I was greatly relieved to find out from my friends with the passenger airlines that they too had their own equally challenging captains. I was worried that all the chromosome-damaged fliers gravitated to the cargo side of the business; evidently the field of misfit captains was equally spaced between both of the airlines, passenger and cargo.

Finally, there were quite a few captains in Anchorage who were "old school" types who held to the belief that there should be three people in the cockpit of an airliner, not two: The captain and his two slaves (I say "two slaves" because most of the older airliner type of aircraft had a copilot and a flight engineer in addition to the captain). Nowadays, since the MD-11 is a two-crew aircraft (generally, unless an RF/O was required), lacking a flight engineer, the first officer did double duty with that type of autocratic dinosaur. There is no doubt that growing up with a somewhat psychotic and totally alcoholic father, and learning how to maneuver around him allowed me the ability to work my way into the personality folds of some of those equally psychotic and chemically well-preserved airline captains, and, actually get along quite well with the vast majority of them.

There was one captain, however, who will remain nameless on these pages and with whom I flew on several occasions from which I saw some truly weird and scary behavior, particularly after what I had thought was a minor disagreement. (He has since been long retired.)

Because of the time and distances involved in flying into or out of Anchorage to get to or from "anywhere" meaningful, a fair bit of time was involved in conversation with your fellow pilot while cruising away the hours. The adventures of many of the miscreant or more conforming captains with whom I flew were as different as their fingerprints. While it was always a welcome pleasure to fly with the mostly sane captains, of which the vast majority were, it was equally wonderful and a true blessing getting to know some of the crustiest of the crusty captains, because, though rough in exterior, most of those men were gentle "giants" (giants, meaning their egos) and remarkably colorful and tender on their insides. My frequent, tactfully phrased, probing questions to them while in flight or at a bar or restaurant elicited some remarkable stories and a rich heritage of aviation…very fascinating and wonderful characters. There is no doubt that many of the "old-timers" with whom I flew had biographies that make mine seem short and boring. The passing of the years has faded the luster, if not the memory, of most of their discourses, however a few stories, due to their uniqueness, will remain forever etched deep within my brain: many tales of wonder, woe, humor, and daytime-soap-like drama, interspersed with real life aviation excitement and bound together by the aura of the men who owned the stories.

In the final analysis, though I went "north to Alaska" worried about confrontation, I left in awe, after flying the Pacific with some of the finest aviators with whom I'll ever have the pleasure to fly and I wouldn't exchange a minute of my time up there for anywhere else in the world.

The one aspect of aviation for which I was not prepared was having to say goodbye to so many colleagues because our career paths diverged. My father never warned me about this aspect of the business when we had our talks about career choices. And, though you might say I should have deduced that from all the years I lived with the old man . . . well . . . I didn't. My dad was a loner, much more so than me, so if he ever missed an acquaintance or friend with whom he flew, I never heard him mention it.

The partings I have experienced with some of my feathered friends has been a particularly hard life lesson because when I was growing up I had a few Huckleberry Finn, blood-brother type buddies move away in the prime of our friendship; I won't lie, given the dysfunction in my family, losing those friends and the sanctity and refuge that their homes provided hurt. These were guys with whom I explored the darkest and deepest parts of the woods that lay across the street from where we lived and where we caught tadpoles, snakes and turtles, shot BB guns at imaginary enemies, and where sacred blood brother ceremonies were conducted. I don't make good friends easily, so the friends I do make mean a lot to me.

However, as I have matured, I have learned to accept the partings and have realized that in the aviation world paths eventually do re-cross and commingle, particularly for the truly intrepid and convicted aviator. And though parting with a well-respected friend and colleague was/is difficult, fortuitous meetings in some out of the way, recondite bar or pub, somewhere in the world do occur, and therein lies a joy that only the parties to those meetings can understand.

These providential convergences are the necessary sutures that maintain the bond between aviation-baptized blood brothers. The bonding of which occurred much earlier in their careers due to aerial escapades that mimicked, figuratively, the Huckleberry Finn–type adventures of their youthful past. These wonderfully welcome, fate-inspired meetings are providence's way of allowing true airmen to connect, weave, perpetuate, and perfect their craft while away from the clutter of their personal lives and the eyes and ears of management.

These impromptu encounters are almost religious in nature. During these trysts the aviator can humbly confess to his aviator-ordained peer of an esoteric flying sin and get absolution thereof, while possibly, returning the favor. The semi-covert meeting roosts always seem to be bound on the inside with dark paneled walls and beamed ceilings. The dim light in them is even more suffused by the ever-present veil of smoke that hangs like a thin, wispy London fog. The patrons appear as dark silhouetted shadows with only the occasional explosion of light from the striking of a match or lighter briefly illuminating their features or the dull red glow from a long drag on a cigarette giving away the location of the smokers. The aviator's true identities are obscured by the bluish/gray shade of the dingy air and shadow embracing them with only the truly intimate being able to make out the character enhancing lines in their faces; these etchings, the lines, are like battle scars. They are caused by years of flying wisdom, dry cockpit air laced with sunshine or moonshine, and worry about weather, low fuel, reroutes, mechanical problems, emergencies, foreign country overfly issues, or tight schedules.

The words of these venerable meetings are recorded for posterity on the walls that surround the participants as the vibrations of their hushed words laminate bits of smoke to the walls. Like petroglyphs on the walls of caves or the hieroglyphics of ancient Egypt, maybe one day in the distant future, those aviator words of wisdom and confession will be decoded and the secret language of the aviator revealed.

CHAPTER 26

What follows next is a discourse on the many topics within the realm of aviation about which my father and I either bantered or delved with great passion and purpose over the years. Very rarely did he and I disagree on aviation related issues, each one of us adding to that "aviation topic du jour" unless, however, we were the subject matter expert in that topic and then the other was edified during that discussion. While all of the aviation world was open to our talks, the one area where I really had to tread carefully was when discussing other pilots with whom I had flown and greatly admired. My dad got pretty jealous if I got carried away complimenting another captain (never with a first officer) and invariably, though he took it okay while sober, once he got drunk I might get an earful of "expletive deleteds" while he denigrated an aviator he didn't even know; such was the bi-polar nature of dealing with my dad.

Previously I had alluded to the differences between the many captains with whom I have flown when I was a first or second officer. To be honest, 98 percent of them (captains) were/are great guys/gals (as of this writing most of the more senior captains with whom I have flown are now retired) but also, let there be no doubt that a few of the more senior guys were pretty crusty...to be blunter, some were downright jerks; the worst ones (though very few) carried a double negative of being "flaming jerks." Because I had grown up with and seen this type of behavior from my own father when he was drunk, the actions and antics of most of those "jerks" did not affect me as much as it did others who may have grown up in Leave It to Beaver (wonderful) type households.

However, no matter what type of captain with whom I flew, good, bad or in between, I critically observed them from the moment we first met to when we parted at the end of the trip. I knew that one day I too would have four stripes and I needed to arm myself with a repertoire of my own and I intended to plagiarize the living hell out of some of the better captains with regards to incorporating their flying and leadership techniques. It was my intent, though, to understand the negative as well as positive aspects of each type of captain to have an enlightened perspective of the mystiques with which all captains are imbued.

The good news is I had a large pool of excellent captains from whom to plagiarize, as there were so many splendid aviators in the employ of my company.

I am an odd person for many reasons, but one esoteric fact about me is that I like to categorize things into what is the best or what is the worst. In my weirdness of doing that rank ordering, and as a lover of hyperbole and extremes, I do have a favorite song, a favorite movie, and a favorite in just about every other category that is mentioned when people are socializing and bring up the topics of favorites.

Extrapolating upon this thread, there a few captains woven into the tapestry of my collective conscious of aviation experience with whom I've flown who I think are among the best of the best.

Before revealing this who's who of commercial aviation heroes, at least in my mind, I must reiterate that, without a doubt, the greatest pilot and influence in my aviation life, and the greatest captain I'll ever know was my father. There is no doubt he had some serious borderline personality issues, but in the aviation realm he was peerless. It sounds so corny to say that your dad is your hero and that he was the best, particularly in today's world where everyone's self-esteem is supposed to be recognized and affirmed, if not enlarged, by not using absolutes, but I don't care, my dad is the best.

The old man was a fighter and a pioneer. He fought through thunderstorms in the like-named alleys of the world without on-board radar and treading where never an eagle would dare to fly. He flew many down-to-minimums four-legged range approaches in the dead of night with a withering load of airframe ice, or accomplished down to minimums PAR approaches in DC-4s with one engine out on foggy days and nights in Europe. He traversed the far north tundra regions of North America in blinding snowstorms to keep the DEW line[61] radar sites supplied with needed provisions so the citizens of North America could sleep securely under the watchful eye of NORAD. There is not one thing I do in my airline job that my father—in some way, shape, or form—did not have some hand in either helping to develop, research, or test fly by the time he retired his flight bag in 1996. Nope, my dad was a scrappy fighter out of the cockpit and an angel in it. I have never met a more natural pilot in my life, in whose aircraft I have personally flown, and my respect for his abilities just continues to grow the older I get.

---

61. Distant Early Warning Line—built in the 50s and became operational in 1957. The DEW line was an interlocking line of radar sites built to detect aircraft approaching Canada and the United States from the North Pole regions.

Below my dad, there are a lot of greats in the category of su-preme airline aviators with whom I have flown—Lou Furlong, Jerry Wolfe, Mike Healy, Dave Morris, Richard Gattis, Janie Aiken, and Darryl Hannah (not the actress) to name but a few for whom I have the utmost of respect. However, as I said earlier, I have met so many great captains at my airline who have taught me so much about flying safely around the world and in all kinds of weather that it would take reams of paper just to describe their fascinating exploits and do their biographies justice.

But there is one captain, Mike Peterson (now retired), who does stand out above the best of the best, and it's not just because he stood six feet and a good bit of change. Mike has more savoir faire than any airline pilot I have ever met, and he was remarkably multi-talented; he could fly a DC-10 better than any captain or FO with whom I flew and then, after landing, he would take his crew to some nice blues/piano bar, in whatever city in the world we were in, and play the piano better than those who were being paid by the establishment to entertain.

If I hadn't seen it with my own eyes, I'd have been doubtful of other's stories, but I did experience his deft ebony and ivory ma-nipulations, as he took the bench at the piano in the rooftop lounge at the Paris Hilton, the first time he and I flew a trip there. When the paid musicians took a break, he seamlessly went from walking to sliding his legs under the piano's keys while his hands began float-ing rhythmically and effortlessly over the keys, as he entered into a lovely jazz rendition . . . I was absolutely blown away. I thought the bar's manager was going to think Mike was nuts, but unbeknownst to me, and prior to my arrival in the lounge, Mike had asked the manager if he could play when the paid help took a break. The manager, as promised, gave Mike a chance to play at the break and pretty soon the peanut gallery, the other patrons, wanted more, and every time the paid entertainers took a break Mike jumped in and filled the decibel void with his lovely notes. Watching him play, was the only time in my life where I wished I had not stopped taking piano lessons at the age of eleven.

But my airline has many incredibly talented individuals who excel at things other than flying. Where Mike rounded out his talent pool was when he met his crew in the hotel lobby in preparation for a trip. He was so professional and oozed so much suave and debonair flair you would have believed he was groomed from birth to be an airline captain. In all the trips that we flew together around the world, his leadership, airmanship, strength of character, integrity, and intuition were/are without equal. Simply put, Mike never seemed to have a bad day and never set a bad example.

So, what is it that sets certain aviators aside, or should I say causes them to rise above the mainstream? What qualities do these "best of the best" embody that make the others seem average or worse?

I will answer that question in the following pages of personal observation, thought, and discourse but just remember this is my book and what follows are my opinions, others may have a totally different mind-set.

If you had flown with my dad, you would not believe how laissez-faire he was when strapped into an aircraft. In all the years and hours we sat side by side, with him either teaching me or me flying with him somewhere as his copilot, I never, ever, saw the man excited. I did some seriously stupid flying/learning mistakes while flying with him and he always seemed to know what I was going to do before I did it and he was never, ever rushed, agitated or startled.

He generally laughed at what I thought was a close encounter with death. Any instructor following him had a seriously tough act to follow, and in fact, only three pilots in all of my career (so far!) have ever come close to matching my father's incredible instructing ability. Gary Haseloh, mentioned earlier, is one of the 3 in the top tier of exceptional instructors I've had as are Mike Danosky (MD-11 F/O checkout) and Jerry Wolfe (MD-11 Captain checkout); truly, those 3 gentlemen were exceptional at their craft.

As I matured in my career, I began to fly ever-increasingly complex aircraft. With the increase in complexity and the ever-challenging and changing rules in which all pilots operate, I have tried, and continue to do so, to learn from the mistakes, or near mistakes, of others, and more importantly from my own (faux pas). A flying career is supposed to be a lesson in continuous learning, constant observation, and honest self-critiquing of one's own performance so you can do better on the next flight and hopefully avoid any potential obstacles and pitfalls that may be in your path.

To be sure I can say that I have tried as best as I can to emulate and project my father's laidback, laissez-faire attitude, as well as his nonchalant, confident, and professional attitude. It was my desire, once I began instructing, to embody those attributes of my father as I progressed in my aviation career, because, quite simply, it served him so well and I was hoping it would do the same for me.

But while some guys, with whom I have flown and really respect, may seem so laid back, what they and my father have taught me is how important it is to really understand and know your aircraft and the environment in which you are flying, to include the rules and regulations, weather, and finally, the geography over/in which you are flying. Knowledge is king.

All of those aforementioned aviators knew well the rules and regulations under which they operated, their aircraft's operating handbook, and other manuals in order to operate confidently, safely and efficiently.

Yeah, all the heroes in my life may have seem laid-back and nonchalant, but inside their brains they are mulling things over and they know their limits and abilities, the crew's (limits), the aircraft's, the ATC structure in which they are operating, the weather they may be flying through, and the topography of the terrain below them.

When aviators enter their office, aka the "cockpit," with the intent to fly a trip, they need to bring a certain mental skill set with them which will aid them in the completion of every flight. Knowing their aircraft and the rules and regulations under which they operate not only makes their job easier, it also, if done without arrogance, communicates to their first officer (or captain) that the person with whom he/she is flying is a dependable, competent, and professional crew member thusly allowing them to feel more relaxed.

Knowing your aircraft's systems and operating limits well really helps when it comes to certain MELs because some are written with the express belief that you know in detail the intricacies of your aircraft's systems and how the application of this or that MEL will affect your aircraft's operation. Many times, when I was a duty officer I saw MELs that were written so vaguely the captain and mechanic disagreed on how to apply them, or, to an even greater extreme, which MEL applied to whatever issue was affecting the aircraft. After Chuck Yeager cleaned the roast beef residue off of his mess dress, his speech at the aforementioned dining-in was enlightening. He was very adamant that a pilot should know their aircraft well, both in its systems and performance. With today's complex aircraft and their very integrated alerting systems, and multiple levels of redundancy, it is a challenge to know the details of your airliner like those of the distant past. But I am trying to stay true to one of aviation's more prominent prophets' words of wisdom, as well as my dad's own implied edification, as well as that of other captains I admire; so far, it has served me well.

Concurrent with knowing your aircraft well, being intimate with the rules of both your company and the regulatory agency under which you are flying is also a must so as to be competent and confident while aviating. It's funny, but when I was learning to fly, I never thought my dad had a clue about the FARs (FAA regulations) as he never seemed to know the answers to the questions I asked him with regards to what I thought were the most basic of FARs. But as I have found out over the years, you really learn well the regulations that apply to your segment of flying and tend to be less clear about others. It's not laziness that causes this forgetting, just normal human nature. I too found, as I inched my way back into general aviation a few years ago, and from where I gestated, that I, like my pappy, had forgotten so many basic rules of flight that I curled up with the AIM (Airmen's Information Manual) on a few rainy nights to reeducate myself.

Wrapped up, immersed, and intertwined with the previous discussion about the technical skills required to be a competent captain/pilot is the somewhat intangible side of human nature and personality. It has been my observation that technical prowess brings a confidence (if not a certain amount of arrogance with some people) that is subliminally conveyed to other colleagues in the normal interaction and discharge of their respective duties as they go about flying a flight together.

But the way you convey this confidence and ego can be tricky. Mike Peterson, my father, and the other wonderful captains whom I have mentioned all had/have an innate ability to be wonderful at ascertaining the psychological makeup of others with whom they are flying and then tailoring their interpersonal skills with them in such a manner that the other person feels at ease and valued.

One very dear friend and colleague of mine, MD-11 Captain Howie Pilcher, is extremely adept at reading people's emotions, and once "in their head," he can quickly evaluate and understand their emotional strengths and weaknesses and then he tailor's his interpersonal skills, while flying with them, to form an effective captain/ first officer team.

In addition, Howie and all the other marvelous captains with whom I've flown and previously mentioned, leave their ego and pride at home when they leave for a trip and exchange that pride for humility and temperance. That's not to say they can't get an attitude, but only when the person with whom they are flying or working displays an arrogance or indifference to their authority that could affect the successful outcome of the flight/trip.

CRM, or crew resource management, is what this somewhat intangible form of communication and personal interaction is called, and it involves so many aspects of communication that I dare not go into it in this book, as it deserves a book all of its own. But before CRM was being defined, refined, and distilled in all of the humanistic laboratories of all the major aviation entities around the globe, the great heroes of my flying life embodied those skills innately.

Finally, and possibly the most least studied and contemplated quality of wonderful aviators, is their wonderfully smooth and accurate manipulation of the flight controls of the aircraft in which they are operating. While an autopilot is the de facto method of flying an airliner for most of the time while it is in flight, every good captain, first officer, or pilot I previously mentioned was an artiste when actually hand flying an aircraft.

Throughout my life, I have looked very studiously at the qualities of some naturally gifted aviators and wondered what makes them so good. Why is one better than the other? I have no one answer, but I have seen a very common thread that I have never heard anyone mention, except of course, my father.

I must, however, put a note of warning upon the following few paragraphs: The observations and opinions of my father and I will probably anger quite a few pilots; it is not my intent to do so, however. As I previously mentioned, in this section of the book you are privy to discussions in the aviation realm about which my father and I delved with great passion and pleasure. What comes next has no longstanding, in depth, concrete or statistical fact to bolster its position, just a small sample size (as experienced between my father and I) of empirical analysis as gathered through a father and his son's respective careers.

My dad flew with many engineering-educated flight test pilots while in the employ of the FAA. I believe it is thought by the general public that an engineering-degreed pilot makes the best kind of pilot; technical, accurate in aircraft control manipulation, mathematical by nature, and most probably a very exacting person when it comes to aviating are some traits that come to mind. However, my father said he always thought engineers were some of the worst pilots because he felt they were rough on the controls when they flew. He said they didn't try to feel an aircraft and didn't seem to want to look at the aircraft as anything more than just a mechanical device that took a certain amount of pressure on the flight controls to make it go up or down, left or right, or either/or at the same time.

When Jack and my father taught me to fly, they said I needed to "feel" the aircraft, to think of "it" as a "her" and as of being alive. In other words, I needed feel her subtle vibrations with each phase of flight, or her change in sounds, to allow my arms and legs to meld into and blend with her flight controls and feel the subtleties of her movements with each movement of the flight controls. My Dad really stressed to not just "move" the flight controls, but to feel them with each manipulation. To expect what should happen when they were moved, not wonder. In looking out in front of me, my father said to project or "see" the flight path that you wanted to fly, as if you saw the arc through the actual sky where you wanted to move. To be sure, at first, I was thinking it was weird, but when I began to fly fighters in the air to air and/or air to ground attack missions I naturally began learning how to visually project my flight path in front of me, and to feel the subtle, or not so subtle vibrations of the Phantom or Viper as she transmitted aerodynamic (or engine) clues to my body as we cavorted about the sky. Feeling and under-standing the vibrations or buffet of my fighter told me of her energy state, engine health, or ability to perform a stressful aerobatic-type maneuver that I might need to do to try and defeat another aircraft or successfully attack a ground target. This whole idea of feeling the aircraft and projecting my flight path seemed odd, but it worked well in practice, and that's what it took to be proficient . . . practice . . . lots of hands-on flying practice. I admit to sometimes worrying that today's pilots are not taught that form of "Zen" flying if only be-cause technology is getting to the point that pilots are more desirous of letting an autopilot operate their aircraft than their own hands.

For me, flying an aircraft is an art, not a science, and the somewhat intangible ideas of "Zen" flying that my father and Jack taught me proved to be an invaluable tool to kicking some serious butt against my adversaries when I flew fighters, dropped a stick of bombs on a target, or even now as I fly a B-777.

And in that realm of the intangible, with regards to being a naturally gifted stick and rudder pilot, I have found that artistically gifted people, whether musicians or artists or both, seem to be better at flying, all things being equal, than most others.

And if you are wondering about my father's talents, he could paint and draw as well as any top-notch artist and he could play the drums, clarinet, and xylophone as if he had gone to the Juilliard School of Music and graduated with honors. In fact, while stationed in the Pacific during the war, he was the bandleader of a "big band" he and the boys had formed in order to entertain the other troops.

If your natural question is, "Why do you think artistic people make better pilots?" it is because I think those kinds of people, of which I am not one, do look at flying as an art form and as an expression of art and are much more in tune with the machine, themselves, and their environment. I think they "see" well beforehand where their flight path is projected and the consequences of a change in direction against the backdrop of the medium in which they are flying. Also, I believe they can feel the capability of their aircraft better than those who have a more pragmatic view of the machine. In my humble opinion, these artists view their aircraft as an extension of themselves, as a paintbrush or an instrument, and not just a machine in which they are operating. But and I must stress this, all of this recent discussion is just supposition on my part as I've never formally set about to analyze why these more artistic types seem to be more natural flyers than the engineers.

"Dirty" Dirks is without question the finest air to air fighter pilot with whom I've ever fought against. While every Instructor, or student, with whom I fought when I was a Fighter Weapons Instructor or student had their weaknesses somewhere in their air to air flying, Dirty was the exception. He always got the best of me, no matter how smart I tried to maneuver, no matter whatever trick I tried, he always was able to soundly win. He was my mentor in air to air and I had the utmost respect for his flying talent across the board when it came to flying fighters. Where "Quisto" was gritty, macho, and a gunslinger type of fighter pilot, Dirty was elegant, exacting and intellectual.

My reason for bringing Dirty into this conversation is due to his other talents. One Friday evening, after a long week of training FWS students, who were in the air to air phase, a few of us instructors were having a well deserved beer in the instructor's area, where our desks were located. There was a whiteboard in this informal lounge and while "we" (the instructors) got to talking about fighter tactics, etc. (actually I mostly listened) Dirty was busy drawing on the whiteboard. I didn't pay attention, initially, to what he was doing until he stepped away from the board and engaged the other instructors in conversation. As he left the whiteboard my jaw dropped…in the span of maybe ten minutes, at the most, he had drawn, with dry erase markers, a picture of an F-4 coming head on, but in a bit of a right bank, with the ground below. I about crapped. I mean, that picture was so detailed and so amazing I couldn't believe it; my father was good at drawing, but Dirty was light years ahead of anyone I personally knew. I found out later he was equally good in the areas of music and math. Dirty was a quiet man, with an amazing brain and with a lot of talent in many, many things. If any person bolsters my argument that an artistic brain allows for a better natural pilot, it's Dirty.

I want to emphasize, not every pilot has to be good in the area of fine arts in order to be exceptional. It is not my intention to stifle anyone's enthusiasm in an aviation career due to mine and my father's opining, particularly if you have no musical or artistic talent. I am not my father's son in the area of music and/or artistry and have managed to garner a satisfying aviation career, acknowledging that I am an average aviator at best. And there are many other aviators much greater than me with no real artistic or musical talent who are outstanding pilots; comparing yourself to others can either make you haughty or depressed, for always there will be better or worse pilots than yourself. I have learned, with age, to be satisfied with whom I am.

However, and keeping Dirty in mind, I have told my children many times being naturally gifted at something is not going to make you the best, it just gives you an edge when beginning your career over those who do not have that innate gift. As an instructor in many aircraft over the years, but most dramatically when I was an instructed in F-4s, I saw the "average joe" rise to the top in aviating skills versus the naturally gifted pilot if only because the average guy, if they were driven, would work and work and work to achieve greatness, while the more innately gifted pilot would rest upon their natural laurels and not try to build upon what God gave him/her at birth. Again, I go back to what my father always said: drive, passion, attitude, and desire can take you very far in life.

As an antithesis to the exceptional captains, there are the less than sterling ones (captains). All airlines have them—the bad captain, captain arrogant, butthole, etc.—lots of colorful monikers and obviously, judging from the type of adjective, it's not very flattering to be considered one of these types of pilots. The good news is the good captains far outweigh the bad ones, in fact, I'd guesstimate that three to five percent of most airlines' captains are what most of us would classify as buttheads. Doing the math, if you have 2000 captains, maybe 100, at most, are bad; in my experience, the actual number at my airline is closer to three percent or less.

Defining the qualities of a bad captain can be pretty subjective, just like defining a good captain, because what makes a bad captain to one person might make him/her average to another. In some cases, I'd guess it's all based upon a person's life experiences and whom they've associated with through the years as to what one thinks is one or the other.

As an example, I said in my reflection upon my years in Anchorage that there were a few grumpy captains up there with whom I know some first officers did not relish flying trips. For me, because of my having been raised by an alcoholic and narcissistic father, it didn't bother me flying with those guys because if they did get in my face with an attitude, I got right back in theirs; as the old man said many, many times, the best defense is a good offense. I usually got along quite well with those guys (I said guys because with the exception of one female Captain, all the rest of the Captain's based in ANC then were male) because I understood their nature. A first officer more sensitive than I and maybe raised with touchy-feely parents, breast-fed until he/she was ten, and not used to the gruffness of some of those dinosaurs might have considered most of those previously mentioned Anchorage-based captains as mentally unstable.

But going deeper, to the bottom of the barrel with regards to despicable and contemptible human nature, are the captains that, no matter what your frame of reference and background, are just plain jerks and on that point everyone would agree. They are the captains with whom all F/Os (First Officer) would like to avoid flying, to include calling in sick just to avoid dealing with them (it happens). I guarantee you that most first officers who've been around a while have a hip pocket list of the bad captains with whom they would rather not be crewed on a trip. While the rank order of who is the biggest jerk captain, and then second, and so forth and so on may not be exactly the same for each of those F/Os, I'll bet the same captains are on each list.

These "jerks," or flaming anus captains, are relatively rare, but nonetheless, and as I previously said, do exist at every airline. Their numbers are very limited, thank God, but they can be very mean-spirited and usually are very senior, though not always. They come across as bullies and seem to derive a certain amount of pleasure in pushing people around. If I had to put specific labels on what their actual traits are it's the fact that he/she is generally unkind to anyone but himself and treats most people, including his/her first officer, with disdain, indifference and sometimes belligerence. In concert with everything they do is an incredible arrogance that permeates them so completely it fully defines them, and indeed this arrogance blinds them to their own harsh behavior toward almost everyone with whom they work.

I have seen this type of aviator yell at an elderly ground support person for no reason other than that the frail old man left the coffee on the ramp, preferring to take the crew meals up to the galley first before going back down for the coffee. Captain Jerk wanted to make his coffee immediately upon arriving at the aircraft in preparation for a flight and the fact that he had to wait a few minutes really angered him so he lit into this very kind and genteel older man. I was pretty upset about this and told this schmuck what I thought of him; it was not a pleasant flight after I did I might add.

There are many negative facets to this type of aviator's behavior and many sad stories to go with each of those facets. Why they want to make life so difficult for other people, and ultimately themselves, I'll never understand, but the one thing I do know is they never seem to change.

There is no point in going deeper on the discussion with this type of pilot, since they are few in number; and it seems that no matter what the company does to try and change the behavior of these individuals, they are smart enough to game the system. When getting checkrides, they play the nice game while under the watchful eye of an evaluator, but once the check airman deplanes, after a one or two leg line check, they revert back to their old selves. In the end, and no matter how many "charm schools[62]" they attend, they always resist change and seem to enjoy being who they are.

However, there is one success story of which I am personally aware.

---

62. Charm School—A derogatory name for CRM, Crew Resource Management training—safety studies through the years have determined that training crews about differences in how each of us interprets, hears, processes and reacts to another's attempts at communication can adversely affect how we react/respond to that communication while operating an aircraft. As many aircraft have crashed over the years due to poor communication, CRM training attempts to provide pilots with tools to overcome communication challenges while operating as a crew.

Many years ago, when I was an MD-11 instructor, I had the good fortune to instruct one of the worst offending of my company's flaming butthole captains (now retired). This captain, who I'll call Captain Difficult, was transitioning from the B-747 to the MD-11 and was a very senior captain who was hired many years ago. I say "good fortune" because experiencing this captain's behavior both in the simulator and then later when he and I interacted during line operations allowed me to see what I can only say is truly Twilight Zone-esque, bizarre, human behavior.

Captain Difficult's initial instructor in the simulator phase[63] of his training on the MD-11 was a new guy who was getting checked out by me. I was observing this new instructor's prowess as we completed the very first simulator of Captain Difficult's series of seven simulator rides before his checkride, which would take place on simulator session number eight.

During the pre-brief, before the actual simulator training session began, and then during the debrief of simulator ride number one, Captain Difficult was argumentative, arrogant and downright obnoxious. He constantly challenged the instructor about his (the instructor's) system and procedural knowledge, constantly saying, "Well, on the 747, we did it this way." He frequently asked questions to which I am convinced he knew the answer in order, I think, to try and stump the instructor, and he was impertinent as hell throughout the whole simulator session. The bolder Captain Difficult got in his bullying, the more timid and withdrawn this new instructor became. It was ugly.

---

63. Simulator phase—When training for an aircraft the first training you receive is simulator training. After successfully completed, you then begin flying the real aircraft with an instructor teaching you as you operate on a revenue trips.

The next day I went to my boss, Warren Travis, an incredibly wonderful man and boss, and told him I saw a potential for disaster with this instructor/student personality mix. Warren knew exactly where I was going with my concerns as he knew very well Captain Difficult's reputation and had actually flown with him in days gone by. Warren was quick to reply that I was now the instructor and that the new instructor would observe me. He added that if Captain Difficult continued with his insolence to have him report to him (Warren) personally.

Armed with a serious Jersey attitude I met Captain Difficult, his poor F/O (with whom he was crewed for the simulator sessions), and the new instructor in one of the designated briefing rooms for the simulators. I told the students that I was now going to be the instructor, that the new instructor would observe me and then, looking squarely in the eyes of Captain Difficult, I launched into a five-minute diatribe aimed at him which included the comment that I didn't give a damn about what he did on the 747, this was the MD-11, and if he wanted to pass his Type Rating Ride he had better listen to me. I ended my extemporaneous speech by telling Captain Difficult that if he didn't like what I just said we could go to Warren right now and get a new instructor for him and his F/O. Shaking his head no, he looked at me with a wry smile and said, "Nope, let's get this done."

And we did. For every simulator period after that initial speech of mine these guys performed flawlessly, both individually and together as a crew, and I have to say that Captain Difficult was the best captain I ever saw go through training with regards to aircraft handling and procedures. He was about as standard and precise of a captain as I'd ever seen on the MD-11. I won't lie, I was proud of them both after having heard they both did very well on their (appendix F[64]) checkrides.

So, fast-forward to a year later, after I trained Captain Difficult. I was trying to catch a jumpseat on one of our flight's to England in order to meet my wife for a family vacation. Captain Difficult was the captain of record for this flight and he had just gotten to the OPS desk, where the paperwork for the flight is reviewed, and upon arriving, his poor F/O and RF/O stood to his side, looking very forlorn. I walked up as Captain Difficult began his preflight study and introduced myself and asked him for a ride to Standsted, UK.[65] Usually, asking for the jumpseat was a mere formality with most captains, you asked them out of respect because tradition demanded the captain be asked personally.

To give you an idea of this process: normally you would walk up to the captain and his crew, introduce yourself and maybe exchange some brief pleasantries to break the ice, and then ask if you could "hitch" a ride with them on the flight. A full 99 percent of the time, and this is even with some of the grumpier captains, they would immediately say, "Yes" or "Welcome aboard" or something to that affect.

Not Captain Difficult . . . now mind you, just a year ago I trained this guy. I figured he and I, no matter what his reputation, on some level, we were brothers and shared a certain amount of karma.

---

64. Appendix F—Before AQP airline training, there were Appendix F checkrides which had to be passed in order to progress to actually being trained on the real aircraft. It was a fairly hard checkride to pass since it concentrated on evaluating each pilot, individually, on their ability to fly and think and not necessarily how to operate as a crew.

65. Stanstead—Fairly busy airport in the U.K. about 30 miles north, northwest of London. Named after the town in which it is located.

So, it was with subdued astonishment on my part when I asked for a ride and offered my handshake to the captain that I got back a very limp hand in return and he said . . . nothing.

The other two guys, the F/O and RF/O, were readily offering up to me that it was not a problem with them if I jumpseated on the flight, and while saying so their heads were rapidly bobbing up and down in a yes motion, like little bobble head figures. I could really tell these guys wanted me to go with them, as I guess they didn't want to be alone this captain and his reputation.

But still, even after saying they were okay with me going, the captain never said a word to me. In fact, he didn't talk at all . . . nothing, not even a grunt, not even to his working crew. He just poured over the paperwork for the flight and never said anything to either the F/O or RF/O, nor asked about their thoughts on the fuel load, weather, etc. No exchange of ideas, restfulness for duty, personal questions about flying time on the MD-11, or where they lived . . . nothing. It was so bizarre. So as the F/O and RF/O stood next to Captain Difficult, almost at attention, I watched and continued to wait for word about approval to fly on the flight, or not.

Finally, though he never said I could jumpseat, he did say, "Let's go," as he gathered up his stuff and started for the door that led to the crew vans that took us to the aircraft.

On the crew van, I tried to talk to Captain Difficult and asked him how things were going and initially he never spoke. He just looked quizzically at me as if I was an alien, or that it was sacrilegious for a jumpseater to talk to him. When I tried to speak to him one more time by asking him if he remembered me as being his MD-11 instructor, he looked blankly at me and said, "No, I don't remember you and stop calling me by my first name, it's Captain Difficult to you."

What an asshole.

Again, not knowing if I was allowed to jumpseat, we were now at the aircraft and actually just inside the entrance door, and again I said to him, in a very authoritative tone, "Can I jump seat or not?"

Looking at me, again with a very blank, no-expression face, he said, "I thought it was obvious, yes."

I then said, "Well, I wasn't sure since you never said anything inside, but I want to thank you for the ride."

With that thank-you, he now looked me squarely in the eyes and said, "If it was up to me I wouldn't be taking you. It's only because the other guys said it was alright, and were so emphatic, that I am allowing this."

He then smartly turned his back on me and walked into the cockpit and closed the door. For the rest of the flight I avoided all contact, to include even looking at him, and once liberated from the aircraft in the UK I rejoiced at my freedom.

But what goes around comes around. About six years after my Standsted jumpseat with Captain Difficult, he busted a checkride for CRM. It was a poignant moment for almost every person that knew of, or had flown with, him. After the investigation as to why he failed his line check, and since he had pretty much pissed off every pilot with whom he flew, or even knew, he was reduced in rank to that of a first officer for six months. I actually got to give him his first officer checkride, and of course he did stellar; there is no doubt he was an excellent pilot.

During my one-sided debrief of his checkride, I asked him if he remembered me. He said, "Yes, you gave me my MD-11 training."

After taking a long pause to put my Jersey attitude in a jar, I said, "I find it absolutely amazing that you can remember that now, maybe seven years since your MD-11 training, but a year after I trained you and when jumpseating with you, you acted like you never knew me. Ya know, you were a real jerk to me and your crew on that jumpseat flight, and neither I nor they deserved it."

I then went on to tell him what I thought of his interpersonal skills, or lack thereof, but wished him well as an F/O and that he had a lot to learn about human nature. He was actually very contrite during the debrief and thanked me for my thoughts and time. To be honest, I thought he was just being gratuitous with his pleasantries and tying to game the system, but…

Remarkably, after serving his time as an F/O and then going back into the left seat, I heard he was a much more accommodating and nicer person with whom to fly, and he was never a problem after that.

He retired a few years after getting back in the left seat.

Miracles do happen.

Though the Captain Difficult–types are always generally predictable (at least in being jerks), there is another type of captain who is much more unpredictable in nature. On a good day he could be quite enjoyable with whom to fly, but on a bad weather day he could be almost as challenging as Captain Difficult. These Dr. "Jekyll"/Mr. Hyde type of captains always fascinated me because of their duality in nature and I wondered what it was in their psyches that causes such bipolar personality shifts when they fly (As a general nature, when I observed these "bipolar" captains, they always seemed to be very nice when out of uniform.).

CHAPTER 27

The first real negative experience I ever saw from any pilot, with regard to having a really bad attitude, outburst of anger, etc., occurred relatively early in my airline career. I was a "plumber" (S/O or second officer) on the 727. We had landed at an airport in upper New York state and were doing a quick turn with the goal of being in and out of that airport in about an hour, whereupon we would head to our final destination for the evening. As I prepared the take-off data (V speeds, runway takeoff capability, etc.) I found that a performance page was missing from the book where I got my takeoff performance numbers. I remembered from my B-727 Flight Engineer training that I needed to call the dispatcher and have him or her give me the missing numbers over the phone. And that is what I did.

As I casually tossed the TOLD (takeoff and landing) data card to the captain and F/O, I told the captain about the missing performance page and what I had done to get the appropriate data. (The captain had been out having a smoke when I went in to call the dispatcher, so I didn't have the chance to tell him at the time.) Upon hearing my words about the missing page, he exploded into a mini-tirade that was beyond belief and said he was not going to leave unless we had that missing page on board. He then told me to call the dispatcher and tell him that "he" needed the page to be on the aircraft or we were not leaving!

"Wow! What a jerk," I thought, as I headed inside to call.

The dispatcher was really on top of his game when I called and said the fax machine in ops was broken, and further explained that we were perfectly legal to depart without the page as long as I got the information I needed. Additionally, he, the dispatcher, said rather pointedly, "If the captain has issues with this then he, the captain himself, should have the balls to call and not have the second officer do it."

As a good messenger, I relayed what I was just told, though I took a deep breath before doing so. There was a serious, heavy atmosphere and a kinda pregnant pause between my relay of the message and the captain biting the bullet and saying he'd take the aircraft, but you could tell he wasn't happy. I am pretty certain when I told the captain that the dispatcher implied that he, the captain, didn't have any balls, it got him moving.

The weather at that New York state destination was very wintery with strong, teeth-rattling cold winds from the northwest, snow flurries and ice and snow abounding on the ramp, taxiways and runways. Did the harshness of the weather concern this captain to the point he couldn't be pleasant if a slight anomaly pushed him out of his comfort zone and into the twilight zone of emotional bizarreness?

And I say twilight zone of emotional bizarreness because six months previously, I had flown with this very same captain on a flight to the Caribbean. It was a four-leg trip flown over three days, and on every flight clear skies and balmy breezes met us at each destination or departure city. On that trip, this very same captain was about as incredibly pleasant and wonderful to fly with as any other pilot with whom I'd flown up until his Mr. Hyde appearance just mentioned.

The rest of that winter wonderland flight was uneventful with no word, neither in apology nor defense of his outburst being uttered by the captain.

I later heard from other crews that this was not the first time this guy had a blowup, and until he retired, which was quite a few years later, it wouldn't be his last; I wish his wife well in "their" retirement.

That was not the first time I would see interesting reactions to what I thought were relatively mundane and normal issues related to flying from A to B. In the years following this event, some of the more notable things I've observed are as follows:

I had one captain explode in anger in the cockpit when he was trying to find a checklist that was layered in with a few other laminated eight-by-ten-inch aircraft informational cards. He literally "flew" (no pun intended) into a rage while looking for "the checklist" among a bunch of laminated checklists we kept in a metal holding bin on the center pedestal in the cockpit of the MD-11. When he couldn't find "the checklist" (I can't recall what one of the many held in that bin he was looking for), he proceeded to throw all of the others about the cockpit while we were in cruise phase of flight. After he threw them he looked at me, as if I was supposed to clean the mess up. I looked at him, the checklists, and then went back to reading my book; he got the message.

I flew with another guy who checked the weather for our destination, alternate, and various other airports in the destination area, on every flight we flew, every thirty or forty-five minutes using either the ACARS or by listening to the scratchy HF VOLMET[66] transmissions, I got tired just watching him as we flew around the world. I can truly say I felt sorry for him and wondered what in the past happened that was so bad, weather-wise, that caused his OCD-type behavior.

Continuing, another captain, who was absolutely one of the most wonderful and pleasant of men while on the ground and during a layover, would get visibly upset, and I mean red-faced to the point I was afraid he was going to have a cardiac arrest or stroke, and would start expelling expletives in vast quantities, every time we got a reroute[67]. God forbid if we were instructed by ATC to "hold" somewhere, because with the assignment of a hold, I braced to give him CPR as he would get extremely upset. However, with that very same captain, I'd seen him many times very jovial in the cockpit as we serenely flew into a sunset or sunrise en route to some faraway destination. Why? I mean why make life so much harder than it already is and get so danged upset with some minor ATC stuff?

Finally, when I was a duty officer I had to talk to a captain who refused to take an aircraft that had a five-inch weld on one of the engine cowlings; the weld was stop drilled as it had cracked again and the length of this weld now put it beyond normal, allowable limits and it had to get specific, company engineering approval for

---

66. HF Volmet—Before aircraft could use ACARS (AirCraft Addressing and Reporting System – in simplest terms a way for aircrews and dispatchers/ATC to text each other with weight and balance, weather, flight plans, etc.) or SATCOM for weather updating, VOLMET broadcasts were continuously broadcast, 24 hours a day. These VOLMET broadcasts gave the weather and forecasts for a select group of airports in the region for which the VOLMET was responsible.

67. A reroute can have two possible meanings; first, it could mean the company changes the destination of one of its aircraft; or secondly, ATC, the crew, or the company changes in the route of flight of the aircraft to its original destination due to weather, turbulence, etc.

continued flight. The cowling was due to be replaced upon arrival at its next destination, but the captain was not budging; he didn't want to take the aircraft. After many minutes of consultation with maintenance folks on all levels the only way he took to flight was when the chief pilot personally asked him. The captain later told me he was worried that the cowling might fly off the engine while they were in flight.

I have to admit I was exasperated from the time spent talking to this gentleman since I guess I was stupidly naive to think it was just not a big deal, flying with this weld for one flight. As I shook my head, another colleague, who knew of the drama involved in cajoling this captain to fly said, "Dude, look at the weather forecast for his destination."

So I did.

"Thunderstorms. So what?" was my unemotional response.

Explaining his flippant comment, "It's been my experience that when thunderstorms or bad weather are forecast to clobber a destination upon our peak arrival times, the number of calls by captains requesting we look at the safety of an aircraft with an MEL goes up."

As I looked at him with my head askew. he muttered, "Hey, dude, I'm just sayin' . . ."

There are many other examples I could give where intrepid aviators did not seem so intrepid, particularly when faced with what one might think is a relatively minor, and legal, anomaly. Without trying to sound too much like an armchair quarterback, I realize they all had their personal and/or professional reasons for their actions, but since I was there and involved on some level with all of the previous examples (and many others not mentioned), I saw first-hand what I thought was a certain reluctance of a few captains to fly with such minor problems that it made no sense, at least to me. Particularly when you contrast them with others I know who flew with such bravado, and with more serious MEL issues, that I told them to take a deep breath and think about what they were doing before they/we departed.

Digressing a bit before I further explore the mysteries of some less-than-intrepid aviators, I'd like to touch on the rather polarizing topic of aviator training.

Many of my colleagues will agree that there are some pilots, both captain and first officer, with whom we have flown who definitely should have chosen another career due to poor flying and/ or judgment prowess, not to mention the possibility of horrible interpersonal skills. I realize that is a harsh, judgmental statement to make, but the observations of some of my more esteemed colleagues and myself over the years have confirmed that there are some pilots who simply should have chosen another career. I am not saying they are dangerous as pilots per se, because most of the ones of which I speak do their darnedest to stay on top of their game, but they also know they won't win any awards for being top guns.

So, looking backward, how do pilots get to be pilots in the airlines? Where do they come from and where were they trained? What standards exist that allow pilots to get where they are? Specifically, how do "bad" pilots get into the mainstream of the airlines?

I'll fully admit that topic alone, pilot training, has, like CRM (Crew Resource Management), been analyzed by institutions and people more qualified than myself, and there must be volumes written on the subject, but since some of you may have ADD/ADHD, I'll grossly narrow and truncate the discussion and limit it to just a few pages. (My father and I talked a great deal about this topic)

A couple of paragraphs earlier, I mentioned the words top gun.[68] Probably the best Navy recruitment film ever was the movie Top Gun, since it romanticized and magnified the business of flying fighter aircraft. Fighter pilots are few in number and generally draw a certain awe from the public due to their profession. I mean what job on the planet seems more romantic, daunting, chivalrous, and derring-do than flying a fighter jet? But when that fighter pilot's days draw nigh and he decides to go into the airlines, does that "ex" top gun pilot make the best airline pilot? Or for that matter, does any military-trained pilot, be it a cargo, bomber, passenger/ VIP transport, etc., make the best airline pilot?

What about a pure civilian-trained pilot? Does the civilian-trained aviator have to automatically bestow laurels upon the military pilot since he/she (civilian-trained pilot) didn't get the same regimented and fundamentally disciplined training in high performance aircraft in which the military aviators are edified?

Within the professional pilot world, be it the airlines, corporate, or commercial pilot realm, there often emerges, and it's usually at one of those private meetings between two or slightly more closely acquainted aviators, a discussion about who makes the better pilot: the military-trained one or the pure civilian-bred model.

There are some of us pilots, myself included, who are a hybrid to the above discussion because we started out in the general aviation realm then progressed into commercial aviation (towing banners in the Super Cub for me) before going to Uncle Sam (USAF) and having "him" pay the big bucks to further refine and hone our aviation, and possibly war-fighting, skills. So, to some degree, I don't

---

68. Top Gun—The U.S. Navy has a Fighter Weapons School like the USAF's and with the same purpose, though utilizing different fighter aircraft. The Navy's School is more commonly called TopGun, though officially it is Fighter Weapons School.

have a dog in this fight. However, since I'm opinionated as hell, from New Jersey, and this is my book, I'll weigh in on this somewhat controversial topic.

I suspect the general public feels the military-trained pilot is the better of the two choices, just like they think a college-educated engineer makes a more skilled aviator. Think of the bonus of an Air Force or Naval Academy-educated engineer who then becomes a USAF/Naval/Marine Corps aviator! My gawd, lay wreaths at his/her feet and bow down! That would seem to be the very tippy-top of a highly modified pyramid of Maslow's hierarchy of desired aviator qualifications!

Yes, I am being facetious, but I suspect that is what most people, who don't know squat about flying or pilots, would believe is the best lineage for a "super" pilot.

Meaning to burst your bubble, if you agree with that last paragraph, what follows may be blasphemy to my USAF/military-trained brothers, but . . . I do not necessarily think the military always produces the best pilot. But, I also don't think the civilian side has a lock on it either. In the end, it's all about attitude, desire, and a strong professional work ethic.

I must also add that I do wish every person who wanted to fly would at least consider trying to get into military service, whether it's the guard, reserve, or active duty. I am a huge proponent that military service should be mandatory for all people after graduating high school/college. I believe it builds an allegiance to one's nation and teaches a modicum of discipline that a lot of younger adults lack, but I digress.

In the dawn of my airline years and while "plumbing" (S/O) on the 727 I flew with two F/Os who "rocked it" when flying the jet. To this day Pete Doran and Brian Tyndall, are two in a group of some of the finest pilots I've ever seen fly a jet, particularly the B-727. Pete is a product of the civilian side of the fence and Brian an ex-Navy F-14 pilot; two outstanding pilots from two separate training backgrounds but each with a flying acumen beyond reproach.

Let me digress a bit to illustrate the difference between my civilian training and the military's...

Right after I soloed, I asked my dad what were my limits . . . what were the boundaries of my flying area and what could I do or not do with regards to me flying that frail little Cessna 150.

In a look only my father could portray, he said, "You have no limits, do what you want, go have fun and explore the limits of yourself." I thought he was seriously nuts or had just taken out a ridiculously high-paying insurance policy on me.

So, with a vacuum of rules from the old man, other than the FAA's (rules), I imposed my own limits and slowly pushed them outward, but not without scaring myself many times in the process.

The fallout from such a laissez faire style of civilian training caused me much tribulation upon entering USAF UPT. I have to fully admit that, initially, the rigid nature in which pilot training was conducted was almost claustrophobic to my free-spirited, civilian-trained background. But, once I embraced and understood the need for the military's style and structure of training, did I truly began to enjoy myself.

The military training pipeline is certainly regimented. Every training flight is graded, and when I went through my training there were six flight checkrides in eleven months: three in the T-37 and three in the T-38 (the USAF has since changed the way it trains pilots[69]). In my eleven months of training at Williams AFB, near Phoenix, I got 170 hours of flying time. In the first five months of USAF training after sitting side by side with my instructor, Sleaze (his nickname and call sign), in the constant noise, variable thrust, and rather forgiving and docile T-37, I went from zero hours to seventy. Then after getting a braver instructor, Kevin (his real name), I flew for the next six months, launching off Williams AFB's three desert runways in a white rocket called the T-38; this time with me sitting in front of the very high performance, tandem seating, supersonic trainer.

I have to say, whatever USAF general decided that the T-38 should be a training aircraft and flown by young, wild and crazy kids with very little flying time but with egos the size of Texas... well, God bless 'em! The T-38 was a blast to fly.

In eleven months, a USAF UPT (Undergraduate Pilot Training) student, entering with only twenty hours of flying time in a small single-engine propeller aircraft (to evaluate his potential to get through pilot training in the first place), will get their silver pilot's wings after roughly 170 hours of jet training (as previously described).

I won't lie, I loved my eleven months at Willie (nickname of the training base). However, there were quite a few students who didn't. I had about 1,400 hours of flying time when I began pilot training. The pressure on me to learn to fly wasn't near what it was on most of the other guys/gals who come with far fewer hours. I knew how to fly and even though all of my flying hours at that time were

---

69. Instead of all students getting to fly the T-37 and T-38, as they/we did when I went to UPT, they are now split into a two-track program. Firstly, the T-37 has been replaced by the T-6, a more modern two-seat, high performance single engine turboprop. Secondly, after being selected for either fighter aircraft or multi engine jet/heavy, the pilot trainee will either go on to fly the T-38 (fighter track) or go on to fly a small Beechcraft corporate jet, T-1 Jayhawk (heavy jet track) in order to get their wings.

in low-tech, low-performing single-engine piston aircraft and the USAF trained us in jets... . . . flying is, well, flying. It's somewhat like driving a car in that the basic concepts of it (flying) apply to every different type of aircraft, no matter how big or small, simple or complex.

What I did have to learn, and which took some getting used to, was the structure and rigidity of the actual flying and the training syllabus. Each aircraft departure route followed an exact "highway in the sky" out to the training areas, which were big, invisible boxes in the atmosphere and defined vertically in feet and laterally in nautical miles (ex. 10,000 to 20,000 feet vertically and with a rectangular area of say ten miles by thirty miles). In those "working (training) areas," other students and I practiced the day's required set of aerial maneuvers after which we flew very precise arrival routes from those training areas back to the air base; there was no messing around, either going to or coming back from those training areas in the sky. I wasn't allowed to peel off and go sightsee over a lake or some mountains or fly low over a forest that looked like it might be fun to buzz. Nope, all of the training aircraft were like little ants following the same path to and from the working areas and separated by a certain distance from each other. Each flight or training ride was supposed to accomplish some specific training objectives for that day's ride. Before we flew, we briefed the flight and the maneuvers to be flown in detail and after we landed we debriefed the flight in detail. Finally, each and every flight had a grade sheet that was submitted by the instructor to record the progress of the student.

What killed me about my year of living dangerously (pilot training), and to be honest my instructors would be more likely say it was they who lived dangerously, was the fact that as most of my classmates of class 8202 were attending graduation ceremonies, one of us (another classmate) was getting his final T-38 checkride. This very eclectic and nice gentleman had the distinction of flunking every flight checkride we had to take on the road to graduation—every one—six checkrides in all. Of course, after the first couple of failures he was given one or two training flights to bring him up to speed and then retook the flunked checkride. But . . . after failing the third checkride, there were no more retraining flights, he immediately went to another (checkride) and it was either pass or you are out. My gawd, how could he deal with that pressure? I would have crumpled. But he didn't, crumple that is, and he made it through.

He was given a transport aircraft as his follow-on Air Force assignment whereupon he would initially checkout as a copilot. The USAF's wisdom, I guess for him, was that being a copilot in "something" might allow him more time to increase his flying acumen to the point that one day he could upgrade to aircraft commander (captain). Plus, to be fair, 99 percent of all pilots graduating from UPT who got a "heavy"/multi-crew aircraft as a first assignment did not go into the aircraft commander (captain) position first, but had to pay their dues as a copilot first before upgrading to the left seat (assuming they were able to upgrade). Whether the aforementioned gentleman eventually got into the left seat (aircraft commander) while in the USAF I do not know, as I never kept career tabs on him.

What I do know is that once he left the USAF, he wound up flying with the same airline as me.

I genuinely—and in a Christian, Budweiser kind of way—love the guy, I do. He definitely has a unique personality and is very eclectic and he is very nice, but, I have to seriously wonder should he have chosen flying as a vocation? Did he really love the profession, or was it his father's influence (his dad was a professional pilot) that may have caused him to choose aviation as a career? I'll never know the answers to any of those, more or less, rhetorical questions, but still, on evenings when I'm staring at the stars out of my aircraft's window while cruising at some flight level, I wonder.

So, just because a guy may have been filtered through the military ranks on his way to the airlines doesn't mean he's better than a pure civilian-trained pilot. There are, however, many military guys who believe that the military-trained pilot is the best in the world. Some say if you take two identical people with zero flying time from the start, that the military route will make a better pilot in less time than the civilian path.

As a civilian-trained pilot, too, I know well that there is not the same kind of pressure on your training as in the military. It's more laid back and more self-paced. Yes, you are critiqued by your instructor after each flight and, as I saw with the difference between my father's and Jack's instructional styles, those debriefs could seem like heaven or hell. Unlike the military, there was never a grade sheet to be filled out after each flight, nor was there the looming checkride at a certain point in your training. Let there be no doubt, if you wanted your private pilot's license, you were eventually going to have to take your private pilot written test and then the practical flying test. And then, in order to progress in your career, you have to take the instrument written test and then the associated flying test with that rating, and then the commercial written test, etc., etc...

But there are no maximum hour requirement (just a minimum), or calendar time restrictions in which to pass these tests and should you flunk a test you can retake it, as far as I know, as many times as you need to pass. It's your dime that is financing your training (or your parents'), so the only limiting factor is money.

In the civilian world, there are colleges that have embedded aviation flying training programs, which work in conjunction and concurrent with the student while he/she gets his/her BS degree in whatever subject they are interested. I actually went to one of those schools, though I had many of my ratings when I started there and elected to continue my flying training using my father since it was hugely cheaper to do so.

So, as you can see, the civilian side of the aviation training world is usually much less structured and regimented than the military, but that doesn't mean you'll get poor aviators from this environment. In fact, if anything, there can be somewhat of a more "worldly" nature to these pilots because they are not trained in such a regimented way, nor do they fly the same routines day in and day out; they tend to be more open to options in how to get from A to B. Continuing, the civilian side can be less forgiving when it comes to operating with shoddy equipment due to the profit motive causing some flight schools to be more stingy about maintaining their training aircraft. This can cause the student pilot to be more apt to have developed real world hip pocket contingencies if an important electrical component on the aircraft fails, or even worse, the engine fails.

While the vast majority of the pure civilian trained pilots that I know at my airline have had, or are having, very successful airline careers there is at least one aviator of whom I know, and similarly, like my USAF UPT classmate discussed earlier, who has failed every checkride he's ever attempted when it came to trying to checkout as a captain.

I couldn't help but feel sorry for him. He's been steeped for so long in a career that expects him, the professional aviator, to eventually upgrade to captain on at least one type of jet during their employment tenure. This poor guy had tried a few times to make it to the left seat over the years and was never able to pass the final checkride that would garner him that coveted position. There is a rather large stigma assigned by the rest of the crew force if you're unable to pass the captain upgrade course, particularly if you fail as many times as this fella.

I'd actually flown with him very early in my career, when I was a "plumber" (second officer) on the 727. He was training to be a first officer, and even in that seat he had a bit of trouble. Years after that initial meeting of ours, and when I was getting my final captain's checkride on the MD-11, he was my first officer on a couple of wintery weather flights to the northeast area of the United States. Though he comes across as very nice person out of the cockpit, he had a tendency, when performing the duties as my first officer, to try to tell me how to do "my" job. He was much more senior than me in relation to his pilot seniority so I guess he felt that he was the "old sage" and intended to add his two cents to every decision I made. I just nodded in agreement since some things are not worth getting worked up over, even if I didn't agree or when it irritated the living hell out of me; tacitly ignoring someone, most of the time, communicates its own kind of subtle message.

In general, he is a likable person, just not very competent as a pilot, and one of his instructors said he wonders how he ever got so far into his career he flew so poorly. There is no doubt he lacked a certain "something" that allowed his brain to connect the dots in the area of good judgment and situational awareness; thinking "out of the box" in an aviation sense was not a quality with which he was naturally gifted nor seemed to be able to learn with any great, or small, measure over the years. The last I heard of him he was retired and I pray in retirement he finds a certain peace to know that he actually was a good F/O and that he takes up a second vocation in something in which he truly enjoys and is gifted.

In the final analysis, I don't buy the argument that military pilots are better than civilian-trained, and since my father, too, had been trained in both the civilian and military sectors, he and I were in complete agreement. As a previous check airman in both the military and airlines I can honestly say I see the positives and negatives of both aviation training pipelines since I've both trained and have given checkrides to a wide range of aviator types from many different pipelines. I must say, I think the regional airline pilots I evaluated or trained (new hires) at my airline were consistently the best of the bunch we hired, if only because of their experience in the Part 121 (airline) world and because they flew repeatedly in high density airports throughout the USA in the course of their regional flying; but the folks from that pipeline too (regionals) also came from either the military or civilian side, so maybe that's a moot point.

Above all, and no matter where your walk in life has taken you, a positive personal attitude has as much to do with your professionalism as an aviator as your training background, if not more. I have flown with military-trained pilots who thought their shit didn't stink but were mediocre pilots at best and have flown with pure civilian guys who seemingly had no ego but who were phenomenal aviators. Time and experience, as it distances you from the womb of your original training schools, whether military or civilian, when mixed with a stalwart personal code of ethics that breeds drive, desire, and a positive attitude will usually always be the great equalizer in the argument of which type of training is better and why certain pilots excel over others.

CHAPTER 28

Previously, I mentioned a Dr. Jekyll/Mr. Hyde type of captain that seemed bipolar in personality when in uniform. This type of captain I call the "anxious aviator." As I alluded to earlier, they were truly the more interesting type of captains with whom to fly and without question seemed to have a deeper sense of trepidation when it came to actually stepping into the cockpit to fly, particularly if the weather was going to be a factor.

Though I can't say I flew with a lot of anxious aviators, the ones with whom I have flown, in my very humble opinion, were very competent pilots. But, I did notice that their moods and the weather would affect their piloting and aircraft operation, so I was constantly on alert when operating with them.

While being generally good aviators when the mood hit them, therein lay their problem . . . their moods. It was in the realm of cockpit interpersonal relations where I tended to treat these guys with a more cautious flair than any other type of pilot. These guys seemed to have far deeper "issues" when in command of an aircraft, than just the plain old difficult captain who was pretty much set in his/her ways and was actually pretty easy with whom to fly once you set the boundaries.

But not so the anxious aviator, their emotional boundaries seemed to breathe in and out, like their edginess when they reported for work. If the weather was not great where we were going, their destination, these guys (I actually never flew with a female anxious aviator, though in truth I have flown with very few women in my career) were generally really tense and edgy from the start. This self-induced stress of theirs at times caused me to believe they may do something rash, like violate company of regulatory policies, so I was kinda hypervigilant when I was crewed with them. Also, keeping in mind their nervous, jittery at times, preloaded tension, I was much more forthcoming in announcing what I was doing before I did it when flying as an F/O with them. I was much more gratuitous in my positive affirmation strokes on what they were doing too, since I thought that might reduce their tension. Finally, I would speak up if I saw something dangerous, but unless it was going to crash, kill, or violate us, I tended to just massage their egos so as to make the flight less dramatic for both of us.

When I was first hired as a banner tow pilot, I firmly believed that everyone in the world who flew an aircraft for a living did so because they were absolutely in love with the profession; so naïve was I.

I observed all the sky kings who occasionally graced our back patio and noted each of their mannerisms. They were awesome guys. But, of particular note was my "other" next-door neighbor, the black sheep, as I called him because of his post-World War II career. This man also flew P-47s in Europe during the war, but as if to highlight and validate the "do what you really like to do" aspect of my father's seldom-spoken creed on how to decide on a career, was the fact that after the war this guy, Mr. Green, never flew again as a pilot. When he told me that he never wanted to fly again after the war ended, I was absolutely dumbfounded. I asked him why he didn't want to pursue aviation as a career. He confidently, if not arrogantly, said he flew to escape the foot soldier's war and he was never that keen on being a pilot in the first place, but chose it to stay out of the trenches. I thought his viewpoint was blasphemous and I was shocked that he could turn his back on such a wonderful gift. As I matured however, I realized that he did what was right for him and the world. He eventually went into real estate, became very successful, and he was quite content.

I realized after hearing this neighbor's story that you certainly don't want someone flying an aircraft when they would rather be doing something else. Thus, this neighbor served as a kind of reinforcing agent to my father's words (about career choices) and my perception that there was a mysterious and esoteric law of "pilot" physics that said only people who really, really liked to fly become and remained pilots . . . all the rest filter down to more earthly and apropos vocations.

A while ago I was on a trip to a faraway destination and after getting to the hotel I headed out to an esoteric pilot refueling station to get my fill of the latest aviation gossip and hot topic rumors of the day. To my delight, as soon as I entered the pub, I immediately saw a very dear aviator friend who I hadn't seen in eons. He too was an airline captain, and we had taken similar paths to get to our respective airlines. We talked about our families and the usual catching-up conversations you have with someone you haven't seen in years. After our initial exchange of pleasantries, I offered up a toast to our careers and then went on some tangent about how great it was that we were where we were at that point in time, captains, flying routes that aviation pioneers before us had forged. In my jubilation of seeing such a long-lost brother I mentioned the advice my dad had given me on how to choose a career and said wasn't it great that we had chosen well. At that point, my dear friend became very somber and said he regretted his career choice, hated being a captain, and wished he never became a pilot...and, after a pregnant pause, he added that he couldn't wait until he was able to retire.

The intensity with which he looked at me, and the unwavering directness in which he spoke, did not give the slightest hint that he was joking, nor was I going to challenge him on the validity of his deeply painful confession.

His words though, his attitude, rocked my world; those anxious aviator thoughts just previously espoused got personal and it was a very dear friend of mine who was affected. I was dumbfounded because as soon as he spoke of his epiphany, I immediately reflected upon our past and the seeming joy I saw in his face as we flew aircraft many years ago.

So, I sat there, on my stool, in the same manner as a shocked parishioner in church might act if a member of the congregation stood up and said he did not believe in God, and similarly, I thought his talk was sacrilegious.

But I quickly collected my composure and soon, deep down in my heart, a feeling of tremendous sympathy for this man began to well up inside of me. I cannot imagine what it would be like to have flown so many years, miles, and hours with contempt for the position.

He said, of his confession, that it was a slow burn sort of process, not an all-at-once hatred for his chosen profession, and for a long while he couldn't understand what it was he was feeling, other than the pure and utter dread of having to fly a trip. He thought his angst in flying might be due to other deeply repressed emotions, not the actual act of aviating itself. However, in the final analysis, he said he was anxious every time he flew, except in the best of weather, and especially hated flying into or out of airports when they were getting creamed with thunderstorms. (What pilot doesn't, I thought)

After hearing of my dear friend's confession, I wracked my brain for days afterward wondering what caused his fall from grace.

As of this writing, and it's been years since his confession, I still am no closer to an answer, just full of possibilities, and I am still shocked.

I don't know what causes a captain to become what I call an anxious aviator, let alone a flaming butthead, but I do know that I don't recall ever seeing any anxious F/Os, though I have flown with a few F/Os that I suspect will be jerk captains (they have to come from someplace).

I know of a first officer with whom I have flown who had been rolled upside down by wake turbulence in a small airliner while on final approach to a major airport. He quite deftly rolled the aircraft back to normal side up, thusly completing a full roll, and landed uneventfully with no harm to anyone or anything, with the exception to maybe all of their underwear. Being none the worse for wear, emotionally, this captain then went on to get hired as a first officer with my airline and was progressing through the ranks when he and I flew together. He was an exceptionally good first officer and no doubt will one day make an excellent captain (once again).

This gentleman wasn't the first pilot about whom I'd heard of that happening. The second time I heard of this very uncommon event, the pilot of the second encounter didn't fare as well as the first. Oh, this second captain did recover the commuter jet without problem, and he too managed to land quite safely, but the event scared him so much he took a position in his company where flying was almost an ancillary duty. He now flies just enough to keep his landing currency.

This brief thread on near-death experiences leads me to ask . . . what of the pilots in support roles in the airlines of the world? What about the instructors, the managers (chief and assistant chief pilots), the office guys (pilots) who have special projects, or the union guys (pilots), etc.? Most of these people were hired to fly the line, not command a desk, so what is up with them? Why did they choose to leave line flying to pursue an alternate career commanding a desk or managing other pilots? Are they afraid or anxious about flying, or does something else drive them into those positions?

I would be a hypocrite to say that all of those non-line flying pilots are anxious about aviating because I too have floated from being in management (duty officer) to being in the training department, and then in standards. Each of the aforementioned positions required me to simply maintain landing currency and not fly the line day in and day out. I can certainly say I love flying the line more than working in the ancillary positions and there are reasons for which I left full-time line flying, fear of flying or anxiousness about aviating not being either of them.

Many pilots choose the niches they choose in their airline for reasons other than concern about violating an FAR, bending metal, crashing, or simple fear of flying.

I myself have been an instructor on the MD-11 or the B-777 for twenty-one years (as of this writing) and have done so because of my kids. After moving to the city/domicile where the main bulk of my employer's simulator training is accomplished, I realized that Liza initially needed my help in raising our children. In conjunction with my desire to spend more time at home to bond with my youngest children, I also wanted to continue to see my children in New Jersey on a regular basis while not taking too much time away from my children in Tennessee. Since my dad was a little lacking in the fathering department, I did feel compelled to be more fatherly than he (my dad) was so that hopefully, my kids won't make the same mistakes I've made; and I pray by being so hands-on with them, they feel more secure within themselves. So, the choice of me being more proactive in raising my kids and spending more quality time with them all requires me to sacrifice a huge amount of line flying to be at home more and those ancillary positions indeed have allowed me the grace of more time with all my children. I believe it is a worthy tradeoff, and I am sure that many other pilots in the departments of the airlines around the world have had to make the same choices.

The decision, going full-time into the training department, was not an easy one to make. My own father was not that excited when I told him I was going to be leaving full-time line flying in 1995 so I could instruct in the simulator, for personal reasons, in my father's eyes that was a huge aviator sin. Since I did give many, many simulator checkrides to management pilots, I cannot say I ever saw many bad pilots in the lot of them . . . a couple were less than stellar, but in fact many were very talented aviators, which led me to believe that maybe they were bored as line pilots and wanted the challenge that being in a training position or management offered. And I would like to add, it would behoove many pilots to get into certain management and/or training positions if only to better learn how their company works or enhance their own piloting skills; breaking down barriers does a lot to increase corporate knowledge between the various departments and dispel myths about the different entities' peoples.

Finally, and let there be no doubt, I do believe, as do many of my colleagues, that there are some pilots who, no matter how you wanna' analyze it, do not like flying as their career choice and do avoid flying the line out of fear and anxiety. What percentage of the crew force that is, very small I'm sure, but after 27 years with my company and with the benefit of much retrospection, observation, and discussion with a couple of my closer connected airline brethren, I have no doubt about the validity of this paragraph's assertion.

My sincerest desire and one of the reasons that I wrote this book is to point out to much younger aviators who may one day read my words and who might be enthralled with the aviation mystique, that the initial glamour of our business does wear off as you age: the seat progression slows, stops, or even reverses itself; the pay will stop growing with seat progression and that too can even reverse depending upon the fortunes of your company; you eventually stop dating all the chicks/guys you can, grow up, get married, have kids, and then what?

You have to ask yourself, what was it that took you to the cockpit in the first place? Was it the pure love of flying? Or, was it money, women/men, traveling, days off, or all of the above?

I wonder how many folks do some serious soul searching before embarking on their careers and look far enough down the road to envision what it's like once you get ensconced "in the burbs" of your career. I know of a lady who got involved in the IT field because her guidance counselor in college told her it was her strong suit in the testing that she had taken before entering college. Twenty-seven years hence, she hates her job . . . she's excellent at it but hates it. She says she does envy me because she knows I love what I do for a living.

And though we all may start our careers with very little emotional baggage, God forbid your marriage begins to melt down, or you lose a loved one, or one of your kids decides they hate you, or your finances go to hell, etc. With all that drama going on at home can you still see the beauty of a cloud-studded sunrise while descending over the mountains when going into Anchorage, Alaska? Or the fascination of arriving at JFK in the early evening to the hustle and bustle of that vibrant city and its environs and then laying over amidst Manhattan's sea of lights and having a beer with the crew with Times Square as a backdrop? Can you still appreciate the beauty of mountains that seemingly climb to greet you as you crest just a few thousand feet above them or monstrous thunderstorms talking to each other at night through continuous displays of lightning?

As pilots, our duties and our office environment, are extremely dynamic and unique as compared to most other occupations. We sit at the front of a large vehicle that takes potentially hundreds of people (or tens of thousands of pounds of cargo), thousands and thousands of feet up in the air, and many thousands of miles at many hundreds of miles per hour. Our office is adorned with all sorts of switches, knobs, multifunction displays, computer input keyboards, indicators, levers, radios, radars, warning lights, regular lights, oxygen masks and much more in the form of "equipment"; We don't realize how daunting and complicated it looks to those who aren't aviators because, in fact, that is our office, it's us, who we are. We may be responsible for a piece of equipment (aircraft) and its cargo (people/freight) that may be worth up to 250 to 300 million dollars (747/A-380, et al), and as for people (as cargo/passengers), there is no dollar value attached. We fly this cockpit/machine through/in all kinds of weather and we generally do it without breaking a sweat. The views, when looking out of our office windows, are usually amazingly beautiful, constantly changing, and priceless. Finally, we are privy to a jet setting lifestyle, while getting being paid, that only the rich and famous can appreciate.

Don't take your career choice for granted, stay interested and enthusiastic. Use the sanctity and magic of flight to rehabilitate and rejuvenate your soul while cruising in the lower reaches of heaven. If you've got problems at home and since you're closer to heaven, God, and the angels "up there", push your boundaries and say a silent prayer to the "man" up there and maybe the holy spirit and an angel will follow you home and help you to sort out some, or all, of your problems. You... are a pilot. Feel blessed, you are special enough to God that He gave you the wonderful gift of being an Aviator; be humble, be thankful, and do not treat others as if you are better, you're just different...embrace it.

CHAPTER 29

The following chapter is a modified version of a short story I wrote after a rather interesting trip I flew many moons ago. I've included it in this book to illustrate both the capriciousness of fate and yet the silver linings that can arise from tragedy.

Only two things in life are guaranteed . . . death and taxes . . . at least so goes the oft-repeated axiom and as of this writing I have managed, so far, to evade a flat line on an EKG display. But in as much as I've managed to stay alive all of these action-filled years of mine, I personally have known or witnessed the passing of more than my fair share of friends, colleagues, or other human beings who weren't as fortunate.

The first death I can remember, a kindergarten classmate, occurred when I was five years old. The second, the first girl I ever kissed, died in a head-on automobile accident one month after the spin of the bottle pointed at her; that was painful. The third, fourth, fifth, and sixth all occurred with me in close proximity as I witnessed the bodies being covered . . . dreadful experience for a twelve-year-old.

There has been no common theme or thread as to what has caused this loss of life, since the reasons for their passing are as varied as their ages and innocence: automobile accidents, medical issues, aircraft crashes, neglect, or stupidity.

Prior to 1993, most of the losses were not too personal, however, the passing of my dear aviation mentor and friend, Jack, in 1993, left me reeling with a hard-to-describe emptiness in my heart and began a series of deaths that affected me deeply.

In spite of these tragedies, in each case I emotionally recovered and moved on with things because, in reality, death is a natural course of life's ebb and flow and "one must get on with the business of living."

There is, however, a corollary to the previously mentioned axiom, and it states that parents should not outlive their children; unfortunately, we don't all have crystal balls that will tell us what life is going to throw our way.

On an evening in late March, I was heading to Tokyo's International Airport. My first officer, Durand Brooks, and I had taken off from Anchorage. This was the second leg of a seven-leg, eleven-day, around-the-world trip on which I was training Durand to fly the MD-11. He had just finished his simulator training, and I was a line check airman, which meant I was qualified by the company to teach new captains and first officers how to fly the MD-11.

The weather that evening was spectacular! It was very clear and though the sun was slowly setting, it was still light enough to see the gorgeous Alaskan wilderness, almost 37,000 feet below.

Takeoff and climb had been routine, and after leveling off I was going through various types of flight management computer (FMC) failures and explaining to my charge how to analyze and, if possible, correct, fix or compensate for said malfunctions.

As Durand was engrossed in solving a simulated navigation problem I had just given him, I heard a radio call on VHF number 2, which we always kept tuned to 121.5, the international aviation emergency frequency, asking if anyone was on 121.5.

I immediately responded, "Aircraft calling on 121.5, this is CSE 17." (Amazingly, almost 25 years before this flight my father, while flying a Convair 880, heard an emergency radio call in the same general area that I was in when I heard this call. In my father's case the radio call was from the pilot of a Comanche that had crash landed east of Bethel, AK. My father and his crew assisted in the rescue of the pilot and his family.)

The voice on 121.5 came back and said he wanted to report the crash of a Super Cub. He said he wanted me to contact "TOP ROCC" (TOP ROCC is the USAF's Alaskan Rescue and Operational Control Center) and Dillingham (a city in Alaska near Bethel) Police Department and let them both know of an aircraft crash. Though we had SAT COM (satellite communication) on the aircraft, I had no idea of the phone numbers of either of those entities, so I told the rather calm pilot that I would report the accident to Anchorage Center and let them handle the coordination.

With that said, the pilot began to give me the following information: The latitude and longitude of the crash site; the color and model of the aircraft; and finally the fact that it was burning and he could not see any survivors.

I cannot impress upon you the calmness of this gentleman, as he relayed this information to me. It was almost as if he saw this type of thing every day and this was just another "ho-hum" accident. I even remarked to the first officer about how calm and collected he was as he spoke and how exact he was in speech, each word having a purpose.

After writing the information, he gave me on a piece of paper. I read it back to him to confirm that I received it correctly and then asked for his tail number as a reference in case Anchorage Center might want to contact him. He gave me the "N number,"[70] and then, as calmly as every other radio transmission he had made up to this point, he said that because it was getting dark, he needed to leave the crash site area and go land at his cabin while it was still light enough to see.

I "Roger'd" him and told him I would pass the information he gave me on to Anchorage Center.

And that is what I did. Anchorage took the information without asking me to repeat anything, and they told me they would call the Air Force and relay what I had told them.

Since the pilot had been so calm in his reporting of the accident, and for that matter Anchorage Center in their receipt of it, my initial excitement rapidly faded and besides, we were 37,000 feet up and moving westward at 480 knots ground speed, what more could we do or what more could happen? The whole "thing" seemed to be over almost as soon as it began.

In an amazingly short amount of time after I reported the accident to Center, TOP ROCC began calling on 121.5 trying to get a hold of the guy I just talked to. Since we had to listen to Center, and both the FO and I were curious, Durand said he'd listen to 121.5 while I monitored Anchorage Center's freq.

---

70. N number—the FAA assigns every U. S. Registered aircraft a registration, N number; kinda like a license plate to cars, but which can be looked-up in the FAA's online data base and details about that aircraft and owner revealed.

As the two parties began their conversation, I turned down the volume of my number 2 radio, as Durand put on his headset, and then he did the reciprocal with his volume, except it was with the number 1 radio. As we flew over the frozen and mostly white-colored world below, chasing a gloriously orange, yellow, and red sunset, I had no idea that on such a wonderful evening as this that the crash of a small aircraft in such a remote place would reach up to rock my world and had already devastated another's.

Durand had been eavesdropping on the conversation below for about two minutes or so when his face made an expression that I took as being one of total surprise. I happened to be looking at him when he made the face, so being the sometimes-impatient person I can be, and also after learning from my kids, I started "miming" to him to give me some information as to what was being said. He understood immediately what my pathetic body gyrations meant and stuck his index finger up, so as to signal for me to wait—which I did . . . sorta'. At least I ceased with the overly dramatic body movements and switched to a more passive aggressive tapping of fingers on the center console.

I wish I hadn't been so impatient. After another few seconds of finger tapping, Durand looked over to me, lifted one side of his headset, and told me that the pilot of the crashed and burned aircraft was the son of the reporting pilot.

What Durand could gather was this: The pilot of the reporting aircraft, the father, had dropped off his son at the field where the accident aircraft was parked. From there the two men were going to fly, each in their respective aircraft, to their fishing lodge where they would rendezvous and spend the night. When the son never showed up the dad retraced his steps and, in doing so, happened upon the crashed and burning aircraft. After circling the wreckage and not seeing any sign of life, and obviously after reporting the accident, he headed back to his landing strip before it got too dark.

The reporting pilot, Mr. Smith (not his real name), said that his son, Luke (again not his real name), worked as a state policeman out of Dillingham's station and today was his off day. He asked if the USAF would call the Dillingham office. The USAF told Mr. Smith that they would begin a recovery effort and gave the gentleman a phone number for him to call when he got on the ground. Durand, being the sharp individual that he is, wrote the number down and gave it to me.

In my heart, there was nowhere to run. The news that Durand gave me literally shook the foundations of my being at that instant. My feelings of grief for this man and his loss, and because of certain memories that I had, were almost unbearable. My Lord, how tragic this was for this man and whatever families they may both have. I was absolutely speechless and sat in the cockpit for a long spell just staring out the window.

The beautiful sunset that I had been admiring just a short time before did not look so beautiful now. Combined with the tragic turn of events, this whole situation now reminded me of a dark Shakespearean play. The sun's red glow represented the blood of a victim upon a white and perfect world, staining it, with the subsequent incineration of that person in the fireball of the crash. As the plane went down in flames, so too was a burning sun descending.

As the evening accumulated, and we flew ever further from the crash site, the growing distance didn't lessen the trauma of the evening. As a fitting end to this morbid play, the gathering darkness of night seemed appropriate as the Grim Reaper swept over the land and gathered up his latest victim.

Since we still had more than half a world to fly around before Durand was finished with his training, I gave "it," training that is, a rest for the remainder of the flight. I just was not in any mood to instruct, other than to give immediate advice on how to fly the aircraft as we proceeded to Japan. Whatever detailed, long-term instructional discussions I had left I was going to save for the remaining five legs.

After a while, I excused myself from the cockpit and left Durand at the controls as I went back to put a meal in the oven.

Once out of the cockpit and out of sight of Durand, I won't be proud and say that I didn't shed a tear or two. I was feeling such remorse for Mr. Smith's loss that it was hard not to grieve without the occasional drop, I just didn't want my first officer to see them. The thought of Mr. Smith and his family and what they were going through, I could imagine it . . . because, you see, I too have outlived one of my children . . .

On January 9, 1997, at 3:30 p.m., my life, like Mr. Smith's, forever changed. My wife was backing out of our driveway when my seventeen-month-old daughter, Autumn-Paige, ran behind her mother's Jeep and was crushed.

I was in the front yard at the time of the accident. I was actually bending down trying to get a house key by the front door. I thought Autumn Paige was by my side since she, Austin (who was three months old then and in a car carrier seat), and I had been out doing errands most of the day and Liza was now heading to the gym after jumping into the same vehicle that the two kids and I had just exited.

I heard a thunk as Liza backed out and immediately looked in the direction of the driveway whereupon, and to my absolute horror, I saw Autumn-Paige lying face-up on the driveway.

I ran over to her, and as I did so, I was screaming at the top of my lungs for Liza to call the paramedics. Liza had stopped backing up after feeling the bump of running over Autumn-Paige but the front end of the car was blocking her view from seeing what caused the bump.

I knew! I knew! Autumn-Paige was either dead or going to die when I ran up to her motionless body. As I approached, I saw that she had a tire track on her forehead and blood was coming from her nose and ears.

I picked up my baby and ran to the middle of the lawn screaming for Liza to call the paramedics.

I held Autumn-Paige close to my chest in my open jacket trying to cradle and thusly comfort her as best as I could. Her heart was beating like a scared hummingbird's, but she was not breathing. I could see the beautiful pink color of her angelic face slowly bleed to an ashen grey; she was dying before my eyes, and there was nothing I could do . . . I was utterly and completely helpless to stop the death of my undeserving to die, innocent, and lovely daughter.

I did attempt to give CPR, since she was not breathing, but it was to no avail, her tiny lungs were crushed and not capable of sustaining breathing, and she did have blood coming from her mouth. Feeling completely helpless and distraught, I continued to hold her as the angels quietly took her soul and her body became limp.

In what seemed like an eternity, but in actuality was only nine minutes after the 911 call, the paramedics took Autumn-Paige from my arms and air evac'ed her to Le Bonheur Children's Hospital.

The human language is inadequate when it comes to conveying the grief that Liza and I felt.

Unless you've been where we have, with regards to your own child's death, you have no comprehension of the pain . . . none. It's indescribable. Don't ever say to a person who has lost a child, if you have not lost one yourself, "I know how it feels." No, you don't; you can't even imagine it. The emotional pain goes beyond any which you have ever experienced.

I can't speak for Liza with regards to her deepest feelings since we've never talked about it, but for me, right after Autumn-Paige was taken from my arms I was engulfed by a feeling of grief and despair so overwhelming and complete that my life, at that point, ceased to exist. As a companion to the despair and grief was a gloom so all-encompassing and invasive that it instantly infiltrated every compartment of my head and heart; mentally, there was nowhere to run. Every time I tried to think of something remotely positive, whether it was thoughts of the future, or past, the trio of gloom, grief, and despair had already preceded me. Sooo much pain, so much. I existed in a void between living and dying, wishing my heart would stop and God would kill me. I hurt so overwhelmingly that there was not one scintilla of a positive emotion left in me; it was just negativity on such a grand scale that it felt like my spirit, the essence of my life force, my soul, was slowly being extruded through my heart and burned to ashes while I watched. Behind every happy or positive thought I tried to think or imagine, to escape the dread, the black cloud of gloom rolled in like a heavy fog and then, to add the coup de grâce, the vision of Autumn-Paige's bloodied face was trumpeted in by the grim reaper for good measure. I was alive, but dead.

And why shouldn't it? Why shouldn't the bloodied vision of Autumn-Paige, be forefront in all of my thoughts? Through my negligence, I had allowed my seventeen-month-old daughter to die a horrible death. I deserved to die myself.

Immediately following Autumn's departure with the paramedics, Liza and I were hysterical with grief and we both lay curled up on the floor in our house for Lord knows how long, inconsolable and incapable of rational thought.

It was only by a policeman's gentle, but persistent, urging that Liza and I go see Autumn-Paige in the hospital that we were able to move at all. The thought of being able to see her was just enough to pull me out of my emotional spiral to hell so that I could compose myself, just barely, and get out the door.

Though everyone did all they could, from the paramedics to the doctors, Autumn-Paige was pronounced dead upon arrival at the hospital. After holding her one last time, my wife and I were driven home, not fully realizing that our life together, our marriage, was over.

You do not recover from the death of a child, you live with it and have to learn coping mechanisms. Like having an incurable disease or affliction, such as arthritis, epilepsy or migraines, you can go for days, weeks or months without an occurrence of the emotional pain that you first felt when your child died and then one day, due to whatever . . . you get hit and have to deal with the torture. And so it is, you live with the loss and avoid the "hot button" things that will recall the pain.

My faith died the day Autumn-Paige died. God did not exist, and He ceased to have meaning in my life. There wasn't a human at that time who could have successfully explained to me why a good

Lord would take the life of a seventeen-month-old child, particularly mine; God got very up close and personal that day, and I hated Him.

In the days and months after Autumn's death, Liza and I grew rapidly apart. We dealt with the grief in completely opposite ways.

Being British and in keeping with the stiff upper lip kind of emotional self-containment that all Brits seem to have, Liza was much more reticent than I to show emotion after our child's death. Why she was that way I don't know—shock, heritage, learned behavior from her parents, who knows. I know I will never understand her lack of emotion and why she was so much calmer than me, but it was what it was and to this day we have never once discussed our differences. I do know, however, that my more openly weepy and melancholy nature irritated her to no end.

As for me, I died every day. I relived over and over the process of seeing Autumn-Paige on the ground, running up to and picking her up, holding her and seeing her bloodied face and crushed body (to this day, almost daily, I relive that moment). I would sit in the shower, crying, with water pouring on me, for an hour at a time, two to three times a day, wearing the same jacket in which I held her as she died. I have no idea why I did this. Maybe I wanted God to absolve me of whatever sin I had committed that caused Him to kill my daughter, or maybe I was trying to make myself clean from my neglect in allowing her to get run over. Each day the pain was there, the same as the day before, I just learned how to function, because quite literally, even though I would have put a bullet in my head after her death. The only thing that stopped me was the fact that I had a three-month-old son, as well as Christina and Kyle, who deserved a father who was not so self-absorbed with his guilt and grief that he couldn't give his children a fair chance at a good life.

Austin did not deserve me having the self-pity and depression that was taking his father away from his life. Each time I changed his diaper or fed him, or played with him I realized that he, Christina, and Kyle were my lifeline to the land of the living, and I totally wrapped my world around Austin and cherished even more my monthly visits with Christina and Kyle; the blessing of my children has been realized over and over as they have aged.

So, returning back to the flight to Tokyo with Durand . . .

I was absolutely beside myself with sympathy for Mr. Smith, and I wanted so much to do "something," but I knew there was nothing that could be done. I thought of the months of intense, emotional pain that the Smith family was going to have to experience, pain that would always lie just beneath the surface, never totally going away. I wanted God to come and wipe his tears away and hold him or bring this man's son magically back to life, but I knew also that none of this was going to happen.

Knowing all too well the personal implications of Mr. Smith's loss, in my own awkward way, I asked God to help this man get over, somehow, his loss and get on with life in a meaningful way. But since I'm probably more of a candidate for hell than most people, I wasn't sure if my prayer was getting through to Thee Chief of chief pilots (God). After a few minutes in the solitude of my thoughts and prayer, I returned to the cockpit.

In the Bible, Isaiah 61:3 reads, "To all who mourn in Israel, he will give a crown of beauty for ashes, a joyous blessing instead of mourning, festive praise instead of despair. In their righteousness, they will be like great oaks that the LORD has planted for his own glory."

There is no doubt in my heart that our—Liza's, Mr. Smith's, and my—lives were in ashes on the day our children died and though I prayed for a miracle on both occasions, sometimes the Lord seems as distant to my requests as the farthest star in the heavens is to Earth. But, in my eternal optimism a poem written by Emily Dickinson comes to my head when faced with certain dread:

> Hope is the thing with feathers
> that perches in the soul,
> and sings the tune without the words,
> and never stops at all,
> And sweetest in the gale is heard;
> and sore must be the storm
> that could abash the little bird
> that kept so many warm.
> I've heard it in the chillest land,
> and on the strangest sea;
> yet, never, in extremity,
> it asked a crumb of me.

The rest of the flight to Narita was very uneventful. However, as if to show the sorrow of crying angels from above, the atmosphere over Narita upon our arrival was filled with moisture-laden, low-laying clouds dripping with heavy rain. Durand did a real nice job of flying the arrival that fed into an ILS and to top it off he landed well on a thoroughly drenched runway 34 Left at Narita.

After getting to the hotel and checking into our rooms, I met my young charge in a very nice wine bar in the hotel to debrief the events of the evening. Were I a younger man, I might have gotten thoroughly drunk, because I so wanted to drown out the thought of the pilot dying and his father's suffering. Instead, being older and wiser, I offered up a toast to an aviator who had taken his final flight. After my second drink, and having finished discussing the mostly finer points of Durand's flying, I bid him adieu and retired to the sanctity of my room for some much-needed sleep.

I awoke at around 6 a.m. Tokyo time, after seven hours of incredible dreaming; I was actually still tired due to the adventures in my dreams! I had one purpose on my mind when I awoke and that was to call the number that the USAF gave to Mr. Smith. With a trembling hand, racing heart and mind, I picked up the phone and dialed the number that Durand had copied down while eavesdropping.

My whole body was literally shaking as I waited for the circuits to connect and cause the phone on the other end to ring. It didn't take long and after but one ring, a U.S. Air Force captain answered the phone with some official military-type greeting. Though he couldn't have known it then, he could have saved his much practiced and official introduction as all I really heard was, "Blah, blah . . . Captain . . . blah, blah." Please do not think I am trying to be disrespectful to the military, or this guy in particular, since I had been in the USAF myself. But, I was so nervous and excited and tired and apprehensive that I could barely contain myself and listening with my ears/brain, in the emotional state I was in at that time was not one of my stronger points. So, after his practiced introduction it was then my turn to tell him who I was and why I was calling. As I ended my extemporaneous, gibberish filled verbal rush I asked, almost in resignation, "I don't suppose you were able to get to the crash site last night, were you?" (Since it was 6 a.m. in Japan, it was early afternoon, the day after the crash, in Anchorage.)

It's been said that the eruption of Krakatoa in 1883 Indonesia is the loudest sound ever heard by humans. Well, let me tell you, my shout for joy after hearing that Mr. Smith's son was found alive is a close second . . . much to the consternation of those in the rooms next to mine! In one of the most ecstatic moments of my adult life, this unknown captain, located over 3000 miles away, told me in a very happy voice that they had located the crash site at about eleven thirty last night and found the pilot alive and with non-life-threatening injuries!

The USAF captain said that when the airplane crashed the pilot was thrown out of the wreckage and because the young man was wearing thick winter clothes, this absorbed quite a bit of the impact forces. In addition, the ejection from the aircraft had the serendipitous effect of sparing the pilot from being consumed by the ensuing post-crash fire. Adding even more serendipity to this mishap, the fire caused the metal of the aircraft engine, and various other now molten metal parts, to retain a great amount of latent heat which, after the flames exhausted themselves, allowed the son to crawl into the smoldering debris and ashes and huddle up against the engine, which was now firmly planted in the ground, to stay warm until help came.

I couldn't believe it! I was so happy I went downstairs to the gym and worked out for two hours just to contain myself! And after that I met Durand at breakfast and gave him the good news! I don't think in my life that my heart has ever gone from being so low and then so up in such a short period of time! In my mind, it was a miracle and I thanked God for saving Luke's life and consequently saving his father and mother from a lifetime of anguish.

That evening, Durand and I "saddled up our ride" and headed for Hong Kong, as I began again his IOE training. In complete contrast to the previous evening's drenching rains, the world was smiling as evidenced by clear skies and light winds.

On the flight to Hong Kong we talked very briefly about the news I gave him earlier, but there was no doubt, my joy was so much more than his that I elected not to discuss what happened again, unless he brought it up first; I did not want to sound like a "broken record." The barrier between he and I on this issue was apparent and was no one's fault. I had personally experienced the dark side of losing a child and I was so grateful for the pain that Mr. Smith was spared. And, it was in this area, of losing a child, where Durand and I were worlds apart and I pray we will always remain so.

Out of the ashes of a crashed aircraft rose the beauty of Mr. Smith's son. And though I was supremely happy about this miracle, the sad fact is that while one child lived, the other one, Autumn-Paige, remained firmly entombed, and no amount of prayer was going to bring her, or my faith in God, back to life.

In the days and weeks immediately following my daughter's passing, the outpouring from my church was beyond all comprehension. Being the loner that I am, I was not huge into socializing and barely knew any of the congregation at my church, but the call had gone out that one of the "flock" (parishioners) had lost a child. The response was overwhelming. For over thirty days after Autumn-Paige's death someone was at our house most of the day and evening, tending to our grief, feeding us food, conversation, and/or faith, or lending an ear for the outpouring of our pain. To this day, I cannot thank the congregation of Grace Evangelical Church enough, and I know I have not done near enough to say thank you.

As the church volunteers were just beginning to settle in for their thirty-day sojourn in our house, an unlikely savior came to relieve Liza and me of some of the pain and grief that we were experiencing. The insight we received by Liza's brother-in-law, Malcolm, was life-changing and had the added effect of renewing my Christian faith; oddly, this savior of my faith was an atheist.

Malcolm is one of the finest men I have ever met in my life. In fact, I secretly wish I could assimilate his unbelievable strength of character and integrity into my own persona.

At the time of Autumn-Paige's passing, Malcolm was an atheist. He wasn't a Bible-knocking or Christ-dissing atheist though, he just said he'd looked at all the faiths and didn't seem to find a reason to believe in any of them. Nonetheless, Malcolm's charm, wit, self-depreciating personality, and humbleness were (and are) so endearing it doesn't matter what he believes. I just love him (he is still alive) and think he is such a wonderful human being. I love being in his presence and hearing his stories of his life in the entertainment world in both Britain and the United States.

The day after Autumn-Paige was buried, Malcolm returned to England to conduct business in London (he and his wife, Kathryn, Liza's sister, live in Southampton, England) while Kathryn and Liza's parents stayed in the USA.

Upon his return to the UK, and after tending to business affairs in London, he drove home, had a quiet evening by himself (he and Kath are empty nesters), and went to bed.

Around two in the morning, he woke up. He wasn't sure why, but he did. He knows it was 2 a.m. because he looked at the orangeish glow from the clock on his nightstand right after he awoke. As he lay looking at the ceiling, desiring to go back to sleep, he saw the room grow darker and shortly thereafter, he lost sight of his familiar surroundings, and very quickly total blackness enveloped every square inch of his world and concurrently he felt as if he was moving.

In short order, light replaced darkness and Malcolm was visually introduced to a new, brighter, more colorful and expansive vista. Where his body was he couldn't say, as he had no notion of his hands or feet or the rest of his body; the only awareness he had was visual—hearing, feeling, smell, or taste were not evident, just a beautiful view of a world he'd never seen before or knew existed laid out before his eyes as if he were suspended in midair.

In the view that Malcolm initially observed he saw neither ground nor stars, just a magnificently pastel-colored sky with clouds, both near and far, and a presence of light that didn't come from one specific place, like a sun; but instead the light seemed to exist in the round, in the same way as air exists all around us.

As he looked around, examining his new surroundings, Malcolm saw a figure. It was a large man, as best as he could tell, wearing a loosely fitting, down to his ankles, white tunic with a head topped with golden colored, long flowing hair. From this figure's back emerged large, white, feather-covered wings that were gently moving, up and down, not giving the impression they could maintain this individual in flight, but, indeed were, judging by the fact that they were well above any observable ground.

As if seeing this huge figure wasn't shock enough, what really caught Malcolm's attention was the tiny form sitting on the back of the "angelic" (my interpretation) figure, between the wings. The angel was at a slight head's up angle to what appeared to be a distant, cloud-layered, multi-colored, horizon and the tiny form gave the appearance of a small child. This child was sitting up and facing forward, as if getting a horsy ride from a very large, in stature, father, except of course they were actually flying. At this time, Malcolm was slightly behind and above the two figures, on the right side, and about thirty feet or so away.

As soon as Malcolm entered this "realm," in his wonderfully astute mind, he said to himself that he better make mental notes of this event, as he knew it was significant and he would want to tell "somebody."

After observing this figure for an indeterminable amount of time, Malcolm suddenly went from being thirty feet to only ten feet or so away and from being slightly to the rear to now being slightly to the front and level with them, where he could see the faces of both. The face of the smallish figure was in shock at Malcolm's close and rapid approach, but seemingly not the angel's; the expression of the child being one of surprise and the angel's showing no change or obvious hint of excitement. Without question though, Malcolm was probably the most surprised, since the face of the child was Autumn-Paige's, at least that was what an inner voice had told him.

Malcolm had not seen Autumn-Paige for over a year before her passing, and at the viewing, he did not elect to see her. He said the sight of seeing her lying in the casket, in a beautiful blue velvet gown, would be too much for him to bear, so he stayed in the anteroom to the viewing area or was outside the building talking to those who came to pay their respects. In fact, Malcolm had no idea of the clothes Autumn-Paige was wearing when she died, or of how many teeth she had grown in her mouth since he last saw her.

In his later description of her to the pastor of my church and to Liza, me, and others, there is no doubt that the child Malcolm was observing was Autumn-Paige. He described her looks in amazing accuracy, from the way she was kneading the hair that flowed back behind the angel and upon which she sat while riding between its shoulders (we had a German shepherd at home and Autumn-Paige used to like to knead Sadie's hair when the dog was lying down), the teeth in her mouth, the tussle of her platinum-blonde hair upon her head, and finally the clothes she was wearing when she died.

When Malcolm went from thirty to ten feet away, it was very evident that Autumn-Paige noticed him since, as I just said, she gave a look of surprise in Malcolm's direction and they briefly looked into each other's gaze. In short order, though, Autumn-Paige began to laugh and looked forward, away from Malcolm. He could tell that the angel and child were communicating, but he didn't know how he knew, he just did. He could not hear anything, but without a doubt the joy and laughter that was expressed from Autumn-Paige's face was matched in reciprocal by smiles and acknowledgment from down below on the angel's face.

Onward, the two flew, angel and child, with nothing but joy showing on Autumn-Paige's face. Malcolm was held captive to a scene that lasted longer or shorter than he knew and from which the feeling he gained, while in this realm, was so indescribably pleasurable that he didn't want to leave.

But alas, God's will be done and He took his dutiful and wonderful atheist back from which he came. The angel turned slightly to the left and began to leave Malcolm, then the sky went oppressively black, and Malcolm was back in his bed in Southampton.

"You don't fall asleep after an event like that," so said Malcolm the next morning when he called to tell us that "something extraordinary" had happened last night, though he refused to elaborate.

He was energized and charged emotionally from whatever happened and caught the next British Airways flight he could to America. He said he was coming to personally tell us of what happened, but first, he wanted to talk to the pastor who presided over the funeral.

For an hour or so, Malcolm and the pastor were sequestered in the pastor's office while Liza, her mother, her father, Kathryn, and I paced the carpet outside. Their voices, Malcolm's and the pastor's, were low enough that no amount of eavesdropping on my part allowed me any discernible bits of intelligence about the topic of their discussion.

Eventually, the door opened up and the pastor came out to announce that, in his professional opinion, Malcolm had been privy to a vision from God. In this vision, Malcolm had seen an angel and, best of all, Autumn-Paige. The scene he saw, of them flying in heaven, was maybe meant to stem the outpouring pain, sorrow, and grief from Liza and me; and secretly, it, in my opinion, was also meant to rekindle my faith that had turned to ashes upon Autumn-Paige's untimely passing.

No, unlike Mr. Smith's son, Autumn-Paige did not rise, phoenix like, from her accident site, nor did she arise, in a living, biological sense at any point after the accident. Instead, in a profoundly more majestic and supremely beautiful passage from this world to the heavenly one she rode, happily, on the back of an angel and commands a far richer, happier, and perfect view of the universe than I do.

My daughter waits for Liza and me in heaven, and nothing, but nothing keeps me more optimistic about death, and resurrection thereof, than the knowledge that one day I will be reunited with her.

You may question the next comment I make, but Malcolm's vision—and in my soul I believe it to be true—was a much prayed for silver lining to an unfathomably dark cloud. Why God chose Malcolm as the one to see this spiritual vision has been the cause of much contemplative thought and introspection on my part through the years. In all of this dialectic, self-absorbed bantering in the deepest reaches of my mind, the only thing that makes sense, in my humble opinion, is that Malcolm was the most credible messenger amongst those Liza and I knew. Had a friend, if she/he was a Christian, told of us of this vision Liza and I would have thought that he/she was making this up to comfort us. But Malcolm was an atheist and had no logical reason to see what he saw, given his total lack of spiritual beliefs, nor could he have known in detail the particulars of Autumn-Paige's looks, dress and habits. He was (and still is) the most honest human I've ever met, with honor and integrity beyond reproach; Malcolm is the only human whose testimony and belief in what he saw that night I would believe.

CHAPTER 30

In the days, months, and years following Autumn-Paige's death, Liza and I grew farther and farther apart.

When I was originally hired to be an instructor on the MD-11, I was brought in to edify my charges only in the simulator. Yes, I was also a company line pilot, too, but since we were so busy training new crews, I spent most of my working time in the simulator and flew "on the line" just the bare minimum to stay proficient.

Working so close to where I lived, and not having to fly the line at this time was a blessing. It was good for Austin because after his sister's passing, Liza kinda left planet Earth for a while as a hands-on mother and I was trying to be there for him at all times until Liza was able to regain her composure and became more active again in his life. Austin and I were inseparable when I was home, and as the years would progress, he and I would continue to have a bond that few parents will ever have with their children; seeing his chubby and smiling face right after coming back from the hospital after seeing Autumn-Paige's body was a contrast that has left an indelible mark upon my soul as to how innocent, needy, and vulnerable children are.

Also, Liza and I had almost immediately started grief/marriage counseling right after our child's funeral. We were given, according to the family counselors directly involved, emotional triage to help us stay functional as spouses, parents, and humans; here too, not flying the line allowed me to work fulltime in the simulator while giving me the flexibility to concentrate on fixing my broken spirit and marriage.

There is emotional pain, and there is emotional pain, but nothing in my life prepared me for having to deal with the death of my daughter and the concurrent crucifixion that was going on in my marriage. For the second time in my life, I had another failing marriage, and it was killing me. I was determined to stay married. Liza was my choice, not my dad's or anyone else's. I hadn't been forced to be with her. I had target fixation on fighting the good fight to stay together and sought to fix the relationship instead of divorcing.

In spite of all the emotional, energy-draining drama, amazingly enough, Liza and I never really blamed each other for Autumn-Paige's passing; at least I never did her. Yes, as the clock counted down toward the change to a new millennium, there were some ugly, emotionally-charged, and very hurtful personal fights between us, however the fights always began with something unrelated to Autumn-Paige's passing. Only on the odd occasion would one, or both of us, throw in some innuendo of fault, like tossing a hand grenade for effect toward the other. But, in general we seemed to have a mutual, unspoken respect to not dwell on who was at fault in Autumn-Paige's death; at that time however, I secretly carried a huge burden of pain, believing I was to blame and unable to forgive myself.

As the year 2000 approached, and the marital therapy we were getting showed its limitations in fixing our marriage, Liza demanded another child to replace the girl she lost. At first, I refused, but then after much harping from her I relented. She had threatened to divorce me, so to try and keep some semblance of peace between us, I agreed. By the grace of God, she immediately became pregnant, and by another wonderful blessing from God, Liza and I were blessed with another girl.

Though I can't say our marriage was any better, on February 11, 1999, Amber Dawn burst forth upon the world, posing almost immediately for the cameras that snapped her picture. If ever a child was born with a natural photogenic quality, it was Amber, and the camera loves her. I do suspect the angels that cared for her while she was in her mother's womb had something to do with her radiance. Amber was truly a pleading prayer answered and an amazing gift from God, and I am convinced He personally sent His angels to tend to His child during her gestation to keep her safe.

CHAPTER 31

As the new millennium approached, Liza's parents flew over to be with us for the last Christmas of the first millennium, AD, and the first New Year's Day of the second millennium.

I only wished I could have been there! My seniority was such that I got stuck flying over that same Christmas and New Year's Day.

Since there were dire predictions that the world might end at the end of 1999, I kept a journal of the trip and have reproduced some of it in this book. What follows are selected entries from that journal.

MILLENIUM JOURNAL STORY

It is December 23, 1999 and in about fourteen hours I will be taking off and headed for Paris and points east.

Christmas Eve, most of it anyway, will be spent on an MD-11 because I will be flying east and my day will be shortened by six hours, so the flight isn't as long as I seemed to imply. I'll have dinner, Christmas Eve dinner, in Paris with my crew, and then I'll spend Christmas Day in a hotel room.

I'd rather be with my kids, my wife, and her parents, in my home but such is the fate of being very junior on the seniority list;

this is not a great mood with which to start a trip. It wouldn't be too bad if, after Paris, I was heading west again, into a setting sun and the rising arms of my son Austin and my third child from Liza, Amber-Dawn, who will be a year old in another month. But alas that is not to be. My fate, and what waits for me, is over the eastern horizon into a rising sun and unknown faces. I will not see the shores of my country until the next millennium.

To be sure, I use trickery with these words as the "next millennium" is not that far away. In plain words, it's only nine days hence.

In emotion, though, it's an eternity. It'll be the turn of the century, the click of a clock, the beat of a heart, 32,000 vibrations of a quartz crystal. It will be the closing of 1000 or 2000 (technically I guess 2001 would be the "technical" end of the millennium, but 1999 seems more in the spirit) years of accumulated human calamity, and maybe, hopefully, prayerfully, the start of a new human consciousness and a reversal of man's continuing fall toward moral and environmental decay . . . yeah right.

So, the clock ticks. It's a new minute, a new hour, a new day, a new week, month, year, decade, century, millennium. I can't imagine I'll feel any different, it's just that I'll be in Hong Kong, most likely with wicked jet lag and a wee bit tipsy.

I am hoping that the Y2K bug's bark is worse than its bite! I do not want to be delayed any longer on this trip than its scheduled "time away from base" so I can see my kids.

Speaking of the Y2K bug . . . much ado has been made of its possible infection and the fate of those countries that may be affected with this human-conceived "virus." The good news is that its incubation period is fixed and known so the necessary vaccine has been taken by most countries to lessen its effects. But there is still a very big question mark in a lot of peoples' minds.

. . .

December 24, 1999 (6:36 a.m., Central Time)

We left 55 minutes late this morning. We were supposed to "push" at 4:20 a.m. Instead, due to an appropriate, seasonal, dusting of snow, we had to wait fifty-five minutes to get de-iced.

As I write this, I am over southeastern Canada (near Saint John's, Newfoundland). The first officer, F/O, Kit Teeter, is sleeping, and the relief F/O, RF/O, is fulfilling his obligation and is in Kit's seat. In about forty-five minutes, I'll be heading to the back for about ninety minutes of "shut-eye." Then Greg, the RF/O, will be in my seat and Kit will be in his rightful position while I'm horizontal in the back. The RF/O position is sorta like being a "jack of all trades but, a master of none."

This is Kit's first looong (thirteen days!) international trip since he's been flying aircraft, and actually this is his second trip since checking out on the Mad Dog (MD-11). He's really excited, as I was when I was in his shoes. "The world is your oyster," as my dad used to say to me when I was just starting out in the aviation world. However, I'm older now and have had my fill of oysters. I've got five kids from two wives, I certainly don't need any more aphrodisiacs. Seriously, I've enjoyed the ride so far and I have no regrets. It's time for new blood to keep the circle of life a circle. Anyway, Kit seems like a good ol' Texan; he has your typical Texas-style drawl, with the humility and sharp wit with which all Texans seem to be born.

The weather in Paris was miserable when we left, very windy with low clouds and rain, and forecast to be the same upon arrival.

Because of this, Kit is really anxious about the arrival and approach, even though it is my leg and I am flying. He was studying the Jepps (Jeppesen is the maker/source of all of my company's pilot's aviation navigation charts) prior to going to sleep and checked every possible arrival for runway 27 Left and the associated ILS approach itself. There are several runways at Charles de Gaulle, but since our facility is on the north side of the airport, the controllers there are really good about getting us on the north runway (de Gaulle has four east/west runways, the south two, south of the main terminal that is, are runways 28 left and right. The northern runways are 27 left and right.

. . .

December 25, 5 p.m. local time (I'm in my hotel room)

Continuing with the flight into Paris . . .

The RF/O, in contrast to Kit's nervousness, awoke about forty-five minutes prior to our arrival. He said he could've slept more, but my calls on the intercom, for him to get up, finally had their effect. After awaking, he cleaned up the mess we all made since our departure and called the company and told them we were in range (with our expected arrival time) and got our gate assignment.

As expected, the weather was crummy. The ceiling was about a thousand feet, which isn't too bad, and maybe three miles in light rain, but the winds were howling from the south. They were from 200 degrees at thirty knots with gusts to forty-two (The MD-11 crosswind limit is 35 knots "Demonstrated", which means you could land in a higher velocity if you were skilled enough), and, with a landing on runway 27, that made for a direct crosswind. And with high wind comes turbulence, lots of it. Approach warned us of reports of moderate to severe turbulence below 4000 feet on our initial check-in, but at the time of this report, we were still above 10,000 feet and it wasn't too bad. All in all, it was shaping up to be an exciting evening!

Aaand, since we're talking about turbulence . . . whoa—those pilot reports were right on the money; it was turbulent on final approach . . . very turbulent. In fact, it was the worst turbulence I've ever experienced on final in my life. I was overriding the auto throttles constantly, trying to keep them from excessive overcompensation of thrust due to the wind shear's additions and subtractions to our airspeed. When I saw the runway at three miles I "kicked off" the autopilot and hand flew until landing.

Since I haven't flown much in the past six months, due to my job as an instructor, (kinda weird to say that actually . . . you'd think we, the instructors, were the most proficient of the MD-11 crew force, but since we are always training, either other captains or first officers, we rarely got to actually "fly" the aircraft…except to maintain landing currency) my heart was really racing as the runway got closer. At one thousand feet AGL on final, the aircraft was crabbed thirty degrees from the runway heading due to the wind. I kept whispering to God that if He helped me land this aircraft without breaking it, I'd be a good boy. And it was during that "profoundly" religious moment, when I was talking to the Man upstairs, that I heard a closer, more heathen voice say, in a Texas drawl, "I'm glad that this is your leg and not mine." Whereupon I responded, "Even if it was your leg it would still be my landing!" That two-sentence dialogue made us all laugh and helped to break the moment's tension.

I told my crew that I was going to use CSE 4 as my "landing indicator." CSE 4, either by pure chance, or grace of God, arrived in

Paris at the same time as us. While we were being vectored for our approach and on downwind, they were five miles ahead and were going to "test the waters" first. My thought, which I voiced to the crew, was if they went around then I was really going to worry!

Our company aircraft landed without incident, I assumed, since I didn't see any flaming wreckage, so now it was our turn. As I said, it was very turbulent on the approach, and as I approached short final I noticed quite a few aircraft waiting to depart. The pressure was on . . . I hate it when people are watching me land . . . I usually plough it on when I have an audience. However, tonight, I actually did manage to get the aircraft down safely and I must say, the landing was very smooth, which surprised the hell out of me . . . and my crew! Even a blind squirrel finds a nut every now and then. But it did take some fast and furious arm and leg work to get onto the runway. Without a doubt, it was the most difficult landing I've ever had to make in my life.

Turbulence is a fact of flying. As aviators, we know what causes it and though riding through it can be uncomfortable at times, not for fear but due to the discomfort, we just accept the bumps and bounces as a normal consequence of the career. But, turbulence in the approach environment and particularly on short final, as you approach to land, adds a totally different dimension to the landing equation altogether; moderate to severe turbulence encountered on approach is a gut check. You are trying to land a big aircraft on a runway maybe 150 to 200 feet wide and from 7500 to 12,000 feet long while the aircraft is constantly being buffeted, left, right, up, and down by winds. The wingspan on the MD-11 is 170 feet, even more on 747s, and the gear may span of 55 feet wide at the mains (main gear, the back wheels). While the autopilot usually does a decent job of managing the turbulent sea of air on approach, the pilot still has to land the jet manually; auto land, autopilot controlled, landings have fairly tight restrictions on wind velocity, particularly when the weather is bad, and even if the wind is in limits, if the turbulence is bad I'm not going to trust my career to the autopilot when it comes to landing. It's a judgment call the Captain must make.

I like to get a feel for the aircraft and warm up my manual flying skills well before landing in any turbulence or high crosswind conditions so I usually disconnect the autopilot early on in the approach to acclimate my brain and muscles for the inevitable wrestling match between me, the aircraft, and the torrent of wind and consequent turbulent, hammering blows upon the aircraft's flight path, particularly if it's really gusting and/or the wind is passing over hilly terrain/buildings.

Essentially, when the air is very turbulent on approach you are kind of shepherding the aircraft to the runway. To explain, you can't precisely follow the electronically transmitted glide slope or localizer because the aircraft is moving around so much either vertically and/or horizontally so you have to continuously wrestle with the aircraft to keep it close enough, and safely enough, with-in the confines of the approach corridor from which a safe landing can be attempted. The closer you get to the runway, the more precisely you have to guide the aircraft and consequently the more you are fighting the aircraft, due to the turbulence. Your goal is to get the aircraft safely to the runway from which a safe landing can be made. There are many times where I've thought, as I'm flying down final.... "If it's not good I'm going around... If it's not good I'm going around..." and I've said that even after touching down. I am always on the alert to reject the landing if the parameters for touching down on the runway do not satisfy my personal limits, let alone those limits set forth by the aircraft manufacturer, the FAA regulations, or the company's policies. So, until I select reverse thrust, going around is always a viable option if the wind/turbulence upsets the delicate balance of landing and stopping safely.

At the hotel, the crew of CSE 4 and my guys met for dinner. We went to Leon de Bruxelles for mussels from Brussels, as we affectionately call the joint. I had the Roquefort Mussels . . . mmm good! In fact, all six of us had something different, so we could each sample the others' fare.

And then the wine started flowing. We initially ordered a bottle of Bordeaux for four of us as Greg and Kit each had a beer to start, a huge beer, actually; I mean, the mugs must have held 32 oz. of the brew! But after their beers they switched to wine...big mistake, as they would pay for that the next morning. One bottle was quickly emptied, so we ordered another. After paying for dinner we went across the street to the Mobillan Lounge/Restaurant. In there we gathered in a corner of the bar, claimed that "spot" as American, and proceeded to consume many more bottles of France's less-than-finest wine.

In short time, the wine had its desired effects as the six of us each became less inhibited. The bar's patrons were a mix of French, American, and English. A Christmas song was started by the Americans and in short order everyone in the bar joined in the chorus of celebration.

Oddly enough, my boss was one of CSE 4's crewmembers. He was called out for the flight due to another crew member going ill. Mike, since he is in management, had to go; to add insult to injury he wasn't being paid extra for the trip. I expressed my condolences to him on not being home for Christmas. As for me, I was on this trip because as a junior line captain, my seniority was so low that my only choice was not if I could get Christmas off, but in which international city I wanted to spend it.

As each of us became less lucid, the noise of our conversations grew and our body movements and facial expressions became increasingly exaggerated. It is an interesting thing to observe. I've found it's definitely easier to tolerate a drunken person when you are yourself inebriated; being sober and relating to a drunk is an exasperating experience!

But on this night, none of us were sober. Mike and I talked about training stuff while the other guys engaged in some unknown discussions of their own, each of us trying to solve the world's and the company's problems.

At one point, toward the end of the evening, I tried to join into a conversation with Greg, my RF/O and the captain, Hermes, of CSE 4. The captain and RF/O got into a very heated discussion about air combat maneuvering and in the difference between the tactics of employing air to air missiles. Hermes, who once flew F-4s in the Air Force, and Greg, who had flown F-18s in the Navy totally disagreed on the subject and things got a little testy. Words were wasted with supporting body animations, hands, simulating airplanes were maneuvering about the bar trying to prove their owner's points. Watches were on fire, being "shot" by the non-watch hand, hair was on fire, tempers were flaring…it was ugly.

In the end, the alcohol won. The combatants would not give in to each other, but the long day and the fatigue we all felt finally caused them to reach a truce.

I slept off the effects of the wine and arose at 3:30 p.m. Paris time. I called my wife and talked to her and the kids and my in-laws, who had come over from England to spend the Christmas with Liza, since she and I were struggling in our marriage due to the loss of our oldest child, Autumn, three years earlier. I wished them a Merry Christmas. I was feeling really homesick.

. . .

Somewhere over Eastern Europe, around 11 p.m., December 25, 1999

After arriving at the airport at 9 p.m., we prepared for a 9:45 p.m. departure, with Kit flying this leg; he hand-flew the departure. The weather was, in contrast to the previous evening, beautiful, with relatively light winds and clearing skies. Kit was a bit behind while preparing for departure; he kept mumbling something about never drinking red wine again. As we alighted from the runway, the winds were almost a direct headwind, a far cry from the previous night's offering.

As I write this, the Texan, RFO, and myself, are over Western Turkey en route to Dubai. We have a five-day layover in Dubai. I like Dubai. There's a lot to do there, although in the summer, which thankfully it was not, it's unbelievably hot.

Our route from Paris to Dubai takes us over Eastern Europe, by Bucharest and Western Turkey, over eastern Cyprus and then into Northwestern Syria, down through Syria by Damascus, through Jordan, into northwestern Saudi Arabia and across it, and then finally over Bahrain for an almost straight-in approach into Dubai. All in all, it's about a 6 hour flight, depending on the winds.

Poor Kit has trouble understanding the controllers. Even though English is the "universal" language in air traffic control, it doesn't guarantee that it is spoken with great clarity amongst the world's controllers . . . or even by Texans with deep southwestern drawls.

I find the French woman, while always "sounding" beautiful, very hard to understand. (I was once told by a wise old sage to never ask a "voice" for a date; he had a funny story to go with that bit of wisdom.) The German controllers, conversely, I find are very precise with their English. Moving farther east, Sofia, Bucharest, Budapest and other Eastern European controllers are generally easy to understand. The Turkish controllers too are very understandable.

I couldn't help but wonder, though, what the controllers were thinking upon hearing Kit's voice. Did they wonder if we had J. R. Ewing, of Dallas fame, flying "shotgun" on our aircraft?

Oddly enough, politics reaches up to us from the nations we fly over to affect how we use the ATC system. For example, when going from Turkey to Cyprus, the Ankara (Turkey) controllers will not hand you off to the Greeks (Nicosia control). You must call Nicosia ten minutes prior to your arrival into their airspace to set up for entry through their domain. Ankara never tells you to contact Nicosia! You just change to Nicosia at the FIR boundary. Goodbye Turkey!

And after giving Greece a "heads-up" about your future transit, you must give Syria, Jordan, and Bahrain prearrival calls too.

For the most part, it's routine. Each Middle Eastern country's ATC system seems to want the same information—departure city, destination, aircraft tail number, and flight level. As I said, some of these controllers are very hard to understand, and poor Kit was really struggling to understand what these guys were saying. I have to admit, it is very difficult, at times, to understand what these guys say the first time, so you ask them to repeat what they said. If you miss it the second time, you're running into dangerous ground. I have seen

Latakia control (Syria) not repeat a third request for clarification. Likewise, I've seen Jeddah (Saudi Arabia) control not respond to repeated radio calls. The Bahrain and Dubai controllers are usually expats (British or Australian) and are very easy to understand, except for Kit—poor Kit. He even had trouble understanding Bahrain's British-sounding controller.

The route from Europe to the Middle East is a well-worn path, particularly the route through Syria and Jordan. Due to airspace restrictions/limits, there are a dearth of jet routes through these two countries and that causes a bottleneck for dispatchers. They wind up having to flight plan their aircraft through the "cradle of civilization" on basically one jet route, kinda like flying a well-traveled caravan route. Visually, you could look ahead and see the many lights of airliners pass over or under you. Quite literally, while flying down the spine of Syria and over Jordan, we must have passed one aircraft every two the four minutes. British Airways, Brunei, Singapore, Gulf Air, Delta, TWA, KLM, Finnair—you name it, it seems like every industrialized nation's flag carrier was represented in this parade of sights and sounds. (Ahhh . . . the sounds. By that I mean the calls they made on the radio to ATC. Let there be no doubt, we could not physically hear them pass by . . . well, sometimes I would make a jet noise with my mouth . . . Hey, I'm still a kid on the inside.)

■ ■ ■

1 p.m., Dec 26, 1999 . . . In my hotel room

As we approached Dubai, the brightening of the eastern sky signaled the arrival of a new day and it also marked the beginning of the end for our flight. The descent and approach into Dubai is nearly continuous and straight in, and we could see the city from

110 miles out. The early sighting of the city signaling clear skies, with approach control saying they had calm winds. The arrival into Dubai was seamless and smooth; a nice bit of flying by Kit.

When Dubai tower told me the wind was still calm, I told them the first officer had no excuse for a bad landing . . . the tower said they would be watching! In the silence of a cool desert morning, Kit landed well and arrived sweetly, keeping in tune with the ambiance of this day's beginning; he may talk funny, but the kid flies a good aircraft!

I think Kit was in awe of being in such a foreign land compared to his beloved Texas! He is so amazed to see the sights he is seeing! It's neat to observe this as it reminds me of my younger days when I went into each new foreign destination with my eyes wide open.

■ ■ ■

December 27, 1999 (writing this on December 28, 1999)

It was my anniversary yesterday. I left Liza a message since I couldn't get her on the phone. I tried to send her flowers, but as is my usual case, it was Sunday, the day after Christmas, when I tried to arrange the flower delivery, and of course the flower shops were closed. So, all Liza got was a message on the answering machine expressing my undying love and my pledge that I would do it all over again.

There are certain neat things about flying around the world, but being away from home on special days is not one of them. Missing my son open his presents on the first Christmas he realizes what Christmas is about, well, it's hard to deal with at times (most times). Liza really has a hard time dealing with my absence too. It's actually been a sore point in our marriage. She knew what my occupation was when dating me, and in fact, she was a flight attendant for a foreign airline when we met. But being young and in love can blind a person to the reality that everyone else sees.

It can get extremely lonely on the road, in spite of what most people think. Once you've been to a foreign destination a few times, the places get old; you can only do the same something so many times. Having a laptop computer can help occupy your mind, as it's something that has multiple uses. At times, I'll write a story on it, play a game, or surf the Web. Or in a more physical way, I'll work out in the gym, take a long walk, or read a book. But in the end, it's always nicest to be at home with my family.

Yesterday, we (the crew) went golfing. I haven't golfed in four years, and then six before that. The Emirates Golf Club, where we went, was spectacular. The weather was sunny (no surprise). I can't say the three of us wowed anybody with our ability to smack a little white ball all over God's green acres, but considering the physical setting and the ambiance, it was one of those nice moments during a layover.

After the golf game, we went back to the hotel, took a break from being with each other, and then met for dinner.

As is typical, for dinner we talked about much of the same as was spoken the night before, (see my previous journal entry) except we did talk about watches and our experiences on the road (flying, of course). We went to bed about midnight.

■　■　■

December 31, 1999

I am writing these very words as we pass over Mumbai (Bombay), India at 37,000 feet. The sun rose about ten minutes ago (about 1+45 into the flight); since we are headed easterly the combination of our 600 mph ground speed added to the 800 mph rotation of the

Earth, at this latitude, made for a rather rapid sunrise; it's kinda like putting the DVD player on fast forward.

The weather is beautiful as we cruise over India. Our route of flight has us cross, from west to east, the lower part of India, about one-third of the way up the subcontinent. Looking out the window over a still yawning landscape, I'm amazed at the aridity. I'm looking at a lot of sharply defined hills (almost like mini mountains) with very little vegetation evident. However, as I write this, the hills are flattening out and I can see more greenery, but it's still not the image of India I've held since my younger days when I saw The Jungle Book. Wherever that little kid, Mowgli, hung out, it wasn't near here.

We are now in Myanmar's (Burma) airspace. No doubt while flying through this short bit of third world airspace Kit is in heinous trouble with the accents of this country's controllers, both in receiving and transmitting. After one of their transmissions Kit will look at me, eyes blank, and wonder what in the hell he heard. Kit maintains that they should speak better English, and well, yeah, maybe so. But considering that the only foreign language either Kit or I can speak is pig Latin, I'll refrain from my criticism. My only solace in all of this is that Kit's lovely Texas twang is so strong the controllers on the ground must surely be shitting gold bricks on the same level as he is up here.

．　．　．

January 2, 2000

I am writing this while on Japan Airlines Flight 702 bound for Osaka. We departed Hong Kong about an hour ago. Two days have elapsed since my last "input" into the diary/journal, and I must say it has been a rather busy 48 hours; I will pick up with our arrival into Hong Kong . . .

After clearing the country of Myanmar without any hassles, I decided to head back to the courier cabin, which is just behind the cockpit, to take a break from flying duties and relax.

I should tell you, that in addition to my normal compliment of Kit, and our "new" RF/O, Jesse, (remember, Greg said sayonara to us after a couple of days in Dubai as he had another flight to operate). I also had two other company crewmembers who wanted to "hitch" a ride with us to Hong Kong. They were supposed to deadhead from Dubai to Hong Kong on the airlines the next day, but they wanted to welcome in the New Year in Hong Kong instead of Dubai, so they asked for a ride.

The sun was well on its way to its daily zenith when I slipped out of the left seat and gave it over to Jesse. The weather, which had been clear all the way from Dubai, was forecast to be the same all the way to Britain's once crown jewel. Sooo, with my shoes off, feet propped up on the leg rest of the now tilted back courier cabin, business class seat, and a fresh cup of java throwing off slight wisps of steam, I settled into a novel that I had been reading since the start of this trip. The other four crewmembers were busily chatting away in the cockpit, excited at the prospects of celebrating the first day of the new millennium in Hong Kong.

I planned on taking a break of about an hour or so and told the guys to get me when we were a couple of hundred miles out. In no time, I got lost in my John Grisham novel and though my body was on an MD-11 my mind was trying to figure out, "Who dun it?" At some point, Kit came back and said we were about fifty minutes out. "No worries," I said to Kit, "I'll be up in about five minutes." My thinking was that fifty minutes was about 300 miles, and since I'd been into Hong Kong a bazillion times before and was very familiar with its arrival procedures so didn't need a lot of time to prepare for the descent and arrival.

In what felt like five minutes, Jesse, the RF/O, came flying out of the cockpit to tell me I needed to get up front, that we were real close and cleared to descend. So up I went! Wow! Talk about time warps!! When I settled into the left seat I saw that we were about 110 miles out of Hong Kong! Can you say "behind"?

I was playing mental catch-up now as I was adjusting the seat to fit my more diminutive frame, as compared to Jesse's. I had not reviewed the arrival, nor the approach, though the weather was "severe" clear and the traffic extremely light. Kit was on top of things and gave me a heads up on a "slow point" on the arrival (which I was still trying to review!).

However, instead of wanting us to slow down, Approach Control asked us to "keep our speed up" on the descent because they said we were leading the pack on the arrival and we were number one in the group of arrivals around us. (Unlike the United States where you must fly 250 knots or less, below 10,000 feet on arrival, in most other parts of the world, ATC can clear you high speed, which means you can keep your speed up to whatever, I guess, feels comfortable for you…except supersonic.) The MD-11 will easily do 350 knots indicated below 10,000 feet, assuming the fuel in tanks 1 and 3, each, exceed 11,500 lbs.; we had about 15,000 in those two, with a total load of roughly forty-5000 pounds. But, since we were level at thirteen thousand feet and had started to slow to 250 knots, due to the "slow point" ahead, I pushed the speed hold function on the glare shield control panel, GCP, and when I did we were at 330 knots, so at that speed we stayed.

And so, it was almost full speed ahead going into Hong Kong. The day was gloriously "sun shiny" as we approached the late British colony. Descending in steps all the way down to 1,700 feet MSL, and still at 330 knots, Kit was getting a bit antsy about our speed. I'm assuming, since this was his first "real" international trip, that he had not done a lot of 330 knot arrivals. I had flown so much international in the past few years I was used to getting high speed arrivals. In fact, when I was a first officer, some of the more crusty, older captains with whom I used to fly when I was based in Anchorage would bet me to see how long I could keep the speed up until it was absolutely necessary to slow down. Amazingly enough, in all of those high speeds I never had to go around, nor were any of the approaches unsafe. I learned a lot about the MD-11 in those days. So, Kit, while not expressing his true concern, did keep asking me when I intended to "pull it back" to something more sedate; had conditions been less certain I would have conveyed my plans, but given the wonderful weather and no traffic, I decided to keep my plan quiet. About seventeen miles from the runway Hong Kong Radar said I could slow down if I wanted. It seemed that they too were obviously wondering when this Yank was going to throttle back.

Due to approach control's subtle prompting, I selected "FMS" speed, the speed at which the aircraft thinks it should be flying, which at that distance and configuration was 245 knots. In a downward drop of my right arm, after pushing the FMS speed button on the FCP panel, I extended the speed brakes to full up to more rapidly slow the aircraft. At 270 knots, I asked for the slats, at 250 the landing gear, the flaps went to fifteen degrees shortly thereafter and then to twenty-eight upon slowing through 190 knots. With each configuration change, and as the distance to the runway got closer, the aircraft automatically readjusted its desired target speed downward.

To cut to the chase, at three miles out we were passing nine hundred feet, on speed and fully configured, gear down/flaps 35, for landing. Due to our very light landing weight, 345,000 pounds, final approach speed was a fairly slow 140 knots. (We were almost completely empty as this flight was a "repositioning flight" to Hong Kong for a charter to Frankfurt)

The approach controller said that a wind shear of ten knots or more, increase in airspeed was possible on final and because of that warning from tower the RF/O thought that I should have added some extra airspeed above our normal approach speed in case of a wind shear encounter. However, since the actual airport winds were reported as less than ten knots, I wasn't really too concerned with what was up ahead. The Paris approach was still fresh in my flying memory, with its serious surface winds and turbulence. So, I guess I was desensitized by the controller's advisory . . . this approach feeling like it was a walk in the park…a nice, sunny park. But, not wanting to have the RFO feel like I was blowing him off, I addressed his concern for more speed by telling him that I did not believe the wind shear report was still valid, due to the actual winds, and really, simply put, I didn't think we were going to have a problem and thusly I didn't feel any additional speed on final was warranted.

As it turned out there was no wind shear, or turbulence of any sort, and we alighted on Runway 07 Right quite softly. (again . . . I'd rather be lucky than good!) Eight hours after leaving Dubai, we were in Hong Kong at 3 p.m. in the afternoon on December 31, 1999.

On the limo ride, from the airport to the hotel, the guys and I discussed the upcoming "whiskey front." We agreed to meet in Someplace Else, which was a local pub, located below the Sheraton Hotel (our layover hotel) in the Kowloon district of greater Hong Kong, at 6 p.m.

It was happy hour when I walked into the bar to look for my colleagues. I had taken a "power" nap in the hopes of rejuvenating myself before the night's festivities, but I had overslept a bit and was thus late getting to the pub. With the associated "2 fer 1" bargain on drinks I readily ordered my vodka and tonics, with a lemon, and began canvassing the bar, a drink in each hand, to look for my feathered friends. While the bar was fairly crowded, it didn't seem any busier than I'd seen it on Friday evenings of days gone by.

My colleagues found me first, and indicated their position with a hearty yell. I pulled into place with them at the front of the bar . . . the boys had garnered perfect position in the pub; they'd gotten there an hour or so before me. I offered a toast to their foresight in getting there early and in grabbing prime real estate in the bar; it was ugly as glasses smashed into each other and "hooahs" were shouted well above the background din of the bar. After the toast, I realized that we had acquired two more people to our original five, another MD-11 crew. I said my hellos to those guys, as we exchanged hearty handshakes and pats on the back.

At 8 p.m., it was still "happy hour" and with all of us "loosened up" from the previous "two" happy hours (6 to 7 p.m., 7 to 8 p.m.) and more people filing in from the outside street and ready to party, the "whiskey front" was fully upon us. The live, "three-man" band (two guys and a lady) was blasting away, playing songs that actually sounded like they were from the original artist, as long as we contin-

ued insulate our ears with alcohol. When I first came into this place
the band was playing, I was sober, and the music sounded really bad.
I suspect their only virtue was the fact that the lead singer, the lady,
was incredibly attractive and dressed in a manner so as to deflect the
listener's sense of hearing to the visual . . . it was quite effective.

Since we were pilots, we talked about the usual stuff that we
talked about in Dubai, but with greater animation given the emotion of it being a millennium New Year's Eve, and of course . . . did
I mention that we had been drinking? War stories were being told,
no doubt for the millionth time, of glory from days gone by. Fighter
pilots, now cargo pilots, were displaying one of their hands with
deadly intent upon their other (hand) as their appendages mimicked their once flown fighter jets in mock combat chasing each
other in exaggerated movement with their hair and watches on fire,
no doubt for the umpteenth time in their lives. Right there in the
middle of the bar we had a mini air war, and the chance of collateral
damage to the "civilians" was very real at that point. What really hit
me emotionally, during a short but deeply introspective moment of
contemplative thought as I saw all of the animated air battles being
fought around me, or the telling of a funny story, was that I and my
colleagues were "my dad and his colleagues" of days gone by. This
was not the first time in my life I've had this "feeling of déjà vu" with
regards to feeling like I was revisiting my dad and his colleagues,
but, on this evening, it was a very enchanting moment due to the
significance of the date. It was wonderful to briefly reflect upon the
memories of my dad and his colleagues, of days gone by, and to
experience the silver lining of having followed in the flightpaths and
journeys of the heroes of my youth.

Once the fires of the afterburning and shot down hands extinguished, either through crashing and burning or ejecting, the flying talk turned to things of the present or near present. The new twist for these middle-aged, ex-knights of the sky was that after their fighter pilot stories, they told "scary" stories of bad weather approaches and aircraft/engine problems while flying their behemoths. Or on a lighter note, one guy might tell a comical story of the misfortune of another aviator or himself. I told the boys my own true story of the night I locked myself out of my hotel room, while on a layover in Tokyo, and I was buck ass naked. That story got a lot of laughs.

As one of the guys was telling a story, I kinda tuned out and looked around the bar. The other, more, earthly humans, most of Chinese descent, were also busily engaged in some form of communication. Most of it was verbal, in either the English or Chinese language, but there was some non-verbal, serious body language occurring in the darker corners of the pub, all of it seemingly aimed at increasing the population.

The atmosphere was truly festive, more so than I've ever experienced in any civilian bar up until now. Even the bartenders and barmaids were in a festive mood, joking with the patrons and pretending to be Tom Cruise's character from the movie Cocktail. As midnight approached, I can't say the crescendo picked up, but more people began to fill the dance floor, which was already quite full.

Then the most unusual thing happened. In every other New Year's party that I've been to, there was a "group" (I mean everyone in the joint) countdown to midnight. The TV would be the pacing guide for the count. But I guess since the Chinese New Year is in February, they weren't quite sure what to do . . . who knows. In any regard, the actual stroke of midnight was pretty anticlimactic. No group yell, no group countdown. The TVs that were scattered throughout the pub, showed some Chinese bigwig shake hands with another bigwig and a mere token display of fireworks; pretty bland stuff.

I suppose with the shock of such a lackluster countdown to midnight, many round-eyed, non-Chinese, patrons gave a some-what belated "Happy New Year!" yell, almost in unison. With that "announcement," people began to make up for lost ground, quickly. People trains were coursing through the bar, their tracks dictated by the areas of the least human resistance in the throng. Champagne was sprayed, quite liberally, on unsuspecting people, and the dance floor was full with all forms of physical movement, some in tune with the beat, if you could call what the band played as a beat, and some not . . . but it was pretty evident that everyone was having a good time!

As amazing as it was inside the bar, outside was a total shock. Imagine hundreds of thousands of people filling the streets, and as festive as those inside the bar…truly an incredible thing to experi-ence. The streets were jam-packed with people yelling, whistling, and chanting. The police, who were on every corner, looked as amazed as I felt. Everywhere you looked there were people, people, people! The lights of the skyscrapers on Hong Kong Island, which was just across the water from Kowloon and my hotel, flashed their 700-feet tall New Year's "messages" and even the many, many boats, of all sizes, in the crowded harbor were whistling and tooting their horns!

I have never seen so many people, so close, and in such a festive mood! It was as if the entire area of Hong Kong was one big bar with people shoving off their inhibitions, like there was no tomorrow; quite simply it reminded me of Prince's song of the 1980s, "1999."

Nothing else I had ever seen in my life before compared to this festival of people, sights, sounds and expression of emotion.

The morning after was not seen. Oh, it passed, the sun rose and began its climb, but with my eyes closed. At noon, I got up and ate lunch, and then Kit and I headed to explore Hong Kong Island.

We took the ever reliable and amazingly cheap Star Ferry (twenty-five cents) to Hong Kong Island and from the bus stop near the ferry caught the bus to Stanley (a little town on the west side of Hong Kong Island).

The ride to Stanley, on the top deck, of a double-decker bus, is the best part about going to Stanley Harbor. Hong Kong Island is essentially a low-slung mountain that rises out of the waters of the South China Sea. Over the years, human development and population growth have slowly encroached upon almost every part of the natural landscape. The road to Stanley goes through the very busy and built up city of Hong Kong proper and then up and over the spine of the island. Once on the other side, the urban complexion changes from business to residential. Initially, apartment buildings, twenty-five to thirty stories in height, grew at random from the sides of the island's slopes, both above and below the road's level. In its journey downward, the road twists and turns, performing switchbacks, all the while going down the steep mountain slopes. At times, you swear the bus is going to go over the edge and you'll be road kill du jour. The vistas provided on the backside of the mountain, after you crested the top, are wonderfully complicated and beautiful. Lush, green vegetation flourishes freely on the mountain as it descends to the deep blue China sea below. Human development is interspersed amongst the natural, mountainous nature of the landscape itself, creating an almost unlimited number of beautiful views from the upper deck seats of the bus as it descended towards Stanley Harbor. It was fun to see Kit's reactions to this new-found world. He was really impressed with the bus ride and the views that presented themselves with the gyrations of the road.

At Stanley, which is a quaint little town on the sea, we walked through the "famous" Stanley Market, famous because flight attendants from the world over have made it that way since it offered some of the best shopping deals in the Hong Kong. Personally, I'm not amazed by the market . . . nope. What brought me to Stanley Market were the Carlsberg beers sold at an Irish pub behind the market. The only way I knew how to reach the pub was by snaking through the labyrinth of shops.

This Irish pub, and a couple of other pubs of either English or German heritage, resided next to a sidewalk and road that itself is on the water's edge. In contrast to the previous night's festivities, the streets were actually filled this time with cars, and the sidewalks sporting their usual complement of people. But without a doubt, the mood of the day was much more peaceful and calm in nature. As we sat drinking our beers, Kit and I chatted with a couple who lived in Spain, were German in nationality, worked for a Swiss company that was based in France but were setting up a spin-off business in China . . . whoa . . . welcome to the new millennium of international business.

The sun set over Hong Kong as I slowly finished my last gulp of the day. Begrudgingly, I got up from my chair . . . one that was firmly and fondly attached to my arse, and then Mr. Texas and I took the bus back to central Hong Kong.

Once back in the city, we went up to Victoria Peak, which is a tourist site of shops, restaurants, and observation decks situated on one of the higher parts of the island and right above the financial district. At night, the view is spectacular. With millions of lights scattered below, the farther ones faintly winking in unequal rhythm, Kit became mesmerized by the sparkle of this once "crown jewel" of Britain now in possession of a new owner. Bidding the night and city adieu, we reluctantly descended the mountain and retraced our path back to the hotel and our rooms.

So, as I write this we are bound for Osaka, Japan on a Japan Airlines 747. We will lay over there for thirty hours or so and then we're scheduled to operate, nonstop, back to our main cargo hub in the United States; depending on winds it's about a twelve-hour flight.

▪ ▪ ▪

January 3, 2000

I'm in the bunk on the MD-11 writing this as we head east over the Pacific bound for the United States. Above me sleeps Kit, and in the cockpit is another crew who will man the controls for six of the twelve hours of this flight. Before I go completely horizontal in my bunk, I wanted to finish this journal.

Three days have passed since the start of the new millennium. The vaccine the world took, to shield it from the millennium "bug," seems to have worked, as no major problems have infected any country—no power blackouts, computer shutdowns, or general anarchy due to old computers with ancient software. So, it is with complete serenity that we fly our computer-controlled jet, guided by electronic air traffic control surveillance over an increasingly silicon-chip-managed world.

I would love to end this journal describing some great epiphany that I had. But the reality is other than the amazing display of humanity I witnessed while in Hong Kong during the New Year's party, it was a pretty routine trip. I said earlier, at the beginning of this journal, that I doubted I would feel any different, and I was right, I don't. The buildup to the year 2000 was like any other human derived event—all hype and no cataclysm, just another reason for one big party . . . right on!

It's been more than ten years since I started flying around the world. I've seen more sights than the average nine-to-five office worker can imagine. I thank God daily for the gift of flight, my career, and the opportunity to bebop about the globe. In those years and during those travels I've seen many wondrous things—the Great Wall of China, volcanoes throwing up, Angel Falls in South America, thunderstorms lighting up the night sky, jungles, deserts, isolated atolls in the Pacific, beautiful cities around the world . . . so many wonderful things. But with the good there was bad: the slums and utter squalor in many parts of the world, children on city streets begging, whole forests being cut down, cemeteries of count-less World War I and II soldiers in Europe, the Holocaust exhibit in Washington, D.C., flying into the Middle East to defeat a dictator's aspirations—so many challenges yet for mankind to overcome.

In closing, I'd like to end on a positive note and state the last words of a poem called Desiderata, which was all the rage when I was in college: "With all its sham, drudgery, and broken dreams, it is still a beautiful world, be careful, strive to be happy."

CHAPTER 32

The new millennium, though not precipitating the end of the world, as some extremists had prophesized, did see the end of my marriage. And with the exceptions of 1997, the year in which Autumn-Paige passed away, and my sophomore year in high school, the years 2000 and 2001 will go down as being the third most horrible period of time in my life.

The arrival of Amber less than a year earlier did not stem the slow trickle of emotional bloodletting from the loss of Autumn-Paige, nor could the grief/marriage counseling we had been receiving. Nothing, no matter how well coordinated and conducted by the psychologists, worked when it came to reintegrating Liza and I as a couple.

Psychotherapy/marriage counseling is only as good as your ability to comprehend and accept what the shrink thinks is/are the causal factors to the dysfunction in your marriage, assuming you've divulged all of the bits and pieces they need to know to make an informed analysis/diagnoses in the first place.

And then the fun part starts . . . fixing what may be wrong with you if it's determined that you have a personality disorder(s) that is contributing to the marital mess. The saying goes that identifying the cause for any problem is 50 percent of the solution; whoever said that has never had to try and fix something that was wrong both in their marriage and their head at the same time. It is very emotionally painful and taxing trying to fix your own self while also trying to stay married, particularly if your partner really doesn't want to be with you. Though not as bad as losing a child, living in your marriage as it epically fails has got to be one of the most depressing and traumatic situations that a person can ever experience in life.

Whatever Liza's motives were in going to marriage counseling, I can't say because I certainly never saw any benefit for us as a couple, as evidenced by the fact that she initiated divorce proceedings a few months after the start of the new millennium. Liza had been in almost continuous counseling since the loss of our child, but, at some point I stopped going. The cause of me stopping was due to the rather harsh comment by a male marriage counselor who was working with Liza and I. (Liza and I each saw a different counselor whereupon twice a month the 4 of us got together to work on reinvigorating our marriage)

The comment in question came after Liza's inquiry to the male counselor, who was an elder at his church, as to why he thought God allowed Autumn-Paige to die.

His unfeeling and cold answer was, "Because of your sin."

The crocodile tears on Liza's face after his answer took days to shut off.

It was after his answer that I understood why certain, very self-righteous and judgmental Christians put a horrible and undeserved stain on the true Christian faith. That "therapist's" answer was out of line, cold, and unfeeling for a woman who had accidently backed over and killed her child.

He never made any attempt to apologize nor qualify his "expert" Christian opinion about whose and what sin it was that caused God to take our child, consequently we never made an attempt to see him again.

In fact, I eventually stopped going to counseling sessions altogether, even with the lady that Liza had been seeing. Since there was no change in our relationship at all, I just couldn't see the point in continuing, I felt like we were beating a dead horse.

So, as the new millennium established a beach head with the calendar and with humanity, Liza and I quickly retreated from our marriage vows while we each began a search for a better life apart from each other.

To cope with the failure of my marriage, I took to the sky, dramatically increasing the number of MD-11 trips I was flying while concurrently serving as an MD-11 line check airman. So, instead of training pilots in the simulator, I would be training them in the actual aircraft. It was a huge change for me since I would now be flying twelve to fifteen days a month, and even though it pained me greatly to be away from my kids that much, I needed the change to stay sane. I was depressed dealing with the death of my marriage and I needed the sanctity of the sky to rejuvenate my spirits, just like it had done many times before.

CHAPTER 33

I have flown with many pilots over the years on seemingly endless flights, and for conversation's sake, during the cruise phase of flight, I will ask them if there is anything that has scared them while flying.

There are a few scary stories of near mid-air collisions, engine failures, fires, or severe in-flight icing, but, by far thunderstorms top the list of more near-death confessions by my aviator colleagues than any other aeronautical hazard.

I too have had my fair share of angry cumulonimbus encounters and thanks to my fighter flying days, I've changed more than my share of underwear due to near impacts with either the ground or other aircraft and the angels have certainly had their hands full looking out for me and many of those with whom I flew during my F-4 and F-16 days.

While spring and summer are the major growing seasons for thunderstorms, winter is when Jack Frost awakens from his slumber to spread his icy chill and imperil aircraft with a coating of ice crystals; there are times that no matter how hard you try, you cannot escape Jack's icy clutches.

Since the inception of aircraft ice forming on an aircraft's external parts has caused many, many fatal crashes. Both the FAA and

NASA have done much research in the quest to learn how to mitigate the dangers of airframe icing on all types of aircraft.

Prior to flying in the military and airlines, I avoided clouds like they were the plague particularly when I flew light, general aviation aircraft and most particularly when it was below freezing outside. I was scared to death of getting icing on my airplane and possibly crashing. The book I mentioned a while ago, Fate Is the Hunter, has a very harrowing story of Ernest Gann encountering severe icing in a DC-3 over eastern Tennessee. And my father too, in his own adventures had to make an emergency landing, in below minimum weather conditions, in Rochester, New York, one winter after encountering the same conditions as Mr. Gann, and in the same type aircraft.

While I can't say I ever came close to the adventures of Mr. Gann or my father with regards to icing, I did have one severe icing episode that got my attention and to this day it is the worst in which I've ever flown.

On December 15, I departed a southern city in an MD-10 (think DC-10 airframe mated with a MD-11 glass cockpit) bound for MHT (Manchester, New Hampshire). This was the first officer's original trip but, for me, I had "bumped" another captain (he gets the trip's pay, I just get my hotel paid for and per diem), the original owner of the pairing, as I wanted to visit my old alma mater and some former college buddies who lived nearby.

Originally, the flight was supposed to go direct to MHT. However, the Northeast had been hammered by its third winter storm, in almost as many weeks, and the dispatcher wanted us to fly to EWR (Newark, New Jersey) first because of some uncertainty about the condition of the taxiways and runways at Manchester.

Upon our arrival in EWR, we were immediately dispatched, as soon as we could unload/load cargo and gas up, to MHT since the field was now open and the weather was improving "rapidly." I do not recall the exact meteorological conditions but I do recall the ceiling as being around 1,600 feet with two miles in "unknown" precipitation.

In thirty-one years of aviating, I had never heard that one before—unknown precipitation—so I asked the dispatcher if he could call the tower and make that "unknown precip." known to the FO and me.

The winds at the destination were from the northwest and fairly light but forecast to gain in strength as the day matured and as a high-pressure system pushed away an unwelcomed low.

Finally, with regards to the weather brief from the dispatcher, he said, "Oh, by the way, there is a forecast for a chance of icing in the MHT area."

"Yeah, I'll bet," I mumbled to him as we exchanged happy holidays and goodbyes.

After an hour of the usual ground stuff in EWR we pushed back from the gate. It was exactly 7:38 a.m. After waiting in the morning rush hour traffic, we departed for MHT with me flying this leg.

The actual climb, cruise and initial descent went about as normal as you can get. We were given a very early descent as we approached the airport from the west, from over New York state and southern Vermont.

At 7000 feet, and still quite a way from Manchester airport, we were just skimming above a vast sea of slightly bulbous, and very dense looking clouds. In contrast, above those clouds there was nothing but blue, the richness of which, in hue, caused you to feel you were looking up, into a deep blue sea.

To add even more visual drama while looking out the front of the aircraft, the early morning sun was almost directly in front of us, warming the cockpit, while just ever so slightly below the aircraft those previously mentioned and fantastically bright white clouds rushed by, their numbers forming a impenetrable barrier between our aircraft and the ground, which we knew lay somewhere below.

The harmony of my daydreaming as we serenely cruised just above the clouds was disturbed by the Ding! of the ACARS. A message from the company, from the dispatcher, said that the unknown precipitation was ice pellets, however, the latest ATIS, again, had "unknown" as the impediment to its two-mile visibility, so I guess ice pellets were designated as "unknown" to the automated weather apparatus that did the hourly observation reports.

In preparation for our descent into the clouds, I asked the FO to turn on the engine and wing anti-icing (the windshield heat goes on at 18,000 feet on all arrivals). In fact, every now and then, as we flew level at 7000 feet, we would fly through an occasional pert cloud, one that was poking its head just a bit higher than the rest, and in that brief meteorological foray we would accumulate a bit of ice on the wipers. This "bit" of ice was just a portent of what was to come.

After maintaining 7000 feet for what seemed an eternity, Boston Center cleared us down to 5000 feet and turned us over to Manchester Approach Control. Immediately upon entering the clouds we started picking up ice. I could see it build up on the wiper blades, which are located at the very bottom of the left and right front windscreens. Since we were the first aircraft into MHT that morning, we were the weather ship for all that followed, and indeed a Southwest flight was about thirty miles behind us flying a similar route. I told the FO to report the icing to the controller.

I will tell you that I did not, nor do I, as I type this, consider myself an expert with regards to the intricacies of airframe and/or meteorological icing. As I said earlier, when I flew civilian aircraft, before entering the military, I never ventured into a cloud in anything but the warmest of days or nights. And though I flew F-16s and F-4s in the USAF, throughout the United States and in all kinds of weather and during all four of the seasons, I can't say I can ever recall, save for one time while leading a flight of four F-4s on a very wintery day, where airframe icing was ever an issue. As far as I was concerned, those fighters were built out of Teflon (the only deicing they had was for the engine intake[s]). Upon being hired by my airline and going through the usual training, for each successive aircraft as I climbed the seniority ladder, I can't say icing was discussed in any depth at all. My company's MD-11/10 flight crew manuals do mention cold weather procedures and limitations, as does our company's flight ops manual, but other than discussions with my dad, about how to deal with wing ice, I can't say I have ever really talked to other pilots, nor had I been instructed in any detail about it (icing). And in practice, before this flight, I felt the aircraft I flew were ice-proof. In my twenty-seven years with my employer, sixteen of those on the MD-11/10, icing had never been a factor . . . ever. In my opinion, icing was only a concern if you flew small general aviation aircraft.

With that said, I will also tell you, because of my "ignorance" about icing, that, at first blush, I thought it was moderate mixed icing that we were encountering and asked Ben, the FO, to report it as such to the controller.

After being turned over to approach control they informed us that we were going to be vectored for the ILS to Runway 35, which jived with the active runway mentioned on ATIS and also was the approached I briefed with the FO.

The approach controller appreciated the icing report and asked us to report any changes in the weather and also asked for the "spot" winds occasionally. Since we were number one for the ILS, I slowed to 160 knots and dirtied up, slats out, in preparation for a slam-dunk approach onto an abbreviated final.

The actual vector onto final didn't happen as quickly as I thought it would. We were taken down to 3000 feet, where we droned a bit, and then finally cleared to 2000 feet and turned onto final and cleared for the ILS.

The MD-10 has six rather large cockpit windows, three on each side. The front four of these six windows are electrically heated with heating coils running between the panes of glass and the last windows, number one and six, on the far left and right sides respectively, which are defogged with warm air blowing on them from inside the aircraft. In my entire life, I have never seen a window, even one that was not heated, get any ice accumulation. Well, I gotta' tell ya . . . today, as we intercepted the localizer, the only windows that we could see out of were the two front windscreens. The other four windows were completely iced over and very opaque; about all they were good for was day/night indicators. Hell, the biggest aircraft in the world could have been about to broadside us, and unless it eclipsed the morning's sun, not that we had a lot of that at 2000 feet, we would not have been able to tell.

I won't be proud and say I was not concerned by this rapid and extensive ice accumulation. I was secretly converting carbon to diamonds with my sphincter muscle and laying them on my seat. I told the FO to tell approach, before signing off, that we were in, now, what I thought was heavy icing. (In actuality, the FAA defines in-flight icing as light, moderate, or severe; "heavy" is not a correct icing PIREP[71]. (I kinda knew that, but I was not about to look for the definitions of icing in our company flight manual at that point and search for the proper phraseology.)

What I have not mentioned, until now, is that, since the time when we turned on the wing anti-ice, we had been getting a continuous "level two" (requires immediate crew attention and subsequent action) master caution alert on the EAD (emergency alert display). The aircraft warning system was telling us that the bleed air from both the number one and number three bleed air systems was not putting out enough hot, engine bleed air for sufficient anti-ice of the wings. However, this had been a problem since the MD-10's introduction to line ops and a new, like BRAND NEW, procedure in the quick reference emergency procedures said that as long as the bleed air temp was above 110 degrees Celsius, it was 180, and the pressure was above 40 psi, it was about 41 to 42, then we were okay (it was not an either/or proposition, they both had to be above the nominal values). I would rather have been Chuck Yeager, zooming through clear air en route to a new supersonic record, than to have been Jack Frost, as I felt I was that day, proving that the Boeing engineers might be right.

---

71. PIREP. PIlot REPort—Throughout the day pilots report to ATC certain weather phenomena that may not be known to the controllers but could be significant to the safety of other aircraft, such as turbulence, icing, or ceilings and/or tops of clouds. Since ATC doesn't know all of the hazards associated with certain meteorological conditions, pilots will report the hazards and ATC reports it in PIREP Reports of which every airman has access.

Established on the final approach segment with flaps fifty and gear down, yeah, I know, you are thinking the less flaps in icing the better, but I needed the drag of fifty flaps, with the resultant power increase of the engines, to keep the bleed air pressure above 40 psi. Anyway . . . established on final the wipers had picked up a lot of ice, but the front windscreens were still very clear, except for the edges. Tower was reporting the braking action as fair, with patchy ice and snow, with no precip. Since we were so light and slow, approach speed was 135 knots,(Vapp[72]), I wasn't worried about stopping on a 10,000-foot-long runway with a rather stiff wind blowing right down the runway. I was worried about airframe ice though, deteriorating the aerodynamic qualities of whatever wasn't de-iced, the tail for example, and the possible extra weight of airframe ice, so I did bump up the airspeed five knots above our normal approach speed. To be honest, I had no idea if that was a valid thing to do, but with the reality of winter encasing my aircraft, at the time it seemed a prudent thing to do.

Instead of breaking out of the clouds at 1,600 feet, down we continued, fully immersed in old man winter's huff and puff, all the while the FO and I discussing the options if we had to go missed approach. I told him if the bleed pressures ever sustained themselves, for even a few seconds, below 40 psi then I was going to hit the go around button and get out of there.

We finally broke out of nature's embrace at 500 feet. The visibility was the reported two miles or better and I disconnected the

---

72. VAPP pronounced Vee APProach—A computed approach speed on final approach for airliners, or other type aircraft. VAPP changes with an aircraft's landing weight. Normally VAPP is 5 knots faster than VREF (Vee Reference) which is 1.3 times the stall speed at that particular landing flap configuration and weight and is the slowest speed you want to fly on approach.

autopilot after clearing the cloud and landed manually. The aircraft felt fine as I flared and stopped.

Clearing the runway was a bit of a challenge since I could not see too well for the turn off, since the side windows were totally obscured with ice, however, after landing they soon began to clear and I did manage to turn off runway 35 and taxi to our ramp.

As I was directed by three mechanics into parking, actually only one working the parking wands while the other two stood nearby, they were all giving me that RCA Victor dog (head tilt) stare as we pulled in to a stop. That got me wondering.

Upon deplaning I walked around the aircraft. I owed the Boeing engineers an apology from my silent cussing of them in flight as the ice accumulated on the windshields because they were right...wherever the aircraft was de-iced there was not a spot of ice, the wing leading edges and wing itself were completely clean, but, where no heat was applied there was about four to six inches of (ice) accumulation, depending on the surface. The tail, which had been a big concern of mine, as I thought it could stall if it picked up a load of ice, was fairly clean but did sport some sizable accumulations in certain places. I was amazed at how relatively ice free the tail was because, unlike the MD-11, it is not de-iced and has no heating applied to it; my concerns about it were, in retrospect, unfounded.

Would I do anything differently if I were to fly into the same weather again? Really, no. Our company's flight operations manual does forbid us to fly in severe icing; but after looking at the aircraft upon block-in, I can't say the aerodynamic qualities of the aircraft seemed compromised in the least. I later heard from some colleagues, whom I respect, that the combined weight of the ice upon the aircraft is the real danger when in icing conditions (assuming you have effective wing de-icing capability) Adding five knots for airframe icing, as I was told by another, more experienced captain, is not a bad idea to account for the extra weight of possible airframe ice, if landing distance is not a factor, but, he said in his career that he has never worried about airframe icing on a transport category aircraft on approach, just ice on the runway.

That icing flight, while seeming ominous as it was occurring, turned out to be a non-event once I reviewed the flight the evening after I landed. It was a nice bit of experience to add to the collage of flying adventures in my synapses.

As I said, there were many times when I flew in the military where I had near death experiences that were not associated with weather. Most of the times when I nearly bought the farm while flying a fighter it was due to either near impacts with the ground or another aircraft; so many close calls with so little time when they occurred to reflect upon the near tragedy. Many times while flying either an air to air combat training mission or flying practice low levels I've passed so close to another fighter I could see certain details about the aircraft, if not of the pilot himself. In one case, I was "popping" over a ridge one morning while flying an F-4 on a Fighter Weapons School sortie in the Nellis AFB ranges, and I was almost inverted (upside down) 100 feet above a notch in a ridge of low mountains called Belted Peak and moving at a rather sedate 450 knots. I was pulling "down," trying to conform my flight path with that of the mountains as best as I could, when, to my utter shock and at the apex in my trajectory through the notch, I passed . . . maaaybeee . . . twenty feet over an A-10 that was right side up and going in the opposite direction; as for detail…I could distinctly see the absolute shock in the eyes of the A-10 pilot as we passed (it was a high overcast, cloudy kinda day and both his and my dark visor were up). But that's the way it was doing that job, you lived to fight another day, even if it was training. You brushed off near death encounters as casually as you brushed snowflakes off of your ski parka and you put your feelings in some obscure compartment in whatever part of your brain holds that stuff.

CHAPTER 34

Though icing, near mid-airs, or ground collisions have scared me and some of my colleagues through these fun-filled and action-packed flying years, by far the most talked about threat to aviators, at least judging from my informal cockpit conversation poll, are thunderstorms.

I don't take thunderstorms for granted while flying an airliner, though I have to say, when I flew fighters I had less fear of flying near and around them than I do an airliner. Most fighter aircraft are built as tough as "brick shithouses" (my father's oft-used phrase) and could easily withstand the stress imparted upon them by the severe turbulence generally associated with a mid-latitude storm. An airliner on the other hand is not built to the same standards as a fighter jet, nor does it need to be, since I've never seen an MD-11 or B-777 fighting in air-to-air battles, flying low levels, or dropping bombs.

If you'll notice, the longest passage, or journal entry I wrote in my first year of flying the MD-11 out of ANC was of an encounter with thunderstorms over a wide area of Pacific Ocean, as I flew from Penang, Malaysia, to Taipei, Taiwan (August 28, 1994). There is no doubt that I, and 99 percent of the pilots I know, are cautious of thunderstorms, and though I am not afraid to fly amidst them when going from A to B, I do show them reverence when doing so.

My first up-close and personal encounter with thunderstorms while flying an aircraft dates back to very early in my career when I was just sixteen years old and trying to fly from that previously mentioned Woodbine Airport, where I first soloed to Knocky's airfield where the well-worn 1963 Cessna 150 in which I was flying (the same one in which I soloed) was based.

One early afternoon I rode my bike to Knocky's, took off in 11Z, and flew to Woodbine Airport for some landing practice and general air work in preparation for my private pilot's license. I still had about nine months to go until I was seventeen and could get my license, so I really was just having fun puttering around the South Jersey skies killing time flying until my birthday and that magic 17 number came up. Like a little boy playing in the sand with his toy trucks and oblivious to the world around him, so too did I play around Woodbine Airport. As I did touch and goes on the same runway in which I soloed, I suddenly became aware of an infiltration of towering cumulonimbus clouds, their numbers and size became so overwhelming I couldn't help but notice them. I quickly scanned the sky in the direction of Knocky's as I did another touch and go and figured I'd better get my butt home before it was impossible to get there, due to those obnoxious, windblown giants.

With my epiphany about the consequences of the interlopers, I immediately left the security of my playground. I stayed low, eight hundred feet or so, and in clear air and deviated at will around the massive, white, and ever-bulging cloud bases looking for a way to the sanctity of Knocky's. But with every turn I encountered a dead end of bubbling and menacing-looking clouds full of energy and enthusiasm and with torrents of rain pouring from their bases, drenching the land below. Again, and again, and again I turned this way or that, every avenue of escape being thwarted by grand canyons of clouds rising 30,000 to 40,000 feet above me. The massing was seemingly complete, and when I saw lightning burst forth from a rather low-hanging bit of cloud, maybe two miles in the distance, I put my tail between my legs and high-tailed it for the security of Woodbine Airport. This sanctuary was still remarkably free of the weather, though it was starting to encroach there too as I landed. Once on the ground I taxied to one of the aircraft ramps and shutdown. There was a payphone near one of the buildings and I used it to call my dad who was at work.

The old man wasn't flying that day, thank the Lord, he was in the weather shop and I had to be transferred to their number after calling flight ops.

When my dad wasn't flying, he liked to go up to the weather office and help the guys. He knew the weather better than Mother Nature and I held his weather wisdom in as high regard as his flying ability. Anyway, when he answered I told him what the situation was, about as fast as light goes from the Earth to the moon. He asked me to slow down to sub light speed in my conversation, so, after telling him about three times and getting a pregnant pause in return . . . he laughed! He thought it was great that I was getting this experience! When I told him about the lightning he thought that was even better and said at least I was getting some good weather experience in preparation for my pilot's license.

With an internal sigh of relief, I asked him what I should do. He said he'd check the weather radar and then call me back. It was always in times of crisis where my dad functioned best and his words were soothing, especially after he told me to relax, everything was going to work out. As I sat in 2011Z, another aircraft landed and parked next to me, he too being chased out of the sky by the tempests canvassing the area. I briefly chatted with the two folks in the Comanche, telling them of my plight and they telling me of theirs . . . misery loves company. About twenty minutes after calling my dad, the pay phone rang and I ran to answer it. The reassuring voice of my father told me that there should be a break in the cells (storm cells) long enough for me to fly "home" in about thirty minutes or so. He said he'd call me when he wanted me to take off.

So, I waited. I wandered around the ramp a bit, inspecting the many single engine airplanes parked there, looking into their cockpits and oohhhing and ahhhing at those that were fitted with the latest in avionics and then dissing the less fortunate that seemed abandoned and forlorn; since I do have a tendency to talk to myself, if anyone was secretly watching me, they would have thought I was talking to an imaginary friend.

After inspecting the aircraft and then putting them in an order as to which one I would want to own first, and then second, and so forth, I peeked into some of the buildings that were adjacent to the ramp. Though it wasn't late in the day, maybe 3:30 p.m., the FBO building was locked up and also not a soul could be found in the open hangar next to the office, which seemed to have a lot of work in progress, with not much work progressing. There was a small boat building company near the ramp that I walked to and there I did find some people with some sort of work ethic. These folks paid me no notice as I looked into their facility and it wasn't until I inspected some of their finished products that were parked outside, that I realized this is where my dad's first boat was built . . . what a small world.

After my nervous meandering and looking at my watch enough times to never allow a pot to boil, I ended up back at my trusty old steed and waited for my phone call. It wasn't a long wait. Funny enough I had been looking to the north to see what the weather looked like and though I could still see many buildups, the bad stuff looked like it had moved to the east. After the Brrrrring! of the phone and my answering it, my dad said the coast was temporarily clear, and he estimated I had a twenty-minute window to get my keister back to Knocky's before another set of storms would block the way. With no time to spare, I started up and took off, leaving the Comanche pilots still sitting there.

Actually, the weather almost looked worse this time, once I began to head toward home, because the smaller "puffy" cumulus clouds were now a lot bigger. But I could see that there was a break in the line of weather in the direction in which I was headed. I could see lightning off to my left, like, all of my left, northwest through southwest, major league lightning at that, about ten miles away at its closest, but with my little engine that could at almost full bore, there was no way those tempests were going to catch me. On my right, the storms that I saw earlier were almost over the beach and no doubt the cooler, more stable sea air was taking the rage out of them and calming them down.

So, with clouds to left and right, I continued home at 100 mph, 800 feet above the ground as my heart raced at a million beats per minute. Once I saw the beautiful grass of my aerodrome from about five miles out, did my heartbeats begin to slow since I knew I would make it to a landing. On my taxi back to parking I briefly reflected upon the flight home and how it really was a bit anticlimactic, save for the incredible display of lightning.

The wind throughout all of this was never a factor and, though blustery at times, I was so used to the sea breezes that affected the shore in the summer that it took a pretty strong wind to bother me.

After landing and tying the aircraft down, I had another tempest, of the human kind, with which to deal . . . Jack DiStefano.

Jack was steaming mad, as he came storming (no pun intended!) up to me and asked me what in the hell I was doing flying HIS aircraft in weather like this and with only a student pilot's license. I had no answer other than it seemed like a nice afternoon to go flying and I got caught down in Woodbine. (My dad had called Jack to tell him what had happened.) There was no appeasing his anger, and after getting my butt chewed out for the better part of ten minutes, I hopped on my ten-speed bike and rode home bewildered . . . not so much by the weather, but by the contrast in emotions between my dad and Jack at times; hell they were both bipolar, and I wasn't sure which one was more whacko. The greatest generation types sure had some anger management issues.

After getting home from work, my father took me to dinner at Rugby Inn, where we sat at the bar and he proceeded to brag to whomever would listen about how his son had cheated death. Yes, he was proud, and I was happy my dad was happy. When Jack showed up to drown his own internal fires of rage with massive quantities of beer, I wondered if these two titans of personality were going to clash over their differences in attitude over my thunderstorm experience. But Jack's anger had been confined to the airport boundaries. The festive ambience of the bar took the edge off of his anger and brought big smiles to his face, which was framed by his jiggling jowls and second chin. The occasional approving slap on my back from each was accompanied by hearty yells; being sober and sitting between two drunk "egos" was not fun.

So, that was my introduction to thunderstorm avoidance.

I've had other very close encounters of a cumulonimbus kind, and even penetrations thereof where the immediate thoughts I harbored while being bounced around by the severe turbulence caused me to have a firm belief that the aircraft was going to break apart. However, most weather penetrations are actually weather avoidances, and in 98 percent of the cases, I've encountered very few surprises or hazards as I've meandered this way and that, using the aircraft's onboard radar to weave my way through a line, or lines, of thunderstorms.

Before I describe the "Oh crap! Were gonna' die!" episodes, I would like to say up front that in most cases flying is very routine, but that doesn't mean it's easy. Most of the aviators with whom I have flown and fly are very competent and experienced. Being blessed with the grace of acumen and exposure to the elements over the years, I am convinced they, my colleagues, are so good at flying an airliner that they make the job appear too easy. This causes the layperson, particularly the airline's management, to think we are grossly overpaid for our services. What management never seems to take into account are the hundreds of decisions that must be made quickly and accurately over the course of just an ordinary, fair weather day flight and that the reason the aviators appear so fluid and competent is because of years of dedication to their art form. These seemingly benign and routine decisions can easily affect the success or failure of that flight and consequently the safety of the crew and the aircraft. The "routineness" of the decisions is not routine at all, but is the result of premeditated or instinctive thought and action gleaned though years of learning and dedication to their professionalism.

However, above the routine of a humdrum flight add thunderstorms into the mix, particularly at your destination airport, and I swear there are times we are not paid near enough to fly some of those trips. In my extremely humble opinion, management gets more than their money's worth out of us pilots on days when our destination is being clobbered by wave after wave of thunderstorms and where some guys get in and land, and some don't and thusly have to divert and land at an alternate airport because they ran low on fuel. It's very stressful during those times, and though the company dispatcher and ATC can help with the decision making and in giving the crew weather and airport updates, they're sitting in a cozy room away from the wind gusts, driving rain, hail, and lightning. In the end, it's the crew making the decision which radar returns to fly through, or which ones to avoid as they attempt to dodge the worst of the tempests all the while trying to figure out what is the safest course of action to complete the flight.

Okay . . . now that I've ranted, I'm going to relive two up close and very personal thunderstorm encounters from my more modern past. In the first narrative, I was leading a flight of four F-4s and thought I was going to fly through hell, and in the second I was flying an MD-11 and did indeed fly through hell.

After leaving the womb of my aviation career far behind in time, geography and career progression, as God would have me do, at one point I was based at McConnell AFB in Wichita, Kansas flying F-4s in an area of the country that is called "Tornado Alley." Just mentioning the state of Kansas, if you are discussing thunderstorms and only slightly weather savvy, can bring chills to any aviator, as it did for me, when I realized I was going to be both trained and then eventually based there.

Prior to the flights I'm about to describe, and since them (the flights), I've had many, many encounters with severe thunderstorms around this globe of ours. In most cases, I've just deftly deviated around the weather using the aircraft's onboard radar. But there are some times when the massing of the cells is so great and extensive in area that avoiding the tempests by a wide area is almost impossible. In those instances, where avoiding the weather with a wide margin is impossible, you have a few options: (1) You can divert and land short of the thunderstorms and wait for them to pass; (2) Perform a huge, fuel-consuming deviation around the entire area of weather (if possible); (3) Hold over an area away from the storms and wait until they pass (assuming you have enough fuel) and then proceed to your destination; and (4) Lastly, pick an area of the weather that looks the least bad between the cells and fly through it, knowing you may fly very close to a cell but also believing that it's not going to be too bad of a ride.

One very notable encounter I had with a tremendously huge line of thunderstorms, with some storms topping out above 50,000 feet, occurred when I was leading a flight of four Phantoms. I elected to use option 4, as just described, and I have to tell you, I initially thought I had made a mistake in my decision to penetrate through the weather once I was actually in it.

The genesis of this thunderstorm encounter started from Nellis AFB, located near Las Vegas, Nevada. Eight of us, four front-seaters and four WSOs had flown into Nellis to pick up four F-4s. We did delay a couple of days in Nellis to fly some local area missions, to include flying low levels and dropping bombs. On the day of departure, heading back to McGuire, we left in the early morning since we planned on flying a low-level to Kirtland AFB, in Albuquerque.

As a portent of the day to come, nearing Silver City, New Mexico, we had to abort the low level due to low clouds, rain showers, and generally poor visibility over the mountains of Western New Mexico. A weather abort was called on the radio and we all popped up above the clouds and reformed in route formation. As we were joining back up, we continued our climb to 17,500 feet and proceeded directly to Kirtland, all 4 aircraft landing uneventfully about thirty minutes after aborting the low level.

After refueling and flight planning, it was our desire to then fly a low level from Albuquerque (Kirtland) to Peterson Air Force Base, located on Colorado Springs Airport, in Colorado Springs, Colorado. We were to spend the night at "C Springs" and then fly non-stop back to McGuire the next morning. The USAF weather briefer in Kirtland said that the clouds where we wanted to fly our low level "should" be good enough for the required 5000-foot ceiling and the required five miles viz. I'd flown that low level once before and the flight amongst the Sangre de Cristo mountains was spectacular, so I was praying for a redux on this flight.

Since everyone in the flight was very hungover from the "last night in Vegas" festivities, no one wanted to actually lead the flight to Colorado Springs. My squadron commander said that his heading indicator was "acting up and unreliable" so therefore he needed to hang on the wing of whoever was leading. The guy who led the flight from Nellis to Kirtland said he'd already led one flight and therefore took himself out of the running. Steve, the number 4 guy was not legal to lead anything other than himself because he was a brand spanking new Phantom pilot.

So that left yours truly.

With bleeding eyes and throbbing head, I quickly did the required flight planning for the flight to the low level start point (we'd preplanned the low level while in Nellis) and then briefed the boys on the entire flight. After about two hours of ground time, we departed the fair skies of New Mexico and headed north by slightly east in a loose route formation bound for a rendezvous with destiny.

It was very evident as we entered the skies over South-Central Colorado that it was looking pretty grim for being able to fly a low-level. Flying at 29,000 feet, the clouds were scattered and broken immediately below us but the lower I looked the thicker and more numerous the cloud layers, to the point it was pretty much solid cloud from 15,000 feet and below. I knew in my heart this was going to be a waste of time, descending in the hopes we could find clear air, but I did it anyway, if only because we were supposed to land at Colorado Springs and spend the night.

I called the boys into close, fingertip formation, and down we went into the relatively smooth, but extremely moisture-laden air mass below. Using our own aircraft's radar and the watchful eye of Denver Center's more all-encompassing weather radar to search the area in front of us, we descended on the eastern side of Colorado Springs, where the flat, great plains spread eastward.

The air traffic controllers at Denver Center were amazingly compliant, as we descended. I asked Center if we could go to this radial and DME[73] or that one while we descended in the hopes of finding clear air, or at least a 5000-foot ceiling so we could fly the low levels, and not once was the controller bothered by my requests,

---

73. Distance Measuring Equipment—An electronic device that tells the aircrew their distance from a VOR station or ILS.

if anything he was extremely helpful, giving me PIREPs to help in my SA. Somewhere approaching 3,000 AGL we broke out of the heavy clouds and were under a very dark and dreary overcast with rain showers visible almost everywhere you looked; it was immediately obvious once underneath the clouds we would not be able to fly the low-level.

Now my attention turned to thinking if C Springs was the best place to land. So, I immediately headed in the direction of the airport, about ten miles to the west, and once I could actually see the environs of the field, I saw a dark and hugely pregnant cloud drifting over the airport and giving birth to drenching rains.

I sent the flight to a private UHF frequency as soon as we were established in VMC[74] conditions because I wanted to talk to the boys about our options. Prior to going to the discreet UHF frequency, I had called Colorado Springs tower and asked them for their runway condition and indeed they said the runway was wet. I knew that, but I just wanted confirmation on what I was seeing as I put our four-ship in an orbit about eight miles east of the field.

Thanks to my father's training early in my career, prior to departing Kirtland AFB I had checked the actual weather and forecasts at a few of the surrounding major airports that we could reach from our intended destination of Colorado Springs. Because the weather was so bad at Colorado Springs, I dared not attempt a landing with the F-4s since it was pouring and the runway was thoroughly wet. At sea level, landing on a wet runway was not a big deal, even in the warmth of summer, but Colorado Springs is around 6000 feet

---

74. Visual Meteorological Conditions—When flying an aircraft, this essentially means you are flying clear of clouds.

above sea level, and the density altitude[75] combined with the wet runway put our landing roll at the extremes of the field; if one of the drag chutes failed to deploy upon touchdown I doubt the Phantom could've been stopped without engaging an arresting cable[76]. On most military fields taking a barrier isn't a big deal, but I was worried about all 4 aircraft having to take the cable and in C Springs the arresting cables were in the overruns of the runway . . . they were not meant for normal or frequent use.

Though the weather was bad and precluded us from flying the low level, and caused me concern about landing at Peterson AFB, by the grace of God on that day we were flying with three external fuel tanks. On most missions in the Phantom we normally carried a single high-speed centerline, external fuel tank capable of carrying 4000 pounds of jet fuel, but the F-4s we'd picked up at Nellis had been configured with three external tanks. The two external wing tanks we were carrying that day added 5000 more pounds of "gas" to our normal complement of 16,000 pounds. of fuel. This added luxury gave me more options as to where we could go and took some pressure off of my decision to divert rather than land at "Pete" field.

While in the orbit below the clouds, and talking on the UHF radio, as if I was face to face with the other guys, I told them of my concerns with regards to landing at C Springs relatively heavyweight, with a wet runway and high density altitude, and I asked them for

---

75. Density altitude is the altitude in the International Standard Atmosphere at which the air density would be equal to the actual air density at the place of observation, or, in other words, the height when measured in terms of the density of the air rather than the distance from the ground.

76. Arresting Cable—A very strong metal cable laid perpendicular to and across a runway. It is used to stop aircraft equipped with a hook (such as fighter aircraft). It serves the same purpose as arresting gear found on aircraft carriers.

their thoughts. I specifically told the squadron commander if there was anything he wanted us to do, or place to go, and assuming it was safe, I'd defer to his desires. He said he was okay with whatever I decided so I briefed the guys on the weather at the various airports for which I was briefed before we departed Kirtland AFB and told them that since we still had a lot of fuel, we had quite a few options. I did add that McConnell AFB was my preference over Tinker (Oklahoma City, Oklahoma), Buckley (Denver, Colorado) or Salina (Salina, Kansas), but said I was open to thoughts. No one dissented about going to IAB, McConnell AFB.

My decision to go to McConnell was based upon their actual weather and the forecast. I also knew from previous flying experience that it would take about 6000 pounds of fuel to fly from Colorado Springs to McConnell (the wind would be at our back, too, which would help) and finally, I knew that around McConnell were other airports, relatively close, that could also be used if for some reason the weather crumped at IAB.

Fuel, in a fighter aircraft, is always a critical issue. It's often said that fighters take off with emergency fuel from the start. Though that may have been true in the early days of jets, it isn't at all like that nowadays with the newer fighters and their more fuel efficient low bypass turbofan jet engines. The biggest reason it's thought that fighters take off with low fuel is because, quite simply, a lot of the practice missions flown require high power settings and consequently use prodigious amounts of fuel rather quickly. Also, let's face it, fighter pilots tend to push the limits of their fuel supply to maximize training time spent on each mission, so it was normal to push fuel reserves and land with twenty minutes of JP-4[77] in the tanks; on

---

77. JP-4—USAF jet fuel designation.

a good weather day, twenty minutes is fine. I have to fully admit though there were a few times when the weather suddenly became horrible, even though forecast to be good, and I had no choice but to fly an instrument approach down to minimums with no viable alternate airport to which I could divert. It's not a life enhancing experience to push the limits of your fuel, but sometimes you had no choice.

The F-4, if left in full afterburner right after takeoff, could consume its entire 12,000-pound internal fuel supply in about nine minutes, or so I've been told; to be honest I've never tried. In fact, in A/B the fuel is consumed so fast the external tank(s) cannot feed quick enough into the main tanks to keep them filled. The fuel flow indicators do not record the accurate fuel flow of the Phantom in full afterburner due to limitations on the fuel flow indicators themselves.

But while flying cross-country, and at much less power settings than full afterburner, the external tanks can easily keep the main fuel tanks full until the external tanks run dry. On this day, with my four-ship leveled off somewhere around 33,000 feet, a nominal cruise fuel flow of 7000 pounds per hour was the norm, not the eighty thousand pounds per hour while in full A/B. Normally I would set 520 knots true airspeed as my target cruise speed and as fuel burned off and lightened the aircraft's weight you could pull the power back to hold 520 knots, and then you could expect to see a 6000-pound-per-hour burn. So, for cross country planning purposes I would flight plan fuel burns at 7000 pounds for the first hour of cruising flight and then six thousand pounds for the remainder of the flight. With three external tanks, like we had on this day, we had 21,000 pounds of fuel which gave us roughly three hours of endurance at normal cruise speed and at the higher flight levels.

Normally, carrying all of that fuel is a pain in the butt as it weighs the aircraft down and limits your maximum combat/training maneuvering capability and Gs available due to the external tank airspeed and G restrictions. Today, however, we were just going cross-country and flying low levels and not going into combat as we went from AFB to AFB, so this extra 5000 pounds was realllllly nice to have, particularly today. (You can always selectively jettison the external tanks if you need to.)

As we started our climb and headed toward McConnell, we left Colorado in the rearview mirrors (both cockpits in the F-4 have rearview mirrors). My external tanks had just fed out as we began the divert and I was now using my internal fuel, 12,000 pounds. But, since this is not a perfect world, not all pilots move their throttles in the same manner, and when you are flying in formation the lead aircraft usually has the most gas, at any given time, assuming you are flying as we were, cross-country (combat is a different situation altogether), and the wingman will have slightly lower fuel balances; the more junior the wingmen, the lower his fuel is than lead's, as they usually haven't learned the varying techniques of fuel conservation as a wingman. As soon as we diverted and started a climb to the flight levels, I took a fuel check . . . as expected, number 4, the newest pilot member of the squadron, was almost a thousand pounds lower than me, with two and three somewhere in between. As I said, I knew from past experience it took about 6000 pounds of fuel to fly the distance we needed to fly to get to IAB, not including deviating for weather though. So that would put us on the ground with about 6000 pounds, 5000 for number four, assuming he could keep his throttle bursts under control. If he started burning too much gas, I could make him the lead aircraft, and the rest of us would fly off of him, thusly allowing him to conserve fuel because he wouldn't have to continuously move his throttles to stay in formation position. Since I didn't expect there to be a wall of water with an attitude enroute to McConnell that I would have to deviate around, I figured we had plenty of gas.

As we climbed from 3000 feet AGL (about 9,000 feet MSL) to FL 330 (33,000 feet MSL) I sent my number 2 aircraft off in search of the real weather at McConnell and cleared him off the ATC freq. we were working on. (Since my number 2 wingman's head [I mean his actual physical head and body, along with his backseater's] was only about five feet off of my left wingtip in close formation as we climbed through some pretty thick nimbus clouds, I was not too worried about losing him, in a physical sense, hence the reason I cleared him off frequency in the first place.)

If you are wondering, my numbers 3 and 4 aircraft were similarly stacked off of my right side, three being a mirror image of number 2, and number 4 flying off of number 3's right wingtip in a similar position as he, three, was on me; the proper term for this is called fingertip, and it's used for flying multiple aircraft, up to four, in weather when the visibility is poor and/or when arriving in the landing pattern for an overhead break.

As a side note to our climb to FL330 and flying in fingertip, somewhere in this climb, since the clouds we so moisture-laden, very thick, and with extremely poor visibility, number 4 lost sight of number 3 and had to initiate lost wingman procedures. The WSO in the number 4 aircraft was very experienced and capable and he was able to talk his junior pilot through the procedures and eventually number 4 ended up about a mile behind and slightly below the rest of us. Using his radar to follow us as we climbed, eventually the thickness of the clouds lessened, and 4 was able to visually see the three-ship ahead of him and rejoined the flight.

As we crested the highest of the low clouds into momentarily blinding and brilliant but welcome sunshine, my number 2 man, after my backseater gave him the appropriate fingers to tell him what frequency we were on . . . and BTW, not the type of road rage fingers you might get while driving in New Jersey traffic . . . informed us that indeed IAB was clear, but . . . there was a severe storm front barreling its way toward the base, with the requisite thunderstorms, and we needed to hurry.

Dang. That USAF weather guy in Kirtland AFB needed some remedial training since he didn't forecast this massing of thunderstorms in Kansas.

As we climbed and headed east at .88 Mach[78] the clouds that had been below us since entering Colorado gave way to clear skies with only scattered clouds down low. But on my entire right side, from the extreme southwest and then then going in front of me to the extreme northeast, I could visually see the wall of weather and had no doubts about the ferocity of the storms. The experience of my years flying out of McConnell and many previous weather penetrations were still indelibly etched into my weather wisdom synapses.

My two biggest concerns, now that I knew we had a hugely imposing line of thunderstorms to penetrate, were: (1) Could I find a hole through which to slip my flight of four aircraft without being tormented by turbulence? ; and, (2) Could we get to the aerodrome before the weather hit?

---

78. Mach is the speed of sound, which is affected by temperature. A jet aircraft's airspeed indicator indicates both indicated airspeed in knots and a percentage of Mach. Thusly, .88 Mach would be 88 percent the speed of sound.

With an old worry behind, landing at Colorado Springs, and two new ones ahead, I again sent my number 2 man off the active ATC freq. and told him to contact McConnell AFB tower and ask them, quite literally, what it looked like out their window, particularly to the west, from whence the weather was coming, and to give us an estimate as to how much time we had before the front hit. Two answered with a quick, "Roj," and off he went, at least in terms of the UHF radio spectrum (the F-4 had only one radio for ATC or inter-flight communications; it worked only in the UHF band).

I will pause from this narrative and marginally educate you on the F-4's radar and its ability for painting weather.

Simply put, the Phantom's radar was not made for weather interpretation or avoidance, but even so, once enlisted in that role and once you learned how to interpret the radar returns, it actually did quite well. All fighter aircrafts' radars are made for locating and tracking other aircraft, big or small, or for ground mapping, or both. Weather avoidance was a complimentary capability due to the nature of the radar and its design; an F-15/16/18 had to use a different, pulse, mode with their radar to "see" weather, whereas the F-4's radar could be used in its normal air to air mode. With that said, the ability for the F-4's radar to see through any thickness of clouds, electronically of course, was not a problem. In fact, the energy put out by the Phantom's radar was so much, because it was designed to detect aircraft at a long distance, I wouldn't be surprised if water evaporated as it hit the radome while we flew in rain (kinda like a microwave boiling water). And on that thread, whenever I led a four-ship of F-4s and we were in close formation, I knew all of the guys had their radars on and their antennas were sweeping left and right (up to sixty degrees either side of center) and I wondered why in the hell with all of that RF energy passing through, around, and bathing me that my kids didn't come out looking like a Picasso painting.

Once level at 33,000 feet, Andre, my backseater, tilted and gained the F-4's radar. I had a repeater of his scope in the front seat, so as he manipulated the radar's search area we talked between ourselves about what area ahead looked the best for penetrating. At first the wall of clouds seemed impenetrable. From sixty degrees left of the nose, to sixty right, all we could see was a mass of commingled storm cells. But I knew from experience, and I explained this to my charge in the WSO's seat behind me, that from a distance though the weather can seem solid, as you get closer, due to limitations in the specific design of each model of radar (F-4, F-16, F-18, etc.), you should see gaps between the cells; some are big gaps, some are small, and some of these gaps can close up as you approach them, so you need to be prepared to turn around if a hole suddenly closes.

As we got ever closer to the backside of the storms, I continued to talk to Andre about techniques on how to interpret the weather returns on the scope and about how best to tilt and gain to optimize said returns and understand the nature of the weather at which we were looking. Andre was so new to the F-4 he'd not had a lot of thunderstorm avoidance experience, so I figured this would be excellent learning for him.

After many minutes of lip biting on my part, I saw that there was a decent size gap between two monstrous cells just north of Wichita. I asked Kansas City Center for a lower altitude, as we approached the weather from the west, since I wanted to stay in the clear as long as possible and the clouds at the higher altitudes were encroaching upon us; I wanted to make it easier on the wingmen by staying in clear air as long as I could.

I did communicate to my wingmen the area of weather that Andre, and I thought would be the best bet for getting through relatively unharmed and they all concurred that it looked like the best area too.

As previously mentioned, the line of storms was marching in a northeast/southwest tilt. I'm sure this slant, in relation to magnetic north, made not a difference to Mother Nature, global warming, or the price of rice in China, but to me it was a royal pain in the butt because my ace in the hole through this mess was about twenty miles or so northeast of IAB, and this meant more fuel spent getting through to the front of the weather and then backtracking a bit southwestward to get to McConnell.

In preparation for entering the clouds, I took another fuel check to give me a heads up on everyone's fuel states. As expected, number 4 was still the low man, holding at one thousand less than me with 5000 pounds total. Since we were only twenty-five miles from our destination, that wasn't too bad, but we still had to fly another twenty miles or so eastbound and then come back southwest, so at best, number 4 would have 3000 pounds on landing . . . thirty minutes at our nominal burn rate of six thousand pounds per hour. If we had to divert to Tinker AFB or Tulsa, both about ninety-five nautical miles south of Wichita, they would land with about 1,500 lbs. of fuel, at best. Not optimum, but since Tinker and Tulsa were clear, I'd let them lead us down there so they could conserve fuel.

I have to say, as we approached the ominous-looking clouds, my optimistic "fat" fuel supply suddenly was looking pretty thin if not right on the edge between risking an end run around and getting in to McConnell or diverting to Salina, which was to the north of us about sixty miles. In fact, if Tinker AFB was not sporting the good weather it did have, I would have done just that, gone to Salina. But, with clear skies, light winds, and no thunderstorms in the area, Tinker was my alternate from IAB once we got on the other side of the storms.

We were now down to 10,000 feet or so, and descending. My wayward number 2 man came back on freq and said the field was VMC (Visual Meteorological Conditions) with mostly broken clouds at around 2000 feet and excellent visibility under the clouds, however, tower estimated we had about twenty minutes before the leading edge of the storms hit the field.

I slightly rocked my wings to bring the boys back into fingertip, as they had been flying in a more relaxed route formation, in preparation for entering the clouds…and then my radar quit.

Crap.

Can you believe it? Of all the times for it to stop working . . . At first, I thought it was my front seat, repeater radar that was the culprit but, in fact Andre said he lost his scope too. I literally, as you might see on TV docudrama, hit my scope in the hopes that it might act like CPR and bring it back to life…unlike TV though, no such luck.

Announcing over the radio "gadget bent," the code words for an inoperative radar, my wingmen immediately picked up the slack and began giving me headings to fly to avoid the bad stuff while my WSO troubleshot our busted radar set.

Since we were only at 9000 feet as we started to enter the clouds, I saw, visually, what my radar had (before it quit) confirmed was a pretty decent hole in the mountains of cloud in front of us.

My visual clue that this area was the place to penetrate as we approached the ankles of these monstrous storms from the west was the ripped-up clouds in an otherwise uniform wall of white. It literally looked like the two cells we were about to fly between were fighting over a white veil and consequently tearing it to shreds, from the ground up. In their fight, they were leaving tatters of cloud in this one geographical area alluding to a weak spot in the storms; or so I was betting, hoping, and praying.

As direct sunshine quickly became obscured by cloud fragments, I couldn't help but take a few deep breaths to try and break the tension within me, as the last time I did this I damn near flew into physical hell on Earth. (That's another story for another day.) I wiggled my toes and fingers and looked over my left and right shoulders at my wingmen to check on their position. Like little ducks nestled in close to mama, they were right there, rock solid and staring at my aircraft, the pilots in each, making continuous and mostly small adjustments with their throttles and ailerons and elevators (stabilator on the F-4) and rudder to stay close enough to see me in the clouds, but yet far enough so as to not hit me. Sometimes these adjustments follow each other in a mixed order, sometimes they are simultaneous, most times they vary between those two extremes; it's a continuous, delicate and minute dance of the flight controls and engines to maintain position on mama duck. Flying on the wing is hard work and mentally very tiring as you must also be thinking about what is coming up and trying to maintain a modicum of situational awareness as your flight progresses.

As bright day quickly turned dark, due to the thickening of the clouds, my wingmen were constantly reassuring me via the radio that the heading we were on looked good on their radars for weather avoidance. Wichita Approach Control had long ago told us that we could deviate at will since there was not another aircraft within forty miles and to let them know when we were turning direct to McConnell. According to my wingmen it would take about ten miles or so to get through the worst of the weather and then we could start edging to the right (south then southwest).

Into the gathering darkness we motored on, at 300 knots, in and out of clouds of varying thickness, and I won't lie and say that I didn't feel a bit uncomfortable flying into this mess without a radar. Sometimes we would blast through thin "whispies," mere remnants of much larger clouds, or maybe they were developing storm embryos, not yet full term . . . who knows. But no doubt our wake turbulence and engine effluent was blasting them apart and either hastening their disappearance or aborting their development; can't say it bothered me either way . . . I've never had a strong emotional attachment to clouds. At other times, we passed through the connecting clouds between the thunderstorms, where I'm sure our passing did little to disturb the nature of the weather behind us. The whole experience was surreal because as we were alternately flying through thick cloud, thin cloud, or no cloud, we were seeing almost continuous lightning bursts all around. Some of the lightning was suffused, embedded within the clouds, and acted like an X-ray machine since you could see the outlines of the clouds within the clouds . . . if that makes any sense. At other times, ragged streaks of lightning, clear in definition were observed, causing me to think I was in Dr. Frankenstein's laboratory where monsters were jump-started to life by arcing bolts of electricity shooting through the air.

As we flew through the skies of Oz, I calculated how much fuel we would have upon our arrival. I had the airfield's TACAN tuned in and it was showing the distance and azimuth to the airport for situational awareness purposes. I was doing my best guessing at this

ROGER BLAIR JOHNSON   541

point, as I had no exact idea as to when we could turn toward the runway. I was figuring though, just to give you an example of the extremely difficult mathematical calculations that fighter pilots use in flight (I'm be facetious), the following—we were doing roughly six miles a minute, 360 kts. ground speed, and were about thirty miles northeast of the destination. I figured we had another six miles, one minute, to go before we could turn southwest toward the airport. So, guessing that we had thirty six miles to go, and at six miles a minute, that would equate to a fuel burn of around 600 pounds (100 pounds per minute, or 6000 pounds per hour, times six minutes of flying time equals 600 pounds. Now, add an extra 400 pounds for slop and then subtract that 1,000 pounds of fuel from the 5000 pounds number 4 said he had when I started this calculating…well, so, I figured the wingman with the lowest fuel state should be on the ground with around 3,500 pounds of JP-4; not too bad actually.

And, with that said, though I dearly wanted to fly at 500 knots to make sure I beat the encroaching weather, neither our fuel supply nor the wingmen could take it (the faster you go the more sensitive the flight controls and though I've flown on someone's wing in fingertip at 450 knots, it's not fun, particularly in the clouds). I figured 300 knots was the best compromise between fuel consumption and beating the storms, so it was at that speed in which we soldiered on.

Just as I was deep in thought in those aforementioned and extremely complex math problems, the sky all around us immediately brightened, signaling our passage through the worst of the weather. To be honest the entire time we ran the gauntlet between the two massive cells the turbulence was, at worst light, so it was indeed a good area for us to have penetrated, and really the passage through was a bit anticlimactic.

Once we broke into the clear, I immediately kicked the boys into a loose route position so they could relax a bit.

Now that we were through the mess of angry clouds, I put the TACAN bearing pointer on the nose and pushed up the power to accelerate to 350 knots. I felt so much better now that I could once again see the amazingly stratospheric ascending and impressive wall of cumulonimbus, this time from the eastern side.

I was now very confident that we would beat the storms to the field, but now I had a new worry, and oddly it was not the towering clouds above us but low-lying clouds below.

If you remember, earlier in the flight my number 2 man said that the field was reporting a 2000-foot broken ceiling. What I was looking at as we headed southwest was a mostly overcast (actually undercast, since the clouds were below us) sky; I wondered just how low the clouds descended.

I had figured earlier, based upon the earlier cloud report, we could fly up initial as a four-ship and then pitch out and land . . . a fairly expeditious and fuel-thrifty procedure. But if we had to split up, plan B, for individual ILS approaches, some of us weren't going to make it before the weather closed the field.

Plan "B" was not on my top ten list of things I wanted to do, so I asked Approach what McConnell was reporting for weather. Their latest report was almost an hour old and it jived with Tower's of a broken, 2000-foot ceiling. Since I was seeing that it wasn't that, I asked Approach for lower. Bringing the boys back into fingertip for-mation, we re-entered the clouds and descended to four thousand feet. At four grand, we were solidly encased in white and I asked for lower again. Since there didn't seem to be any other aircraft flying, my request was quickly granted, but even at 3000 feet we were still in the muck.

I had pretuned the ILS to runway 19 right's frequency while in the thunderstorms, so I asked for and was cleared to intercept the localizer as we approached the field from the northeast. We were now eighteen miles out and still firmly in the clouds' grip. I asked approach to take me down to their min. vectoring altitude. That altitude was about 2,500 feet and at that altitude, about 1,500 feet above the ground, I could see breaks in the clouds and the ground below. Upon seeing the ground and noticing the visibility was pretty good underneath the clouds, I immediately cancelled my IFR clearance and descended to get fully into the clear air. With my cancellation to Approach, they bid me sayonara and told me to go to tower's frequency.

At twelve miles out, and lined up on runway 19 right, I told Tower where we were. They cleared us to land on the right side (McConnell AFB has two parallel 10,000-foot runways).

Since we were only about a thousand feet AGL, we could not fly up initial and pitch out as I initially had planned; we had to do straight-ins from this altitude. Just seeing the runway made me feel incredibly relieved and took a ton of bricks off of my chest. But I could see lightning to the west and a roll cloud out there . . . until we were all safely on the ground we weren't home free yet. With the new wrinkle, low clouds, spoiling my arrival and landing plan, and not wanting to break up for ILS approaches, I told number 4 to "drag."

If you remember, number 4, at least the frontseater, was the "new guy," so I was sure he had no idea what "drag" meant. When

I first talked to tower and saw the low ceilings I told them we were going to do a "shotgun" approach. This was vernacular that came out of my ass as I hadn't used the term "shotgun approach" in a couple of years. But we used to do these oddly named approaches when I was on active duty for the exact reason I wanted to do one now . . . low cloud and straight-in approaches while in a formation. In essence, all you did was have the wingmen, in turn, starting with number 4 and then number 3, etc., slow down as rapidly as possible to landing/approach speed at two-mile intervals, or thereabouts. Since I was the lead aircraft, I flew on at 300 knots as each aircraft rapidly slowed and hopefully this would give us the required 3000-foot (offset, alternate sides of the runway) spacing we needed to land behind each other. In theory, and practice, it worked well, but it was not something we did a lot in my guard unit in Jersey.

Since I had told tower we were going to do a shotgun approach, I knew that would key the other flight members as to what my plan was and, with that said, though I knew the number 4 "pilot" was clueless as to what this meant, I knew his backseater, the WSO, was not and I hoped he would brief the "greenhorn" on what the plan was. When I told number 4 to "drag" at twelve miles, the word "drag" being the command to slow down, I was looking directly at him to see what his reaction would be . . . I really, really hoped that they would immediately slow down as I didn't want to have to brief this over the radio at this point!

To my immediate relief, no sooner had the ga sound of drag gotten out of my mouth than number 4 was dropping back rapidly, his speed brakes fully deployed. That was a relief . . . the rest of the guys I wasn't worried about.

And so it went, at roughly two mile increments, I dropped the guys off one by one with number 2 leaving me as we approached six miles to go via the TACAN-indicated DME.

At that point, I was doing 300 knots; the final approach/landing speed was around 150 knots. While the Phantom may be a flying brick to some, it does have a pointy end, and merely pulling the throttles to idle and going to fully deployed with the speedbrakes isn't going to kill 150 knots or so of excess speed in four miles (the TACAN is located midfield, about 5000 feet from the approach end of either runway). Though my father never trained me to fly fighters, he did show me how to go down and slow down via cross controlling the flight controls of an aircraft (also known as "slipping") and I am here to tell ya, the F-4 can be cross controlled quite easily. The first fifty knots I "killed" using speedbrakes and slipping the aircraft; using a lot of left aileron to fight against a lot of right rudder which caused the aircraft to fly somewhat sideways on its way to the runway. Keeping the speedbrakes extended, the next 100 knots were lost with the aid of the landing gear and full flaps which were extended at their 250-knot limit. By the time the runway met the wheels I was on speed and well within the normal touchdown zone for landing; I had four thousand pounds of JP-4 remaining in the tanks.

As we rolled out on our landing roll into a strengthening headwind, I could hear number 3 ask tower if he could land on the left runway because he was having trouble getting spacing on number 2. Tower approved this and as I turned off the right runway, and headed east, toward the left runway, number 3 rolled past the intersection I was approaching.

Crossing the runway after number 3 went by, I taxied to the transient ramp to park after being cleared by tower. As I shut down my engines on the ramp number 4 was taxiing into parking.

As Andre and I got our bags out of the travel pod (a long since converted napalm bomb canister that we used to carry our personal effects) and closed the canopy, I felt some plump-sized raindrops hit my head. By the time number 4's canopy was closed, the wind had shifted from the south to out of the west with a roll cloud fast approaching the western edge of the airfield while lightning segregated the very blackish western sky. As soon as we walked into base ops, the monsoon started in earnest with sideways pelting rains and amazing displays of lightning accompanied by very loud and sharp reports of thunder. Settling into seats at base ops in preparation to going to the base hotel, I casually asked number 4 how much fuel he had when he landed . . . 3000 pounds he nonchalantly said; just enough I thought . . .just enough.

I said in my August 28 MD-11 journal entry that I had a rather bad encounter with a seemingly benign green dot a few months earlier (in the journal entry) while flying from Tokyo to Singapore. What follows is my worst-case scenario, so far in my career, for thunderstorm avoidance, or lack thereof, and was a huge lesson learned for me and, no doubt, the captain too.

To be sure most seasoned pilots have had at least one close encounter with a thunderstorm in which they may have had to change their underwear.

What follows is mine.

I was a brand-new first officer, of sorts, flying with a new MD-11 captain. We were going from Tokyo to Singapore and had an 8 p.m. departure time. After meandering through the rather large terminal we found our way to the gate where our company van was wait-ing. Since cargo aircraft don't normally pull into gates at passenger terminals, transportation of some sort is required to get you from the terminal to where the aircraft is parked, hence the reason for the van. The paperwork for the flight was in the van when we got in it and the Captain poured over the flight release, weather, and NOTAMs as we made our way to the cargo side of the airport. A line check airman, who was jumpseating with us to Singapore, greeted us as we climbed onboard the aircraft. Oddly enough, this guy was to give us a line check on our flight, in two days' time, from Singapore to Taipei via Penang. (Normally he would have flown on the airlines down to SIN but to give himself more time in SIN, he instead decided to jumpseat on his own company's aircraft . . . in about 3 hours time I'm sure he wished he had taken the airlines.)

The weather in Narita was pleasant enough, as we did our usual preflight thing and departed. I was the pilot flying, but because of being rushed and busy when we got to the aircraft, I was never able to actually look in depth at any of the reports of weather along the way and/or weather maps. I asked the captain how "it looked" (the weather) as we progressed in our preflight duties and he said, "Fine." As we climbed into a dark, evening sky I never would have suspected this might be my last MD-11 flight.

We were level at 33,000 feet. The captain liked to fly with the overhead cockpit lights on when it was dark and when at cruising altitude, and it was not adverse to company policy. Also, he and the check pilot knew each other and they began to have a nice little chat as we cruised serenely south while I kept track of the fuel log and did that "pilot stuff." I had my NAV display[79] scale set to 320-mile range (it'll go to 640) and the radar was set for level tilt as we bid sayonara to the Japanese mainland and headed toward the Philippine islands.

Mike had just finished talking to his friend, and I used that social pause to ask him about a tiny green radar return innocently displaying on the nav display at about forty miles. In fact it was the only thing showing on the entire display, that one itty bitty green dot. The captain said that since it was green it was not a factor and to not worry about it . . . which I did . . . not worry about it that is. I never bothered to briefly turn off the overhead lights to try and visually see if we were heading for a build-up and I couldn't see any lightning through the semi-opaque (due to the cockpit lighting on full) windshields. So, on we sailed, blithely, contently, like lambs heading for the slaughter.

As the green dot disappeared into the bottom of my nav display, indicating we were about to merge with it, I was looking back at our line check airman as he had just laid down in a sleeping bag on the floor of the courier cabin (the cockpit door was open and this is well before 9/11, so cockpit security was not near as Draconian as it is now). As I looked forward again, I saw St. Elmo's fire begin to dance upon our windscreen and I thought that was odd as I only saw that phenomenon when penetrating high clouds very near thunderstorms. Then, I smelled the distinctive sting of ionized air attacking my nostrils followed by an immediate pounding of rain upon the windscreen. Since we had so many clues to the nearness of convective activity, the captain was now fully integrated into the goings-on

79. NAV Display is a modern aircraft all have electronic, flat screen, multifunction displays that display an abundance of flight information to include their programmed route of flight, wind speed and direction, ground speed, time/ distance to the next navigation point, mandatory altitudes for certain waypoints, etc.

of the flight and subsequently turned off the overhead lights to get a better look out of the front windscreen. Though the switch he hit was only supposed to turn off the overhead cockpit lights, tonight it seemed like it was doing double duty because as soon as the lights went out the turbulence hit us with the intensity of Thor's sledge-hammer . . . all hell broke loose.

With the first smash of the updraft against us, I had no doubt the aircraft was going to break apart. The odd thing to me was how sudden we went from being in relatively smooth, level flight to severe turbulence. Unlike flying into the gradual buildup of a jet stream's sometimes tumultuous winds and associated turbulence, there was very little gradient leading up to this hellish storm's crescendo. The first gust we "hit" was as severe as all of the others, and as bad as the last, there was no discerning the edges of the thunderstorm from the center with regard to the intensity of the turbulence.

The first jackhammer hit against the aircraft was an updraft of such magnitude that it immediately pitched our nose ten degrees skyward and at the same time pushed the entire aircraft rapidly upward. Concurrent with the upward movement of the aircraft, the captain and I were violently driven down and into our seats with such incredible force I kinda bent forward at the waist with my head falling toward the yoke before I was able to straighten up. I wasn't expecting such turbulence in such an innocuous-looking (accord-ing to the radar) cloud, and the initial violence of the turbulence was very disconcerting and scary. The almost continuous up and down drafts and their force upon the aircraft, and our bodies, was extremely violent and caused me to wonder if the aircraft structure could take such repeated abuse. I am not ashamed to say I thought we might die. In that initial wallop of the updraft against the aircraft, as the nose went up the left wing went down sixty degrees causing the captain's and my upper body to be immediately tilted off of center, but as soon as the aircraft's nose went up ten degrees it almost immediately reversed direction and went precipitously nose-low with the entire aircraft following as we entered a horrendous downdraft that dropped the aircraft like it was but a puny toy in the hands of an exceedingly large and volatile giant. The downward thrust of the aircraft lifted me uncomfortably high off of my seat causing me to think I might hit the overhead panel with my head, and with catastrophic results to my scalp sure to follow. The auto-pilot immediately gave up the ghost and disconnected in protest at the manhandling the sky was giving it. I corrected the unusual attitude by grabbing onto the flight controls and tried to gain some semblance of controlled flight. My dad had always told me to fly attitude in a thunderstorm, to just keep the aircraft as level as you can and not worry about maintaining a precise altitude

"Keep the ship level as best as you can," were his words.

Well, as I was doing this, keeping the aircraft level, the captain was yelling for me to re-engage the autopilot and let it fly! And let me add, the captain was not yelling because he was mad, he was yelling because the noise from the very heavy rain was deafening and I would've sworn the nose of the aircraft was getting a "shot peening" treatment; my Lord, it was distracting and disorienting, it was so loud.

I yelled back to the captain that the autopilot had its chance to fly and it quit, so why should I trust it again? But he was really, really adamant, so I re-engaged the autopilot and kept my hands and feet like shadows on the flight controls in case I needed to take over again.

As I said, the bouncing/pounding was positively horrible and would not allow you to see the instruments with any clarity, and it was quite easily the most violent turbulence I'd ever experienced up to that point in my career (as of this writing it still is). The gyrations assaulted every physical dimension of our immediate space/time continuum: rolling, yawing, pitching and airspeed increases and decreases, all being encountered in amplitudes that defied rational aeronautical and meteorological description, particularly since the aircraft in which we were flying was designed with reasonable, but certainly finite, structural standards. One moment, we were being forcibly shoved into our seats and then as soon as the blood rushed from our brains, it was reinserted, with a vengeance, as our seatbelts contained the upward movement of our bodies toward the overhead panel . . . no matter how tight I tried to cinch my lap belt it never seemed tight enough to keep me from an uncomfortable upward movement as negative G was encountered.

As much as the aircraft and our physical bodies were being assaulted, so too was our psyche. Since most pilots have some tendency to be control freaks (some more so than others!), given the nature of the profession, this situation was mentally taxing as there was not a lot we could do about it. We were bounding helplessly through a wicked sea of turbulent air and, other than monitor the autopilot's ability to keep us relatively level and override the auto throttles to keep them from wildly excessive power corrections, we were at the mercy of Mother Nature and not in control of the situation anymore; it was a very helpless feeling.

The airspeed indicator, like every other part of the aircraft, showed wildly opposite movements; one moment we were indicating an over speed and then, as fast as it increased, it reversed itself and dropped precipitously into the region of an aerodynamic stall. (While the actual airspeed was fluctuating radically up and down, the MD-11 has a ten-second trend indicator next to the airspeed readout, and this green airspeed trend line was showing increases or decreases such as I'd never seen before.) The butterfly effect, in a very obvious sense, of the airspeed changes was the crazy fluctuations in the auto-throttles; they were alternately going from idle thrust to climb power and then to idle again! Hence, I held on to the throttles as best as I could, given the turbulence, and overrode the automation to keep it from abusing the engines.

After engaging the autopilot, I chanced, for some reason, to look back and see how our jumpseater was faring, and in retrospect, it was quite funny. He was still horizontal, as if in a sleeping position, but was looking directly at me, eyes as big as half dollars. And while that may not seem so odd, his body was at least four feet above the air mattress upon which he had been sleeping! And going further, in the time that it took for me to look forward, check on the autopilot's flying ability, and then look back, Don was now firmly planted on the floor and scrambling to get out of his sleeping bag. I have to fully admit that in spite of thinking that might be my last flight in an aircraft, I did laugh to myself due to the look upon his face and his antics, as he was bounced around in the back. I've often wondered if God wanted to bring me a bit of humor while I was immersed in a dark sea gloom to lighten the mood; I'll never know.

There was no lightning visible, as we bounced our way through this "innocuous green dot," and I find that amazing given the violence of the up and down drafts, but, none was observed.

I had no real conscious thoughts, as we raced through hell. Monitoring the autopilot while hanging on and hoping the aircraft didn't break apart, were all I could think of or do. One lifelong question of mine, however, was answered on that night, so I guess I can say some good came out that thunderstorm encounter. Unlike all the Hollywood movies I've seen where they show a person's life flash before their eyes when they think they are going to die . . . Ha! I saw none of that; no regrets about things I did or didn't do and no technicolor movies showing the highlights of my life. I was kinda bummed actually, all those years believing I'd get a synopsis of my life if I was getting ready to die.

And then, as quickly as it began, it ended. The absolute mayhem lasted, maybe, all of sixty seconds, but for all I know, it could have been only thirty . . . I'll never know. I can tell you, though, it was the longest continuous period of time in my life that I feared for my death.

We went from severe turbulence to absolute calm in a couple of seconds. Since the cockpit floodlights were out when we entered this malevolence, almost as soon as the turbulence ended I could see stars winking at me through the now very clean windscreen, and let me tell ya, I'd never been so happy in all my life to see stars as I was then! In fact, the moon was up and illuminating the ocean below, and not a cloud could now be seen . . . how bizarre. I almost wondered if I had fallen asleep and had a bad dream. But alas, no such luck, the look on the captain's face seemed frozen in an expression of concern, still illustrating how I felt.

The jumpseater, who I had last seen magically levitating above the floor, was now wide awake and in the cockpit, rambling to anyone who would listen and wanting to know what in the hell happened. Now, ya gotta' figure that since this guy is a line check airman, and though this was not a line check we were getting on this leg to Singapore, in a couple of days, when he does give us our line check, he's gonna' have a serious negative bias toward us. I mean how do you dig yourself out of this hole? We had just flown through a very small, but potent, thunderstorm or at least one in full development, and it was the captain's and my fault . . . there was no excuse.

To tell you that I kissed this guy's ass for the rest of the flight down to Singapore is pretty much an understatement; I acted as if this MD-11 was his very own personal private jet, and I was a corporate pilot intent on keeping my job with a very fickle owner. I offered to make him dinner, coffee, snacks, whatever, just to help calm him down. Actually, in doing this it helped to calm me down and took my mind off of what I perceived was a near death experience. After an hour of nervous talk, he eventually succumbed to his fatigue and climbed back into his magic carpet ride of a sleeping bag, but not before directing me on how to use the radar to thoroughly scan the sky ahead. I can't say he didn't tell me anything I didn't already know, but if it reassured him, then it was time well spent for me.

The rest of the flight was smooth and uneventful and the though the captain and I talked a bit about what happened and how to prevent it from happening again in the future, to this day we've not ever really personally shared how we truly felt.

And by the way . . . the checkride to Taipei? Though we did encounter a few thunderstorms en route, they were deftly avoided, and overall the flight went really well.

To this day, those encounters with Mother Nature's iron fists have left an indelible impression upon me. Even though I was cautious before, now every time I fly around or near thunderstorms I analyze both the storm(s) and the area around which I am deviating with more scrutiny than I do future ex-wives.

And that's what it's all about, learning from your past mistakes, or others', and applying that insight and knowledge to future endeavors. Flying is all about risk, what is acceptable risk and what is not (acceptable risk). Experience, training, knowledge and intuition all help to make that assessment.

As pilots, we live in a never-ending environment of learning, at least we should feel that way. My Dad stopped flying with at least 35,000 hours under his belt. On his last flight, and during a quiet moment, my dad told me, "Son, I was still learning to fly up until I set the brakes on my last flight"; he was seventy-five years old and never had an accident, incident or violation. I'd say he practiced what he preached.

CHAPTER 35

As the first year of the new millennium dragged on, my and Liza's divorce lawyers increased their coffers, supposedly fighting for the benefit of their respective clients.

Though Liza and I spoke very little during this time, my dad and I were talking, via rather lengthy phone conversations on a regular basis and I would detail to him the latest goings-on in my world of aviation. He had retired in 1997 due to a weakening heart, and he was very keen on wanting to know what was new. At times, I might be the one dominating the conversation, and then there were times when he relentlessly rambled on about his past. So, as the conversations progressed into autumn of 2000, our discussions were inter-mixed between both of our flying experiences, present and past, and let me tell ya, there were some very poignant conversations during that period. Premonition hinted to me that our time together, even if it was just talking on the phone, was nearing an end.

My father was a prideful man in his retirement. He knew the "torch of the aviator" had been passed to his son after the lost his medical and could no longer pilot an aircraft, and he was very bitter. Losing his wings was a fatal blow to him, and I knew it would cause a rapid decline in his will to live. Flying was his life, it defined him and who he was. Without flying, he was a mere mortal, but with it he was a demigod, and nearly invincible. He lamented to me many times on the phone about how being grounded was killing him. All I could do was just listen with sympathy to his complaining, from which he might then go on a tangent and repeat some oft-told story of his daredevil flying days. I silently prayed, as he rambled on, that our conversations would help ease an old, bold and proud aviator's pain. I did use some of his more melancholy moments as an opportunity to talk about how my faith sustained me in troubled times, hoping the pagan might see the light, and he did, at times, respond in a positive manner to my Christian words of solace.

I rarely saw my parents after I moved out of the area, hence the many phone conversations with my father. Instead of seeing them, my monthly visits to South Jersey were relegated to spending time with Christina and Kyle. I'd washed my hands of hoping my mother and father would ever exhibit any real change in their very self-centered behavior, and since they showed no genuine interest in any of my kids, I stopped bringing them by. Also, my mother smoked like a chimney, and she would become incensed if I asked her not to smoke around the kids, since she would do so anyway, just to show me that she was the parent, and I wasn't going to tell her what to do.

On a personal level, with regards to my mother, she was not really interested in much of what was going on in my life. Quite honestly, as shallow as my father could be, my mother was worse. I truly did love her, but given the emotional distance between her and me, I only spoke on the phone with her occasionally, just to see how she was doing since she rarely liked to talk to me.

Ironically, it was a phone conversation with her that did cause me to rush out to visit them on December 7, 2000. I had been talking to my father, and my mother, very uncharacteristically, grabbed the phone and started chatting to me about some of the most nonsensical things. She made no sense, and I said to her, I think, "I need to come see you guys," whereupon my mother blurted out, "Yes, you better!" When my father got back on the phone, I asked him how long mom had been acting so odd, and without missing a beat, he said, "Hell, all of my life."

Upon arriving at my parents' house on the morning of the seventh, I could immediately tell that something was wrong with my mother. She was disheveled and smelled as if she hadn't showered in days. My father was his normal self, bitching about his wife and life, but I could tell by the stains on the wall above each of their normal sitting places in the living room, many drinks had been thrown back and forth between them, indicating that they had indeed not changed.

After greeting the two of them, and taking them to brunch where I further analyzed my mother, I decided to take her to the emergency room for evaluation. About an hour after June disappeared into the bowels of the ER facility, a very stunned and apologetic doctor told me that my mother had a very invasive type of brain cancer, that it was inoperable, and he gave her four to six months to live . . . in fact, it turned out to be three weeks. She passed away on January 1, 2001.

Both my father and I were in utter shock at how quickly my mother went from walking and talking to death.

I wish I could say my mother's passing was sad to me, but to be honest, for her I was relieved. She was free . . . from her husband, her kids, and from a lifestyle she never wanted. For reasons I'll never understand, she accepted the misery of living a life she loathed and being surrounded with everything she despised, never venturing out and having the courage to reach for her own dream by leaving the hell her husband dished out. I really felt sad for her and to this day I pray that she is in Heaven, because to be honest, I have no idea if she was a Christian or not, in spite of the fact that she taught me the Lord's Prayer.

After June's burial, I brought my father back to the area where I lived and then put him in a very nice assisted living facility near my apartment. He'd had a minor stroke, well before my mother's passing, and needed some help with certain daily activities, but for the most part his mind was still very sharp and he spoke with amazing clarity and memory recall.

Of course, my father hated his new digs, saying it was filled with nothing but old people, and he said he lived for the times when I liberated him from the home after I'd return from a trip. It was arduous having him as much as I did due to his physical needs, his almost constant negativity about living with old people, and the added stress of caring for my youngest two kids. There were times after my mother died where I wished I had let my oldest sister deal with Ken's crap, but in actuality the last few months I had with was a wonderful blessing.

The silver lining of our final 6 months together were the many insightful and wonderful conversations we had over lunch or dinner in some "pilot type bar." Maybe it was premonition on his part, but during that time together the old man revealed many things about his father, mother, career, etc. that he never before told me. Without me even asking, I had many questions answered as he rambled on about this or that ancient episode in his life when he was either a villain or a saint. And, never did I need to prod or goad him into confessing his sins, he just seemed ready to divulge some of the darker sides of his life. I knew there was more though, even after all of those sidebar conversations, I knew that somewhere in his deep past there was a kernel, a seed from hell that magnified his emotions to the extreme when he was drunk. My mother once told me she was convinced something profound had occurred in his younger life that ignited an unquenchable anger that caused him to view the world as his enemy when he was intoxicated…unfortunately she died without him ever revealing to her what it was, and it was possible, given his rapidly declining health, that he would take that secret to his grave.

CHAPTER 36

As a hot and humid summer began emerging from a beautifully dry spring of 2001, the compartmentalizing of my emotions, given all that had occurred since the passing of Autumn-Paige in early 1997, had reached its limit.

I was spending so much time and energy on all of the elements of my life: Flying international trips on the MD-11 and consequently being eternally jetlagged; dealing with my father's grumpiness as I tried to mend long ago broken fences; having my kids, as well as my father, whenever I was not flying; and finally dealing with a divorce that was gutting me with each request from one of the attorneys for either records, or money, or both . . . so much on my plate, it was crippling me emotionally and mentally.

I was on a long west coast layover in the spring of 2001 when the enormity of my life of flying and living between heaven and hell hit me. I won't go so far as to say I had a nervous breakdown, but I can say when I entered my hotel room after that particular flight west I remained in the room for almost 2 days, deeply depressed, feeling very sorry for myself, and maxed out with everything that life had been throwing at me since birth. I thought of all of the crappy things I had done to hurt people over the years, things I dearly wished I could have personally gone to each of those persons I hurt and apologized. Then there were the years of abuse from my parents that Gail, Linda, and I endured. It wasn't fair, we didn't do anything wrong, why couldn't they have just split up and stayed apart instead of putting us through the torment of their hatred of each other. And then there was my father's abuse and drunken hatred directed towards me; the absolute evil in his eyes when he emotionally and mentally ripped me to shreds while drunk, or the times when he physically attacked me. I was his son, how could he do that to his own flesh and blood? I just couldn't understand it. So much pain. There was the daily vision of my daughter and her bloodied face as I held her after she had been run over, the pain, oh my god the pain; and then there was the divorce I was going through, but didn't want, and the financial stress that was beyond belief…all of it. There was not one emotional stone left unturned or a box in which I had not stuffed some deeply painful emotions from my youngest memories that wasn't emptied in those 48 hours… all of it, all of my life was relived in that compressed 48 hour time capsule. I asked God to forgive me more times than I can count for all of the bad things I had done in my life and conversely asked Him why He allowed so many bad things to happen to me; the paradoxes explored with God in those two days was epic and the releasing of pent up feelings was hugely healing. I came face with many fears, long held regrets, and probably most importantly forgave myself and Liza in the accidental death of Autumn-Paige.

When I returned from that trip west, I renewed a ritual I had long ago abandoned…that of going to a little chapel, on the inside of a large Catholic church, where I would pray. So with my father and kids in tow, I began to slip off to this lovely little chapel and while my father was left to his own thoughts and prayers in a pew near mine, and Austin and Amber quietly played near where I knelt, I would pray the Lord's Prayer and then follow up with other issues I wanted to bring before God. I can't say the world's problems, nor all of mine, were solved during those visits, but that quiet time did bring me peace and strength to face each new day with hope.

In addition to my church revival, I renewed my visits to Dale, the therapist that Liza and I had gone to for marriage and grief counseling. I had gained some insight in those 2 days out west and needed some of Dale's wisdom to help me unlock the mysteries of my own dysfunction, dysfunction that began rearing its ugly head when I was in the USAF and was only getting worse. And, since my father was now in town, I asked Dale if she would be interested in seeing him too, since no doubt he and my mother had much influence on who I was.

My father's two visits to Dale were interesting and, in many ways, a wonderful godsend to me personally as it allowed Dale to come full circle with me, to meet my life's greatest human blessing and curse. It allowed her to personally get to know and study a man that I came to both despise and covet and from whom most of the hell and dysfunction arose in my sisters' and my lives. For my dad's part, he loved seeing Dale. He loved talking to her and, my lord, he was dripping with charm and effervescence upon their first meeting and wanted to see her as much as he could. After those visits, Dale said she had seen enough of him to confirm what she had suspected all along.

In her summation of my father, she said he was a very sweet and charming old man who was "extremely narcissistic." Bringing my mother into the fold, she said my mother was no doubt as narcissistic, if not even more so, that my father; the aforementioned being based upon my father's comments about his wife and their marriage and mine (comments). She said it's bad enough when one parent is narcissistic, but having two can make it challenging for the children as they grow and mature.

In my ensuing sessions with Dale, while leaving my father in his assisted living home, she helped me discover how the sins of my mother and father affected my sisters and me.

Her analysis of what and who I'd become, my personality type, was not easy to hear and accept. She said there was no doubt I was my father's son and best student since I had some of his traits, both the good and bad. Getting even more specific, she further explained how my mother's dereliction of duty to me after I was born affected my psyche and caused me to have certain deep-seated insecurities above and beyond the influence my father had upon me. With each session Dale gave me coping strategies on how to deal with psyche deficiencies within me that, though they would always be there, just knowing their affect would allow me to live a more normal life and become more wholesome. It was liberating to know that some of the emotional feelings I had felt in daily life, were normal and had my parents been better at parenting, I would have known that.

CHAPTER 37

My father's health had begun to decline almost as soon as my mother was buried. Though my mother and father had endured a very contentious marriage for a ridiculous amount of years, it was all my father knew and once his wife and caretaker was taken from him and he was moved from his house, he began to wither. I saw the decline in him and wished I could have done more to see him, but I had to fly a heavier than normal schedule to pay for the lawyers, my future ex-wife's lifestyle, my kids' needs (all four), and finally support my own self.

In spite of the almost continuous emotional and financial drama and struggle, I was always happy when I went off to fly a trip. As with my father, flying was an escape from the real world, and I still found every take-off exhilarating and each new foray into the wonderful blue world above us a wonderful adventure. However, a crack in my emotional mindset about the joys of flying did appear after Liza and I split. I noticed that I was missing my kids so much with each trip that I found myself pining for them to the point I couldn't wait to get home so as to spend time with them. Also, it was evident that even though I could temporarily escape to the sky, the same ole problems always greeted me upon my arrival; as Dale had been trying to pound into me, there was no real escape from my issues other than to face them head on and defeat them, yet for far too long I'd chosen to run.

I do believe my increasing desire to personally care for and spend time with all of my children was answered prayer. On many nights when I was low and hating "me" for the villain I felt like I'd become and my lot in life due to my failed marriages and other toxic relationships, I begged God—and I mean begged—for Him to not let my kids be affected by the same issues that plagued me. I wanted that proverbial chain of dysfunction to not be just broken, but smashed to bits, and with no chance of reassembly.

About a week before my late mother's birthday, June 19, my father was taken from the assisted living complex, which he still loathed, and gently laid in a bed in a very nice nursing home close to my apartment. The decision to move him was based upon his rapid deterioration in health combined with a worsening depression that was spiraling out of control. His spirit was draining from him right before my eyes and there was nothing I could do to cheer him up. As he lay in the nursing home, being fed through his stomach, I cried in the shadows of his room while he slept due to the sadness I felt for this icon. This narcissistic giant, sometimes tyrant, who had most of his life manipulated those around him while torturing his own soul as well as that of his wife, was rapidly dying; he now seemed so weak and utterly incapable of hurting anyone. The maelstrom, the storm that had sustained his fight all of those years was dissipating, leaving him deflated in ego, pride, and zest. It may seem odd to feel such emotional pain for someone who had caused my mother, my sisters, and me such pain, but I felt as if I was watching a majestic yet ferocious lion slowly pass away, and I was deeply saddened.

On the morning of my mother's birthday, the nursing home called to tell me that my father had been transported to the hospital due to a heart problem. Upon my arrival in the ER, I was taken to my father's side. His heart was beating erratically and failing, but as I held his hand and sat by his side, he was very alert and talkative. The attending nurse was cute as a button and ever true to form my father was laying on the charm with her trying to show a brave face, as the angels and demons played a tug of war with his soul. It was there, in the ER, as my father could see the dawn of Heaven rapidly approaching, where he confessed to me the deal he had made with the devil, his mother, many, many years before and the cause of all his inner strife.

When America became involved in World War II my father, since he had his pilot's license, wanted to join the Army Air Corps and be a fighter pilot. His mother, Elsie, the seemingly genteel woman who was the brains beside the brawn in she and her husband's very successful trucking and storage company, made her son vow that he would never fly an aircraft in combat. She said that she feared losing her only child and, to add a numbing ruthlessness to her understandable motherly plea, she said he would be excluded from her and Harold's will if he defied her wishes (they were very wealthy). Extremely reluctantly, Ken agreed with her desires though he had a huge amount of emotional conflict within his heart and head as he struggled with the implications of obeying his mother.

The emotional pain of capitulation to Elsie's desires profoundly affected Ken throughout his entire life. He said he always wanted to be a fighter pilot, but his mother's decree and his consenting to her sealed any chance of him ever becoming one. The fact that his life-long dream was shattered by him relenting to his mother, ate at him.

But, as my father divulged revelation after revelation to me in the ER, he said there was an even deeper issue beyond his broken dream of ever getting fly a fighter. He said he came into the Army Air Corps already able to fly, in fact he trained military pilots while he was instructing at Wiggin's. Because of his flying experience and skill, he could've easily gotten any aircraft assignment he wanted. But, in fact he, he said, he was afraid of flying a fighter in the war because he was afraid he would've been killed flying in combat. He said his mother's demand for him not to fly in combat was his "legitimate" ticket out of harm's way, certain battle, and into the relative safety of flying transports. All of his life, he said, he had to live with his cowardice and it literally ate his soul alive.

His confession was my "A Ha!!!" moment. I knew as soon as he told me that this was the key to his anger and bipolar nature for all of my life. I had always wondered what fires of torment burned so hotly with-in his soul that no amount, and kind, of liquid could quench. It was those fires, caused by his belief that he was a coward, that caused him to be so cruel for so many years to his wife and son. As my father lay on the very precipice of death, I finally got closure.

After revealing his deepest of secrets, and while still holding his hand, I prayed the Lord's Prayer over him, told him I loved him and that he was my greatest hero. Whatever lingering bitterness, anger or resentment I harbored against him melted that morning with his confession.

There is no doubt that after we prayed and my father confessed of his long-held secret, I could see a marked change in his face. After being liberated of his guilt through his confession to me, long attached demons fled his heart as angels rushed in to comfort him. And in concert with his confession and new found faith in

Jesus, a smile appeared on his face for the first time in many, many months. He was glowing, such as I had never seen in him before, even though his heart was rapidly failing. After a few more minutes of a slowly muting, one-way conversation (from him to me) with words of humor or endearment, to include an "I love you," barely making it out of his vocal cords, my father closed his eyes just as his heart stopped beating.

After his passing, I walked to my car and, in the silence and solitude of my vehicle, I cried and cried. I missed my dad, the good side of him, the hero, the aviator. I lost my mentor and toward the end of his life, my sounding board when I needed aviation wisdom.

I am not a pastor, but I can tell you that my father, broken as he was, went to Heaven in peace after accepting Christ as his Lord and savior that morning. In addition, he died lighter in heart knowing he had shared his emotionally painful and spirit killing secret with me; a secret not even his late wife knew. And though that secret had been a dark cloud in his soul for most of his life, in telling me, the cloud was finally lifted, and with its lifting it revealed the most wonderful of all the silver linings of his and my life, as he smiled his way to heaven when he finally closed his eyes; like my mother, he was finally free . . . and now so was I.

EPILOGUE

As I close out this memoir, it has been ten years since Austin and I flew that fiftieth birthday flight. We eventually made our way a little to the west of the small field from which we alighted and flew over the mighty Mississippi. As we banked to and fro above the swollen river we chased flocks of Egrets, trying to join their formations, and investigated interesting looking coves, oxbows, and buzzed obscure and isolated sandbars. I very much enjoyed the complexity of my surroundings on that day and the memory rush I experienced; I truly wished my father could have seen me taking flight with my son, he would have been very proud. That flight acted as a kind of time machine, helping me to reset my mental gyros to a slower pace and decompress emotionally due to my very hectic and complicated professional and personal life back then. Finally, it allowed me to reflect upon some of the more traumatic moments in my life and to try and come to grips with their ramifications…

Liza and I finally did divorce six months after my father passed away, almost to the day. It was an extremely emotional, spirit-killing, and at times very contentious process, made worse for me due to having to deal with both of my parent's illnesses and subsequent deaths.

A friend of Liza's called me just a few days after the divorce was final. She said she wanted to help me get closure on my anguish as to why the marriage counseling sessions failed and as to why Liza and I actually divorced. This friend said that after Autumn-Paige passed away Liza struggled internally with the loss and decided she wanted a divorce, she just wanted to see if we could have another girl before doing so (divorcing). There were more complications to the above divorce scenario than I have mentioned, details that need not be written here, but suffice it to say, Liza and I started with a struggling marriage and it was Liza who, wisely, finally put it to rest in December, 2001.

I was initially bitter after hearing of Liza's premeditation on wanting a divorce, but in retrospect, it was a silver lining (the divorce). While in our marriage, on most days, she and I were indifferent to each other living as roommates and on those days there was always an undercurrent of anger, angst, or bitterness. On the bad days, of which there were many, Liza and I were horrible to each other. We were just a bad match with no common ground for spiritual and emotional growth and should never have married; our jet set dating life was a glitzy façade to a poor foundation upon which to marry and have children.

Because I flew a Super Cub during the flight with Austin, a couple of times thoughts of Luke, the young man who crashed in Alaska while also flying a Super Cub, came to mind; that was a fateful evening indeed so many years ago. I am happy to report that I have maintained a casual contact with Luke's father, and Luke returned to flying a year after his accident and now has three lovely children. I pray the Lord continues to protect he and his family from any further harm.

At one point, I looked down at the massive Mississippi and realized it started out as millions of rivulets, which congregated into thousands of streams, which eventually amalgamated into Old Man River, which eventually empties into the mass of water that is the Gulf of Mexico.

All of us have a similarity with old man river. Just as the Mississippi has rapids, short lengths of flow where the current is tumultuous, confused and chaotic, so too do we as humans have chaotic flows in our timeline where our days are stressful and our future is muddied. Eventually though, the rapids give way to serenely smooth, long stretches of slow flowing waters that allow a wonderful calm between the maelstroms. By the time the river nears its end and long after the last series of rapids have abated, the current has gracefully slowed and its course ends unceremoniously when it empties into the vastness of the Gulf of Mexico.

In concert with my personal life, though delayed until I was 16, my flying career started as a trickle. As I got more and more experience, like the rivulets that add more and more to form a stream, so too were my flying adventures, and the edification from them forming a river of knowledge. As I got, and get, older and more experienced this torrent of flying wisdom collects into a vast pool of collective knowledge from which I can draw when faced with a difficult flight.

In forty-two years of flying, so far, I have seen so many wonderful sights, flown so many wonderful aircraft, and have had the great fortune to tread the upper reaches of the world's troposphere with so many wonderful pilots, and with it all I have learned so much. Words cannot express my gratitude to God for blessing me with such a wonderful career.

As I turned eastward and headed back toward the little grass strip from which Austin and I alighted, he had fallen fast asleep. He did that a lot when we flew, and I didn't mind; I did on occasion when I flew with my dad.

The end of my career is drawing nigh, and though I pray I have a few more years flying with my airline before I retire, I'd love more than anything to get back into general aviation so I can fly just for fun—no schedules, no pressure, just the enjoyment of being airborne and loving the view. Just as I started, so I want to finish.

Both of my sisters have passed away since that 50th birthday flight and as I was putting the finishing touches on this "run-on" memory.

Gail never recovered from the trauma of being raised in our house of hell. Her excessive drug use and many overdoses, along with her promiscuity led her down a road from which she never could exit. She had a very brief marriage, right after graduating high school, which ended a year or two after it began; she never had, nor ever wanted children. After that marriage, she and my mother began sleeping with the same man, a carpenter, who had come to do renovation work on our house while I was in college; I don't think my father ever knew of that bizarre tryst. Eventually, she went to live with Linda in Hawaii and after Linda had divorced her first husband. At some point while living with Linda, Gail had a complete emotional breakdown and was institutionalized for a few months. After being diagnosed with paranoid schizophrenia, due to the excessive use of drugs, but refusing to take her medication, Linda asked her to leave her apartment because she was so unpredictable and destructive. Leaving Hawaii, she naturally settled in Hollywood, living in a condemned apartment building with other, near homeless people. I used to visit her on my Los Angeles layovers when I began to fly in the airlines. I regularly gave her money for groceries/sundries and took her out to lunch or dinner while visiting her; there are no words to describe the pain I felt every time we met, if only because I would always think of the incredibly sweet sister she was while we grew up.

When Linda remarried and eventually moved to upper New York State, Gail would begin to spend her winters in Las Vegas (she left Hollywood for Las Vegas after being kicked out of the condemned building) and the summers with Linda in New York (Gail did collect about 850 dollars a month in some sort of disability payments). For most of the time she was roaming about in Las Vegas she was homeless, living on the street, but she would keep in touch with Linda and I even as she wondered; there too I would quite regularly send her money. At some point in her homelessness in Las Vegas she decided that it was better to stay in New York year-round than battle with the other homeless people and she permanently moved in with Linda and her fiancé sometime after my divorce. Sadly, Gail kept losing her balance and falling during the summer of 2013, and was admitted to the hospital. She was eventually diagnosed with Mad Cow disease. Being a very long drawn out and terminal illness, I had to make to the decision to end her life support since Linda could not bring herself to do it. Though she is free, and I know she is in heaven, I cry when I think of all the things Gail and I did when we were very young...swimming, playing in the woods with all of the neighborhood kids, catching tens of fireflies and releasing them into our house (that was not popular with our parents). She had so much potential and was so beautiful, both inside and out; it's painful to think about the hell she went through for most of her life.

Linda, for her part, was the best of us 3 kids. She really was. While young my mother placed a heavy burden upon her shoulders, to take care of Gail and I while she, our mother, played around with her married boyfriend after our father left.

After moving to Hawaii and then divorcing, and after Gail left for Hollywood, Linda remarried another army soldier and they moved to Germany. At about that time I had begun to fly internationally and Germany was one of my frequent destinations. Linda would pick me up at my hotel, when I had a long layover, and we would drive around taking the roads least traveled. She was such fun and always full of laughter! We really had some wonderful days as we drove about, not really knowing where we were going, but finding a lovely destination with each quaint German town we entered.

After a couple of years overseas Linda and her husband moved to Watertown, NY, near Ft Drum, New York. Unfortunately, her second husband ditched her almost as soon as they arrived stateside and they divorced. Picking up the pieces, Linda moved into her own place at the same time as Gail rejoined her. She, Linda, also started a position at a new Walmart Supercenter in town where she was initially hired as a manager of the shipping/receiving dock; she would work there for 25 years.

The sadness I felt for Linda, and the pain I knew she carried inside, was from the constant rejection of her by her own mother. Her mother's disdain for her own daughter was demonstrated one weekend, in late 1993. Linda was down from New York, visiting and staying with me in Linwood, NJ. We actually went to dinner, if you can believe it, with my mother and father. We were at some casino in Atlantic City and having a very nice time when my mother told Linda that she needed to lose some weight (Linda was generally heavy for most of her life). After hearing this Linda looked down at the table, with tears immediately dropping from her eyes, and said, "I know I'm a little heavy, but I've always been this way and I like who I am."

Without missing a beat my mother sternly said, "Well I don't want to see you again until you lose weight, you're too fat." And with that my mother lit a cigarette, held her head high and gazed far into the restaurant as my father and I looked at each other in shock. That wasn't the first time my mother embarrassed Linda in public.

Linda didn't deserve that from her mother. She lived with so much internal hurt and pain accrued over the years. She was always, always so loving to me and so amazingly sweet to everyone; I never understood why she never fully broke down, but she always remained solid and strong, at least in my presence. She was always acting like my mother, tender and sweet, always patient with me when I vented about something. There were the special times when we reminisced about the hell we lived in as children. She would laugh when I made a snide, yet comical, observation about our mother or father, but then in an instant she might burst into tears when a twinge of a bad memory would surface; but her tears would be shut off almost as soon as they began, she hated dwelling on the negative. Many times, on the phone, or in person, a symbolic effigy of our mother took many darts as Linda and I tried to rid ourselves of the pain of our past and slay, in an imaginary way, the ice queen who was our mother. My father too took hits from me during those late night, self-help sessions but Linda never saw that side of my father, his wrath upon me; she just saw the arguing that they both did while in Absecon and felt that our mother was more to blame than our father.

Linda eventually met another guy after being in Watertown for a year or so, actually Gail set them up as she (Gail) met Bill while they both waited for a bus. Bill and Linda were inseparable after their first meeting and lived together until she died of cancer in mid-summer, 2018; I was sitting next to her as she passed away. The pain of losing her is still heavy upon my heart as I write this, but, she too was a wonderfully lovely and very sweet Christian. It is a wonderful blessing to know that both of my sisters are holding each other in heaven and finally, "up there" they have found true, unconditional love and acceptance and one day we will all be reunited.

Finally, and to end on a high note, my oldest son, Kyle, is the one who decided to become a pilot, though not without having to go through Marine Corps Officer Candidate School first. He is presently in flight training at NAS Kingsville; he hopes to fly F-18s or F-35s as a follow-on assignment.

It is not lost on me that Kyle is a third-generation pilot and, as was the tradition with my father and me, he and I have almost weekly talks as he learns to fly the Navy way. The better news is that Kyle is a very emotionally stable and strong young man, a loving husband, and not afflicted with any of the dysfunction that has affected me.

Even before his walk with aviation began, I gave Kyle the same spiel that my dad gave me about how to choose a career. But as his and my talks progress I intend on expanding upon the wisdom my father passed down to me, since I intend on including the notes, warnings, and cautions about his career choice, deeper things my father never mentioned.

Lastly, and most importantly of all, I told Kyle, as we were talking the night before his first T-6 checkride and solo (he was nervous) that somewhere in my learning-to-fly days I began singing, very qui-etly, "a song." I sang "my song" as I preflighted the aircraft and then while taxiing for takeoff; to this day, even as I captain a flight on the B-777, I still quietly sing that song.

After his checkride, Kyle called to tell me he "rocked it," the checkride, and his check pilot said it was one of the best flights he'd seen, even with crosswinds that were so strong they almost canceled the flight. When I asked him if he had sung a song while preflight-ing he said, "Yes, I did!

And do you want to know what I sang?" he asked, ending on a high note. "Sure, son, what was your song?"

"The Lord's Prayer."

"And we know that in all things God works for those who love him, who have been called according to his purpose" Romans 8-28, NIV

ODE TO AVIATORS

Slightly louder than the sound of a whisper but less than that of a spoken word, if you listen with discernment, you can hear my engines' faint roar.

Looking unto the heavens to see from where this hushed thun-der comes, immersed in a star-studded field of shimmering jewels, you can see my flashing lights run.

Onward I fly while pulling a bit of wispy cloud-fabricated thread, my colleagues and I stitch this world of ours together from end to end.

From the coziness of my cockpit, well above the highest eagle's lair, I've seen sights that no earthbound person could imagine or even try to dare.

Bursting through a cloud-speckled sky, I've seen singular shafts of the sun's first rays splay through holes in the cloud, heralding in dramatic announcement the laboring birth of a new day.

Leaving the day behind and into the darkness I've flown, discovering the secret places where the stars, the moon, flaming meteors, and the aurora borealis roam.

While leaving a thin white trail of ice crystals behind me over the vast oceans, I've serenely cruised, whilst plying the tempests of the seas below, many a sailor through the ages has been battered and bruised.

Between, around, and sometimes through Mother Nature's bubbling, mountainous, and thundering legs I've threaded, while fierce bolts of lightning all around me have streaked and flashed, as I've witnessed up close and personal the sky become tattered and shredded.

I've looked down upon Angel Falls and have seen from where its sacred waters flow, and I've peered endlessly in immense wonder at the vast deserts and remote mountain ranges of this planet where nary a human go.

Dinner in Paris, breakfast in Dubai, the next day it may be lunch somewhere in Mumbai; after that, Tokyo? Sydney? Beijing? Or New York? Sometimes I don't know what's next, but I'm sure to pass through Shanghai or Hong Kong with the possibility of Kazakhstan's Almaty as my night's rest.

With my fellow airline brethren canvassing the stratosphere twenty-four/seven, we connect and make this world a better place by bringing people, goods, and services through the lower reaches of heaven.

Out of the misdeeds of providence or fate's fickle ways, some friends and colleagues through the years have met with tragedy and have been denied their expected full allotment of days.

But cry for them I shan't for the Bible says one thousand years on Earth is but a day when you have risen; so pour me a frosty one my mates, now with heavenly wings of your own, for in no time at all I'll be joining ye, and we'll be toasting to our careers while in heaven!

Made in the USA
Middletown, DE
27 October 2022